HERE TODAY

San Francisco's
Architectural Heritage

HERE TODAY

San Francisco's
Architectural Heritage

Text by Roger Olmsted and T. H. Watkins
Photos by Morley Baer and others
Sponsored by the
Junior League of San Francisco, Inc.

CHRONICLE BOOKS/A PRISM EDITION

A Note on the Ninth Printing:

In the ten years since Here Today *first made its appearance, some of the fine old buildings pictured or described have been demolished. Others are threatened. Still others have undergone a change in status by becoming historical landmarks.*

The pages at the back of this book list all such alterations of which we are aware in San Francisco, San Mateo, and Marin counties.

The softbound edition was printed on Warren's Patina by Associated Lithographers and bound by Roswell Bookbinding, in Phoenix.

NINTH PRINTING   1978

Book design by James Stockton

CONTENTS

Preface

San Francisco

Introduction

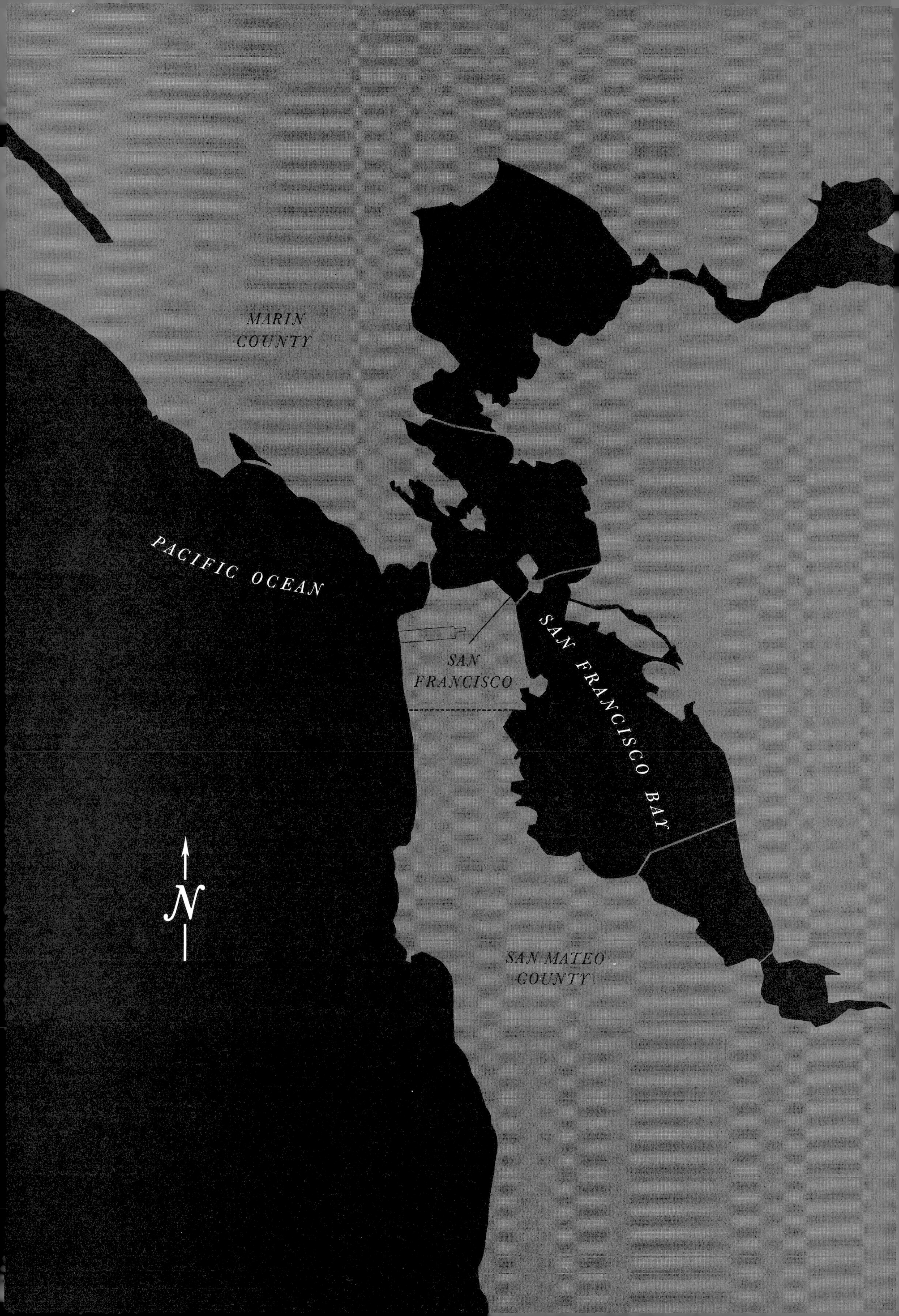

MARIN
COUNTY

PACIFIC OCEAN

SAN
FRANCISCO

SAN FRANCISCO BAY

N

SAN MATEO
COUNTY

PREFACE

Members of the Junior League of San Francisco, Inc., became concerned in 1962 about the increasing destruction of fine old buildings in San Francisco, San Mateo and Marin Counties. Some spontaneous preservation was evident, but the League recognized the need for a broader base of awareness and interest.

Many concerned American cities had already passed legislation and formed commissions to safeguard historic buildings and districts. Of special note were measures taken in the Vieux Carre, New Orleans; Beacon Hill, Boston; Society Hill, Philadelphia; and College Hill, Providence.

The San Francisco League, after discussions with local and national organizations, concluded that the first step toward selective preservation must be to discover as many as possible of those buildings most worthy of being preserved. The Historic Sites Project and Committee was set up in 1963 to identify the architecturally and historically significant buildings built prior to 1920 in the three counties.

The Committee selected a group of Community Consultants which included John Campbell, Margot Patterson Doss, Dr. Elliot Evans, John Pack Hunter, Carter Keane, Mrs. Richard Keating, James McCarthy, Herbert McLaughlin, Ted Moulton, Norman Murdoch, David Myrick, Charles Pope, Dr. Frank Stranger, Wesley Vail and John Woodbridge.

These advisors included within their ranks members of the American Institute of Architects, California Historical Society, National Park Service, Marin County Civic Library, San Francisco City Planning Department, San Francisco Planning and Urban Renewal (SPUR), San Francisco Redevelopment Agency, San Mateo County Historical Museum, Society of Architectural Historians, the California Heritage Council and Society of California Pioneers. Without the advice and support of the consultants, the project could not have been carried out.

To educate the more than two hundred participating League members, a series of lectures on research techniques, architectural history, preservation, and San Francisco history was held. Certain architectural books were required reading, and kits were prepared with instructions and background information. Certain project members were assigned books from a bibliography selected with the help of Irene Simpson of the Wells Fargo History Room, and James Abajian, California Historical Society librarian.

The impressive files of Dr. Joseph A. Baird, Jr., (principal lecturer, and author of *Time's Wondrous Changes*, which was of inestimable help) and James Beach Alexander, records of the Historic American Building Survey of the National Park Service, the AIA, and the Barclay-Jones Urban Design Survey at the Bancroft Library were combed for information.

Other members interviewed knowledgeable residents to gather information on specific buildings. These people in San Francisco included Mrs. W. W. Adams, George Cabaniss, Jr., Kenneth Cardwell, Mrs. Ernest Charleston, Richard Dillon, Mr. and Mrs. James Hancock, Mrs. Paul Hassel, Mrs. William E. Hilbert, Bernard Kearney, Miss Nora Kenyon, George Livermore, H. Putnam Livermore, the late Mrs. Alfred McLaughlin, John Papa, Dr. Albert Shumate, Mrs. Max Stern, Miss Ruth Teiser, and Paul Trimble.

In San Mateo, Blanche Coates, Miss Susan Gale, the late Alvin Hatch, Merritt Hosmer, Richard Schellens, Mrs. William Steele, and Harry Tracey were especially helpful as was the board of the San Mateo County Historical Association. In Marin County, those interviewed included Mrs. Harry B. Allen, Mrs. Robert Bastian, Frank Galli, Mrs. John Harlan, Miss Lucretia Little, Mrs. John W. Mailliard, Jr., Mrs. Donald Marvin, Mrs. Louise Teather, and Parker Woods.

Dozens of League members went out into the three counties to research buildings on a block-by-block basis.

Each county was broken down into sub-areas. San Mateo (six) and Marin (five) were divided easily by townships; San Francisco was subdivided into ten areas according to City Planning land maps. The convenient sectional maps, showing lot sizes, block numbers and typography, were made available by Miss Phoebe Hearst Brown, Senior Planner with the Department of City Planning, who lent support throughout the project.

In organizing the survey, criteria suggested by the National Trust for Historic Preservation were used. These included, among others:

1) Age
2) A fine example of a particular style
3) A work of a notable architect or builder
4) The site of an historic event
5) A building associated with a famous person

The visual survey was important for four reasons: 1) it confirmed that a building mentioned in previous research was still standing and noted its condition; 2) it turned up many architecturally significant buildings that had not been discovered in previous research; 3) it provided working photographs for the files; and 4) it enabled the surveyors to note construction materials and architectural style.

Buildings were judged as examples of their styles although some buildings defied easy classification. Each building was also judged relative to its particular area. Thus, an Italianate residence in the Nob Hill area (where most were destroyed by the 1906 fire) would be of more interest than an identical Italianate structure in the Western Addition, where many still stand.

Furthermore the condition of a building became important in visual surveying. What was in poor condition one day, a week or month later could be vastly improved by general restoration, such as painting or repairing of the exterior. Therefore what was by-passed at the time of visual surveying might have been considered at another more opportune time.

All buildings found in the research phase and in the visual survey were recorded on individual data sheets (with photographs attached). This data sheet was developed from those used by the Historic American Building Survey and from the College Hill Survey (Providence, Rhode Island). All other pertinent data were clipped to the sheet.

Once the visual survey was completed, the material was appraised by the Community Consultants, who graded each building. Those favored by a majority of the consultants are included in this book. Those receiving the highest marks are in the main text; the others are in the Appendix.

It was difficult to research the older San Francisco buildings since the fire of 1906 had destroyed most city records. Fortunately those of the San Francisco Water Department survived.

The helpfulness of the Water Department's Customer Service staff made much of the research in San Francisco feasible. Until recently Charles L. Hynes was Supervisor of this Department, now headed by Marvin Simon. Other helpful Water Department personnel include B. W. Roblin, Eugene Stluka, Patrick Sullivan and R. W. Wilson.

The Assessor's Office was of additional help in San Francisco. Assessor Joseph E. Tinney and Chief Assistant Assessor Raymond Leavitt made available the building cards. These helped verify the dates of post-fire construction. Earlier buildings had been dated by the staff on the basis of architectural style. Samuel Ducca, Chief of the Real Property Valuation Division, and his staff were helpful as was John J. Feeney, Director of Public Services and Information, ably assisted by David Lasley and John M. Walsh.

In Marin County the Assessor's records and Court House files were used. In San Mateo similar research methods were employed. In all three counties dates were substantiated, when possible, by owners and by consideration of architectural styles, which are generally accurate within a decade (see glossary).

In San Francisco, block books were made available by the San Francisco Real Estate Board which listed the owner of each lot in 1905 as well as subsequent owners up to 1965. Special thanks also go to the Board for the privilege of using their Plat Map Book and the Realty Ownership Directory.

The library of the California Historical Society was helpful to the teams working in all three counties. Dates could, in some instances, be verified through its formidable photographic collection. Librarian James Abajian also gave generously of his personal knowledge as did his assistant, Mrs. M. K. Swingle. The complete collection of city directories at the San Francisco Public Library was helpful.

The Society of California Pioneers' Curator, Dr. Elliot Evans, contributed much help, as did the Society's librarian, Mrs. Helen Giffin.

The increasingly fine collection of San Francisco material in the Special Collections Room of the Main Library, under Mrs. Ruth Hanson, was an important resource.

The staff of the San Francisco Maritime Museum, directed by Karl Kortum, gave valuable assistance. Special appreciation goes to Mrs. Matilda Dring, photo archivist, Mrs. Robert Mozley, and Miss Jane Bradford of the museum staff.

The Chinese Historical Society of America made the Chinese community aware of the Historic Sites Project. Its member, writer-historian Nanying Stella Lee, personally researched the previously unexplored buildings of Chinatown for the League project.

In San Mateo, the help of the San Mateo County Historical Association and Museum was invaluable, particularly that of Dr. Stanger, San Mateo County historian and former Director of the Museum; Leslie O. Merrill, Director of the Museum; and Mary Woodhead. The *Redwood City Tribune* files produced information as did the many articles by Mrs. Marian Goodman. In Marin, Parker Woods made available the resources of the Marin County Historical Society. Information of importance was also gathered from the files of the *Independent Journal*, Wells Fargo Bank, County Library and Mill Valley Library.

The research material from which this book evolved will be deposited in appropriate local libraries at a later date.

It is the hope of the Junior League of San Francisco, Inc., that its survey will create a new basis for awareness of the West Bay's vast architectural heritage and a desire to retain the best of that architectural past. If the citizens of San Francisco, San Mateo and Marin Counties appreciate this heritage, they will surely insist on retaining their distinctive buildings so that they are Here Today and not gone tomorrow.

Historic Sites Committee of The
Junior League of San Francisco, Inc.

Mrs. Alden Crow, General Chairman

Mrs. Peter Platt, San Francisco County Chairman

Mrs. Joseph R. Hutchinson, San Mateo County Chairman

Mrs. Stevens Manning, Marin County Chairman

Mrs. Ricardo J. Alfaro, II

Mrs. Richard S. Bodman

Mrs. Watrous Brennan

Mrs. Stuart K. Choate

Miss Mary Franck

Mrs. Hood M. Harris

Mrs. Gordon M. Hazlett

Mrs. Frank Hinman, Jr.

Mrs. Kent Kaiser

Miss Sally Moseman

Mrs. Alan H. Nichols

Mrs. Richard C. Olds

Mrs. Allen Vejar

Miss Helen Janet Wilson

Note on How To Use The Book

In presenting this material, we have attempted to make a vast amount of data comprehensible by grouping the material geographically. The three main divisions are San Francisco, San Mateo and Marin Counties; then within each county the material is presented in geographical subdivisions. A map at the beginning of each chapter serves to locate the area covered in that chapter in relation to its county.

The architectural terminology used has been taken from Dr. Joseph A. Baird, Jr.'s book, Time's Wondrous Changes. *A visual description of the principal styles and a glossary of terms can be found at the back, immediately following the Appendix. The drawings and the glossary have been adapted from* Time's Wondrous Changes *with the permission of Dr. Baird and the California Historical Society.*

1868 view of San Francisco

INTRODUCTION

San Francisco is a city of strong light and shadow. The great modern architectural critic, Lewis Mumford, has described it as an interplay of whites and darks, a kind of Mediterranean city of thoroughly human scale and contrasts. It is comprehensible from most of its approaches, a powerful work of man — with his rules and squares — yet it also seems almost a natural phenomenon.

A city is more than its collective architecture, but its architecture generally manages to reflect its character. That San Francisco should be known everywhere as a great city is testimony to the intensity of its total character. It is a city that was known to any man who could read his own name at a time when Tokyo and Bombay were geographical abstractions to most men. It was then a tangible goal to people who never harbored the ambition to visit Edinburgh or Milan. When the Gold Rush made San Francisco a city, everybody knew of it — and few have forgotten the name since.

A universal image of San Francisco was created in the Gold Rush years, but gold alone was not responsible. After all, Sacramento was the gathering place for the miners, and who had heard of Sacramento in Patagonia or Burma? Herein can be seen this suggestion of character — for it was views of San Francisco, not Sacramento, that were published by the score in illustrated magazines and newspapers all over Europe in the early 1850's.

Nor did the image of gold maintain through a century the reputation of San Francisco. The special character of the place must be held responsible. When the city again became an international byword after the earthquake and fire of 1906, it was not just the magnitude of the disaster that aroused wonder, but its qualitative importance. The idea of San Francisco meant something to people elsewhere, meant something more to them that a plain accounting of the number of buildings burned or their appraised value. A city that was something of a vision, something of a symbol, was gone — for the moment.

Though the natural setting of San Francisco is dramatic, its early inhabitants were struck by the barrenness of the site. San Francisco is not a city of trees; but the forests and groves planted on Mount Davidson, in Golden Gate Park and the Presidio, vastly enhance areas that were once thinly cloaked with brush.

1

Typical row houses in the Mission District

Trees did not come early to San Francisco; as late as the middle 1860's the city was still almost barren, and not until the 1880's and 1890's did the present groves begin to appear.

The builders of San Francisco spared little time for planting trees, and less for some of the amenities of modern city planning. The grid pattern of streets, laid willy-nilly over steep hills, was a practical necessity when it was essential that a city be laid out rapidly and that property lines be quickly and easily determined. This done, San Franciscans proceeded to move tens of millions of cubic yards of earth to level parts of the hills, fill up parts of the hollows, fill the coves of the waterfront, and make the streets conform (when possible) to acceptable grades.

The staggering amount of cutting and filling accomplished as early as the mid-1870's was one of the chief wonders of the city. The same haste that had led to adoption of a street plan not really suitable to a city of hills resulted in reconstruction according to the same plan after the destruction of a major part of the city in the 1906 disaster.

That San Franciscans have always been in a hurry does not distinguish them from the citizenry of many other American cities. What does distinguish them is that to this typical quality they add a collective awareness. J. S. Hittell, the historian of San Francisco, writing in the middle 1870's, identified this remarkable self-consciousness with the experience of the Gold Rush and the early years of city-building: "The early American settlers in California, instead of being, and many persons at a distance supposed they would be, the mere offscourings of a low rabble, were, in a large proportion, men of knowledge and capacity. . . . At brief notice they organized a state, complete in all its parts. As if by magic, their touch or their influence created magnificent cities.

By their help, a village so insignificant

The extraordinary Queen Anne at 2007 Franklin Street

2

that it had scarcely a mention on the map, grew till it became a leading center of population, commerce, industry, wealth, luxury, and of intellectual, political, and financial activity. They saw the indigenous chaparral give way to tents, these to cloth-lined wooden buildings, and these to public and private palaces that rival the homes of European princes.

"The men who took part in most of these wonderful changes, and witnessed all of them, feel that California, and especially San Francisco, has an interest for them such as no other country or city could have acquired, in our age at least, nor do they lament that they did not live in some better time in the remote past. No golden era of romance or chivalry, no heroic period of Greece or Rome provokes their envy, or in their conception, outshines the brilliancy of the scenes in which they have been actors. This is the very home of their souls."

Much the same attitude can be found in the post-Earthquake period—from the poem about "The Damndest Finest Ruins" to the climactic celebration of the 1915 Exposition. The self-consciousness exhibited was not just civic chauvinism, for it had a strong historical orientation. The survival of much of this spirit down to this day would also seem to be the result of its historical flavor: it has not been a spirit contingent upon the continuance of the latest building boom. It is no acci-

Side view of 946 Eddy Street

San Francisco's architectural character is known throughout the world.

dent that San Francisco was the first great city in the country to resist violently the encroachment of the freeway builders.

In their conscious appreciation of the character of their city, many San Franciscans are highly aware of the importance of both the past and the physical qualities their city draws from the past. It is not enough merely to preserve a few monuments or "historic buildings." The double-decker freeway running in front of the Ferry Building symbolizes the bankruptcy of this traditional approach, as does the wholesale destruction of a large part of the old Western Addition in the name of "Redevelopment."

San Francisco is going to lose more than it can afford if it does not protect its architectural character. In particular, the many delightful frame houses that we generally tag "Victorian" are one of the important elements in the "feel" of San Francisco. Thousands of other buildings of some merit also contribute to the lively atmosphere of the city. These old buildings cannot last forever, but all too often ruthless real estate speculation is responsible for their destruction. The replacement of buildings of distinction by plastered boxes cannot be viewed with indifference by people who love San Francisco.

It is the purpose of this book in part to sketch the architectural heritage of San Francisco and the suburbs of the Peninsula and Marin, in part to identify the more outstanding buildings and residences that establish this heritage. By this date there is probably no argument as to whether or not it is desirable to save older buildings and neighborhoods of merit. It is hoped that this book may help to demonstrate what of San Francisco it is vital that we save.

R. R. Olmsted

May 1, 1968

PRESIDIO/FORT MASON

SAN FRANCISCO

I n the cities of the old world there are tracts of park and woods—the legacy of kings indifferent to the requirements of progress. Peculiarly, among the cities of America, San Francisco has been the benefactor of this unsought heritage. In San Francisco, perhaps the last city on earth that one would think monarchical, nearly a twentieth of the land still is occupied by what was once the King of Spain's Presidio.

Together with Golden Gate Park, the Presidio favors San Francisco with an expanse of parkland that might excite envy in any great urban center. Yet, like Golden Gate Park, the Presidio was formerly a wind-swept desert of scrubby brush and flying sand.

Today, the Presidio is very much a great park, with its winding roads passing through open groves of cypress and eucalyptus, with clusters of attractive houses set amidst spacious lawns and luxuriant plantings, with substantial barracks arranged about broad parade grounds.

The Army's Corps of Engineers classifies many of the most pleasant buildings as "obsolete"—or so they reported in a recent analysis of the 1700-odd structures that are scattered about their 1400-acre principality. Apparently a large and influential number of people think otherwise, for some substantial pressure or interest prevents the Army from declaring portions of this militarily useless post "surplus" and selling it off to land speculators.

Seen in historical perspective, there is nothing unusual in the Presidio being militarily pointless. The reservation is getting on toward two hundred years old now, and at nearly every point in that long history it has been obsolete. The cultivated obsolescence of the Presidio today is thoroughly charming, and the Presidio as a whole is an invaluable part of the public domain.

It was not always so. It was only in the early 1870's that the extensive tree planting program began, and as late as 1900 large parts of the reservation were still barren. In Spanish times all the Presidio had was a view—small compensation for the fogs and winds of summer and the rains that melted adobe walls in winter.

In the decade or so following the establishment of the Presidio (officially, September 17, 1776), the buildings were temporary by even the modest standards of Spaniards used to the rigors of the northern frontier of Mexico. By 1792, when the British explorer George Vancouver visited San Francisco Bay, a few permanent improvements had been accomplished.

The tiny church impressed the British captain most favorably; it was "neat, in comparison to the rest of the buildings . . . being whitewashed with lime made from sea-shells." The commandant's house was the other notable structure, a low adobe with unglazed windows in the front wall. Vancouver wrote later that it "ill accorded with the ideas we had conceived of the sumptuous manner in which the Spaniards live on this side of the globe. . . ."

Truly, the Presidio at San Francisco was the last outpost of the Spanish Empire. As such, it was a likely setting for the celebrated romance in 1806 between Concepcion Arguello, daughter of the *Comandante*, Don Jose Arguello, and the Russian Chamberlain, Nikolai Petrovich Rezanof.

The *Officers' Club* at the Presidio is said to be the building in which Rezanof wooed and won Concepcion. The creature comforts of the place have improved wonderfully since Arguello entertained his guests on the dirt floor. But while many sources identify this building as "the first in San Francisco," there is almost nothing about it to suggest its ancient vintage.

It is doubtful that any vestige of the structure dates from 1776; 1791 or 1792 seems the earliest date to which the remaining (and almost totally concealed) adobe walls can be ascribed.

The present building is the result of a restoration project of the Civil Works Administration in 1933.

Built of materials shipped around the Horn in the course of the construction of the fort at Fort Point, the *Old Station Hospital* on Lincoln near Funston Avenue was the first permanent building completed by the U. S. Army in the Presidio area (possibly excepting a small powder magazine). Since its completion in 1857 the hospital has

Behind the WPA facade in this picture lies the Arguello adobe of 1792 now buried in the walls of the Officer's Club

been in continuous use as a medical center, though since the construction of old Letterman Hospital in 1899 it has been relegated to use as the post dispensary and dental clinic. The setting of this attractive building still retains enough of its pastoral quality to suggest the days of the 1860's when ladies of the post cultivated a garden nearby to keep the patients in fresh vegetables, and among the medical equipment was a cow to provide fresh milk.

The changes in the main building since its construction have been minor; the ground has been excavated from around the brick basement, making the hospital appear to be three stories, rather than two, and the upper veranda has been glassed in. An addition which is most eye-catching is the hexagonal three-story tower adjoining the north side; apparently built as an operating area, it still serves for minor surgery.

A row of handsome *brick barracks* lines the west side of the *main parade ground*. These barracks (built 1895–1909) are of simple but strong design. The monolithic effect associated with barracks-type buildings has been avoided by a thoughtful choice of materials (deep red brick and brighter red roof tiles), the use of open front porches, and by breaking the line of the hipped roofs with dormers. These buildings have been used as enlisted men's barracks during five wars — the Spanish-American, the two World Wars, the Korean War and Viet Nam — and are still rated good for twenty-five more years.

The red brick *stables* (built 1913–1914) on *McDowell* and *Patten Avenues* were probably built for the horses of the Field Company of the Signal Corps attached to the Presidio. As horses disappeared from field use, the Army managed to save a few, and for a time the stables housed the ponies of the Army polo team at the Presidio. Today one of the buildings is a veterinary hospital and the others are used for storage, classrooms, and an auto craft shop.

The most impressive example of military architecture in the San Francisco Bay region is the masonry fort at *Fort Point*. Built during the 1850's, and somewhat similar in plan to Fort Sumter, it is one of the best remaining examples of the multi-storied fortification of its period.

This great brick battleship occupies the site selected in 1776 by Colonel Juan Bautista de Anza for a presidio. Those who had to live at the Presidio of San Francisco thought better of the location about a mile to the southeast, but the idea of erecting a fortification at the narrows of the Golden Gate was a logical one.

The original Spanish fort, which had been abandoned long before the American conquest, stood some 60 feet above the "modern" fort, the bluff at the point being cut down to bedrock as the first step in the construction that was undertaken in 1853. In 1861 the new three-story

These barracks have seen five wars and are still in good shape

brick and granite fort, mounting over 120 heavy guns, was complete.

Three tiers of galleries supported by brick arches, with gun ports pierced through the outer walls, form the sides facing the water. Living quarters for the garrison were along the inside of the wall facing the land. On the ground floor were mechanics' shops; the second and third floors, supported by fluted iron columns, housed the officers and artillerymen. In the central courtyard were furnaces for heating shot.

After 1868 the U. S. Army imitated the wisdom of the Spaniards and withdrew the garrison to the Presidio proper. By the time that the old photograph on Page 13 was taken (about 1886), the fort was obsolete, but it was not until 1893 that work was begun on a new series of reinforced concrete batteries to replace the old Columbiads and Rodman guns at the Point. In 1914 the fort was officially abandoned, though during the First World War it housed some German prisoners, and during World War II it mounted a light battery and searchlight.

Today the ironwork is rusty, the mortar and stone weathering away, the remarkable masonry of the spiral granite staircases unseen except by participants in rare special tours.

At present, the Fort Point Museum Association, having acquired a long-term lease from the Army, is hoping to raise the money needed to rehabilitate Fort Point for use as a military museum which would hold memorabilia re-lating to California and the West from 1861 to the end of the Indian Wars.

Fort Mason (formerly Black Point) once captured the eye as does the Black Point on the northwestern shore of San Pablo Bay. Its steep, scrub-covered slopes suggested a logical site for a secondary battery to command the anchorages of the port, and it was put to military use by the Spanish in 1797. The existence of this branch fortification of the Presidio down to the American occupation later became the basis of the government claim to ownership of Black Point.

In the beginning, however, the fortification of Alcatraz, directly opposite Black Point, suggested that the Army had no intention of using the site. As a result, some early residents built houses on the brushy point that were among the most pleasant in the San Francisco of the 1850's. Perhaps Black Point may be considered San Francisco's first suburb.

Remarkably, some of the atmosphere of suburban Black Point has come down to us to this day, thanks to the decision of the Army, shortly after the outbreak of the Civil War, to fortify the point against any Confederate invaders.

Some of the houses on the Point were razed for the fortifications—among them the "Fremont House," a cottage occupied around 1860 by Mrs. John Charles Fremont while her husband (then California's most famous citizen and unsuccessful candidate for the Presidential nomination on the first Republican Party ticket) was away at the Mariposa gold mines.

The Station Hospital (left) has been in service since 1857. The brick stables (below) were built in 1914 and once housed polo ponies

11

But the best of the "squatters'" houses were saved and turned into quarters. And for this reason, and because stingy post-Civil War Congresses looked more favorably upon "repairs" than upon new construction, some of the earliest of San Francisco's homes (much modified by later additions) are still in use at Fort Mason.

Three of the four oldest buildings at Fort Mason are built around houses constructed for Captain Edwin Moody and Joseph Brooks, both of the Gold Rush mining company that came to San Francisco on the ship *Balance*. Moody and Brooks built their homes at the Point in 1855. The Brooks house (or a little part of it) is now *McDowell Hall*, the Fort Mason Officers' Club.

The original house is said to have been split in two after the Army occupied the post in 1863 with one part removed and a new quarters for the commanding general built onto the remaining part and the existing foundation. Subsequent improvements have resulted in a structure that dates mostly from the 1880's (with internal renovations that bring us right down to today); yet the building preserves an air of dignity, antiquity, and character.

Quarters Two (directly north of McDowell Hall) is thought to have been built around the removed part of the Brooks house. *Quarters Three* was built for Captain Moody, later one of the founders of the San Francisco Yacht Club. Moody sold the house in 1857 to Major Leonidas K. Haskell, a close friend of the Fremonts. Haskell was also a close friend of David C. Broderick; because of this, the house figured in one of most dramatic political incidents of the Gold Rush period. It was to this house that the dying Senator Broderick was brought after his duel with California Supreme Court Justice David S. Terry on the morning of September 13, 1859. *Quarters Four* was built for Major Haskell about 1855, and sold to banker Joseph Palmer of Palmer, Cooke & Co., presumably when Haskell bought Moody's house. Both Quarters Three and Four have been very much modified from their original appearance by the addition of second stories, bay windows and trim of a later period.

Together with the row of small enlisted men's quarters across the road, the four old officers' quarters form one of the most interesting groups of early residences in the Bay Area. If this area evenually becomes a park, these houses would make excellent civic buildings.

Fort Point as it looked about 1886. At far left, a granite staircase at the fort

PACIFIC HEIGHTS

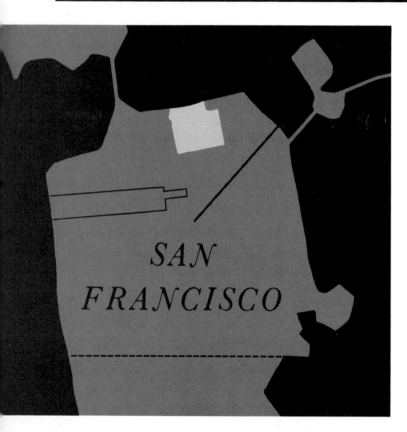

SAN FRANCISCO

Nowhere is San Francisco's ever-changing face more apparent than from the hills that form Pacific Heights. The beauty of the Bay and its islands, of the hills of Marin County and the East Bay combine to create a setting that has naturally drawn people who want to live not only in, but with, San Francisco.

A narrow definition of Pacific Heights might include only the area west of Van Ness Avenue that is, in fact, on the heights. For the purposes of this book the definition has been broadened to cover the area extending from the Bay on the north (including the Marina District) to California Street on the south, and from Presidio Avenue on the west to Van Ness on the east.

Variety is a characteristic of Pacific Heights. Residence

there has never been the exclusive prerogative of the wealthy. Some of the grand mansions of the post-Comstock era (1880 and later) were built there—but so were many more modest houses. Today men of substance still live there, but so do the less affluent, for many aging mansions have been converted to flats, apartments and "residence clubs."

When the hysteria of the Gold Rush was still a recent memory, the land from Van Ness Avenue to the Presidio between Pacific Avenue and the Bay—a patchwork of nurseries, vegetable farms, and open fields—was called Golden Gate Valley. Within the northwestern confines of this area was "Cow Hollow," once all that its bucolic name implies.

But by the 1870's, the old city could no longer house the successful in a fittingly splendid fashion. Many built impressive residences outside the city, but the land west of the city proper beckoned attractively, and in Golden Gate Valley homes appeared with increasing rapidity.

The highest crests of the ridge which became Pacific Heights were blessed with excellent views of the Bay. Houses built here were spacious and oriented toward the view. On the lower slopes, where views were less spectacular, houses were crowded more closely together.

What is now the Marina District was once largely part of San Francisco Bay, until completion of the tidal land fill project which provided the site for the 1915 Panama-Pacific International Exposition. After the Exposition closed, all but one of its magnificent buildings were demolished, to be replaced during the 1920's and 1930's by the present residences and apartments. The survivor was architect Bernard Maybeck's most enduring monument.

The Palace of Fine Arts (on *Baker Street*, between *Bay Street* and *Marina Boulevard*) was the thematic focus of the Exposition. A great rotunda of a Roman Classical character, with Corinthian columns and carefully-detailed cornices, was placed at the center of two out-curving colonnades of similar design. Behind it, a curved shed provided a setting for the fair's fine arts exhibits. The whole ensemble was given Baroque grandeur by its scale and focused organization; an artificial lake added atmosphere and foreground reflections.

The Palace met with such success that after the Fair was over, nobody had the heart to destroy it. Maybeck thought its "staff" sheathing, cornices, and figures might last indefinitely in the mild San Francisco climate. But by the 1940's chunks were beginning to fall from the structure like leaves from autumn elms.

Because the Palace of Fine Arts had dominated the city's northwestern skyline for so long, and because of its sentimental associations for so many, a number of proposals to restore Maybeck's triumph were advanced. The State of California offered two million dollars for restoration if the city would match the sum, but San Francisco voters refused. Then Walter Johnson, a nostalgic San Francisco financier, offered the city two and a quarter million dollars, if other sources would match his gift. This time the money was raised.

Now the Palace has been reconstructed in pre-cast concrete, with special attention to tone and texture, in an attempt to duplicate Maybeck's masterpiece. While no ultimate use for the complex has yet been determined, it is hoped that it will eventually house one or more of the city's cultural organizations.

Also in the Marina is *3640 Buchanan Street*, formerly headquarters of the San Francisco Gas Light Company, which purchased three square blocks fronting San Francisco Bay in 1884. In 1893, the company constructed three brick buildings, an oiler dock and two storage tanks. Only the handsome brick Richardsonian structure at 3640 Buchanan survives.

The building changed hands over the years, reflecting the consolidation of the various utility companies, until it was purchased and converted to an antique store, Merryvale. The most impressive interior feature is the main room which once housed two great gas compression cylinders. A magnificently simple coffered redwood ceiling, accentuated by large redwood beams, is further dramatized by exposed brick walls which come up to meet it. Just to the south, a walled Garden Center replaces a formerly landscaped area of the gas plant.

Perhaps the most unusual building in all San Francisco is the *Vedanta Society's Old Temple* at *2963 Webster Street*, corner of *Filbert*. The Vedanta Society of Northern California was founded in 1900 by Swami Trigunatitananda. Its congregation was (and is) made up almost entirely of Americans.

Vedanta is the highest of the six Hindu systems of reli-

The old Vedanta Temple at 2963 Webster Street may be the most unusual building in San Francisco. It was built in 1905 and its various architectural aspects are an attempt to capture the Vedanta belief that all religions are paths to one goal

gious philosophy; one of its basic tenets is that all religions are true and effective paths to one goal. Swami Trigunati-tananda, working with architect Joseph A. Leonard, sought to capture this essence of Vedanta in one building. The temple, commenced in 1905, is a remarkable combination of Queen Anne, Colonial, Medieval and Oriental features.

The first two stories of the temple, except for the lobated arched windows on the ground floor, are normal examples of the Period Revival bay window architecture common to the day; but the third floor and its roof, added in 1908, are quite spectacular. Moorish columns support cusped mughal arches which extend around the entire top floor, forming an arcaded balcony.

The roof, however, displays the essence of Vedanta most

strikingly: on the southeast corner looms a crenelated European castle tower; at the northeast corner is a double-bulbed dome on a round tower styled after old-fashioned Bengal temples; next to it rises an octagonal dome like that of a Shiva temple, and beyond that, a cluster of pointed domes represents in miniature a temple of Banaras; the whole is climaxed by a dome in the style of the Taj Mahal.

In the northeast corner of the Pacific Heights area is Blackstone Court, a blind alley which intersects Franklin Street just south of Lombard at an angle. One of San Francisco's oldest homes is *11 Blackstone Court*, a two-story frame structure dating to about 1851. Its origin is not clear, but Captain Nathaniel Blackstone lived here as early as 1853,

Octagon House, 2645 Gough Street, was built in 1861 on the strength of a then-current belief that an eight-sided house was lucky

16

Dairy rancher James Cudworth built the Victorian houses
at 2038 Union (left) and 1980 Union (below) which are now
part of that street's new distinctive shopping area

according to legal documents concerning disputes over the land title.

Until its recent remodeling, the delicate split pilasters (with modified Tudor arches above) on the second-story veranda and the casement windows—characteristics of the occasional touches of Victorian Gothic on certain early San Francisco houses—substantiated the early date.

Also of interest is *30 Blackstone Court*, built by Charles Abraham about 1885. This house is discussed further in the Appendix.

Octagon House, 2645 Gough Street, is an unusually well-preserved example of a mid-nineteenth century architectural form. Based on ideas in Orson S. Fowler's popular book, *A Home for All*, it was built for William C. McElroy in 1861, and is one of two remaining examples of its form in San Francisco (see p. 47).

In addition to the octagonal shape, Fowler also advocated the use of concrete walls. These were then often sheathed in another material, in this case redwood siding. The octagonal shape is here accentuated by wooden quoins and the slightly inclined octagonal hipped roof which carries the eye upward to the octagonal cupola.

Formerly situated across the street (at 2648 Gough), Octagon House changed hands many times until 1953 when the National Society of Colonial Dames of America purchased it from the Pacific Gas & Electric Company for one dollar and a promise to move it. The present site was donated by the Misses Lucy H. and Edith W. Allyne, the

From the servants' quarters in its back garden meals were sent to 2460 Union Street through a covered passageway

house was moved, and architect Warren Perry supervised an extensive reworking. Octagon House presently serves as a museum and library as well as the center of the society's activities.

Union Street just west of Van Ness Avenue has become a distinctive shopping area with block after block of antique stores, art galleries and other specialty shops. Many of the buildings, generally Victorian in feeling, have been rehabilitated and give the street a pleasing atmosphere, augmented by new plantings. Several of them would be considered architecturally significant in any area of the city. Interestingly, these were all built by James W. Cudworth, a prominent dairy rancher and one of San Francisco's first Supervisors.

Mr. Cudworth's own house, *2036–38 Union Street*, definitely dates to 1874, although the present owner believes it is even older, in part because of the height of the ornamental palm tree in the front garden. The largest farm house still standing in an area once devoted mainly to dairy ranching, the house itself is enhanced by its unusually large surrounding grounds.

The former residence has recently been sensitively renovated to accommodate specialty shops and offices. Exterior details reveal a shift from Italianate (especially the pipe-stem colonnettes framing slanted bay windows) to Eastlake (the chalet style trim under the main gable).

To the rear of the property is Cudworth's former barn, also recently restored and remodeled in keeping with the original structural form, although it has been moved to a new foundation.

The Little Place, 1980 Union Street, a recently unified complex of three buildings, was also built by Mr. Cudworth. Two of these are identical; according to legend, they were purchased by a father as wedding presents for his two daughters — thus, they are known as the "wedding houses."

The three structures appear to date from the 1870's or early 1880's; they were recently restored to house small shops, and restaurants.

The Episcopal Church of Saint Mary the Virgin, 2301 Union Street, was built in 1891 to house the small Pacific Heights congregation led by the Reverend William Bolton.

The fountain in the brick-lined courtyard rises from an artesian spring, supposedly an Indian watering place with curative powers which drew people from miles around. The gurgling of the underground brook can still be heard near the altar. The church proper is a simple late Victorian Gothic wood structure with shingled sides; during remodeling in 1953, Warren Perry changed the entrance from Steiner to Union Street.

Another early Union Street residence, *2460 Union Street*, was probably built about 1872. It formerly stood on a knoll in the center of the lot, then the middle third of the square block, with access from both Union and Filbert Streets.

In the 1890's, the property was owned by Henry Wadsworth and George F. Bowman. Later, when it was subdivided, Mr. Bowman acquired the house and moved it to the Union Street side of the lot.

A Mansard roof particularly distinguishes this house and relates it to similar houses of the later 1870's. Double-arched windows in the upper center and double-arched doors below suggest work of the 1860's. The bracketed gambrel roof section over the center of the house is unusual before the 1890's, but may here be interpreted as an 1870's variant of the steep gables on Victorian Gothic houses.

The deep back garden with its many old and lovely trees has a brown shingled cottage, formerly the servants' quarters and kitchen, from which meals were sent to the main house via a cook's lift through a covered passageway.

A century ago, Pierce Street was a country road leading down to Washerwoman's Lagoon and *2727 Pierce Street*, better known as the *Casebolt House*, was the manor house of Cow Hollow. It stood alone in the sloping fields, overlooking vegetable gardens and cow pastures, a barn, a windmill and a rustic lake with waterfall and island.

The entrance was later enriched by a double-arched gateway through which carriages ascended the double driveway. Although the spacious lawns have been converted to ground cover, the house and its impressive setting remain uncompromised, and the delightful "upper" garden at the back is a handsome addition to the entire neighborhood.

Henry Casebolt was a Virginia blacksmith who, with his wife and his eleven children, settled in San Francisco in 1851 and soon prospered. His intricate three-story wooden mansion was built in 1865–66.

Massive ships' timbers support its four corners; mast-like uprights run from the mudsill up through the attic and are reinforced by heavy beams placed diagonally. Italianate at its most opulent, the Casebolt house is not confined by any rigid stylistic formulae. The rusticated exterior was originally flecked with black paint to give the effect of stone and, though that feature has since been changed, the house still exudes strength.

Before his death in 1893, Casebolt sold the house and it passed through various hands until it was purchased by the present owners in the 1920's. They have maintained this fine old house in perfect condition for the past forty years.

Another Victorian mansion, the *Sherman House, 2160 Green Street*, was built in 1879 for Leander P. Sherman, founder of Sherman Clay and Company.

A huge, three-story music and reception room forms the entire west wing of the house. In this skylighted room is a platform on which such music greats as Paderewski performed; from a balcony high in one corner of the room, singers like Madame Schumann-Heink and, earlier, Lotta Crabtree (who lived next door to the west), entertained.

The beautifully-preserved house might be called Vic-

torian Baroque; it has an abundance of quoins, brackets, dentils, and balustrades. Front windows on the main level are arched and trimmed with pierced work, and the impressive Mansard roof is further distinguished by scalloped shingling. Terraced gardens and a splendid view to the north add to its environment of high quality.

A chaste and charming precursor of today's high-rise complexes exists at *1950, 1958,* and *1960 Green Street.* This three-story, three-unit apartment house was built about 1875 for a former Baltimore shoemaker, Isaac Hecht. It is said that the building was moved here about 1891; the balustraded balconies now visible from Green Street were originally the back door entrances while the bay windows, now at the rear, originally faced the street.

The building is Italianate in style; lofty flat-arched windows with "squeezed" pediments on the main floor (strip-corniced on the upper floor) underlie a bracketed cornice line. The overall effect is high and narrow, as the Italianate dictated, yet eminently functional.

The multi-domed *Holy Trinity Russian Orthodox Cathe-dral, 1520 Green Street,* was built in 1909 after the original cathedral—the first in the United States—was destroyed in 1906. The rambling frame church is not completely traditional Russian Orthodox in style, although blue domes and the many small stained-glass windows create a general medieval effect. This is actually an adaptation of Baroque Period styling of a quite Classicist type.

The interior atmosphere is more Russian with numerous icons and murals, and four tryptichs. Of especial interest is the massive 5000-pound bell, cast in 1888 in a Moscow foundry for use in the original cathedral at 1715 Powell Street. Of silver, brass and copper alloy, the bell was a gift from Czar Alexander III of Russia.

An unusually charming example of the fanciful Mannerist-Baroque, verging on Art Nouveau in wood and plaster, is *2413-17 Franklin Street,* between Green and Vallejo Streets. The building, which houses three flats, was erected in 1902. Numerous exterior ornamental details and intricate ironwork, especially the balconies and their traceried grillwork, express an animated turn-of-the-

The Casebolt House (left) is 1866 Italianate at its most opulent. 1950-60 Green (below) is an 1875 version of an apartment house

21

century fantasy which proved quite influential in San Francisco. Particularly the unusual French doors and curvilinear overwindow are echoed throughout the city.

The square wooden mansion at *1772 Vallejo Street* was an ex-sailor's wedding gift to his son. Ephraim Willard Burr came to California after he left the sea and eventually went into the wholesaling business. The New Englander prospered almost immediately, and went on to become one of San Francisco's earliest mayors.

The Italianate mansion on Vallejo Street, with slanted bays and a Mansard roof, was designed by Edmund M. Wharff and built in 1875 as Burr's wedding gift to his son, Edmund. During the 1906 earthquake, the house slipped off its foundations and ninety-three jacks were required to lift it back. As one of the best preserved residences of the period, it is a fine example of the transition of style in the later 1870's.

The *Musto-Morrissey House, 2700 Vallejo Street,* was designed and built in 1915 by architect Henry Smith for Clarence M. Musto, a descendant of Joseph Musto, who was one of the West's largest importers of marble—which explains the extensive use of that material in this Baroque mansion.

2413–17 Franklin (above) was an early-day pacesetter. 1772 Vallejo (below) was an 1875 wedding gift from a mayor to his son

The interior stairs and hall are of white Alabama and black Belgian marble; one fireplace is Numidian Pavanazzo marble, another Italian black and gold; a statue of Daphne and Apollo is Carrara marble; the large terrace is light pink Tennessee marble. A lovely ornamental cornice and striking green glazed-tile roof cap the relatively severe three-story main structure; two projecting Baroque wings frame the triple arches and paired columns of the entrance facade.

A house which one might expect to find tucked away in some bosky dell in Marin County is *2828 Vallejo Street*. This three-story home of redwood shingles and red sandstone was also a wedding gift, from shipping magnate William F. Babcock to his daughter and her husband, Dr. Charles Brigham.

The house, dating from the 1880's, originally occupied the site of the James L. Flood mansion at 2222 Broadway. When Flood bought the property in 1911, Dr. Brigham and his wife had the house moved in sections to its present location, set back from the street and enhanced by a walled garden.

San Francisco's Convent of the Sacred Heart has assimilated three of Broadway's most interesting old homes. The brick mansion at *2252 Broadway* was built around 1905 for Andrew B. Hammond, a lumber and railroad millionaire. The handsome residence was eventually purchased in 1956 by the Convent for use as a boys' school.

The three-story Italian Renaissance mansion at *2222 Broadway* was erected in 1912 from a design by architects Bliss and Faville for James L. Flood, son of the Comstock King. Corinthian columns encircled with fine incised spiral fluting flank the delicately-ornamented door and carefully-detailed cornice above. The window frames are derived from Northern Italian palace architecture. Tennessee marble is the principal structural material, although the base is of granite. Distinguishing features include a superb metal door screen, attractive quattrocento lamps and copper eaves. Flood's widow gave the house to the Convent in 1938. It has been used since 1940 as a school for girls.

The sedately elegant mansion at *2200 Broadway* was designed by New York architects Hiss and Weekes and built in 1910 for Joseph D. Grant, president of the Columbia Steel Corporation, board chairman of the California-Oregon Power Company and for many years chairman of the Save-the-Redwoods League. The brick and white stone Baroque mansion was purchased from the Grant family in 1948 by the Convent, and has been used since 1950 as part of the order's school complex.

Another Flood residence has also become a private school. The three-story Neo-Italian Baroque home at *2120 Broadway* was built in 1900–01 for James L. Flood. It served as his home until the sumptuous residence at 2222 Broad-way was completed in 1912, when he gave the house to his sister, Cora Jane (affectionately known through the years as "Miss Jennie"). In 1924 Miss Flood gave the house to the University of California, and in 1928 Sarah Dix Hamlin purchased it for use as a girls' school.

Although built during the high tide of Period architecture, this building retains a somewhat Victorian ingenuousness that relates it clearly to the James C. Flood house on Nob Hill (see page 66). The boldly-articulated two-story central motif of portico-like elements with rhythmic columns creates an obvious focus; pedimented windows recall the seventeenth century's reliance on Renaissance details in a Baroque context.

The two-story house with slanted bay windows at *1782 Pacific Avenue* was built in 1869 by lumber tycoon William C. Talbot as a wedding gift for his daughter. An unusual feature is the foundation which is supported by underground "flying buttresses" of brick. In 1905, Jacob Goldberg purchased the house and added a wing in keeping with the original style. The home is now a decorator's office and residence, and the shingled carriage house in the rear serves as a garage.

2828 Vallejo was also a gift—from a shipowner to his daughter

*Two of Broadway's showplaces, the Grant and Flood mansions
(above and right), are now a Catholic school for girls.
1782 Pacific (far right) was another wedding gift house*

At one side the present owner has created a Classical
Revival guest house which adds a third stylistic flourish to
the ensemble. The main house is an excellent example of
the Italianate town house, with pipestem colonnettes on
the first floor bays and other Mannerist Italian detailing;
the brackets at the roof line are clearly Victorian.

The massive brick structure at *2550 Webster Street* was
built in 1896 for William B. Bourn, President of the Spring
Valley Water Company. Architect Willis Polk, who also
designed Bourn's palatial Peninsula estate, *Filoli*, created
a powerful variant of Georgian forms for this residence
on property which then embraced the entire block. The
house has been maintained in superior condition perhaps
because it has had so few owners during its life.

One of the oldest houses in Pacific Heights is the *Leale
House, 2475 Pacific Avenue.* Dating possibly from the 1850's,
it was originally the farm house for a twenty-five acre dairy
ranch. Set back from the street on a high rise of land, enhanced by lawns and a few trees, the beautifully-preserved
house looks small but actually has four bedrooms, a library,
living room and dining room.

John Leale, a famous Bay ferry boat captain, purchased
the property in 1883. The false-fronted late Italianate

24

facade would seem to date from that time, although it could conceivably date from the 1860's, and the interior may be even older. Captain Leale had an elaborate play house built for his children which was later converted to a replica of a pilot house where he met with friends after his retirement.

The *Music and Art Institute, 2622 Jackson Street,* is reputed to have been Willis Polk's first major commission. Polk came to California in 1889 and designed this two-story Period house five years later as a "country" home for industrialist George W. Gibbs. By the time it was finished in 1894, the surrounding area was already so developed that no rural atmosphere existed.

Many features of the house, which is built of Oregon gray sandstone with a roof of glazed tiles, suggest Polk's later work. The most overt example of this is a semi-circular portico based on the round temples of ancient Rome, here with Ionic columns and a half-domed surface with a coffered interior. Terraced gardens were planned for the lot, which originally extended down the hill to Pacific Avenue, but the area's building boom disrupted these plans.

The building was purchased by the Music and Art Institute in 1947 as a center for the study of music, drama and opera.

The soaring red brick Jacobean-Georgian manor house at *2600 Jackson Street* reflects the generosity of Irving Murray Scott, a pioneer design engineer. Scott commis-

2475 Pacific (below)—an Italianate house bigger than it looks to be. 2550 Webster (right)—a Georgian house as big as it looks to be

This great brick manor (below) at 2600 Jackson was also a wedding gift. 2209 Jackson was once part of 1863's Tucker Town

The Spreckels mansion at 2080 Washington was built by George Applegarth who later designed the California Palace of The Legion of Honor

sioned Ernest Coxhead to design this residence for his daughter Alice in 1895 upon her marriage to Dr. Reginald Knight Smith, and members of the same family occupy the house today.

This was one of the first houses wired exclusively for electric light in San Francisco. The style is modified seventeenth century English. A long low dormer window, and chimneys on the north and south, break the line of the steep roof. All windows are composed of small leaded panes, while a three-foot-thick brick wall with an arched entrance over the gate extends from the glassed-in portion of the living room on the Jackson Street side.

A remnant of one of San Francisco's earliest real estate developments, originally bounded by Webster, Buchanan, Jackson and Washington Streets, can be seen at *2209 Jackson Street.* These cottages, built between 1861 and 1863 by John W. Tucker, a pioneer jeweler, were collectively known as Tucker Town.

Flanked by slanted bays, 2209 Jackson's entrance is clearly Italianate. (The present facade probably dates from a decade or so later than the original Tucker Town.) A brick livery stable stands behind the house in an area which has been enchantingly revised for modern use into a kind of mews.

Further east on Jackson Street is the former Whittier mansion, now the home of the *California Historical Society, 2090 Jackson Street.* Built in 1895–1896 for William Frank Whittier from a design by Edward R. Swain, this red sandstone Richardsonian residence, with Period (essentially Classical) details, is one of the few examples of almost unchanged late nineteenth century elegance in California.

Particularly notable is the Jackson Street facade, with its rhythmically-columned portico and massive pediment above between two modified Richardsonian Queen Anne towers. Also significant is the fact that this was one of the first town houses in California to be built of stone on a steel framework.

Most of the mansion's many rooms have carved paneling, predominantly mahogany, golden oak, primavera, and tamano. The vastness of the interior is indicated by the fact that *each* of the mansion's four levels has 3500 square feet of usable space, with a large attic above. The Historical Society has preserved the mansion's glory with great care, revitalizing this noble residence with new uses and minor interior changes that enhance its turn-of-the-century splendors.

Behind and below the Whittier mansion, at *2209 Pacific Avenue,* is the Historical Society's library, now called *Schubert Hall.* Constructed in 1905 of wood and stucco, the house is Baroque in style, with turn-of-the-century touches in the windows, which also incorporate handsome iron grillwork. The Society purchased the building (originally built for John D. Spreckels, Jr. as a wedding present from his father) in 1961.

The massive stone mansion at 2090 Jackson (below) is now occupied by the California Historical Society. 2579 Washington (right) is a cottage of the 1880's

29

The *Haas-Lilienthal House, 2007 Franklin Street*, is among the great houses of San Francisco and by all standards one of the finest examples of late nineteenth century architectural opulence in California. The house, enhanced by the large garden lot to the south, was built in 1886 for William Haas, a Bavarian merchant who came to San Francisco in the 1870's, and has been a family residence for all of its more than eighty years.

A fascinating combination of wooden details was erected upon the brick foundation, with sharp gables, dormers, and sidings which range from horizontal lapped types on the first floor, to fish-scale shingles on the third. The structure is dramatically capped by a corner Queen Anne tower, the top of which contains an additional room reached by an interior staircase from the attic. The wood trim of the house is richly ornamented with Eastlake, Baroque and even late Italianate forms, and stained-glass panels adorn the second-story windows. An iron fence with granite retaining walls and pillars still borders the sidewalk.

The elaborate exterior is more than matched by the interior, with floors of tile and marble, marble fireplaces, golden oak and mahogany woodwork, stamped leather walls, and a dining room dominated by an oak-beamed ceiling.

Three blocks away stands a completely Period mansion, the *Spreckels House, 2080 Washington Street*, which commands one of the prime views in all Pacific Heights. It was built about 1912 for Adolph Spreckels, son of sugar magnate Claus Spreckels, and architect George Applegarth's design reflects Mrs. Spreckels' French heritage. The mansion was Applegarth's first major work for this family—which later commissioned him to design the California Palace of the Legion of Honor.

Formal gardens were intended to cascade down the hill to Jackson Street, but they were never completed. Spreckels did, however, create landscaped islands on Octavia Street between Washington and Jackson, to avoid noisy descents by the "modern" automobile. Designed in the

The Swedenborgian Church of the New Jerusalem (preceding pages), 2107 Lyon Street, is based on an Italian village church

This group of row houses was put up in the early 1870's in the 2600 block of Clay Street and remains in fine condition

manner of a French palace of the later Baroque, the white stone house occupies nearly half a block. A major entrance on Washington Street has been removed, and the interior has been revised to suit the family's present needs.

Washington Street possesses a number of smaller but equally interesting old buildings. Among the most charming of these is *2355 Washington Street*, a three-story wooden Italianate Mansarded house built for Augustus Starr about 1882, and later the residence and office of Adolph Sutro's daughter, Dr. Emma Sutro Merritt—one of the first women to practice medicine in the nineteenth century.

The cottage at *2579 Washington Street* was built in 1884, apparently for Frederick Helbush. With its late Italianate trim and quasi-Gothic spikiness this represents a fanciful version of the San Francisco one-story false-fronted house of the 1880's. The wood trim is pierced with curvilinear Eastlake patterns; fish-scale shingles cover rooflets over the door and windows. The miniature castellated ornaments over the door's roof possibly allude to the "H" of the first owner's name.

The tree-shaded Eastlake-Queen Anne residence at *3020 Washington Street* is somewhat less visible. This three-story clapboard house was built in 1886, possibly by William Pluns, a carpenter and builder who lived in the house. The exterior retains its original charm, although the original entrance on the west is now on the east and a former coach house has been removed. Extensive remodeling of the interior has left little of the original character with the exception of the colored glass windows and nineteenth century moldings.

Complementing this gabled and towered residence is the former firehouse next door, *3022 Washington Street*, built in 1893 to house Engine Company 23. Closely related in style and age to the firehouse at 1152 Oak Street, 3022 Washington is very late Italianate with Victorian Gothic overtones, most apparent in the tower formerly used for drying the fire hoses. The interior, now a residence and studio, has been remodeled to accentuate its original purpose in a striking, yet comfortable manner.

In 1867, the Reverend Joseph Worcester came to San Francisco from Boston, where his father, the Reverend Thomas Worcester, had founded the New Jerusalem Church, based on the teachings of Emanuel Swedenborg. Worcester's first congregation worshiped in Druids Hall on Sutter Street, but in 1894 he participated in the planning of the present *Swedenborgian Church of the New Jerusalem, 2107 Lyon Street*. The church is based on Bruce Porter's sketches of an Italian village church in the Po Valley near Verona, and Porter also designed its two large stained-glass windows. The actual architectural drawings (from Porter's sketches) were done by a young man named Bernard Maybeck in the firm of A. Page Brown.

The church was completed in 1895, and reflects the Swedenborgians' central theme, presenting natural objects and incorporating them into the structure and grounds. A heavy tile roof, for example, is supported by massive bark-covered madrone logs. The sturdy maple chairs used for worship were made by hand, without the use of nails, and their seats were woven of tule rushes from the Sacramento River Delta. The walled gardens are symbolic; each detail was selected for its international or universal significance.

Architecturally, the church is simple and direct, characteristic of both its spiritual sources and the concepts of Maybeck. Only the charming wall belfry suggests any period; the low arches and roof line are otherwise utilitarian and neutral.

Pacific Heights possesses a large number of what might be termed group houses, so similar in style and preservation that they dominate their immediate area, and often set the tone for an entire neighborhood.

An unusually fine group of frame row houses is *2637, 2643, 2649, 2655, 2661, 2667* and *2673 Clay Street;* all built in the early 1870's, all with similar essentially Italianate, stylistic characteristics, suggesting that they were not only built at the same time, but by the same contractor. The use of redwood may be partially responsible for their preservation, but much of the credit must go to owners who have joined together to maintain these houses in mint condition.

Another well-maintained row is *2209* through *2253 Webster Street.* The Italianate slanted-bay houses were constructed about 1878–79 and again reflect the thinking of one contractor-builder. This row differs from that on Clay Street in varying from single-family residences to flats to small business offices partly due to the proximity of a large hospital.

Another group of Victorian flats and houses is on Pierce Street between Sacramento and California. This row, *2002* through *2032 Pierce Street* and *2695 Sacramento Street*, lacks the overall architectural unity of the earlier single-family residences of the Clay Street row nearby. Three of the buildings show the flavor of the 1890's.

2028–30 and *2032–34 Pierce Street* reflect a late blending of Italianate, Stick and Eastlake with a few hints of Colonial Revival. Both feature fish-scale shingles which accent the peaked roofs and Victorian trim. The Queen Anne structure at *2695 Sacramento Street*, which uses its corner lot to advantage, was also built in 1894 but is more heavily ornamented than the adjacent twin houses. Period regularity is minimized by the two steep, almost medieval, gables that break the roof line, and by the salient corner tower. Colonial Revival garlands festoon the whole exterior.

The architectural strength of the row lies not in these late Victorian flats, but in the chaste Italianate-Stick buildings, *2002–04, 2006–08,* and *2010–12 Pierce Street*, built

The Italianate slanted-bay houses (above) in the 2200 block of Webster Street were built in the late 1870's by the same contractor. The 2000 block of Pierce Street contains some fine specimens of Victorian Gothic but the best of them are the trio at 2002–12 Pierce (right), all built between 1878 and 1882

between 1878 and 1882. Their uncompromising verticality and almost Mondrian-like surface interlineations create a prismatic crispness that adapts itself to any modern paint or decorative treatment.

The row of five identical one-story wood Italianate-Mansarded cottages at *1805* through *1817 Baker Street* was constructed in 1882 by builder William F. Lewis and is typical of tract housing of the time. A common feature of these residences is the use of the flattened Mansard roof, an unusual element in houses this size. (The roof of 1817 Baker was originally similar to the others, but was severely damaged in 1906 and never rebuilt in its original form.) Again, the owners have restored the houses most attractively, adding charm to the entire neighborhood.

The twenty-six hundred block of California Street pos-

sesses a row of fine old houses, all originally built and owned by Edward A. Selfridge.

His own residence, built about 1878, stands at *2615 California Street.* This two-story Stick-Style Victorian structure shows much architectural detail typical of the age, such as the omnipresent Classicism of the Corinthian-columned entrance, the gabled roofs (a carved but flat sunburst fills the gable above 1880's-type squared bay windows), and Eastlake scrollwork in the entrance portico. During the 1930's architect Julia Morgan divided the house into three units. She was also responsible for the bay-like effect to the west of the entrance which now balances the facade.

In 1892 Selfridge added six small two-story cottages to his property. These houses, *2603* through *2613 California Street,* are predominantly Colonial Revival with Queen

The Mansard roofs on these identical 1882 cottages at 1805–17 Baker Street are rare in such small houses

1969 California (right) was to have a twin next door but it was never built, hence the half arch intended to span a common driveway

Anne towers. They were later allowed to fall into disrepair, and were marked for condemnation by the city.

The row was purchased in 1959 by a far-sighted realtor who refurbished the houses without substantially altering their external appearances. They now make up a striking complex called "California Mews." A community row garden at the rear links the houses and opens their small individual back yards to a common center.

In 1849, the less than one hundred Jewish immigrants to San Francisco met to celebrate Passover at the Hotel Albion. The congregation called itself "Sherith Israel," or the "loyal remnant of Israel." From such humble beginnings grew the congregation that built *Temple Sherith Israel, 2266 California Street,* in 1905.

The Temple survived the earthquake so well that the city used it as a Hall of Justice for two years following the disaster. The Temple, of gray limestone in the Romanesque

tradition, has an especially impressive Byzantine dome. The interior is enhanced by intricately-carved woodwork of Honduras mahogany and by outstanding stained-glass windows.

That captivating architectural curiosity, *1990 California Street,* is as representative an example of Stick-Eastlake and uninhibited Queen Anne as can be found anywhere in San Francisco. This extraordinary "castle" was built in the early 1880's for Mrs. Faxon Dean Atherton. Nowhere is the restless irregularity of late Victorian design more clearly evident. The house vibrates with a picturesque asymmetry and steepness of roof line. The facade displays a great variety of different treatments, from quite plain to intricately carved. It remains today, outwardly unchanged, a vestige of California Street's eminence in late Victorian prestige.

Next door, *1976 California Street,* complements its large

The 1800 block of California (above) exudes formal elegance.

neighbor although their architectural styles are quite different. Elaborately Stick-Italianate in style, 1976 California was built in 1883. Both 1990 and 1976 California are on the edge of a style's demise; their super-active surfaces are ready to burst all bounds. 1976 California is the last phase of Italianate with Stick; 1990 California moves into Queen Anne.

The interior of 1976 California retains its original moldings, paneling and brass and crystal chandeliers. The front reception hall contains a fourteen-foot plate glass mirror, reputedly shipped around the Horn from England.

Across the street is a modified English Tudor Gothic residence, *1969 California Street,* built in 1915 to the designs of Willis Polk. This house was built for Mrs. Joseph O. Tobin (Constance de Young) next door to the former de Young mansion, now demolished. The design also contemplated a twin to this house for Mrs. George T. Cameron (Helen de Young), but it was never built, as Mrs. Cameron moved to the Peninsula shortly after 1969 California was completed. The former Tobin residence still includes half the Tudor arch which was to span the driveway between the two houses.

The complex of houses radiating from the northwest corner of California and Franklin Streets comprises one of San Francisco's most valuable and architecturally distinguished districts. Each house is admirably set off from its neighbors by spacious lawns and gardens, immaculately maintained as are the residences themselves.

One outstanding residence here is *1834 California Street,* built in 1876 by pioneer wholesale grocer Samuel Sussman.

Approximately twenty years later, the three-story Italianate house was purchased by financier John C. Coleman, who modernized it according to the dictates of the 1890's. The house stands in that form to this day.

The town house at *1818–20 California Street* was built in 1876 by Louis Sloss, an organizer of the Alaska Commercial Company. The Italianate slanted-bay-window house originally had an elaborate balcony over the entrance, and the once-ornate fence posts were enhanced by finials.

Edward Coleman in 1895 built a home near his brother John's at *1701 Franklin Street*. Edward's is a massive, three-story, triumphantly-Queen Anne-Colonial Revival house with balustraded balconies, garlanded friezes and a corner tower—all on a brownstone base.

The very correct brick Colonial Revival (Georgian) house at *1735 Franklin Street* has little in common with the other houses in this group. Built in 1904 from a design by architect Herman Barth, it gives the solid appearance of a manor house. The construction is brick veneer over wood; even so, it survived the fire and earthquake of 1906 in fine fashion. The owner of this property purchased both the Sloss home and the Edward Coleman home to ensure that the parklike integrity of the area would endure.

Another enclave barely removed from Van Ness Avenue's commercialism is on Sacramento Street between Franklin and Gough: *1911, 1913, 1915, 1919,* and *1921 Sacramento Street* are all related in style. The most recent, 1919 Sacramento, with its small dormers, Palladian first-floor window, and columned portico at the front entrance, is Colonial Revival in style and was built in 1895. The other four were built in the late 1860's or 1870's. All the latter are basically two-story Italianate designs. The pointed-arched Gothic windows and pedimented Italianate windows which contribute so markedly to the charm of these town houses have been well-preserved. The three houses have been painted in dramatic complementary colors.

These fine early San Francisco homes are in the 1900 block of Sacramento St.

RUSSIAN HILL

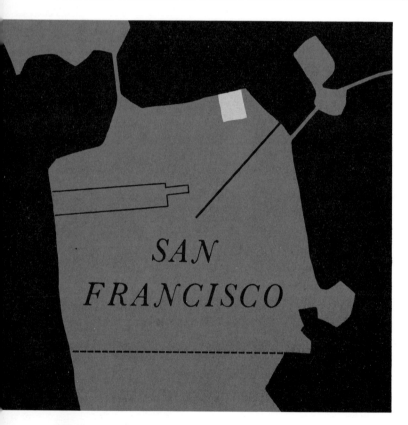

SAN FRANCISCO

Russian Hill has been called the most magnificent natural site for residences in San Francisco. An adjunct of Nob Hill (the saddle connecting them being the high "pass" of Pacific Avenue), it can be loosely defined as the area bounded by the Bay on the north and Pacific Avenue on the South, by Taylor Street on the east and Van Ness Avenue on the west. Both for its view and comparatively easy access through the gap to North Beach, it early became a desirable place of residence. Russian Hill afforded just sufficient removal from downtown to attract people of moderate means but superior tastes, those "Bohemian" enough to value a view over the convenience of nickel horse-cars.

Today it is much the same in character, but more crowded. High-rise apartments now dot the hill but its most beautiful sites remain, as from the beginning, largely in the hands of discriminating San Francisco families.

In the present development of the *Ghirardelli Block, Larkin and North Point Streets,* at the foot of Russian Hill can be seen that imaginative combination of renovation and preservation that can produce something invaluable to a city.

Domingo Ghirardelli, San Francisco's premier chocolate maker, was intimately associated with two crowning jewels of the city's recent enthusiasm for the preservation and lively use of blocks of buildings of beguiling and historic architecture—Jackson Square (where the Ghirardelli building forms the core of the superb restoration) and Ghirardelli Square, the modernization of the wonderful red brick pile he began to construct in 1893.

The nucleus of the Ghirardelli Block is the three-story building originally built as the S.F. Pioneer Woolen Factory in 1864. This old structure is easily distinguished from the later buildings not only by its plainer surface treatment, but because it is not aligned on the same axis as the later buildings—as can be most easily seen from the Polk Street side of the block.

Ghirardelli purchased the old woolen mill in 1893, although he died before the factory was moved from Jackson Square in 1897. In the next two decades Domingo's sons added the increasingly elaborate buildings that make up the present block, finishing in 1916 with the Clock Tower Building at the corner of Larkin and North Point, an impressive structure patterned after the Louis XII wing of the Chateau Blois in the Loire Valley. All the buildings were designed by architect William Mooser, whose father had designed the original woolen mill.

Ghirardelli Square (right) is a magnificent example of the way in which a city's architectural heritage may be preserved and its value enhanced by intelligent restoration

*Some Russian Hill homes survived the
1906 fire when their owners refused to be dynamited.
High-rise apartments dot Russian Hill
today but many of its most beautiful old homes remain*

In the early 1960's, the fate of this attractive industrial block was much in question; the value of the land had advanced steadily while the old buildings were becoming less and less suitable to an up-to-date plant. The obvious probability was that the Ghirardelli Block would be demolished to make way for high-rise apartments.

At this point, William M. Roth bought the block and retained the distinguished architectural firm of Wurster, Bernardi & Emmons to remodel it as a center for high quality shops and restaurants. Only one of the old buildings was razed—the frame "box factory" on Beach Street—and this was replaced by a handsome modern building executed in a style consistent with the older structures.

Altogether, Ghirardelli Square is a triumph of imaginative planning and sensitive use of existing buildings of architectural merit. The great success of this project has had a profound effect on the Aquatic Park-Fisherman's Wharf area, as developers seize upon the possibilities inherent in other old buildings.

If the Ghirardelli block has been the most obvious and important element in the Aquatic Park area's restoration and development activity, it is the still incomplete State Park program, sponsored by the San Francisco Maritime Museum, that has been the true cornerstone. Al-

though the old *Haslett Warehouse Building, 650 Beach Street,* has not yet been converted into the projected railroad museum, its purchase for this purpose (and the creation of a nineteenth century park on the block bounded by North Point, Hyde, Beach and Larkin, as well as the reconstruction of the Hyde Street Pier and the mooring there of representative historical vessels) has had the effect of "nailing down" the historic character of the district.

The Haslett Warehouse, built just after the 1906 earthquake, is not a structure of remarkable distinction. It is merely a handsome, clean-lined, good quality, turn-of-the-century warehouse. But that this good red brick building should be considered worthy of indefinite preservation and museum use inevitably suggested the potential value of the other big brick buildings in the area. Further, it has become increasingly obvious that the axis formed by the transportation museum committed to Aquatic Park and the existing Fisherman's Wharf complex must before long become the greatest tourist attraction in one of the greatest tourist cities of the world.

On the *Hyde Street Pier,* the San Francisco Maritime State Historical Monument, a small office has been installed. It is hoped this will be only the first of several buildings that will eventually "reconstruct" a San Francisco waterfront scene

of the late nineteenth century. This building was the foreman's office at the Tubbs Cordage Company, out in the Potrero District. A simple, hipped roof structure with Italianate details, the little office is thought to have been built in the early 1860's; it was donated to the Maritime Monument when the Tubbs Company closed its old rope walk a few years ago.

One of the best of the adjacent buildings is that of the West Coast Advertising Company, at *781 Beach Street.* This two-story brick structure, built in 1912, has been a winery, soap factory, and warehouse. With its handsome arched windows, this building is one of the more attractive properties fronting on the Aquatic Park development.

Another eminently successful restoration is *"The Cannery,"* a building once owned by the California Packing Company at *Beach and Leavenworth Streets.* Built around 1909, at the same time as the Haslett Warehouse next door, this building has been remodeled into a shop-and-restaurant complex comparable to Ghirardelli Square. With the renovation of this old building, the Fisherman's Wharf-Aquatic Park area is all but framed with large, brick industrial buildings of powerful design, elegant use, and permanent value.

Set far back from the street, almost hidden from view,

Careful remodeling preserved the charm of 765 Bay

The Thomas Church cottage at 2626 Hyde dates from the 1850's

44

the house at *765 Bay Street* is reputed to date from the year before the gold discovery at Sutter's Mill. Originally a simple vertical board-and-batten house, it was moved twice (presumably during the decade of the 1850's), winding up on its present site enlarged and remodeled with a front and decorative details sent out from Salem, Massachusetts. In the 1930's, the present owner extensively remodeled the interior consistent with the old architecture. The charm of this interesting antique was heightened by the skillful landscaping of Thomas Church, who planned the garden around existing old fruit trees.

The home of Thomas Church himself, at *2626 Hyde Street*, is a peculiarly attractive building that almost certainly dates from the middle 1850's. The original cottage—a four-room, two-story house of simple design—is said to have been built by a Scottish architect for his bride. A building is shown on this exact site on the 1856 Coast Survey Chart of San Francisco, and it is very likely this same house.

Some time in the 1860's the house appears to have been remodeled in its present Victorian Gothic style. While Church enlarged and remodeled the house in 1954, adding such striking features as the curving double staircase leading to the front door, the decorative treatment that characterizes the house is original. The unusual friezes under the eaves are old hand-cut designs, rather than the machine-made "Eastlake" of the 1880's.

A block up the hill, at *2540–50 Hyde Street*, is an unusual row of six cottages which march up a slight rise at a right angle to the Hyde Street cable line. Not visible from the street are the charming little gardens at the back of the houses. The houses were built around 1900 by Lucius Solomon, and they possess a Victorian feeling in its most simplified form.

One of the oldest homes in the city is the residence at *825 Francisco Street*, originally constructed by R. C. Ruskin of lumber salvaged from ships abandoned at San Francisco in the Gold Rush. In 1854 the house was enlarged by a new owner and probably reached its present form at a much later date.

It is said that the house was saved from the 1906 fire by means of wine-soaked sacks applied to the roof and walls. In 1908 its front lawn held grandstands erected by the city so that distinguished guests might view the entrance into the bay of the Great White Fleet on its round-the-world cruise. The front of the house appears much as it did in the 1850's, while the interior has been extensively remodeled.

In the 2500 block of Leavenworth are several homes dating from the 1880's, the most interesting of which is *2500 Leavenworth Street.* An attractive junior-size gingerbread villa, it was built in 1881. An almost integral decorative detail is the carefully-sited ornamental palm, the out-

*825 Francisco (top) was built from ship's timbers
A cottage row (center) at 2540–50 Hyde Street
2455 Leavenworth (bottom) is typical of its time—1908*

door equivalent of the potted conservatory plant.

A handsome shingled house in the style best exemplified in the work of Bernard Maybeck and Julia Morgan, the residence at *2455 Leavenworth Street* is of the type that is apt to be described casually as "Swiss Chalet" in derivation. This four-story home was built in 1908 for Mr. A. G. Langenberger.

On the other side of the block from the fine old house at 825 Francisco Street, on the east slope of what used to be known as the Chestnut Street Hill, stand two handsome homes dating from the 1860's. A photograph of 1867 shows three houses standing amidst fruit trees on this part of the hill—the house on Francisco and the neighboring houses at *930 and 944 Chestnut Street.*

The house at *944 Chestnut Street* was built in about 1863 by artist Alexander Edouart. Eschewing the popular Italianate style, Edouart built a two-story frame house of rather Georgian character. Two years later, he sold the house to a real estate man, Francis Spring.

Francis Spring lived in the house until his death in 1896. In 1918 artist Bruce Porter bought the home for his bride, a daughter of the philosopher William James. Porter, with his designer's eye, considerably remodeled both house and garden.

In 1926 Porter bought the house next door, at *930 Chestnut Street*. A two-story Italianate structure, it had been built in about 1861 by James C. Cary, whose family occupied it for sixty-five years. Today, beautifully maintained and embowered by lush foliage, the Cary and Spring Houses are among the most delightful of the city's old residences.

On the western slope of Russian Hill, in the twelve hundred block of Lombard Street, are a number of old buildings of considerable character, two of which cannot be seen from the sidewalk.

At *1215 Lombard Street* is an attractive, two-story shingled house set well back behind a garden. Built around 1886, its architectural details suggest that like some of the other houses on the street it may originally have been a standard Stick Style house, to which shingles were later applied. At present the house is divided into apartments and is handsomely restored and maintained.

On the other hand, *1245 Lombard Street* may have been built as early as 1884 in a distinctive shingle style. This house is also well restored; rooms have been added to the rear, but the present owner is confident that the facade is basically the same as when the house was built.

An especially impressive pair of three-story shingled apartment houses stand at *1263–67 and 1269–79 Lombard Street*, the former originally built as flats, the latter originally a single-family dwelling. Both structures seem to have been built around 1877. Behind these large buildings are a pair of attractive cottages, *1261 and 1271 Lom-*

1263 Lombard Street (above) was built around 1877
1215 Lombard (right)—shingled Stick Style

This one-story house, 2531 Larkin, really has two stories

bard Street, also built in about 1877–78. Both are of simple Italianate style, 1261 having the usual horizontal siding, 1271 being shingled.

Around the corner, at *2531 Larkin Street*, is an outstanding example of the interior remodeling of an old house. This little single-story-and-basement home was built in 1876, and to all appearances looks as though it has only been "restored." In fact, its architect-owner has converted it into a two-story house with almost double the space of the old building. The second floor, which contains the living spaces, was achieved by dropping the twelve-foot ceilings to eight feet, thus concealing the second story behind the high parapet of the old facade.

Perhaps the most famous residential street in San Francisco is the twisting stretch of Lombard Street between Hyde and Leavenworth. The amazing curves of the descent make the street something of a tourist attraction. The red brick paving is wonderfully set off by the banked masses of flowers planted in the segments of the right-of-way left vacant by the curves in the street—a happy example of neighborhood planning and maintenance.

At the top of the hill is the very intimate and attractive house at *1098 Lombard Street*, a home that from the street gives the impression of an elegant, woodsy cottage. It was built in 1919. The lot once included almost half a block, and still includes a garden (walled from public view and sweeping down the Hyde Street side to Chestnut Street) which is almost large enough to qualify as a park.

The ten hundred block of Green Street, on one of the three crests of Russian Hill, is one of the most remarkable blocks in the city. The outstanding building on the block is the octagon house at *1067 Green Street.* One of the two remaining octagon houses in the city (once there were five), the "Feusier House" was built in 1857–58 by George Kenny and sold in 1870 to Louis Feusier, a companion of such San Francisco celebrities as Leland Stanford and

Mark Twain. The plan was developed from the general scheme of Orson S. Fowler, a phrenologist who had succeeded in identifying well-being with the shape and construction of one's domicile. The addition of a Mansard roof, providing a third story, and a small, octagonal cupola during the 1880's does not seem to have affected the original style of the house.

Next to the octagon house, at *1055 Green Street*, is an elegant little villa originally built in 1866. This house was remodeled under the direction of Julia Morgan in 1916, and it is Miss Morgan who must be given the credit for the beautifully balanced facade, with its three arched French doors and wrought-iron balcony.

Somewhat reminiscent of an old farmhouse, *1045 Green Street* is a three-story brown shingled home of uncertain date. It may have been built as early as 1867 or as late as 1887. There is also the possibility that it may have been moved to this site immediately after the 1906 fire.

The house next door, at *1039–41–43 Green Street*, more certainly was moved to its present location after the great fire. A narrow, three-story Stick Style building of the 1880's, it consists of three large flats. The curving staircase leading to the second-floor entrance is quite unusual.

1033 Green Street is an elegant Italianate house, with its slanted bay and arched windows and doorway. Built prior to 1891, it also may have been moved from a different site.

On the other side of the street, a most striking building is the firehouse at *1088 Green Street.* This structure was built in 1907. The facade is entirely different from the prevailing firehouse architecture of the period, being half timbered and having a steeply pitched roof and ornate front dormer. Always a neighborhood center and landmark, the firehouse was saved by Mrs. Ralph K. Davies, who bought it from the city in 1956. The interior now houses a small museum and a large "party room" that is often used for charity functions.

These two Italianate cottages of the 1870's are behind 1263 Lombard

There is an unusual shingled house at the corner of Jones and Union Streets, with a handsome shingled apartment house next door. The house at *1960 Jones Street* occupies the site of a residence built by Henry H. Bruns in 1879. After the 1906 fire, which destroyed this house, Bruns' son-in-law, William H. Middleton, built the present structure.

One of the most unusual features of the house is the use of mullioned windows of a small diamond pattern. At the time this home was built (1907), the widow of Henry Bruns erected the large apartment building next door.

Macondray Lane, a privately-maintained street running from Leavenworth to Taylor between Union and Green Streets, has an old Bohemian reputation. The bucolic atmosphere of this country lane on Russian Hill attracted artists and writers (such as poetess Ina Coolbrith), and for many years some of the city's leading newspapermen. The most historically interesting of its houses is *15–17 Macondray Lane*, which dates to at least 1872 but is thought to be older, perhaps having been shipped around the Horn.

At Taylor and the Green Street steps stands an almost monumentally impressive shingle apartment building, *900–910 Green Street*, containing seven large flats. Built in 1910, the building rises five stories high on Taylor, decreasing in height as it backs up the hill. The front on Taylor is broken up into many surfaces by squared and slanted bays, a corner tower effect being created by the angled bays. The back of the house is only three stories high, the vine-

Mullioned windows distinguish 1960 Jones Street

covered walls forming a garden courtyard opening onto the Green Street steps through a covered gate.

Immediately above the gate *920–30 Green Street* is an older brown-shingled residence of attractive demeanor. Gables and porches and the rustic setting characterize the house. It was built by Hans H. Christiansen, a police sergeant, in 1895. In about 1903 it was purchased by J. M. Moss, one of the city's best-known citizens. Moss appears to have remodeled, and perhaps enlarged, the house, and it was he who later designed and built the apartment building below.

Further down, *840 Green Street* is an unusually attractive town house, brown-shingled and in the romantic and vaguely Gothic style popularized by Maybeck. It was built in 1907. Clean-lined, its facade dominated by a simple but elegant bay window accented with narrow, vertical panes, it is the kind of home that is at once distinctive and unassuming. Author Charles Dobie once lived here.

The ten hundred block of Green Street in 1915. All the houses are still standing today

The highest point in downtown San Francisco, the 1000 block of Vallejo Street, is one of the city's most attractive residential neighborhoods. It is the only area of frame construction that lay entirely within the limits of the 1906 conflagration and yet survived. There are three narrow residential streets at the top of the hill: Vallejo Street, which is approached from Jones Street by a pair of ramps designed by Willis Polk; Russian Hill Place; and Florence Street, another cul-de-sac, leading off Vallejo to the south.

The influence of Willis Polk in the architecture of this block is great, and here he apparently found an opportunity to try out one of his concepts of thematic architecture. A group of fine homes was projected on property owned by Norman B. Livermore. The seven tile-roofed, Mediterranean-style villas were all built in 1915–1916. Polk designed the row to the north, which have their entrances at *1, 3, 5, and 7 Russian Hill Place;* Charles F. Whittlesey (architect of the Pacific Building on Market Street) did the group to the south, at *1085 Vallejo Street and 1740, 1742 Jones Street.*

Whittlesey tried to handle three houses as a single unit, while Polk did his four as obviously separate houses of somewhat different appearance. Altogether, the development is one of the most successful of its kind attempted in San Francisco.

Willis Polk's own home was the romantic shingled house just beyond the circle at *1013–1015–1017 Vallejo Street.* It is said that when Mrs. Virgil Williams commissioned her house in 1892, Polk agreed to do the job for the eastern twenty feet of the sixty-foot lot. The result was two houses under one roof—the Williams house, *1019 Vallejo Street,* being the larger, western portion of what appears to be a single building. Polk's house was much bigger than it appears, as the hill drops off so steeply that it is seven stories high in the rear. It would also seem that Polk got the better part of the bargain so far as the view was concerned.

The Horatio P. Livermore home, at *1045 Vallejo Street and 40–42 Florence Street,* is a grand shingled house built around 1860, and later remodeled by Willis Polk. At the height of its glory this country house on the highest nob of Russian Hill was situated on an exceptionally large lot, planted with fruit trees to provide a park-like setting.

In 1917, shortly after the death of Livermore, his widow decided to turn over the main house to the Norman Livermores and build another house on the eastern edge of the property. Julia Morgan was commissioned to design this home, perhaps the best example of her residential work in San Francisco.

The new house at *1023 Vallejo Street* was on varying levels, as the ground dropped off steeply. In the shingle style for which Miss Morgan was famous, it is notable for repetition of large, arched, mullioned windows. It is almost hidden from the street, access being through a narrow "panhandle" of the lot.

On the north side of the street are two severely plain shingled houses which were built around 1884 for D. P. and Emily Price Marshall, although the name of the Reverend Joseph Worcester of Swedenborgian church is often erroneously connected with the houses. The two houses, *1034 and 1036 Vallejo Street,* are quite elegant despite their plainness, the sharply peaked roofs and small windows of the upper floor being reminiscent of old New England. The home at 1036 Vallejo is sometimes remembered as the one-time residence of Colonel Rowen who carried "The Message to Garcia," during the Spanish-American war.

At *1652–56 Taylor Street* is the "House of the Flag." Part of the original portion of the house, behind the building fronting on Taylor Street, appears to date from the 1850's or early 1860's. In the late 1890's the old home was purchased by Mr. Eli T. Sheppard, and in 1903 he built the new addition on Taylor Street.

On April 19, 1906, as the great fire swept up the slopes of Russian Hill, the Sheppards and their tenant, E. A. Dakin, were forced to evacuate, but not before Dakin hoisted a large American flag over the house in a gesture of defiance. Soldiers of the Twentieth Infantry Regiment saw the gesture and made a spur-of-the-moment decision to save both house and flag. With water the Sheppards had stored in the bathtubs after the earthquake, with seltzer bottles the family had purchased for emergency drinking water, and with wet sand from a construction project, they snuffed out each flame while the fire swept through all the other houses on that side of Taylor Street. Days later the Sheppards learned from newspaper photographs that their house had been saved.

Another nearby house with an unusual history is *1637 Taylor Street.* Apparently dating back to the 1860's, the house is said to have been cut in half to carry out a community property decision, the husband electing to remain with his half, the estranged wife removing her half to the Potrero.

The two houses at *1629 Taylor Street* and *1020 Broadway* are built on a large lot owned until after 1906 by attorney Charles H. Parker. After the family house was destroyed by the fire, two of the Parker children divided the lot and built their own homes in 1909. Both are attractive shingled residences; both were owned at one time or another by poet Sara Bard Field Wood and her husband, Charles Erskine Scott Wood.

On the steep hillside at *1032 Broadway* is a house built by James Atkinson in about 1853. Originally a frame Italian villa, it was extensively remodeled by Willis Polk in 1900.

Russian Hill remains a charming mixture of old and new

These 1884 "look-alikes" are at 1034–36 Vallejo

Willis Polk designed two houses under one roof at 1013–19 Vallejo

This Polk villa is one of four he built on Russian Hill Place

Willis Polk also designed 1 Russian Hill Place in 1915

TELEGRAPH HILL/JACKSON SQUARE

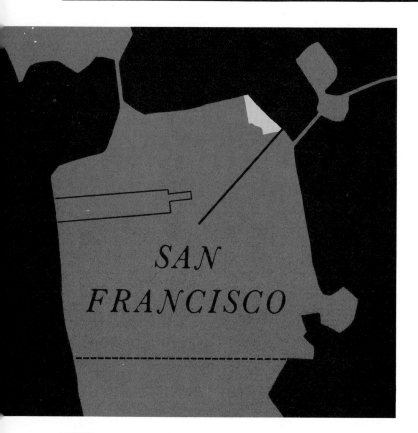

SAN FRANCISCO

The only major part of downtown San Francisco that was spared by the 1906 disaster consisted of three enclaves of completely different character, but which had in common a geographical association with Telegraph Hill. One of these enclaves was on the southern and eastern slopes of the hill itself, another was a small part of the waterfront warehouse district at the foot of the hill, the third was a small part of the business district of Gold Rush times located just south of the hill and just north of the present financial district on lower Montgomery Street.

Some of the earliest business buildings in San Francisco still stand in the block of Jackson Street between Montgomery and Sansome, now known as Jackson Square. The restoration and enlightened use of these fine old buildings

in recent years has paid off handsomely in economic and aesthetic, as well as historical, terms. The development of the Square as a headquarters for dealers in fine silks, hand-blocked wallpapers, and furniture has provided remarkably distinguished quarters for a business that trades in distinction.

The impression conveyed by the renovated Jackson Square is that of liveable urbanism. The two-and three-story brick buildings let light into the street and in no way overpower the pedestrian. Yet this is no "main street" setting; it is distinctly and consciously metropolitan.

One elegant Jackson Square building is the former A. P. Hotaling warehouse at *451–461 Jackson Street.* A fine example of the Italianate style popular in San Francisco business blocks of the '60's and '70's, the Hotaling warehouse employs the powerful Baroque device of alternating pointed and arched window pediments. The ornamental pillars of the first floor are of a cast-iron pattern produced by a San Francisco works. All of the windows were once fitted with iron shutters, the heavy brick construction and shuttered openings comprising "fire-proofing" in that day.

Hotaling was one of San Francisco's leading liquor dealers, and he erected this headquarters and warehouse in about 1866. As the business flourished he added an adjoining structure on Jones Alley (now called Hotaling Place), the rather similar two-story building on Jackson adjoining to the east, and the three-story building across the alley at *463 Jackson Street.* The warehouse at 463 seems to have been built around 1860. It is in the same general style of *451–461 Jackson,* but more restrained in ornamentation. In this case the pediments over the windows are less elaborate, and all of those over the second floor windows are arched, while those of the third floor are pointed.

The cast iron pillars employed in these and many other buildings of the period now permit an almost totally glazed facade for the first floor, a characteristic that makes such buildings eminently eligible for modern shop use. At the time the style of these buildings was characteristic of San Francisco, they, too, would have had glass fronts had they been used as stores; as warehouses, they had floor-to-ceiling iron doors, which greatly facilitated the handling of heavy goods.

A magnificent example of the textural properties of old brick is seen in the former French consulate at *432 Jackson Street*. Combined with the surface qualities of the brick, the pattern of Romanesque arches of the first-floor facade, and the flat, recessed arches of the second-floor windows, the plane trees of recent vintage enhance an inherent interplay of light and shadow.

Said to have been the first French consulate building in San Francisco, the structure was erected about 1865. In keeping with this romantic flavor, its later tenants included Ina Coolbrith, poet laureate of California, and a school of languages conducted by a Professor J. Mibielle. Further, Balance Street, which flanks one side of the building, was named for the *Balance,* a Gold Rush ship which ended her last voyage landlocked forever by the encroaching wharves and streets of the growing city.

What was once the Ghirardelli Chocolate Factory stands at *415 Jackson Street*. Domingo Ghirardelli moved his burgeoning chocolate business into this building in 1857. He also moved his wife and family into the spacious second story quarters: which illustrates an important characteristic associated with the handsome commercial architecture of old San Francisco—that the upper floors of business, or even light industrial premises, very frequently were used as flats by the owners or other prosperous citizens. The combination of business and residential use in the downtown area is one that is only now being revived as one of the answers to the problems of urban living and of full-time use of scarce and expensive "core city" lands.

The buildings at *441, 402 and 470 Jackson Street* would be worthy of special note were they located in a less distinguished block, but details concerning them must, in this case, be removed to the Appendix. A final Jackson Square building that should be noted is the one that originally housed the bank of Lucas, Turner & Co. at *498 Jackson Street*. Built in 1854. this Italianate structure was originally three stories high. The first-floor Montgomery Street facade is of white stone, the remainder of the building being plain red brick. This Montgomery Street face, with its elegant flattened arches and central doorway surmounted by a chaste classical pediment, has a substantial air well befitting a bank.

William T. Sherman, soon to earn a reputation as one of America's greatest generals, was the resident partner in the bank, and it was his native caution in fiscal matters that kept it strong in the midst of one of the city's most turbulent periods.

Hotaling's warehouse, elegant ornament to Jackson Square

53

*This fine old brick building
at 432 Jackson dates from 1865
and housed the French Consul*

*449 Pacific now houses
an art gallery but was once
the local firehouse*

Around the corner on Montgomery Street between Jackson and Washington Streets is a row of buildings of the same ancient vintage as those of Jackson Square. The most striking of this set of four adjacent buildings is the two-story brick structure now identified as the Belli Building, *722–724 Montgomery Street.* According to its owner, attorney Melvin Belli, there is reason to believe that at least part of the brick shell of the building dates from before the disastrous fires of 1851; certainly, there seems little doubt that the building is one of the earliest still standing in the downtown district. In December of 1857 the Melodeon, a resort of variety entertainment, opened for business on these premises.

The building had long since fallen into neglect when it attracted the attention of Belli in 1958. Since then he has lovingly rejuvenated this relic of Gold Rush days. The antique texture of the brick and cast iron architectural ornamentation is enhanced by window boxes and vines, a handsome wrought-iron gate, and colorful gas-lamps. The effect is highly nostalgic, but old Montgomery Street was never quite like this!

More characteristic of early Montgomery Street is the next door building, *726–728 Montgomery Street,* also restored by Belli. This three-story, unadorned brick building looks very much like many San Francisco business buildings of the very early '50's. It was built by Joseph Genella about 1853–54 for his chinaware business. As in the case of the Belli Building, the foundation is constructed of heavy, criss-crossed planking which "floats" in the sand of what originally was the beach of Yerba Buena Cove.

The *Golden Era* Building at *732 Montgomery Street* also appears to date from the 1850's. The cast iron pillars in the front bear the marking "Vulcan Iron Works 1892"; as the building is obviously much older than this, it seems likely that the front was remodeled to provide wider openings for warehouse use. The *Golden Era* was the most substantial literary periodical published in San Francisco during the 1850's and 1860's. Bret Harte, Mark Twain and Thomas Starr King were among its celebrated contributors.

Slightly out of the Jackson Square environment proper is the excellent development of *One Jackson Place.* Though relatively recent in construction (1907), this building retains the essential integrity of solid brick warehouse construction. It is now combined with sympathetic decorative modern treatment.

Originally the Nordwell Warehouse, *One Jackson Place* was occupied from the date of its construction by the Zellerbach Paper Company. The warehouse is actually two six-story buildings, separated by a tunnel and courtyard—a feature that was intended to expedite deliveries, but which now provides an excellent focus for renovated office and shop frontage.

The United States Custom House, at *555 Battery Street,* occupies half of the block between Jackson and Washing-

These two Gold Rush Era brick buildings on Montgomery Street just off Jackson were restored by their owner, attorney Melvin Belli

ton streets. Not only does it provide a great contrast in size with the buildings we have been discussing above, but one can see some interesting contrasts in the handling of some of the same architectural devices. For instance, the alternating rounded and pointed pediments that are so prominent in the largest of the Hotaling buildings on Jackson Square are carried through the second floor of the Custom House as a major ornamental device.

Where the building tends to come off badly is in the degeneration of decorative detail into "decor." The otherwise chaste style of the building is spoiled by a profusion of eagles and shields that are out of scale even in this very large building. The Custom House was begun in 1906 and finished in 1911 by the architectural firm of Eames and Young, of St. Louis.

The notorious Barbary Coast was one of the most un-lamented victims of the 1906 fire, which swept the area between Jackson Square and almost the crest of Telegraph Hill. The only one of the Coast's pre-quake saloons still standing was at one time "Diana's"—now "The Brighton Express"—at *580 Pacific Avenue*. This building, with its attractive arched doorway and windows, may have been built in the 1860's. Curiously, the formal and apparently balanced facade is not quite symmetrical—as though the bricklayers had traced the facade out on the ground with a stick, agreed to the general appearance, started building at one end, and failed to come out even. Presumably only the bare shell of the building survived the fire, and even much of that may be a reconstruction.

Just one year after the earthquake, in 1907, an imaginative entrepreneur opened a dance-hall at *555 Pacific Avenue* that dared San Franciscans not to come and celebrate their survival in its circus atmosphere. It passed through several owners until designer Alexander Girard turned it into a furniture display room in 1959. Girard brought the old days back with "stop 'em dead" color combinations that the Barbary Coast had never seen. The circus-like arcade facade, with its beveled glass oval insets in swinging doors, the fan-lights, and the gilded dimpled rosettes, is not be taken too seriously architecturally but it is the best possible example of pointing up amusing and delightful details with unexpected color.

An exceedingly elegant building is the former house of Engine Company #1, at *449 Pacific Avenue*. This Italian Renaissance-style firehouse, with Tuscan columns and pilasters surmounting the large Roman arch, has very pleasingly balanced proportions. It was built in 1877 although the present facade is post-1906, and the building, which now houses an art gallery and an advertising agency, is still

One Jackson Place was built in 1907 but still exemplifies the solid brick warehouse style of the 1850's. It is really two six-story buildings separated by a tunnel and a courtyard. It has been modernized without destroying its essential character

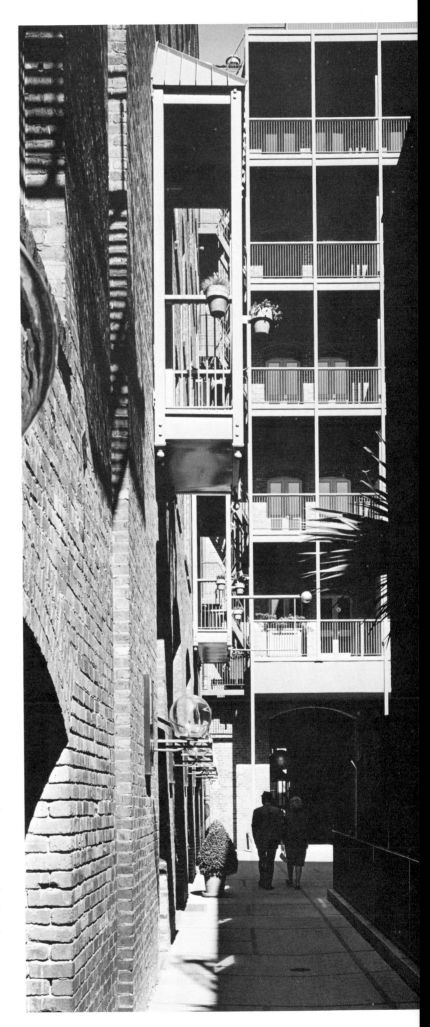

57

*580 Pacific — last of the Barbary Coast, (above) and
the Custom House — a profusion
of eagles and shields*

redolent of the romance of the oldtime fire department.

Just two blocks away, the *Transamerica Building, 4 Columbus Avenue,* is a brilliantly white, three-story, Period Italianate structure built in 1911. Originally the first floor was occupied by the Fugazi Banca Popolare Operaia Italiana, and the upper floors contained a hotel. The Bank of Italy (now the giant Bank of America) took over in 1928, and in 1938 the Transamerica Corporation, a holding company associated with Bank of America, began using the building as its headquarters. The building is best described as a delightful wedding cake, symbolic of the marriage of North Beach and Montgomery Street.

The Columbus Tower, 920 Kearny Street, originally called the Sentinel Building, is a fine example of the renovation of an old office building to modern standards. Built in 1907 to the design of Field & Kohlberg, this little brick flatiron with its white glazed surface is associated with memory of the dubious "Boss" of early twentieth-century San Francisco, Abe Ruef, who seems to have been associated in promoting the building and had his offices there after he was paroled from San Quentin in 1915.

The building was taken in hand by architect Henrik Bull in 1958. While Bull's large, arched, first-floor windows and colorful mosaic tile surface do not qualify as true restoration, the remodeling does blend with the rest of the structure and quite simply lifts the ornate building onto a clean-lined pedestal. It must be accounted a good idea, because it works.

Telegraph Hill is perhaps the most "San Franciscan" of all the city's residential communities. Gold Rush settlers didn't mind the convenient but vertical "commute" to the original "downtown"—and even to this day the hill overlooking the north waterfront attracts residents with Bohemian tastes and strong legs.

At the foot of Telegraph Hill is the rambling frame structure formerly occupied by the Telegraph Hill Neighborhood Association. This compound, at *1736 Stockton Street*, was begun in 1907, when Bernard Maybeck was commissioned to design a building to house a dispensary, club room, and flats for the nurses and settlement workers of the Association.

The building was enlarged in 1909, 1913, and 1928. It is far from certain that Maybeck had anything to do with the additions, but they were executed in a compatible style, and it is entirely possible that he did draw the plans. Though the Neighborhood Association moved to new quarters in 1954, the building's new owner has preserved its integrity.

The *Church of Saint Francis of Assisi, 610 Vallejo Street*, stands on the site of the little frame parish church that served San Francisco's Catholic community in Gold Rush days. The cornerstone of the present building was laid in December, 1857, and the church was dedicated in 1860. Of a simple but strong Victorian Gothic style, Saint Francis is closely related in architectural character to Old Saint Mary's. The 1906 fire left the walls and ninety-five foot towers more or less intact, and these were incorporated in the present church which was dedicated in 1918. Thus the exterior of the church today is virtually identical to the structure of the late 1850's. It was the city's first parish church.

Telegraph Hill derives its name literally: in 1849 a semaphore—"telegraph" in the parlance of the time—atop the hill signalled the arrival of ships to the merchants and townspeople whose livelihoods depended upon quick intelligence of commercial importance. The houses on the hill were little more than shacks, yet today many of these cottages are thought most valuable properties indeed. For Telegraph Hill has the distilled essence for which San Francisco is famous: it has a view and it has character.

Architecturally and historically, the little old houses on Telegraph Hill are of particular interest in that they carry a strong flavor of the San Francisco of the 1850's, before the Italianate and Stick Style rows came to dominate residential streets. Early San Francisco was something of a jumble, and so is Telegraph Hill. The photograph on page 62 of the view from Telegraph Hill in about 1862 gives a good impression of the hill's casual, almost haphazard, style.

Columbus Tower (top) is one of our last "flatirons"
Transamerica Building is an Italian wedding cake
The panorama of Telegraph Hill (next page)

59

31 Alta Street today (left)

31 Alta Street (center left) in 1862
291 Union Street (below)

62

The house to the right of center, with the double-decker balcony, is still standing, at *31 Alta Street*. This house is one of the oldest residences in San Francisco, having been built by a Captain Andrews in 1852. The balconied facade of this plain house is quite characteristic of the early 1850's, and very similar homes may be seen in the earliest photographs of San Francisco.

Originally, the dining room and kitchen were in the brick semi-basement, the living room on the second floor, the family bedrooms on the third floor, and the maid's quarters in the attic. From before 1860 to 1935 the house was owned by the Maass family, glove makers.

The houses at *9 Calhoun Terrace, 287–89 Union Street*, and *291 Union Street* all date from the late 1850's and early 1860's and are also part of this early heritage of Telegraph Hill. They will be discussed more fully in the Appendix.

Old Telegraph Hill is preserved most completely in the Filbert Street Steps and Napier Lane. On the Filbert Steps, the most eye-catching house is the one at *228 Filbert Street*. Built around 1873, this house is an expression of a rather

simple "Carpenter Gothic" style, with bargeboard, finials, and Gothic arches reduced to straight lines over the windows.

Second in interest to *228 Filbert* is *224 Filbert Street*, a cottage that appears to date from 1863. This house is a good example of the very simplest type of home of its period. The roof line is unusual, being in the pattern of an old-fashioned barn roof—that is, with the center peaked up sharply and the outer edges at a flatter pitch.

The house at *222 Filbert Street* is one of the best looking in the row, but seems to be of later date—1875 at the earliest, perhaps 1880 or a little after. *230 Filbert Street* is a very plain little cottage of about 1883.

Running north from the Filbert Steps, Napier Lane is one of the most enchanting little streets in San Francisco. The houses in the lane date from about 1875 to 1890. The lane provides a good architectural insight into the appearance of old Telegraph Hill, although now colorful flowers and plants have been added.

The oldest house (1875) in the lane would appear to be

This house at 228 Filbert Street (on the Filbert Steps) was built in the 1870's and is an example of a simple "Carpenter Gothic" style highly popular among Telegraph Hill dwellers of that day both for its looks and its relative economy

10 Napier Lane, a very simple Italianate structure similar to *293 Union Street* (1860's). Other houses which should be noted along this charming boardwalk are *15* (1884), *16* (1872), *21* (1885), *22* (1876), and *32–34* (1890, and considerably remodeled).

Like most of the crest of the hill, the old warehouse district at the foot of Telegraph Hill escaped the flames of 1906. In the 1850's and '60's this small area had been one of the most desirable dock and warehouse locations on the waterfront, for here was good, solid land close to deep water. Hence the big warehouses associated with Lombard Dock, Greenwich Dock, and India Dock were almost alongside the famous clipper ships that called here.

Only one of the famous brick warehouses of this period still stands in more or less pristine condition—the North Point Dock Warehouse (later, and currently, known as the Seawall Warehouse) at *1501 Sansome Street.* It was built around 1853, and soon became the favorite berth for such famous clipper ships as the giant *Great Republic.*

The Seawall Warehouse, with its broad arched doorways and windows (and original iron fire shutters), is a particularly handsome example of heavy commercial architecture. In over a century of active use, the great weights placed on the foundation have caused the building to sag a bit here and there, but it would be good for another hundred years were it not scheduled to become a victim of redevelopment.

A powerful expression of brick construction is seen in the building occupied by the Merchants Ice and Cold Storage Co. at *Battery and Lombard Streets.* The owners moved into the existing building in 1896, and though the building does not appear to be substantially older than this, it is entirely possible that evidence of a much older structure uncovered during various remodelings relates to the Greenwich Dock Warehouse. In the horse-and-buggy days, drays drove right into the building through the wide arches, and one can see the ruts their iron tires wore in the stone paving of the floor. To some extent the majesty of this great brick pile has been injured by the placement of square (and outsized) aluminum frame windows wherever it was desired to install modern office space.

Another very strong brick warehouse, dating from about 1898, is at *1265 Battery Street.* Like the Merchants building, this structure is characterized by the repetition of massive arches. But the use of pilasters with Ionic capitals and other "downtown" architectural devices robs it of some of the elegant simplicity of the former building.

A small red brick building of considerable quality stands on the northwest corner of *Battery* and *Union.* The building may date from 1874, though the earliest reliable photographic evidence available does not place it any earlier than 1880. It has been used as a seamen's hotel and saloon during most of its years. Dwarfed by the large warehouses all around it, yet looking stately and clean of line, this little building shows off its good brickwork and good proportions very well. The interior has been restored by the present owners so as to show off the brick work from the inside as well as the outside.

The distinctive red brick warehouse at *1075 Front Street* was built in 1892 (gutted in 1906 and subsequently rebuilt) for the Cowell family of Santa Cruz and has been used until recently to store quarried materials. The most unusual features of the building are the cast iron shutters and the complementary massive iron doors at street level.

One of the most architecturally interesting of the waterfront buildings is *50 Green Street,* built for the Fuller Paint Company in 1907. Here the theme of large first-floor arches is carried almost to a logical conclusion, giving the building a very light appearance. Most fortunately this fine building has been carefully remodeled to provide space for a number of businesses.

On the verge of the original San Francisco waterfront, at *Vallejo* and *Front Streets,* stand two brick warehouses which were built in the early 1850's, partially destroyed in 1906, but rebuilt almost precisely on the original plans. Reconstruction centered around the still-standing portions of the above-ground brick, incorporating the corner-structure. Also followed were the old window pattern (omitting a few of the original piercings,) and the existing foundation and basement layout.

These twin warehouses of Gold Rush times today bear the colorful designations, Pelican Paper Company and Trinidad Bean and Elevator Company, and are distinctive examples of waterfront building of 1854, with their sandstone-framed doorways and handsome arched basement ceilings.

Altogether, Jackson Square, the heights of Telegraph Hill proper, and the brick warehouse district at the foot of the hill comprise a district of unusual architectural variety. The "comeback" of the Jackson Square area raised hopes for the preservation of the best old buildings in this sector, though the warehouse district faces the dangers of demolition in whole or in part if present plans for the projected International Market Center are carried out.

These cottages along the boardwalk of Napier Lane (left) are a delightful memory of the Telegraph Hill of the 1870's and 1880's

NOB HILL

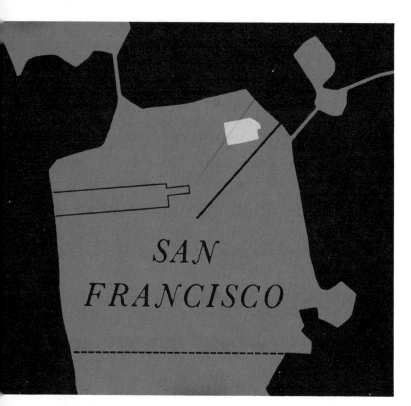

SAN FRANCISCO

The San Francisco of the early 1850's faced directly eastward, toward Yerba Buena Cove and Goat Island. It had little choice for the waterfront was the gateway to the city, and the direction of most natural expansion (west toward the ocean) was blocked by the very steep heights that made such commercial streets as California, Clay, and Washington impassible starting with the block or so beyond Stockton Street.

The proximity of these heights to the center of the city — a matter of a few blocks — counted for little in making them desirable for residence in an age when transport meant horse-drawn carriages and horse-drawn streetcars. Further, the early and permanent development of the grid pattern of streets and town plots prevented the natural development of easy access roads along contour lines.

It was Andrew S. Hallidie's invention of the cable car that turned the "Clay Street Hill" into Nob Hill, home of the railroad and Comstock millionaires of the 1870's. The Clay Street cable road of 1873 and the California Street line of 1878 made this magnificent location at last accessible.

The name "Nob Hill" seems to have come into general use about the time that the mansions of the late 1870's were rising, and its derivation has been attributed to "nabob" or "snob." More likely, "Nob" was simply "Knob," but the more colorful derivation is certainly appropriate, for the palaces of the rich dominated the top of the hill on California Street in the decades before the 1906 conflagration. The Nob Hill householders of the 1880's and 1890's were not the sole proprietors of the State of California — but they may well have represented the majority interest.

All of the great mansions but one were destroyed in the fire of 1906. The survivor was the Italianate-Baroque brownstone palace of James C. Flood, which was gutted, but stood with its shell intact. Bought by the Pacific Union Club in 1909, it was remodeled by Willis Polk and is today one of the architectural landmarks of San Francisco.

The Flood Mansion, at *1000 California Street,* was designed by Augustus Laver and built during 1885–86. Flood, not to be outdone by the magnificoes of New York, ordered the building constructed of Connecticut sandstone. As one of the four proprietors of the "Big Bonanza" of the Virginia City mines, he was quite able to afford a reputed $1,500,000 on the house.

As it stands today, the house that Flood's mining millions financed is a much handsomer building than the long-departed homes of the other Nob Hill millionaires. In part this is the result of good initial design, but at least as much credit should go to Willis Polk, who restored the building, as to Augustus Laver. To accommodate the Pacific Union Club, Polk added the impressive wings on either side, and incorporated a third floor by raising the floor line four feet (at the same time removing the central tower in front). A close look reveals these changes as flaws in the majesty and proportions of the building, yet the general effect is a structure more pleasing than the original.

The memory of the Stanford and Hopkins mansions, which took up the block bounded by California, Powell, Pine, and Mason Streets, is preserved by the Mark Hopkins Hotel, the Stanford Court Apartments and the massive wall which surrounds most of the block and is most impressively visible along Pine Street. Constructed of interlocking blocks of granite dioride quarried in the Sierra during the middle '70's, this great gray wall appears virtually indestructible, and it proved so in the 1920's when George D. Smith, builder of the Mark Hopkins Hotel, tried and failed to remove it by blasting.

The name of another Nob Hill Croesus of the golden age of millionaires is perpetuated in the *Fairmont Hotel* (occupying the block bounded by California, Sacramento, Powell, and Mason). James G. Fair, partner of Flood in the "Big Bonanza," apparently planned to "move up" from his Jones and Pine Street residence to something grander on the superb Fairmont site, but he died before he had the opportunity to match his fortune against that of his princely contemporaries.

His daughter, Tessie Fair Oelrichs, sought to correct this oversight by building the grandest hotel in San Francisco—in fact one of the grandest hotels anywhere. She

Bonanza King James C. Flood's brownstone mansion at 1000 California Street is reputed to have cost $1,500,000 in 1885

retained the firm of James and Merritt Reid to design a 600-room Classicist Baroque and Mannerist monument, and in 1903 the granite glory of Nob Hill began to rise.

The building was less than a month from its grand opening when the earthquake shook it and the fire gutted its lush interior. But the shell of the hotel stood, and the renowned Stanford White (of Pennsylvania Station fame) was employed to do up the inside in even greater splendor. One of the great architectural experiences left to San Franciscans and visitors to the city is the sight of the awesomely opulent lobby of the Fairmont; here is a fragment of the Golden Age preserved almost intact.

In order to provide some impression of the frame palaces of the Nob Hill residents of the 1870's and 1880's, we present the accompanying view of the blocks now occupied by Grace Cathedral and Huntington Park (with vistas of the underdeveloped neighborhood and the murky spaces of the Western Addition). The rather chaste David D. Colton residence stands at center, the gingerbreaded Second-Empire mansion of Charles Crocker beyond it. In the foreground (right) is the hillock which was to be leveled for the future Flood mansion (present Pacific Union Club).

It also illustrates one of the most astounding domestic vendettas in San Francisco history. The strange, high-rise blank wall in the center—which appears to be nestled into the dog-leg of the Colton house, but which is actually situated across the street on the corner of the Crocker property—is the celebrated "spite fence" of Charles Crocker. It seems that when Crocker bought up his block he ran up against the wiles and greed of an undertaker named Nicho-

After the 1906 fire, only the shells of the Fairmont Hotel and the Flood mansion remained

Nob Hill today (next page)

The blank wall in center was Charles Crocker's "spite fence"

las Yung, who stubbornly held out for what Crocker considered an excessive price for his house and lot. Baffled in his efforts to buy out Yung, Crocker erected a three-story plank fence around Yung's establishment.

The Crocker heirs after the 1906 fire gave the land on which their father's house had stood to the Episcopal Diocese, and on this site stands *Grace Episcopal Cathedral, 1051-Taylor Street.* To those who admire reinforced-concrete Gothic cathedrals, this massive church, for which George Bodley drew the plans and which Lewis Hobart executed, may be considered the finest example of that style in the west. The cornerstone of the cathedral was laid in 1910, but it was not considered completed until 1964, when it was consecrated.

A superior use of materials is found in the Cathedral

Grace Episcopal Cathedral was begun in 1910 and not finished until 1964. The Cathedral House in the foreground was built in 1912

House. This four-story, late English Gothic building offers a surface texture and finish far superior to that of the cathedral proper. Built as the Church Divinity School of the Pacific in about 1912, it later became a graduate school for priests and is now used for cathedral offices. Unfortunately, this handsome structure stands smack across the grand approach to the cathedral, and must probably be removed at some future date.

At *1021 California Street* is a delightful little French "petit palais" designed by Colonel George Schasty, a New York architect, for Herbert Law about 1911. The building is somewhat larger than it looks, standing a full five stories high in the rear, where the lot drops off steeply. Built of concrete, scored to imitate stone, the heavy classical elements of the facade are delicately relieved by the tall French doors of the second floor and the elegant iron-

work of the door and window grilles and the railings. The fanciful effect of the structure is further heightened by employment of the currently popular technique of picking out decorative architectural details in a contrasting color.

At *1110 Taylor Street*, just north of Sacramento, is a little Classical Revival cottage said by a former resident to have been the house built by James C. Flood for his coachman, William Keating, and therefore dating back to the days of the great mansions. It is hard to imagine a frame house surviving the 1906 fire, but perhaps it was merely damaged and reconstructed along its former lines. This little home was in the Keating family until 1936, when it was purchased by its present owner.

Across from the coachman's house, at the corner of *Pleasant* and *Taylor Streets,* is a very large gray shingled apartment building of distinguished ancestry and appearance.

The town house at right was built in
1910 at 535 Powell and was once occupied
by Tessie Wall, a prominent madam.
The "mini-mansion" below at 1021 California
is a full five stories high in the rear

The tiny cottage above at 1110 Taylor
was probably built for James C. Flood's coachman.
1202 Leavenworth (right) was built
in 1910 by famed architect Julia Morgan

Notre Dame des Victories, at 564 Bush Street, was inspired by a Byzantine-styled church in Lyons, France, and built in 1913

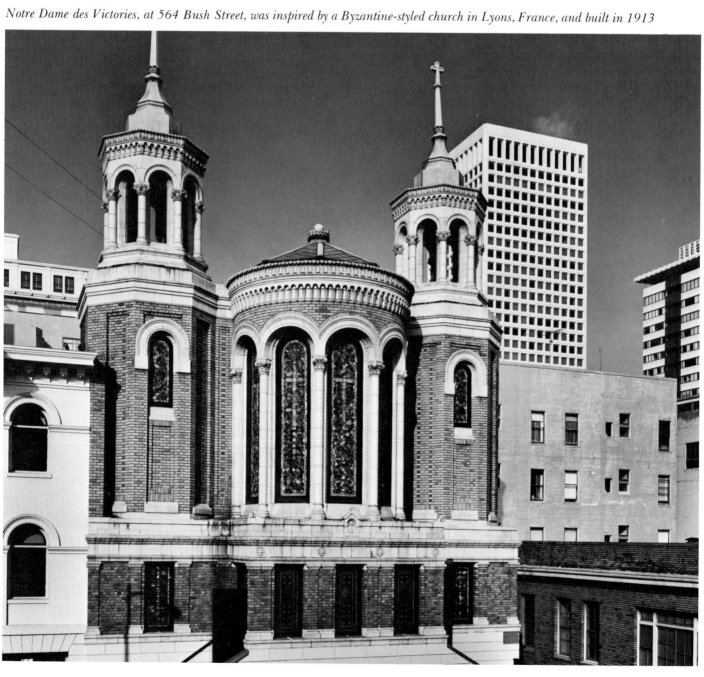

Designed by the firm of Bakewell and Brown for artist Emil Pissis and built in 1908, this utilitarian structure, with its restrained Baroque touches, contains seven flats and one apartment, all but two of which are different in arrangement.

The handsome "California Style" apartment house at *1202–1216 Leavenworth Street* was designed by the outstanding Julia Morgan, first woman architect to graduate from the Beaux Arts in Paris. A student of Bernard Maybeck, Julia Morgan is most celebrated as William Randolph Hearst's San Simeon architect, but her solid Bay Area reputation rests upon her excellent Maybeck-type residential designs.

The shingle and stucco structure was built in 1910 for Minerva C. Miller, and was intended to provide an income for her three daughters. One of the characteristics of this fine building is the large number of windows. Miss Morgan (as well as Maybeck) designed houses which distinguished between the indoors and the outdoors, and great spreads of glass were no novelty to them. Few "modern" buildings have close to the window area of this outsized vine-covered cottage.

A post-fire structure of importance at the western fringe of the Nob Hill district is the *Old First Presbyterian Church, Van Ness Avenue* and *Sacramento Street*. This handsome brick edifice of modified Byzantine style houses the congregation of the oldest organized Protestant group in California. The present building is the sixth church built by this congregation. It was designed by William Hays, Sr., an architect of the University of California, in 1911. The church is very solid and massive in aspect, as is suited to this development of the straightforward basilica style of Roman times. The facade is dominated by a huge rose window, a Gothic device which in this case is in turn dominated by a Greek cross, an element which again picks up the Byzantine theme.

At *831–849 Mason Street*, across from the Mark Hopkins Hotel, are four town houses designed by Willis Polk in 1917 and built in collaboration with Mrs. John Proctor. At the time, these town houses were proclaimed a "new style". The ground floor and second stories of these houses are indeed elegant, and deserving of emulation as a "new style", but the upper stories trail off to a very flat and ordinary appearance.

An elegant "town house" in the grand manner can be seen at *535 Powell Street*. This Second Empire home was built around 1910, and was bought in 1912 by Frank Daroux for his bride, the fast-living Tessie Wall, who said that she would rather be a lamppost on Powell Street than own all of San Mateo County. Daroux, a gambling figure and Republican political boss of the Tenderloin, set Tessie up in this town house as a move toward respectability.

In 1917 Tessie and Frank were divorced, and a few months later Tessie shot her ex-mate. In recent years the building has been used as a medical office. It stands a monument to an architectural idea that never did catch on very well in San Francisco.

One of the most handsome club buildings in San Francisco is *The Family Club, 545 Powell Street*. An Italian Renaissance structure of brownish-red Roman Brick, this distinguished structure was designed by Clarence Ward and built in 1909. The high, arched first-story windows, with their white facings, surmounted by square second-story windows and a decorative overhanging cornice (also in white), combine to produce a substantial yet airy feeling, an effect of dignity yet informality.

Another carefully designed club on Powell Street is the *University Club, 800 Powell Street*, at the California and Powell corner once occupied by Leland Stanford's stables. A four-story brick building, constructed in 1909 to the design of Bliss and Faville, this is a larger, somewhat similar variant of the Renaissance forms used in the Family Club. A strongly arched portal, arched windows and a large overhanging cornice give it a generic resemblance to an Italian palace, although the material here is brick rather than stone. Most American men's clubs seem to owe their Florentine and Roman appearance to Mckim, Mead and White's use of these modes.

The *Metropolitan Life Insurance Building, 600 Stockton Street*, is a studiously correct neo-Classical Baroque edifice of almost Federal proportions. The original central portion was designed by the LeBrun Brothers in 1909. Additions were made in 1914, 1922, 1930, and 1954, all in a style compatible with the original. The building is of steel and reinforced concrete covered with dazzling white terra cotta.

At *564 Bush Street* is the church of *Notre Dame des Victoires*. Designed after Notre Dame de Fourvieres of Lyon, this French church is an example of 19th century French tastes in the Byzantine mode. Built in 1913 under the supervision of architect Louis Brochoud, the church occupies the site of the first French church in San Francisco.

Chinatown was wiped out by the fire of 1906 but quickly rose again as this old photo shows

CHINATOWN

With the large immigration of Chinese to California during the Gold Rush times, and for decades after, a compact Chinese colony swiftly developed just above the foot of Nob Hill, on those streets that were just a little too steep to be convenient for heavy commercial traffic in the age of the horse.

Old Chinatown was not an area of remarkably distinctive architecture even before the fire of 1906. Its complete demolition in the fire gave rise to the popular fancy that it was gone forever. But in the absence of any coherent planning powers, Chinatown rose again, this time as a more self-conscious entity in the architectural sense, but as the same oriental slum underneath.

Perhaps the most widely misunderstood aspect of Old Chinatown was the existence of the "tongs." Hatchet men, gambling monopolies, opium, and slave girl traffic come to mind at the mention of the word. Yet, the real *raison d'etre* of the "tongs" was somewhat more mundane. The essential economic power behind these regional organizations of Chinese immigrants stemmed from a system that was close to labor contracting; the merchants of the "tong" advanced passage money to Chinese of their home districts, through agents in China who were officers or employees of the organization. In exchange for this service, the immigrant was a virtual peon until his debt was paid off. His family association found him a job, gave him a place in society, and acted as union agent, welfare department, and burying society in his behalf.

The celebrated "Six Companies" represented the alliance (sometimes breached in notorious "tong wars") between the rival claimants to the loyalty and dues of the Chinese population in general. If for no other reason, then, the headquarters of this old California institution is worthy of note. Located at *843 Stockton Street,* and now known as the Chinese Consolidated Benevolent Association Building, this edifice of "Chinatown Renaissance" architecture

76

has purple overhanging eaves, a blue enameled vestibule, and red and yellow splashes in the window casings. As befits the quiet old age of the Six Companies, the upper floor houses a night school in which Chinese youth is instructed in its cultural heritage.

Not too remarkably, the first building of "authentic" Chinese architecture after the 1906 fire was devoted to the authentically Yankee enterprise of a telephone exchange. The Chinese Telephone Exchange Building (now, since the advent of digit dialing a branch of the Bank of Canton) was erected at *743 Washington Street* in about 1909. The site of this pagoda was, of all places, the spot upon which Mormon Sam Brannan printed the *California Star,* first newspaper published in San Francisco.

Hardly less up-to-date in purpose than the telephone exchange building was the Chinese Chamber of Commerce, built at *728–730 Sacramento Street* in 1912. In its general form, with heavily bracketed third-floor balcony, wrought iron railings, columns rising from the balcony, and decorative cornice with bold dentils, this structure has the general characteristics of the two buildings mentioned below.

At *834–840 Washington Street* is a good example of "Chinatown Renaissance" in the four-story, balconied structure belonging to the Oak Tin Benevolent Association. This building was constructed in about 1909.

Of the same style, but more impressive in the proportions of its facade, is the Tin How Temple of the Shiu Hing Benevolent Association, at *125 Waverly Place.* This temple is one of the oldest institutions of its kind in America, the original altar having been brought over with some of the first Chinese immigrants to California during the early days of the Gold Rush. The old temple, of course,

burned in 1906; since the construction of the new Shiu Hing Building in 1911, it has occupied the top floor, the association using the lower floors for other purposes.

The largest, and perhaps the most famous, Chinese joss house in America is the Kong Chow Temple of the Kong Chow Friendly Society at *520 Pine Street.* Established in the middle 1850's, the temple was destroyed in 1906 and rebuilt anew in 1909. The temple has a very small street frontage, appearing to be nothing more than a story-and-a-half gate; the main portion of the building is located on a much wider plot in the rear, and as the photograph shows is a full three stories tall. As can be seen, this exceptional building has some most interesting and excellent architectural detailing.

The most famous landmark of Chinatown is not at all Chinese in character—for it is Old St. Mary's Church, at *Grant Avenue* and *California Street.* This red brick Gothic structure has some Chinese antecedents, though, as the granite for its foundations was imported from China, a practice not at all unusual in the Gold Rush years. Brick and iron for the church came from the East Coast, as did the bell, and stained glass from Europe.

St. Mary's was dedicated at a Christmas midnight mass in 1854, and until 1891 was the cathedral of the Archdiocese. The great fire gutted the church in 1906, but the walls and tower remained intact. The church was rebuilt promptly, and in the 1920's was extensively remodeled and enlarged towards the rear.

Yet Old St. Mary's stands very much today as it did in the Gold Rush decade, somewhat overshadowed, to be sure, by new skyscrapers, but still San Francisco's best-loved ecclesiastical landmark.

Three landmarks: Old St. Mary's Church, Grant and California, Tin How Temple, 125 Waverly, Kong Chow Temple, 520 Pine

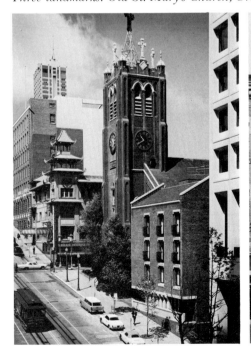  

DOWNTOWN

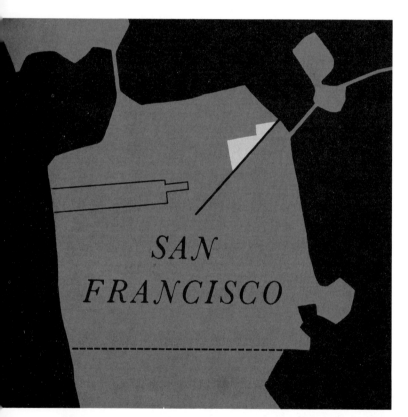

From the top of the Fairmont or Mark Hopkins you can still see about half of the geographical reason for the concentration of San Francisco's downtown. Immediately before you is the steep slope of Nob Hill—much too steep in horse-and-buggy days to permit heavy commercial deliveries. To your left, Telegraph Hill hems in the downtown. A good part of the rest of the original topography is vastly changed.

Straight ahead, to the east, almost half of the land you see was once part of Yerba Buena Cove. The pressures of space and the advantages of a waterfront location pushed the city front from a point just beyond Montgomery Street to within a few yards of the present Ferry Building by the mid-1850's. The central city did not creep up the hills or push through the Columbus Avenue gap toward North Beach so much as it moved out into the bay.

It also moved toward the southeast—at your right from our vantage point on Nob Hill. Here the original city was defined by high sand ridges just north of Market Street, which tended to stall the original southward development along Montgomery and Kearny Streets at around Bush Street. Market Street was a line of sand hills, and south of Market were parallel ridges.

The leveling of these sand hills (with much of the fill going to extend the waterfront) advanced the business district south to Market Street before 1860, and in subsequent decades the commercial area spread up Market, occupying the more level blocks around the foot of Nob Hill. The total effect of these changes has been, in 120 years, to move the center of gravity of the core city no more than a few blocks to the south. Market Street formed what is to this date a permanent boundary to the downtown core.

Before the turn of the century, the downtown was characterized by three-to-five-story buildings of Italianate and Second Empire inspiration, structures that were apt to be architecturally compatible and that frequently formed whole streets that had some unity of design but diversity of purpose. One of the most remarked-upon peculiarities of the downtown was that San Franciscans of some substance frequently lived in apartments over commercial premises. The 1906 fire wiped out what was left of the multiple-use character of the financial district, and the area was rebuilt with larger buildings of single purpose.

The only scrap of the downtown San Francisco of a century ago is the Jackson Square area. The notable buildings in the rest of downtown San Francisco which date from before 1906 are large structures, of sufficiently recent and substantial construction to have been worth rebuilding after they were gutted by the fire.

The outstanding pre-fire building of the financial district is the *Mills Building, 220 Montgomery Street,* designed by the famous Chicago firm of Burnham & Root and erected in 1891–92. This ten-story, foursquare brick structure picks up the Richardson Romanesque style in its massive, intricately-carved, arched entrance, in the arches crowning the modified Corinthian pilasters that delineate the vertical line of the building, in the repetition of the Romanesque arches in the ninth-floor frieze, and in the squat columns between the windows of the top story. Yet the building as a whole is a powerful expression of the style that was developing in Chicago in the heyday of Burnham and Sullivan and the young Frank Lloyd Wright.

The Mills Building was built by Darius Ogden Mills, a Forty-niner who parlayed a Sacramento shop into a partnership in William C. Ralston's Bank of California, and went on to become one of the authentic financial moguls of late-nineteenth-century America.

Willis Polk supervised the reconstruction of the Mills Building after the fire of 1906, and was also in charge of the additions to the rear of the building, which he executed in the same style as the original. In 1931 the adjacent twenty-two-story Mills Tower was completed to the design of Lewis Hobart.

A very good large office building, of more interesting detail but of weaker conception than the Mills Building, is the *Kohl Building, 400 Montgomery St.* Designed by Percy and Polk in 1901, it shows Polk's preoccupation with extravagant details as well as advanced construction. A rather plain structure up to the tenth-floor cornice, it suddenly turns into a riot of bold variations and exaggerations of Baroque and Classical styles (partly lost with the removal of numerous lions heads in the recent interest of public safety).

The building is constructed around a steel frame, the interior employs metal lathe and plaster, the sheathing is of a handsome greenish-gray Colusa sandstone. Perhaps the first "fireproof" building in downtown San Fran-

*The Mills Building (above), 220 Montgomery,
was built in 1892 by one of the first tycoons.
The Bank of California (above, right) was finished in
1908 and intended to be a true temple of finance.
The Kohl Building (right) was designed by Willis
Polk and shows his love of intricate detail*

cisco, it survived the 1906 fire intact above the fourth story, while all other buildings, once ignited, were gutted.

Alvinza Hayward, also one of Ralston's Bank of California associates, put up the building which was later purchased by the Kohl interests. It has been said that the unusual "H" shape was the result of Mrs. Hayward's superstitious regard for initials—a story not out of character with the nature of San Francisco's first generation of millionaires.

The tallest building in the financial district at the time of the 1906 earthquake was the *Merchants Exchange, 465 California Street.* This fifteen-story, steel-frame structure, with Tennessee granite and brick sheathing, was designed by Willis Polk in 1903; it traces its ancestry back to a three-story brick building of 1851 located about two blocks north on Battery Street. The original Merchants Exchange furnished a library and meeting room and posted information on arriving ships and cargoes. The latter-day skyscraper was intended to provide some of the same services to the business community.

The great hall of the Exchange, now modified as a bank office, is still decorated with some of the best and most appropriate San Franciscan murals—paintings executed by William Coulter, a leading maritime artist of his place and time. Other touches of period architectural art can be seen in the bronze eagle heads and lamps of the exterior, designed by Julia Morgan. Miss Morgan can also be credited with the inspiring interior appointments.

The days are gone when the merchants of San Francisco gathered there over one thousand strong to approve the plans for the 1915 Exposition or to condemn the 1934 general strike, and the Merchants Exchange is now just another building. But the great glass-roofed foyer and the adjacent meeting hall are reminiscent of that former era.

The Bank of California, 400 California Street was founded in 1864 by William C. Ralston, D. O. Mills, and their friends with two million dollars capital, an astonishing sum for that time. The bank that Ralston built on the site of the present structure was a magnificent Classical-Italianate palace, torn down prior to 1906.

The present bank, designed by Bliss & Faville and completed in 1908, is a most impressive granite-surfaced Corinthian temple of finance, with a magnificent main banking room of Roman proportions and Tennessee marble facing. Arthur Putnam did the marble mountain lions at the rear of this room, and the ram's head at the entrance.

The Royal Globe Insurance Building, 201 Sansome Street, is a structure well suited to illustrate the wonderful curiosity of a great many of the older buildings of the downtown,

The Hallidie Building (left) hides behind a curtain of glass. 130 Bush (right) is a tiny "skyscraper" a scant 20 feet wide

The Palace Hotel, opened in 1875, dominated the downtown area. The present hotel replaced it after the 1906 fire gutted the original

buildings which for the most part lack the distinction of the Royal Globe, but which still possess details of interest that are apt to be sadly lacking in new buildings of the second or third class. Built in 1909 to designs by Howells & Stokes, of New York, this Georgian-style building mixes red brick and white marble with dark green terra cotta. The eye can hardly escape the contrasts of the materials, and is inevitably drawn to the imposing entrance with the great marble clock supported by the unicorn and the lion above.

The lobby is of particular historical interest: the five carved marble door frames were originally part of the Torlonia Palace in Rome. (This Palace was built in 1680 by Carlo Fontana for the Bolognetti family but dismantled to provide space for the Victor Emmanuel Monument.) A notable stained-glass skylight depicting the crests of various English insurance companies is visible from the eleventh floor.

On Sutter Street are two older buildings that show how long ago it was that the "glass wall" which many identify with modern architecture was developed. The first of these, the *French Bank Building, 108 Sutter Street,* is a ten-story steel-frame structure built in 1907 on such a narrow frontage that its mostly-glass exterior is not immediately obvious. The huge window area is set off by the sandstone sheathing of the vertical members and ornate bronze grillwork over the lower parts of the windows.

The Hallidie Building, 130 Sutter Street, appears to outdo the most extreme recent designs, though it was built in 1918. But in fact the shimmering, all-glass facade is a curtain hung in front of a building of quite conventional architecture, a building in which the "real" front wall is visible a few feet behind the facade. Built by the University of California as an investment, the building was named for Andrew S. Hallidie, inventor of the cable car and a Regent of the University. As a further reflection of the building's ownership, the ironwork was originally painted blue and gold.

While it is questionable to what extent architect Willis Polk may have anticipated the wave of the future in the building, there can be no doubt that it is smashingly effective. The integration of exterior fire escapes into a pattern of almost Victorian decorative ironwork cannot fail to delight anyone, and the pure lightness of the glass facade has rarely, and barely, been matched in any other building.

The problem of how to terminate a tall building has bothered architects ever since the vertical line of the skyscraper became the dominant theme. The verticality of the Gothic early suggested itself as a suitable style, and an amusing and generally successful example of this treatment can be seen at *130 Bush Street.* The amazingly narrow structure was built around 1910 for the Liberty Mutual Insurance Company. A scant twenty feet wide—but ten

The burned-out Mutual Building after the 1906 fire. Willis Polk's elaborate Hobart Tower (left)

Today's Mutual Building (now Citizens' Federal Building) and annex

stories tall—this building uses the Gothic line to make a virtue of a fault: it soars, it ends in satisfactorily airy spires, and, interestingly, seems to have almost as much glass as the latest modern structure.

One can see an even more interesting attempt to satisfactorily terminate a tower in *The Hobart Building, 582 Market Street.* This is an instructive example of the lengths to which an architect can go to fit the surroundings and still produce something original and desirable.

Willis Polk designed this building around 1914 and it is said to have been his favorite. The lower bulk of the structure is very plain, so non-committal that it could get along with almost any building on Market Street. Above this basic structure, Polk reared a tower almost as much higher, a tower standing free of the margins of the plot (which is odd-shaped and filled by the lower building), a tower that is finished on all sides in magnificently ornate style unmatched by any of its neighbors. The visual effect of the rays of the setting sun on the rich detailing is one of downtown San Francisco's remarkable sights.

The Palace Hotel, 633 Market Street, was built by William C. Ralston, a man who so perfectly expressed the spirit of his time and place, particularly in its more generous and carefree aspects, that he was a legend in his own time. Ralston poured the resources of his Bank of California into a wonderful variety of pet schemes—of which the Palace Hotel was the most visibly ostentatious.

When the Palace opened, on October 2, 1875, it was the most lavish hostelry in the world. The seven-storied, bay-windowed hotel, built around a central court that piled tier upon tier of marble colonnades, contained 800 rooms, all furnished with the best that supposedly unlimited money could buy.

The old Palace resisted the 1906 fire to the extent of defying the wreckers who sought to bring down the gutted structure; but the massive brick walls finally succumbed to the wrecking ball, and in the post-fire years a new Palace, of the same general proportions as the old, but lacking the wonderful bay windows, was erected. Gone, too, was the old carriage entrance and the central court, though the space occupied by the latter was converted to the still-famous Garden Court. It remains one of the city's major landmarks.

The Citizens' Federal Savings and Loan Building (originally the Mutual Building), at *700 Market Street,* provides an excellent example of preservation combined with a thoughtful modern enlargement. William Curlett designed the building in 1902 on a site which did not include the corner lot. When the present owners decided to renovate the structure, they purchased the corner lot and commissioned Clark and Beuttler to design a new annex. This addition is modern in materials and basic concept yet entirely compatible with the original building's Mansarded

86

The elegant and powerful Hibernia Bank Building was erected in 1892 and lauded as the most beautiful structure of its day

style. Sensitivity and imagination have given the owners an exceptionally fine Market Street headquarters.

The James Flood Building, 870 Market Street, is one of the distinguished office blocks of Market Street. Designed by Albert Pissis for millionaire James L. Flood in 1905, it was newly completed when it was gutted by the 1906 fire. Traces of the discoloration caused by the great heat of the fire can still be seen in the handsome sandstone arch of the main entrance, but the very substantial structure resisted the fire sufficiently to allow reconstruction with the original twelve-story walls after 1906.

One of the most engaging of the Market Street structures is the *Pacific Building, 821 Market St.* Built to the design of C. F. Whittlesey Co. in 1908, this nine-story building was at that time the largest reinforced-concrete building in the world—a tribute, no doubt, to the impression wrought by the earthquake and fire. The Moorish style of the building is highlighted by green Italian tile, a colorful contrast to predominant Market Street gray.

The Hibernia Bank, One Jones Street, is yet another de-

*The Ferry Building tower, which is modeled
after the cathedral in Seville, opened in 1898.
The glass-domed interior of the City of
Paris, a Union Square landmark, dates from 1909*

*Arthur Brown's City Hall (preceding pages)
is the centerpiece of one of
the great architectural complexes in America*

lightful and scholarly effort by Albert Pissis. At the time
of its construction in 1892, the bank was lauded by Willis
Polk and like-minded admirers as the "most beautiful
building in the city." The building "clearly declares its
purpose and the interior arrangement is plainly expressed
by the exterior," Polk wrote. Polk's admiration has not
been entirely displaced by time, for the Hibernia, like the
Flood, is elegant and powerful.

The upper limit to "downtown" Market Street is the
general area of the Civic Center. That the Civic Center
should be so far from the traditional commercial and
financial center of the city is an accident originally determined by the location of Yerba Buena Cemetery. When
the city undertook construction of a giant city hall in the
1870's, this plot running west from the corner of Market
and McAllister was the most suitable piece of city-owned
land available. When the city hall all but fell to pieces in
the 1906 temblor, the new civic center was placed in the
approximate position of the old, but on a larger site just a
little to the west.

There can be little arguing that the Civic Center as it
stands today is one of the great architectural complexes in
America, and much the grandest collection of municipal
buildings. It is the realization of the dream promoted by

90

Daniel Burnham, James D. Phelan, and other turn-of-the-century advocates of the "City Beautiful."

Begun in 1913 under the aggressive and flamboyant leadership of Mayor "Sunny Jim" Rolph, the Bakewell & Brown *City Hall* is the centerpiece of the complex. This Classicist Baroque monument was directly in the mainstream of then-current notions of what a government building should be. The giant dome, heroic central stair, the profusion of columns, the finely-finished detailing – all these were seen as the perfect expression of the wealth of a free people.

In more recent times it has been fashionable to question the validity of such non-functional extravagances, and to question even more the value of design derived from dead architectural styles. In part, such criticism is to the point; a truly original and brilliant conception such as the Wright-designed civic center in Marin immediately establishes itself as belonging in a higher league. At the same time, what ordinarily passes for "functional" or "modern" in the eyes of public officials and their architectural help is apt to be totally unimaginative. A comparison of the San Francisco Civic Center with the new State Mall in Sacramento will quickly establish the superiority of the work of Arthur Brown Jr. and his followers.

Arthur Brown Jr. also designed the *Civic Auditorium*, begun a little after the City Hall, but rushed to completion in the interests of being available for the Panama-Pacific Exposition of 1915. The *Library*, begun in 1916, is the work of George W. Kelham. As in the City Hall, a grand stairway dominates the interior arrangement—a vastly impressive touch which unfortunately does nothing to improve the use of the building as a library.

The eastern terminus of Market Street is the celebrated *Ferry Building*, the very symbol of San Francisco itself. Designed by Arthur Page Brown and opened in 1898, the building is an early example of the classicist-monumental style that Polk and Burnham and Brown envisaged as appropriate to a grand and beautiful San Francisco. The tower of the building was modeled after the Giralda Tower of the cathedral in Seville. The powerful facade, with its great arcade, is suggestive of the classic Roman.

In the days of its glory, before the bay was spanned by bridges, the Ferry Building was the heart of the metropolitan region. As many as 50,000,000 people a year passed through the Ferry Building, making it the busiest transit station in the United States. The identification of the building with the city of San Francisco is so complete that it is certain to be preserved indefinitely—although its authority as a fitting termination to Market Street has been seriously compromised by the frightful Embarcadero Freeway, which slashes across its front.

That part of the downtown district north of Market and west of the financial district is not favored by a great many old buildings of particular distinction, but Union Square has two famous San Francisco landmarks, the City of Paris and the St. Francis Hotel.

The City of Paris, Geary and *Stockton Streets,* is one of the city's oldest retail institutions, dating from the day that Felix Verdier sailed through the Golden Gate in a chartered brig named *Ville de Paris.* In 1850 Verdier was selling goods from the deck of his brig, and the family business has prospered ever since. The present site was occupied in 1896, the present building erected in 1909. In the design of the building architect Clinton Day picked up decorative themes from Parisian prototypes. The mezzanine windows and the friezes separating the floors are pleasant and lively. The wonderful glass dome of the central court forms the perfect cap for the four-story Christmas tree that each year (for over fifty years now) delights San Francisco youngsters.

The St. Francis Hotel, on *Powell* between *Post* and *Geary Streets,* is one of the great hostelries of the city. Built in 1904, when it was felt by some members of the Crocker family that San Francisco could use a major hotel somewhat more up-to-date than the old Palace, the basic structure was designed by Bliss and Faville to an Italian Renaissance theme. Only two years after the hotel opened, its interior was completely destroyed by the fire following the 1906 earthquake, although the basic structure survived. Undaunted, the owners immediately opened a "grille" in the damaged building and within forty days established the St. Francis Annex in Union Square. This temporary building accommodated guests until November of 1907, when the restored and expanded St. Francis opened.

All profits from the St. Francis Annex were turned over to the city and the Hotel company had Union Square restored after vacating the Annex.

A third wing was added in 1908, making the Saint Francis the largest hotel on the West Coast.

The St. Francis Hotel and Union Square before 1906.

91

SOUTH OF MARKET

SAN FRANCISCO

South of Market was San Francisco's first industrial area. As early as 1851 the shore beyond First Street was the site of several foundries, and the first steamboats launched at San Francisco were knocked together on the beach there. The little depression between the sand hills on Market and Howard Streets, better sheltered from the winds than most of barren, treeless San Francisco, was dubbed "Happy Valley," and here rows of little frame houses, many of them prefabricated in the East, housed the city's first industrial population.

The superior climate of the South of Market district suggested Rincon Hill (now largely buried under the Bay Bridge approach) as a desirable residential neighborhood. By the middle 1850's the hill was dotted with compara-

tively elegant homes, and despite the continuous development of the surrounding industrial area, Rincon Hill remained San Francisco's most fashionable neighborhood into the 1860's.

Rincon Hill was ruined as a desirable neighborhood by a promoter convinced that his fortune would be made by cutting Second Street through the hill so that heavy wagons might ply between downtown and the recently-constructed Pacific Mail docks at Second and Brannan Streets. In 1869 he managed to get the "improvement" authorized and the sixty-foot-deep cut all but demolished the value of Rincon Hill property.

The most elegant — and curious — of San Francisco's early residential developments has left the only traces of Rincon Hill's fashionable history. *South Park*, with its elliptical common and curving frontages, still wears out its existence as the focal point of the block bounded by Second and Third Streets, Bryant and Brannan Streets. The "London Roman" townhouses of the 'fifties had disappeared prior to the 1906 fire, to be replaced by very ordinary brick commercial structures — but the latent elegance of the setting suggests that in coming years South Park may regain its fashionable past as the locale of decorators, furnishers, architects, and others who are prone to seek distinctive surroundings.

South Park was the brain child of George Gordon, an Englishman who set out to create in 1854 a residential square modeled along the lines of similar squares in London. Within two or three years sufficient affluent citizens had built there to establish it as a stylish domicile of the gentry. The plan of the residential park was never fully accomplished, for the decline of Rincon Hill set in before more than half of the park was built.

After 1870 South Park was involved in the general ruin of Rincon Hill, but was for a few years less directly affected than were blocks laid out in the usual pattern. The interior frontage of the block still makes it a quiet enclave in a heavy commercial and industrial area, and it is just this unusual layout that holds promise of its eventual renaissance.

Two of the handful of important buildings which survived within the limits of the burned area of 1906 are found South of Market—the Old Mint and the Post Office. Both of these structures came through the great fire intact, and are of unusual distinction.

The "Old Mint," Fifth and *Mission Streets,* is a massive monument to the Federal Baroque-Classical Revival style of architecture. There is nothing quite comparable to it west of the Mississippi, except the old post office in Portland. Designed by A. B. Mullett, architect of the amazing Old State, War and Navy Building in Washington, D. C., the mint was commenced in 1869 and completed in 1874. The structure is built of brick, the exterior of the base and the Doric columns of the portico being Rocklin granite, the facing of the rest Columbia sandstone.

In keeping with the clean-lined exterior, the interior is not exceedingly elaborate, though such touches as fine bronze hardware, cast-iron balustrades, and rose marble fireplaces bespeak an age in which craftsmanship was inexpensive. A startling characteristic of the interior, suggestive of the essentially utilitarian and industrial purpose of the building, is the treatment of the ceilings; shallow brick arches that carry the floors are not concealed by a hanging ceiling (being only plastered by way of finish in the case of the main floor), and the ceiling of the upper floor is formed by exposed corrugated metal arches.

Time has not dealt gently with the Old Mint. For years pieces of the sandstone cornice fell off at odd intervals, and recently the whole cornice was removed in the interests of public safety. Yet it remains an outstanding monument to an age in which a great public building was supposed to express the power and the majesty of the nation and reflect the pride of a free people.

The Post Office and United States Court of Appeals Building, Seventh and *Mission Streets,* is a superlative governmental structure that has been maintained and improved by its occupants—no doubt because high court judges admire space and grandeur. This granite Mannerist-Baroque building was designed by James Knox Taylor, architect for the Treasury Department. The building was authorized in 1893, and it is said that the depression that immediately followed permitted the appropriation to cover considerably more elaborate interior finishing than had been planned initially.

Indeed, the interior of the building, which was completed in 1905, is of a splendor most often associated with "Byzantine." Workmen from Italy were imported to execute the detailing of the interior, and they left nothing unfinished, whether in bronze, in wood, in marble, in mosaic, or in etched glass. Altogether, the building is a magnificent example of the lavish display of public wealth which the public should expect to find in some of the more important buildings it finances.

The Pacific Gas & Electric Co. substation, 222–226 Jessie Street, tucked away in a dead-end alley between Market and Mission, is one of San Francisco's few great examples of the architectural possibilities of the brick facade. Originally built in 1881, and subsequently enlarged twice, the substation was damaged in a fire in February, 1906, and almost destroyed in the earthquake and fire of April, 1906. Rebuilt in 1907, the building owes its present character to Willis Polk, at that time head of the San Francisco office of D. H. Burnham and Company, the Chicago firm that had prepared the 1905 plan for the conversion of San Francisco to a model of the "city beautiful" along the lines of Paris and Washington. As a result, it is not altogether surprising

These fine "London Roman" town houses graced South Park in 1856

that the architectural ideas of Polk and Burnham should have been applied to an electric substation in a South-of-Market alley.

This noble structure is a simple (but quite sophisticated) exercise in the development of balance, line, and texture. Though the eye focuses on the ornamental, vertical, and symmetrical piercings and moldings, it is the horizontal line of the rough, red wall that catches the breath. Yet, of course, it is the elaborate applied inventions that make the plain surface more than just another brick wall. This is a building that many San Franciscans have never seen, and it is worth going out of one's way to look at it.

Fronting on Mission, with its back pushed up almost to the front of the Jessie Street Substation, is another brick structure of merit, *St. Patrick's Church, 756 Mission Street.* St. Patrick's was dedicated in 1872 as successor to an earlier St. Patrick's that occupied the site of the Palace Hotel. The tower and walls survived the fire of 1906, with the result that this good example of Victorian Gothic architecture still presents much the same appearance it did in the San Francisco of the mid-nineteenth century.

Opposite the Embarcadero, *11–21 Mission Street* is one of the last buildings that convey any of the flavor of the more modest commercial buildings of pre-1906 downtown San Francisco. This building was put up in 1889 by Hipolyte d'Audiffred to a design well-calculated to "remind him of home." Hipolyte's grandson recalls that the family building was saved by the barkeep of the first-floor saloon ("The Bulkhead"). As the great fire swept toward the waterfront, a corps of dynamiters ahead of it. For two quarts of whiskey per man and a hose cart full of wine, the firefighters were willing to take the chance that the d'Audiffred Building would spread the flames across East Street (later the Embarcadero) to the piers. As it happened, the fire spared the building, leaving it the only structure intact on the landward side of East Street.

The "Old Mint" expresses the power and majesty of the nation

In the last few years this building's upstairs rooms have housed artists, composers, and poets giving it some of the reputation of the old Montgomery block.

The rapid development of the South of Market district (Happy Valley, South Beach, Steamboat Point) in the 1850's made the next solid ground south of the Mission Bay mud flats attractive as a location for new industries. But it was not until after 1865, when the "Long Bridge" across Mission Bay was built along the lines of Fourth Street and what is now Third Street, that access to the Potrero became easy.

The location of industries led to the settlement of a good-sized working-class population on Potrero Hill. At the same time, a number of the owners and managers of industrial operations built houses for themselves there. The Hill is favored by the best weather in San Francisco and its heights provide the sweeping marine and city vistas that San Franciscans buy dearly in some other neighborhoods.

Some of the most interesting of the old houses of the

Potrero are located on the thirteen-acre tract centered about Eighteenth and Pennsylvania Streets that was purchased by Captain Charles Adams in the 1850's. Captain Adams's own home at *300 Pennsylvania Street* was completed in 1868. This is a very handsome house indeed. Of Italian villa derivation, it seems to have just enough in the way of decorative architectural devices (such as the pipe-stem colonnettes of the bay windows, the bold brackets at the roof line, and the quoining) to create a strong visual interest without detracting from the dignity of the building.

The oldest surviving home in the Adams Tract appears to be the chaste but forceful frame Italianate residence at *301 Pennsylvania Street* built around 1865. The house is now shorn of its entrance porch and the delightful octagonal cupola which crowned its roof.

At *400 Pennsylvania Street* is another large but simple Italianate built for the Crowell family about 1870. It is somewhat similar to 301 Pennsylvania but has an off-centered entrance. It is worth noting the degree of architectural balance maintained in this structure despite its departure from the regular plan, which the squared facade implies.

The Long Bridge built in the middle 1860's also extended across the base of Potrero Hill and leaped the flats and swamps of Islais Creek to the base of Hunters Point, thus making the present Bayview District almost as accessible to the city as the Potrero.

Across Innes Avenue from the Anderson and Christofani boatyard, last of the many small building and repair yards that made Hunters Point a center of maritime activity before the turn of the century, stands the restored headquarters of an industrial institution once vital to the well-being of the boatyard workers and the scow schooner sailors of San Francisco—the Albion Brewery.

About 1868 John Burnell, an Englishman who came to San Francisco by way of the failure of some Canadian adventures, staked out the site at *881 Innes Avenue* in the interests of gaining control of some good springs which broke above ground there. By 1870 he had built a stone brewery, with a three-story tower which is still a modest landmark of the area.

The unusual buildings were bought by a sculptor, Adrien Voisin, in the late 1930's, and restored as a dwelling. The springs, which are conveyed into caverns beneath the old brewery building, are still commercially exploited by the "Mountain Spring Water Company."

On the western slope of the Hunters Point heights, in the Bayview district proper, are two very large residences which are distinctive examples of the restrained Italianate style of the period. At *1562 McKinnon Street* is a fine, two-story house built about 1867 for a prominent San Francisco physician. This house is very much the same in character

The P. G. & E. substation on Jessie Street—brick at its best (next page)

The main Post office at Seventh and Mission is a government building of unusual splendor inside and out.

St. Patrick's Church on Mission Street

as the Adams house on the Potrero, with a somewhat different treatment of the window openings. At present, it is very handsomely kept up, and represents a striking contrast to the sometimes run-down structures around it.

An even larger house than that on McKinnon Street, one perhaps identifiable as a mansion, is the Sylvester house at *1556 Revere Street.* Perfectly square and balanced, with massive, arched pediments over the upper windows, the building (given the surrounding structures) must almost certainly at first strike one as having some institutional purpose. Originally built on Quesada Street, in perhaps 1870, the house was moved to its present location in 1913, the lumber from the original carriage house having been used to construct the present lower (garage) floor.

One of the most interesting Hunters Point-Bayview landmarks is the *South San Francisco Opera House, Newcomb* and *Mendell Streets,* built in 1888 by the Masonic Lodge. The "Opera House" (theatre would be a more accurate designation) opened during Christmas week of 1888 with a performance of a play called *Little Puck.* Subsequently it was the scene of many traveling theatrical events, particularly during its early years; autographs of such famous showmen as David Belasco can still be seen beneath the stage.

Long since fallen on evil times, the old Opera House has been a meeting hall and warehouse, and was recently on the verge of destruction. Purchased by a sympathetic owner, the Opera House has momentarily been "saved". Mayor Alioto has announced plans to fully restore the Opera House to be used as a neighborhood center. The building is essentially quite well-preserved, and the stage curtain, with its advertisements from the 1890's, is still in place.

The Opera House, together with the Baptist Mission across the street *at 1606 Newcomb Avenue,* is an example of the Italianate shifting into the Stick Style of the 1880's. The vertical lines of the building are accentuated by the application of strip pilasters and corner moldings; a suggestion of Gothic reappears; lathe-turned ornaments are applied. Still, in the Opera House and the Baptist Mission the decorative details are reasonably chaste and substantial.

All Hallows Church, Third Street, at Newhall and *Palou,* is a large, wooden Gothic church very much in keeping with the more notable old buildings in the neighborhood. It was built in 1886, to accommodate the overflow from another parish. Perhaps the most interesting architectural feature of the church, aside from the shingled steeple surrounded at its base by many small delicate spires, is the row of six lancet windows on the Palou side.

300 Pennsylvania — an elegant survivor from 1868

This stone studio was once a brewery.

The South San Francisco Opera House once sheltered the famous showman, David Belasco

The d'Audiffred Building at the foot of Mission Street as it looks today.

MISSION

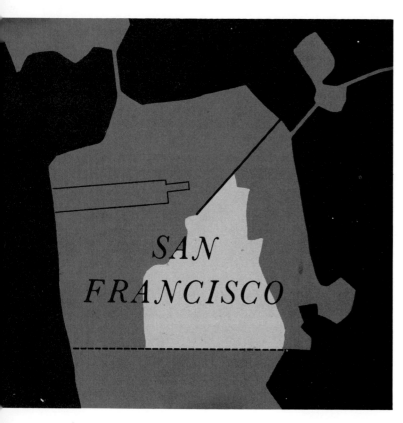

As the Mission district, like the adjoining Potrero and Bayview districts, was favored by its climate and its location athwart the easiest route to San Mateo County and southward, it attracted numerous settlers of some substance in the 1870's and 1880's; as a result the district has many old homes of considerable distinction. From 1850 through the 1880's, the Mission was something of a resort area to San Franciscans; both elbow room and climate suggested the location of such diversions as race tracks and pleasure gardens in the southeast section of the city.

Indeed, in the early 1850's there was almost nowhere for a San Franciscan to *go* of a Sunday unless it were out to the Mission itself—a circumstance that led naturally to the installation of roadhouses in the vicinity of (and even next

door to) Mission Dolores. A franchise to build a plank toll road along the line of Mission Street, thus affording easy travel between the little town of San Francisco and the Mission, was granted in 1850. In 1853 the city's first Sunday resort, Russ's Gardens, was established at Sixth and Harrison Streets—to be followed eventually by many others over the next thirty years.

The days of the Mission as a resort lasted only a generation or so, but one of its early characteristics has been retained to this day. The Mission is the most self-contained of San Francisco's districts, and outer Mission Street is like the main street of a small city. Traditionally, Mission residents have been particularly conscious of their community, and this sense of identity is otherwise found only in North Beach or, in days long past, "South of the Slot." It may be that this characteristic is swiftly on the wane, with the great influx of new people during the past decades, but the Mission still seems to be a city within the city of San Francisco.

Appropriately, the Mission district contains San Francisco's oldest building, *Mission Dolores at Sixteenth and Dolores Streets*. The cornerstone of the church was laid by Father Palou in 1782, and the building completed in 1791. An excellent example of the late Baroque ecclesiastical style of Mexico, with intimations of Classical Revival, the old church building appears today much as it did at the time of its construction—when Indian neophytes laid up its adobe bricks, shaped fastenings out of tough manzanita, and lashed the redwood roof trusses together with rawhide strips.

Indian artisans, using reds made from cinnabar and yellows from ochre clays of the Peninsula, executed much of the interior decoration, including the lively ceiling. The elegant carved wood and painted canvas *retablos* (screens behind the altars) were imported from Mexico. The church bells, presented by Mexican Viceroy Mendoza, are dated 1792 and 1797. The church has withstood three major

*Mission Dolores (above) is San Francisco's
oldest building. Details of the
historic structure seen from the
adjacent cemetery.*

earthquakes, and not until 1920 was major renovation necessary. Fortunately, Willis Polk was retained to handle this job; he accomplished such things as reconstruction of the roof without finding it necessary to throw away the old trusses and tiles. Further, Polk restored architectural details which had been altered previously.

Across the street from the old Mission is *Notre Dame School, 347 Dolores Street,* a convent and day school for girls erected in 1907 on the foundations of an earlier convent that had been dynamited to contain the 1906 fire east of Dolores Street. The school is a Mansarded structure of frame and stucco, with very pleasing proportions. The main steps and the wonderful iron gate and fence are from the original building.

Two very old houses that have maintained their original appearance can be seen side-by-side at *220* and *214 Dolores Street.* The "Tanforan Cottages," so called because members of the family of Toribio Tanforan occupied them from 1896 to 1945, are simple frame structures with modified late Classical Revival facades. Though very nearly identical in appearance, they were not constructed at the same time; 214 Dolores is said to have been built a little before 1853, 220 not long after that date. This dating is questionable, though, as the first substantiated date is 1866, when Revilo Wells, owner of 214, had water piped in.

There is still a small carriage house behind 220 Dolores—occupied as late as 1940 by one of the Tanforan carriages. The large gardens of these houses have been well-maintained and contain many specimens of turn-of-the-century San Francisco taste in flora.

A reminder of the days when the Mission was carved into good-sized tracts is found just off Dolores Street at *1876 Fifteenth Street,* about in the middle of the tract acquired by Andrew Thompson in 1852 and called by him *La Quinada.* A gold miner in 1849, Thompson soon settled down as owner of a popular saloon adjoining the Mission Dolores, and later built a substantial brick home (with adjoining grocery store and saloon) at Fifteenth Street and Dolores.

When the earthquake and fire demolished this establishment, Thompson purchased a comparatively new house on Haight Street and moved it to the site at 1876 Fifteenth Street. This home, of the Italianate era, is larger than it appears to be—there were 13 rooms on the top floor, and the building presently contains seven apartment units.

Nearby in the One Hundred block of Guerrero Street, is a series of older Italianate houses. The three at *120, 122, and 126 Guerrero Street* were built about 1878, apparently by the same builder, as they are substantially identical. Together with the flats adjoining *(104–114 Guerrero Street)*

Notre Dame School replaced a convent destroyed in the fire of 1906

and the house at the corner of Guerrero and Duboce (*102 Guerrero Street*), these buildings form an outstanding row, particularly in that they are handsomely maintained and are located where thousands of motorists see them each day.

The trio at 120, 122, and 126 Guerrero are fine examples of the restrained Italianate, their many decorations being just subdued enough to avoid an overcrowded effect. The pipestem colonnettes of the slanted window bays and the columns of the entrance are cabled in their lower third to break up what might be an excessively strong vertical line in these high narrow houses; the single upstairs window over the doorway repeats the theme of the entrance; only the entablature of the portico seems somewhat out of character with the rest.

The Mission District has several interesting churches — aside from Mission Dolores itself. Among the attractive old churches of the Mission, perhaps the most outstanding was the former Swedish Evangelical Lutheran Ebenezer Church at Fifteenth and Dolores Streets. Designed by August Nordin and built in 1903–04, the building was outgrown by the congregation about ten years ago, and

This Italianate trio on Guerrero Street was built in 1878

has changed hands. Substantial alterations have been made on the exterior. The shingles have recently been removed and the exterior is now sheathed in stucco.

A very pleasant shingled church of imaginative design is *Saint John's Episcopal, 120 Julian Street*. This church was built in 1909, on the site of a previous church that had been dynamited to slow down the 1906 fire. Its architectural style is sometimes called Tudor Lantern—a form of late medieval gothic style adopted for the parish churches of England.

At *3243–3245 Twenty-first Street* is a very distinctive example of the Eastlake style, with its Stick addition and riot of turned-wood decorative devices. This house was built after 1880, and was long ago converted to a multiple dwelling. It is the trim of this house which is of particular interest.

Moving outward, south of Mission Street, one finds the interesting Thirteen Hundred block of South Van Ness.

The most unusual home on the street is the mansion at *1348 South Van Ness Avenue*, a Stick-Queen Anne residence built in 1886 for Frank M. Stone, law partner to Aaron A. Sargent, former United States Senator from California. The house was designed by Seth Babson, one of the very few professional architects in nineteenth century California.

The Stone house is interesting not only for its general architectural appearance and location, but because its rich interior has been little changed since it was built. If one were to describe the interior, one might not get beyond the front hall: the floor is inlaid with black walnut and mahogany, the ceiling is Port Orford cedar with redwood moldings, the hall fireplace and its mantle include over three hundred pieces (including carvings and columns), the newel posts of the stairway are topped by globular lamps. . . . The fireplace of the drawing room is finished in gold and bronze tiling, with a mantle of cocobola wood. The frescoing of the ceiling is in the form of a sunburst—

106

Saint John's Episcopal Church, which was built in 1909, is an example of the Tudor style architecture common in English parish churches

the golden rays diverging from the window in the tower, while into the rays "flies a bright-hued, peacock-plumaged bird, the legendary *wahoo . . .* which ever seeks the rising sun." The rest of the interior is equally grand.

Across the street, at *1381 South Van Ness Avenue,* is a large house with squared bay windows—beautifully restored in recent years. This residence was originally designed and built by Charles I. Havens, City Architect of San Francisco, for his own use in 1884. When the present owner bought the house, it was run-down; its elegant appearance now is a tribute to the wonders that fresh paint can work.

A rare brick residence of its period is at *1232 Treat Street.* Built in 1885 by John McCarthy, who had come to San Francisco to supervise the masonry of the Palace Hotel, it is quite unusual in that it executes the popular late Italianate style in brick rather than frame. Almost completely covered with vines, the exterior is much the same as it was during Mr. McCarthy's later days as San Francisco's lead-

ing masonry contractor. His accomplishments include the Mills Building, deYoung Building, and Appraisers Building.

As the Thirteen Hundred block shows, South Van Ness was once a residential street of some elegance. Few buildings of note are left in the blocks nearest Market Street, but two worth attention stand side by side at *822* and *834 South Van Ness Avenue.*

The house at 822 South Van Ness was built in 1883 as a wedding present from Claus Mangels, an in-law relative and business associate of sugar magnate Claus Spreckels, to his daughter. Designed by German architect Henry Geilfuss, the house was basically of the late Italianate style —with the bays now changing from slanted to the square shape, and details becoming more elaborate.

Originally, the house had two stories, like its plainer neighbor at 834 South Van Ness Avenue which was built about 1887. In 1913, it was sold to the Sisters of the Holy

107

This Italianate house dates from 1883 but the somewhat different third story was not added until 1921

This Queen Anne residence was built in 1883 for lawyer Frank M. Stone and is of additional interest because of its elaborate interior. Among the materials present are walnut, mahogany, cedar, redwood, marble, gold and bronze tiling and cocobola wood

Cross as a residence for the nuns teaching at Saint Charles School. In order to improve the accommodations, it became necessary to enlarge the building, and in 1921 a third story was added—which accounts for the peculiarity of the second-floor cornice line.

After the Sisters left, about a decade ago, the house changed hands several times before becoming a residence for Indian boys. It is one of the last links with the past glories of the neighborhood.

Liberty Street, which runs (with a slight interruption) from Castro Street to Valencia, is one of the few remaining San Francisco streets where one can find whole blocks of single-family Victorian homes more or less intact. Most of these houses are of fairly modest size—that is, about the right size for a family by today's standards. Two of the somewhat larger and more elegant old homes are found in the block between Dolores and Guerrero Streets, at 109 and 159 Liberty. Though both of the homes have been divided into apartments, they have in recent years been handsomely restored.

Judge Daniel J. Murphy was the long-time owner of *159 Liberty Street*, built in 1878 and generally similar in character to the Italianate houses of the period. The slanted bay is to one side, the entrance, with its single window above, to the other. The portico is unusual with its split

108

This 1870 mansion is at 109 Liberty St.   *Susan Anthony visited 159 Liberty in 1896*   *Interior view of "Nobby Clarke's Folly"*

pediment framing a golden eagle—reminiscent of a high Georgian design.

Appropriately, this house on Liberty Street appears to have been a hotbed of the women's suffrage movement, for an old invitation reads: "Mrs. D. J. Murphy cordially invites you to meet Miss Susan B. Anthony, Rev. Anna Shaw, and others interested in the 'Woman's Suffrage' question, for a social chat, at 159 Liberty, Mission, on Friday evening next, March 27, 1896. . . ."

Even older is the handsome house at *109 Liberty Street,* built in 1870 and owned by Mr. James Lunt at the time of Susan B. Anthony's visit. Essentially, the plan of this house is not radically different from that of 159 Liberty, at least in the facade. The entrance is off-centered, like houses of the late 1870's and early 1880's; but the rather capricious, elaborate pediments over the windows give a vigorous look to the structure.

Another example of the flat-facade Italianate is at *1366 Guerrero Street.* Built around 1880, this house shows the emergence of the "stick" theme in the flat pilasters flanking the windows and in the vertical strips at the corners. Its general feeling and plan adhere more closely to the earlier style than to the full-blown Stick Style of the 1880's, which tended to rely much more heavily on profusion of applied decoration.

Not long after its construction, this home was bought by Frank G. Edwards, Fire Commissioner, importer, later

printer and publisher. The Edwards family occupied the house continuously from 1884 to 1948, gradually selling off the adjoining lots that had been planted as gardens and orchards. Among the frequent house guests of the Edwards' were the Wright Brothers (Orville and Wilbur), who visited 1326 Guerrero whenever they were in San Francisco.

This house was carved into apartments after the Edwards family sold it, but fortunately was not dealt with violently, either on the inside or the outside. A recent owner reconverted it to a single-family residence and restored it to its original splendor. It has since been reconverted to apartments.

A good place for viewing a mixture of frame Victorian houses of the Mission is the last two blocks of Fair Oaks, between Twenty-fourth and Twenty-sixth Streets. Perhaps the most unusual of the lot is the house at *387 Fair Oaks Street,* which may be described as a late Eastlake, with use of period motifs. Built in 1897 by S. A. Born & Co., it was bought by Edward J. Smith, a Mission druggist and later coal dealer.

Featuring an unusual bay window tower, with a curious slanting bay overhanging the wide and deep entrance, the facade of this house is a riot of garlands and scrolls. Like many of the homes of its same date, it is so exuberant that it adds genuine warmth and humanity to an increasingly dull cityscape. The house has been in continuous use as a single-family residence; despite the crowding of its neighbors, it may go on forever.

At *394 Fair Oaks Street* is a large home of the middle 1890's which also combines some features of very late Eastlake, Queen Anne and approaching Period architecture—in a restrained fashion. This house was built by a contractor, William Shaughnessy, for himself. In 1914, sometime after Mr. Shaughnessy's death, the big home was remodeled into three flats; in the intervening years further interior remodeling has been undertaken, but the building as a whole retains much of its original character. The octagonal tower can be seen here as an excellent architectural device for a home on a corner lot.

In the next block of *Fair Oaks*, at *435, 455, 463,* and *464,* are four good examples of the Stick or Strip development of the Italianate, built between 1878 and 1888. Some details regarding these houses will be found in the appendix.

At *3780 Twenty-third Street,* near the corner of Church Street, is an Italianate house of simple and stalwart design built around 1869. Originally located at the corner of Church and Twenty-third Streets, it was moved to its present location around 1900, when the grading of Church Street threatened the foundations. The large parcel of property which included the original and present sites of the house was bought by George T. Pracy in 1869, and was afterwards laid out with gardens and groves watered by a windmill that tapped a spring rising in the vicinity of Twenty-fourth Street and Castro.

The house has been continuously occupied by the Pracy descendants; altogether, its roof has at one time or another sheltered six generations of the family. After the house was moved, Pracy's daughter, Mary Ann Schneider, built three cottages on the former site. These "stock" residences of about 1901, located at *1081, 1085,* and *1091 Church Street* are of interest not because they are particularly unusual, but because they are so typical of tract homes of that time.

Among the surviving mansions of the general Mission area, the Alfred Clarke house, at *250 Douglass Street,* is particularly interesting, both because of its style and the style of its original owner. "Nobby" Clarke was an Irish sailor boy who put into San Francisco aboard the American ship *Commonwealth* in the fall of 1850. Naturally, he tried his luck in the gold mines but soon returned to the city, where there was more money to be made as a stevedore.

Clarke's up-to-then unpromising career improved when he joined the police force during the 1856 Vigilance excitement. By 1887, when he resigned from his position as

"Nobby Clarke's Folly" at 250 Douglass cost $100,000 in 1892

110

clerk to the Chief of Police, he is said to have saved some $200,000. He bought seventeen acres at the head of Eureka Valley, and there erected the mansion known at the time as "Clarke's Folly."

The four-story, multi-towered house cost around $100,000 to build in 1892. The architectural style reflects the frequently eclectic fashion of the day, but may most briefly be described as Baroque-Queen Anne. Of interest is the shingle pattern, in which bands of plain shingles are alternated with bands of scalloped shingles. The interior decor is best judged by the photograph on page 109.

The Clarke family did not live in the house for long, and by 1904 the building was the "California General Hospital," advertised as "an Elegant and Commodious Hospital" with large grounds, no other buildings in the block, and "Sheltered from the Cold West Wind." At a later date it was a rooming house for Standard Oil Company employees; at present it is an apartment house.

A house with a considerably more exotic background than the "Nobby" Clarke mansion is found at *196–198 Laidley Street,* at the corner of Miguel, overlooking the gap between Diamond Heights and Bernal Heights traversed by the old San Bruno Road and the original line of the San Francisco and San Jose Railroad. This three-story, frame, Second-Empire-and-Italianate structure was built by an attorney, Cecil Poole, about 1872.

Around 1900 the house was bought by Teresa Bell, associate of the legendary "Mammy" Pleasant, and wife of millionaire Thomas Bell. An obscure web of intrigue, blackmail, and murder had spun itself out, leaving Teresa the survivor and a millionairess by the time she occupied this house. Teresa died in 1916; today her house is given over to apartments.

One of the most unusual structures in the outer Mission area is a conservatory on the property at *236 Monterey Boulevard.* This handsome and utilitarian frame and glass building was constructed before 1918 by Frank Merrill, an inventor and inveterate star-gazer. Behind the late Victorian house on the property, Merrill built a steel observatory tower (still standing) which revolved on steel balls. His interest in rare plants and birds led to construction of the conservatory. His daring plunge into the aircraft business led to ruin, and in 1919 the bank sold his property. The conservatory and six of the original eight lots which comprised the small estate were later resold as a unit; by good fortune, the conservatory has been beautifully maintained and has become something of a landmark in the area.

Conservatory interior at 236 Monterey Blvd.

WESTERN ADDITION/TWIN PEAKS

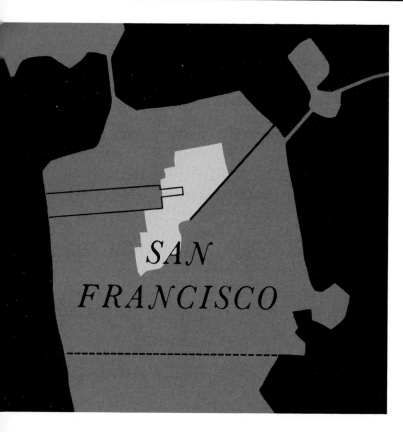

SAN FRANCISCO

The term "Western Addition" originally referred to the area between the city's surveyed boundaries (extending to Larkin Street) and the western limit set by the legislative charter granted in 1851 (present Divisadero Street). The area was opened for development by the Van Ness Ordinance of 1855, which cleared title to lands in actual private possession, extended the standard grid pattern of streets, and set aside a number of public squares.

In the years immediately following the 1855 Ordinance, the Western Addition remained fairly open country, with a few huts, houses, barns, and fresh water ponds here and there, the whole patterned by footpaths and rutted trails. The heart of the area did not begin to develop into a prime residential section until the 1870's and 1880's.

The substantial quality of this early development was modified after the turn of the century as many large older homes were cut up into increasingly smaller apartments. One possible reason for this was the hasty development of Fillmore Street as the city's principal temporary shopping area in the months immediately following the 1906 fire. Nevertheless some of the finest of the old buildings remain.

Near the southernmost edge of Pacific Heights stands the Shumate House, *1901 Scott Street.* This thoughtfully-detailed Italianate residence was constructed in 1870 for John F. Ortman, the present owner's grandfather, who had come to San Francisco from Germany in 1852. Mr. and Mrs. Ortman had picnicked here, and were so taken with the beautiful trees that they determined to purchase the property for their home. Aside from the elegant Italianate simplicity, perhaps the building's most notable feature is the large south garden which is still watered by the original well.

Like the Shumate house, the two-story structure at *1900 Webster Street* is not only Italianate and beautifully preserved, but has also remained in the same family through the years. It was built for Pierre Bonnard Berges, a Frenchman who sailed to California in 1855 at the age of sixteen. In 1884, Mr. Berges commissioned B. W. Hendrickson, a pioneer San Francisco architect, to design this house. The family still has Mr. Hendrickson's carefully drawn plans, twelve pages of specifications on linen.

The most interesting exterior feature here is the group of four blind windows on the Pine Street facade. Mr. Hendrickson felt the proportions of the building required relief on this austere side, yet additional windows would have hindered the interior placement of furniture. The blind window is common to the Italianate, but unusual to San Francisco, and highly effective in its use here.

The area in and about Bush Street has a number of important buildings which vary widely in age, style and

112

This Italianate residence, shown here in a turn-of-the-century photo, was built in 1870 at 1901 Scott by the present owner's grandfather

use. The Stanyan House, *2006 Bush Street*, for example, among the oldest structures in the Western Addition, was built about 1852 for Charles H. Stanyan, one of San Francisco's leading citizens. Stanyan, as chairman of the Outside Lands Committee, had been one of those responsible for the acquisition of Golden Gate Park. This simple, well preserved Victorian Gothic house has been held by the Stanyan family ever since.

Around the corner, at *1907 Buchanan Street*, is an Italianate cottage, also part of the original Stanyan property but moved from its former Bush and Hyde site in 1875. About 1885, the Stanyan family had a row of flats, *2000* through *2012 Bush Street*, built as income property where part of their spacious garden had been. These are good examples of the late-Italianate and Stick styles.

The imaginative Venetian Gothic-inspired edifice with a Romanesque portal at *1881 Bush Street* houses the Zen Soto Mission. The structure was originally designed by Moses Lyon for use as a synagogue. In 1898, the members of Ohabi Shalom (formed in 1863 by former members of Temple Emanu-El, who had withdrawn to establish a more conservative congregation) purchased the land at Bush and Laguna Streets. The temple was then built to hold one thousand persons, and formed the center of a complex of related buildings.

The heavily-painted wood of the temple's lower facade is scored to simulate rustication; fan-shaped stained-glass windows arch over the tower doors and second-story windows. The central part of the superstructure in the original building is now gone, but it is not difficult to imagine what it looked like before alteration.

One of the most photographed rows of houses in San Francisco is *1801* through *1845 Laguna Street*. These homes, built between 1887 and 1890, have been painstakingly restored and refurbished by their owners. Stylistically, they represent the frenetic mixture of detail characteristic of the late 1880's—combining somewhat modified Italianate, Mansard and Stick-Eastlake details.

Another interesting architectural area in the Western Addition is the south side of Bush Street in the block between Fillmore and Webster. A remarkably unchanged row of Italianate houses, *2115* through *2125 Bush Street*, was constructed about 1874. The stock detailing of rounded- and triangular-pedimented windows, the effective use of console-supported porch elements and the dignified repeat of cornice line distinguish these handsome survivors. This same block has a small row of slightly later houses, *2103* through *2107 Bush Street*, which continues the uniformity of the street facade. Finally, *Cottage Row* which dips down toward Sutter Street, between *2109–11* and *2115–15 Bush Street*, represents one of San Francisco's few residential walkways comparable to an English mews.

England's medieval architecture is represented by the stone Trinity Episcopal Church at *1668 Bush Street*. This imposing and dignified Gothic edifice, of Colusa sandstone, was designed by A. Page Brown, somewhat after Durham Cathedral, and built in 1892. The bronze angel which supports the lectern near the chancel and two of the smaller stained-glass windows were designed by Louis Tiffany.

Equally imposing in its way is the rambling Stick structure at *1409 Sutter Street* constructed in the early 1880's for Theodore Payne from a design by William Curlett. The two-and-a-half story building has, in turn, been a residence, restaurant, an alcoholic rehabilitation center, a Y.M.C.A. branch and a Pacific Gas & Electric Company office. In 1934, it was converted to its present use as an antique gallery and interior design studio.

The easternmost reaches of the Western Addition include three impressive churches. The First Unitarian Church at *1187 Franklin Street*, designed and built in 1888, is the oldest, and the congregation's most renowned leader,

Refugees in Alamo Square at Hayes and Steiner the morning after the 1906 earthquake watch the fire consuming downtown San Franc

2006 Bush has been in the Stanyan family since it was built around 1852. The 1800 block on Laguna (below) is typical late 1880's

Four blind windows were added to 1900 Webster (left) by its architect in 1884 to relieve the bareness of the wall

Thomas Starr King, is buried in the church yard. His efforts on behalf of Abraham Lincoln in 1861 contributed significantly to California's decision to remain in the Union during the Civil War; after that, he was the main force behind the U.S. Sanitary Commission in California, forerunner of the Red Cross. Architecturally, the church demonstrates the more correct eclectic feeling of the late nineteenth century. The gray stone edifice is of modified Gothic design although invested with the massiveness of the Richardson-Romanesque. Except for the bell tower, destroyed in 1906, the church looks much as it did in 1888, though some minor interior changes were recently made.

St. Mark's Evangelical Lutheran Church, *1111–1135 O'Farrell Street*, now surrounded by high-rise buildings, retains its isolated dignity. This vigorous example of what might be called the "creatively eclectic," with Romanesque and Gothic details, was constructed in 1894 of red brick and Bedford stone to the design of Henry Geilfuss.

St. Paulus Evangelical Lutheran Church, *999 Eddy Street*, designed by J. A. Kraft and built in 1894, is a reproduction in wood of the Cathedral at Chartres. The position of the spires has been reversed and the authenticity of stone and thirteenth-century stained glass are lacking, but general resemblance to the facade of Chartres is unmistakable.

Some other examples of the typical Italianate San Francisco home can be seen on Eddy Street. The two-story house at *819 Eddy Street* was designed by P. R. Schmidt and built for Frederick D. Stadtmuller in 1880. The house remained in the Stadtmuller family until 1951; then, like many of the large old homes in the Western Addition, it became a boarding house. In 1963, new owners began a highly successful program of Period interior renovation.

Built eight years later, and more elaborate than the Stadtmuller house, is *946 Eddy Street,* which is complemented by *948–54, 962* and *964 Eddy Street,* all built between 1878 and 1888. The row is enhanced by palm trees and low wrought-iron fences.

One of the most charming sights in the area is the Italianate town house at *807 Franklin Street,* with its columned entrance and arched doorway below a balcony and balustrade. Careful restoration and dramatic repainting display to advantage the gently-arched windows in slanted bays, string courses above first and second stories, and small carved medallions; the iron fence in front adds a final touch of the 1870 character.

Some nine blocks further west on Eddy Street stands one of the city's smallest church building, Old Saint Patrick's Church, *1822 Eddy Street.* Said to be the oldest frame church in San Francisco, it was first erected in 1854 on Market Street where a portion of the Palace Hotel now stands. After the site was purchased for the Palace, and "New" Saint Patrick's Church on Mission Street was completed, the building was moved in 1873 to Eddy Street between Octavia and Laguna Streets and rechristened Saint John the Baptist Church. It served as a pro-cathedral for Archbishop Patrick W. Riordan from 1885 to 1891 when a larger Roman Catholic Cathedral was completed. That same year, the church was moved for the last time to the north side of Eddy between Scott and Divisadero Streets.

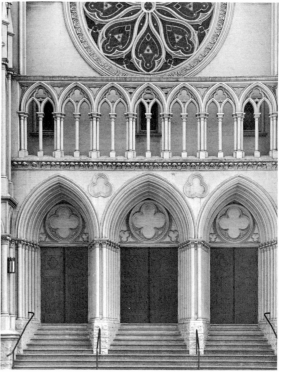

The church at 999 Eddy is a wood copy of Chartres
1409 Sutter (left) was an alcoholic treatment center
2115–2125 Bush (far left) is remarkably unchanged

Here it served as the Holy Cross Parish Church until 1899, when the present Holy Cross Church next door was completed. Now used as a Parish Hall, the building still reflects the essential character of the 1850's although the interior has been modified to accommodate its new social and educational function. Stylistically, the structure is Classical Revival. The stained-glass windows over the entrance which interrupt the pediment were probably added to the building in 1873 and the windows on either side of the entrance have been enriched.

Few buildings are left on McAllister Street that echo its more pleasant years. One of these rare buildings is the old firehouse at *1051 McAllister Street*, built for Hose Company No. 6 in 1876 and now slated for demolition by the Western Addition Redevelopment program. The most notable feature of the firehouse, presently a storage facility for the Art Commission, is the fifty-foot hose tower in the rear, once used for the "drip-drying" of wet hoses.

An almost astonishing departure from the standard architectural tone of the Western Addition stands at *1347 McAllister Street*, a wonderfully Baroque little apartment house built near the turn of the century. With its French doors and oeil de boeuf windows, projecting cornices and ornate brackets, it is one of three similar designs in San Francisco.

Also interesting is the row across the street at *1376* through *1392 McAllister Street*. Built in the 1890's, the houses are of a general Queen Anne style, combining rounded corner towers (with some spires) and Neo-Georgian details, anticipating the Colonial Revival.

Alamo Hill, which lies between the older Western Addition and today's Haight-Ashbury, was a popular residential location in the 1880's and 1890's. While the Stick Style is as evident as in the Western Addition, many larger homes are reminiscent of the *Beaux Arts*.

Some typical architecture of the Western Addition can be seen in the streets around Alamo Square. For example, the three-story Italianate building at *633 Laguna Street* (now with a brick lower story), was built in 1879 for Laura A. Mowry, a widow with vast real estate and commercial holdings in this area. Presently used for commercial purposes, the building retains a hint of the spaciousness it once had as Mowry's Opera House (later Mowry Hall). It

These Italianate houses at 962–946 Eddy (below) are handsome survivors of the 1880's

was here that San Francisco's Board of Supervisors met for eight months after the 1906 disaster.

The square block formed by Fillmore, Grove, Steiner and Fulton Streets contains four interesting buildings of about the same age, but differing in style. The two-story house at *820 Fillmore Street* would be unusual in any part of the city, but it is particularly eye-catching in this environment. This vigorously non-conformist structure gives the definite impression that the architect viewed a Persian mosque through Queen Anne spectacles. It was built in 1895 by C. A. Worth.

Within sight of Alamo Square is the three-story apartment house at *926 Grove Street* which lends an air of spacious elegance to the area. Reminiscent of the 1890's, it was built for vintner John L. Koster. It includes features common to the Baroque, Italianate, Queen Anne and Colonial Revival. A private residence for forty years, it became, in turn, the Jewish Community Center, the Jewish Educational Center, a boys' school and, in 1943, a thirteen-unit apartment house.

Another elegant home is *940 Grove Street*, once a combination residence and art school, and now the home of

Old St. Patrick's Church (built in 1854) once stood on the site of the Palace Hotel. Mowry's Opera House (below) is a relic of 1879

the French-American Bilingual School. Built about 1894 for Edward Probert, an English diplomat, its basic character is Stick-Eastlake with a suggestion of Colonial Revival in the entrance porch.

Bordering the Square is *850 Steiner Street*, a three-story home built in 1899 which features rounded-arched windows in the Queen Anne corner tower, balcony with balustrade, and colonial details as well as stained-glass windows more typical of the Victorian era.

One of the more picturesque examples of the Stick Italian Villa is *1198 Fulton Street*, the most imposing building in the area. Designed in 1889 by Henry Geilfuss as a residence for William Westerfeld, a noted baker and confectioner, this enormous wood *palazzo* is the closest San Francisco equivalent to the Carson house at Eureka; both are exceptionally picturesque versions of the towered villa form, here seen in uncompromising Stick expression with the characteristic squared-bay window of the 1880's.

About the turn of the century, the residence was purchased by John J. Mahoney of Mahoney Brothers—builders of the present St. Francis and Palace Hotels and the Greek Theater in Berkeley. After the Mahoneys sold the building in 1928, it was leased for almost twenty years to various tenants before eventually becoming a rooming house. It has recently been purchased for restoration.

Further south, on Steiner Street, is a group of row houses built between 1894 and 1895 by Matthew Kavanaugh, carpenter and builder, as single-family dwellings. While the houses, *710* through *720 Steiner Street*, are constructed around identical floor plans and are similar in style, the builder obtained individuality by altering a doorway here and a window there.

The very large Ohlhoff House at *601 Steiner Street*, on the corner of Fell, is one of the most striking examples of the period when Queen Anne met and often conquered the Colonial Revival. It was built in 1891 as a residence for James Scobie, a railroad contractor and later a prominent real estate man. About 1900, Mr. Scobie sold the house to Nicholas Ohlhoff whose grandson, James Broughton, has immortalized the house in a drama, *How Pleasant It Is To Have Money*. In 1958 the Protestant Episcopal Church purchased the building for use as a rehabilitation center.

Of oak and redwood, on a brick foundation, the house has two Queen Anne towers, partially shingled in the more regular patterns of the 1880's, and a multitude of lofty gables. The detail borrows from the late Eastlake and early Federal Revival all combined with the inevitable bay. Inside, one finds mahogany-paneled doors and walls, parquet floors, stained-glass windows, coved ceiling, plaster carvings, rosewood paneling and maple doors with mahogany and, occasionally, rosewood veneer.

Even more fascinating architecturally is *201 Buchanan Street*, built in 1883 probably for the family of John Night-

This Stick style Italian villa at 1198 Fulton was built in 1889 and once housed the builder of the Palace and St. Francis Hotels. 710–720 Steiner (at left) were all built in 1894 by carpenter Matthew Kavanaugh

123

201 Buchanan (right) is an 1883 example of the fusion of Eastlake and Stick details. The 1891 Queen Anne house at 601 Steiner (below) is noted for its intricately carved doors

ingale, a former president of the Society of California Pioneers, who came to San Francisco in 1849. The piquancy of Eastlake and Stick details are here fused in exuberant chalet styling; a Mansarded tower rising over the center has startling similarities to the use of pyramid roofs now fashionable in contemporary Bay Area work.

The two-story Stick Style home at *294 Page Street* was designed and built in 1885 by Henry Geilfuss for Charles Dietle who sold it to John DeMartini in 1906 for a bag of gold which DeMartini had managed to salvage from his business after the great fire. The elegantly-preserved house has both the uncompromising vertical rhythms of fully-developed Stick and some of the fantasy which underlay the Italianate. Comparatively shallow squared bays accent the flat but crisp articulation of this house.

The district which centers around the intersection of Haight and Ashbury Streets with Haight Street as an east-west axis, developed somewhat later than the Western Addition. Although the Stick Style is apparent here, many more of the houses seem to reflect the more rococo characteristics of the 1890's, and an even greater number seem to date from immediately after the 1906 fire to 1920. Still a number of outstanding Period structures remain.

The oldest residence in San Francisco may be the Abner Phelps House at *329 Divisadero Street.* As with all very early San Francisco houses, the date of construction cannot be positively ascertained; it is generally believed to date from about 1850 (though some say 1860). The earliest published account of the history of the house states that it was "built in 1850 by John Middleton & Sons, one of the first real estate concerns in this city; and constructed of lumber framed into sections brought around the Horn from Maine, there being no sawmills here at the time."

However, a direct descendant of Abner Phelps declared in 1961 that the house had been purchased in New Orleans in 1850 and shipped around the Horn in sections to ease the homesickness of Phelps' bride, the former Augusta Roussell of New Orleans. This latter explanation seems more reasonable as the house is raised on a high foundation, in the manner of southern river-front cottages of the eighteenth and early nineteenth centuries and has the two-story facade veranda often seen in Louisiana at that time.

It is certain that Phelps, who had been a colonel in the Mexican War, lived in the house with his family around 1851, and it is possible that John Middleton put the house

This finely-detailed Stick style house at 294 Page Street was built in 1885 and changed hands for a bag of gold after the 1906 fire

125

together when it arrived. Phelps chose as a setting a 160-acre plot at the foot of Buena Vista Hill, a part of which is now the Panhandle of Golden Gate Park. Phelps traveled from here to his law office on Montgomery Street through Hayes Valley. Divisadero Street was then a cow path to pastures in the Mission district.

The house has been moved twice: first, from its site facing east on the western side of Divisadero to a much smaller lot farther west, then to its present location, facing south. Despite the Divisadero Street address, the house is actually situated in the middle of the square block and today can be glimpsed only from Oak Street.

In the middle of the next block south on Divisadero Street stands a particularly good example of how later nineteenth century residential architects used the advantages of a Mansard roof – providing an extra story and roof together. Squared bays with Stick strips, a chastely Classical portico with balustrade and minimal emphasis on ornamentation give *280 Divisadero Street* a quietly dignified appearance. Built in 1885, the house has been thoughtfully restored in recent years. Its wide lot permitted a carriage drive down the side; the carriage house and former turn-

around have since been transformed into an apartment with terraced garden.

There are two structures of uncommon interest in the westernmost portion of the Haight-Ashbury district. The first is the Georgian-detailed, hipped-roof house at *1901 Page Street*, built in 1896. The general style of the house is Colonial Revival. One of its more notable owners was the late novelist, Kathleen Norris.

The old firehouse at *1757 Waller Street* was built in 1896 to house Hose Company Number 30 and was used as such until 1959. It has since been carefully restored as a private home. Built of granite and wood along the simplest of elongated lines, the building exudes the character (despite its youth) of a structure of Gold Rush days.

Buildings in and about Buena Vista Park vary greatly in style and age. Most compatible, in terms of era and architecture, are two close neighbors at *1080* and *1081 Haight Street (One Buena Vista East)*. The former was designed by a German architect named Raven between 1885 and 1890 for Dr. John C. Spencer. At one time it boasted its own plant for distilling and purifying water and, to the rear of the lot, a childrens' playhouse (converted to a garage in

329 Divisadero, hidden in the middle of a square block, is believed to date from 1850 and may be the oldest house in San Francisco

*Novelist Kathleen Norris once lived at 1901
Page (top left). 1081 Haight (top right) is an
1890 "flatiron". 280 Divisadero (left)
has a fine Mansard roof. 11 Piedmont (above)
is all that's left of an 1860 dairy farm*

This old photo of 3224 Market shows it before the turn of the century and Market Street's extension up and over Twin Peaks

129

1909). The Queen Anne tower has a lofty polygonal accent while Palladian windows and a triple-arched porch entrance suggest the approach of Period sources; the overall effect is one of late Victorian variety. The second building, now apartments, was constructed in 1890 in the "flatiron" pattern common at that time in commercial architecture but unusual for the area.

An imaginative use of the basic Eastlake-Stick Style can be seen at *130 Delmar Street*, near the edge of Buena Vista Park. This two-story redwood structure with scalloped shingles, slanted bays, deep overhanging eaves, and carved fan-shaped embellishments, was built in 1890 by E. N. Fritz.

Easily the most ornate structure in the Buena Vista Park area—markedly similar to 1901 Page Street—is the mansion at *737 Buena Vista West*, built in 1897 or 1898 for Floyd Spreckels. The top floor for a time provided studios for authors Ambrose Bierce and Jack London. The house, of wood on a stone foundation, is laced all around with a garland just beneath the roof; an imposing rounded entranceway, with four composite columns, is crowned with a balustrade. The style is exuberant, freely-interpreted (fan-lighted windows, round windows with garlands below) Colonial Revival.

The house at *11 Piedmont Street* is all that remains of a once-prosperous dairy farm. Originally built nearer the bottom of the hill about 1860, the house was moved to the far corner of the property in 1888. Its pristine whiteness suggests New England, and its renovation by the present owner retains its character of practical Italianate elegance.

Hidden behind a massive hedge is the two-story home at *49 Park Hill Avenue*, built between 1880 and 1885 for a doctor who also had his office here. Originally situated on a much larger parcel of land, the house is still surrounded by woods. Its most distinctive architectural feature is the polygonal corner tower surmounted by a multi-angled roof. Also of interest is the charming "Victorian" garden complete with an inviting gazebo, added by the present owner.

Long before Market Street's upper reaches were crowded with apartment buildings, the house at *3224 Market Street* was built in 1875 for Adam Miller. Mr. Miller purchased the land later known as the Mountain Springs Tract around 1868. The house has probably been enlarged (as the vintage photograph indicates) and a large window was installed in the central portion of the facade forty years ago to improve the view. Miller's daughter married Behrend Joost, president of the Mountain Springs Water Company, and for several years the house served as company headquarters.

Bernard Maybeck's rapport with nature was such that it is hardly surprising that most of his San Francisco homes are centered about the Twin Peaks and Forest Hill districts. These areas bordering Sutro Forest lent themselves well to his talent for blending living space with the charms of the outdoors.

One of the finer Maybeck residences in this city is situated in the Haight-Ashbury District. This rustic home, at *1526 Masonic Avenue*, sits in striking contrast to its neighbors. Built in 1910 for E. B. Power, then Assistant Attorney General of California, its exterior is simple in form and detail. The only exterior motif is the arrowhead design, symbolizing Mr. Power's great interest in the American Indian, used in the shutter of a gable window.

This simplicity leaves one unprepared for Maybeck's interior: massive beams, natural redwood paneling, infinitely-detailed joinings, a mammoth fireplace and the inspiring two-story, cathedral-ceilinged living room. Other interior details normally supplied by Maybeck were designed to the Powers' specifications: copper hardware and fixtures replace the usual brass and a series of three triangular shapes for decoration appears instead of Maybeck's diamond pattern.

A small rustic cottage which incorporates living space with outdoors charm is *196 Twin Peaks Boulevard*, one of the earliest homes on the steeper slopes of Twin Peaks. Maybeck was commissioned to design the cottage for Miss Alice Gay in 1917—with the express stipulation that it could cost no more than four thousand dollars. Maybeck managed to keep well within his budget; but, in so doing was forced to subdue the superb motifs and wood carvings usually so essential a part of his buildings. Redwood was used throughout, however, and the large living room has a beamed ceiling.

South and west of Twin Peaks lie three additional Maybeck structures, all built in the wild area of Forest Hill between 1913 and 1919. Maybeck designed a number of buildings for friends and for organizations of particular interest to him. A case in point is his residence for Edwin C. Young, whom Maybeck knew through the Bohemian Club. Begun late in 1913, the home at *51 Sotelo Avenue* was completed in 1914 and is considered the first Maybeck building in the Forest Hill Tract.

Because the house is built into the side of a hill, its dimensions, particularly in depth, are especially impressive. Some Maybeck students feel the exterior of this house represents the beginning of his movement toward fanciful rather than essential forms and patterns, as the ornamentation here seems applied rather than integral to the structure. If this is true (and the projecting beams which form a lattice across the front seem to suggest it) his style had certainly lost none of its strength. Nor are his hallmarks missing: the balconies, a necessity in Europe where he studied, are perhaps more notable here than in any of the other residences discussed—they not only ring the living room on the second-story level just under the cathedral ceiling, but are also used outside.

The Forest Hill Club House at *381 Magellan Avenue* was designed by Maybeck and built on weekends by members of the Forest Hill Association, residents of the area. The facade of the structure, completed in 1919, is more restrained than Maybeck's other works, but the interior is Maybeck at his best. The high ceiling with its massive beam work is one of the architect's most inspiring.

More thoroughly typical of Maybeck is the home at *270 Castenada Avenue*, designed for S. Erlanger and begun in April, 1916. Although this is among the most visually pleasing of Maybeck's structures, it is less-inventively articulated inside than others. The cathedral ceiling here is truncated by the presence of a second floor bedroom directly over the dining area.

The interior is less formal than the exterior would imply. Repeated rhythms of sharply-pointed gables reiterate Maybeck's and other architects' allegiance to early American seventeenth century homes. Much of the strength and purity of Old Salem is here, but to the ageless traditions of massive framing, wooden board or shingle sheathing and small-paned leaded windows, Maybeck has added a freedom, a thrust of interior to exterior, that is inescapably his own.

Bernard Maybeck designed 1526 Masonic in 1910 and 381 Magellan in 1919. Both are excellent examples of his work

RICHMOND/GOLDEN GATE PARK SUNSET/PRESIDIO HEIGHTS

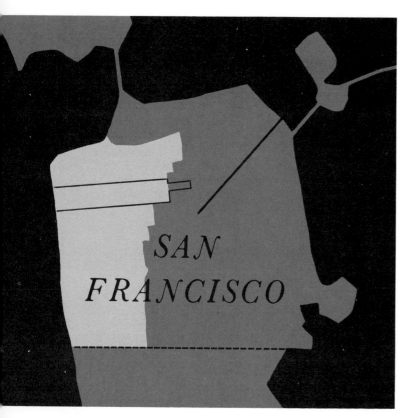

W est of the hills that ring the central city of old San Francisco lies the great rough rectangle of the Richmond and Sunset districts. Stretching from the Presidio to Lake Merced, and from Lone Mountain and Mount Sutro to the Pacific Ocean are a thousand blocks of pleasant homes, some of them of notable age and distinction. Bisecting the rectangle is one of the world's great parks. And snug against the rectangle's northeast corner lies one of the city's most attractive architectural enclaves, Presidio Heights.

For a while, in the latter part of the nineteenth century, the westward spread of San Francisco's residential area stopped short of the Richmond and Sunset—for the simple reason that a large part of these districts was a restless

jumble of sand dunes. Twin Peaks and Mt. Sutro cut off the Sunset from the city. The Richmond was artificially isolated by the cemeteries centering around Lone Mountain (site of the present San Francisco College for Women). The cemeteries were described in 1865 by Frederick Law Olmsted as, "a burial ground on high elevation, scourged by the wind, laid out only with regard to the convenience of funerals, with no trees or turf, and with but stunted verdure of any kind, and this with difficulty kept alive."

As a result of this comparatively unfavorable aspect and the availability of land elsewhere, the eventual opening of the Richmond district did not precipitate a stampede of new residents. The oldest houses in the original district (Arguello Boulevard to Fifteenth Avenue between Geary and California Streets) are small and scattered, and while many are still standing, they do not dominate the neighborhood.

Some of the typical early construction in the Richmond can be seen on Third Avenue, between Cornwall and Clement Streets. Most interesting in the row of four identical homes at *211, 213, 215,* and *217 Third Avenue* built by J. R. Chapton in 1893. The interesting pointed turrets, the diamond shingles, and the entrance porches with colonnettes and arches identify these uniform structures as indeed separate castles.

The long, narrow neighborhood adjacent to the Presidio, with its short, dead end streets off Lake Street, is probably the most charming part of the Richmond. The proximity of the Presidio and the quiet streets make this strip particularly desirable; indeed, the largest houses in each of the short blocks tend to be those at the far end, adjoining the Presidio.

The house at *2 Sixth Avenue* is characteristic of the size of the homes built on the lots adjoining the Presidio wall. This big two-story shingle structure on a high brick foundation was built for Mrs. Elise Kelley Drexler in 1914. The broad, balanced gables and overhanging eaves of the house, its heavy, timbered balconies supported by large brackets, are suggestive of Maybeck, though the style seems somewhat more heavy-handed.

In 1903, when Ansel E. Adams, the famous landscape photographer, was barely a year old, Charles and Olive Adams built the chalet at *129 Twenty-fourth Avenue* shown in the old photograph on page 134. As Nancy Newhall has written in The Sierra Club's *The Eloquent Light*, "Doubtless on one of their bicycle trips to collect wildflowers for 'Ollie' to paint on china, they found the steep hillside above the thickets of Lobos Creek from which they could look down over the dunes to the tumultuous surf on Bakers Beach. . . ." Having found the spot, they made their dream

of a "farmhouse in the city" come true. On the barren slopes they planted a tiny Norfolk Island pine, which was Ansel's first Christmas tree, a tree which now towers before the house. These same slopes were transformed into an "astonishing garden—a brilliant foreground for the often sombre majesty of the country."

The house was badly shaken up in the earthquake, and it was later necessary to turn it around and place it on a new foundation in order to prevent it from sliding down the dune. Today the heavy foliage surrounding the house makes it very difficult to photograph—indeed almost impossible to see from the street.

A truly exceptional variation of the stock San Francisco "tract" home of the late 1890's is the graceful Queen Anne

This Queen Anne house at 451 Twenty-fifth Avenue is typical of the 1890's

House at *451 25th Avenue.* The present owner of this immaculately-maintained residence, a member of the California Heritage Council, accurately describes the house (built in 1897) as, "a middle-class home, sort of custom built." The round tower, the ornamented pediment, the arched entrance with its small composite columns are among the more expensive touches that distinguish it from the frequent rows of otherwise similar houses found in many parts of the city.

The most famous San Francisco resort for over a hundred years, the *Cliff House* is a landmark of the first importance, however undistinguished the architecture of the present structure which dates from 1908. The Cliff House site, with its spectacular view over the Ocean Beach and the adjacent Seal Rocks, has been a tourist attraction for more than a century. The first Cliff House was put up in 1863.

The beauties of the place were described by Mark Twain in the *Californian* about a year later: "When we got to the Cliff House we were disappointed. I had always heard there was such a grand view to be seen there of the majestic ocean, with its white billows stretching far away until it met and mingled with the bending sky; with here and there a stately ship upon its surface, ploughing through plains of sunshine and deserts of shadow cast from the clouds above; and, near at hand, piles of picturesque rocks, splashed with angry surf and garrisoned by drunken, sprawling seal-lions and elegant, long-legged pelicans.

2 Sixth Avenue was built in 1914 and shows the influence of May

This then-isolated 1903 chalet was Ansel Adams' first home

134

"It was a bitter disappointment. There was nothing in sight but an ordinary counter, and behind it a long row of bottles with Old Bourbon, and Old Rye, and Old Tom, and the old, old story of man's falter and woman's fall, in them."

In 1881 Adolph Sutro, a firm believer in and supporter of healthy, family-type recreation, took over the old roadhouse. When it burned in 1894, Sutro characteristically rebuilt it in the grand manner. Whereas the old Cliff House, even with its numerous additions, was no larger and no more eye-catching than the present structure, the gingerbread palace that Sutro built was at once one of the most conspicuous and fanciful monuments in the west. Six stories high, surmounted by towers and turrets, this jig-saw masterpiece was the fitting termination of Victorian San Francisco. But it survived the palaces of Nob Hill by only a year, burning to the ground in 1907.

Nothing else that man has built in the San Francisco region can match the vision, art, and labor that has produced Golden Gate Park.

In 1866, Frederick Law Olmsted, designer of Central Park in New York City, came to San Francisco to discuss park planning, at the request of the Board of Supervisors. He offered a series of suggestions, none of which were specifically acted upon but all of which emphasized the importance of parks as part of the urban environment.

Olmsted's ideas moved the city to reserve a major portion of the so-called Outside Lands—lands outside the original pueblo limits and not specifically given to San Francisco as successor to the Pueblo of Yerba Buena—for a major park. In 1869, Order Number 800 provided for establishing a park of at least one thousand acres. A committee finally determined on the acres now known as Golden Gate Park and the Panhandle, surely the greatest investment the city ever made.

The notion of park planning on a grand scale implanted by Olmsted had taken root, and the first Park Superintendent and Engineer, William Hammond Hall, proceeded to draw up a magnificent plan in accordance with Olmstedian principles.

This house at 45 Scenic Way, is one of a distinctive trio designed by Willis Polk in 1915

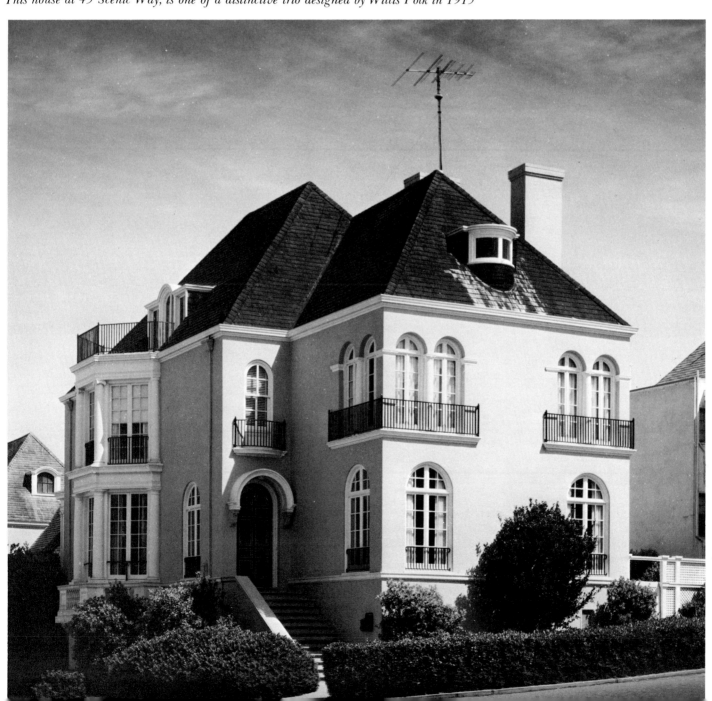

CONSERVATORY
ERECTED 1878 HRS 8 AM 4 50 PM

During his tenure, Hall did what he could and did it brilliantly, though there was in fact no need for a great park in San Francisco in the early 1870's, and appropriations were therefore grudgingly given and proportionately small. Not until the late 1880's was need for the park more clearly recognized, and at that moment San Francisco suffered a stroke of luck. John McLaren went to work at Golden Gate Park, and in 1887 was elevated to the position of Superintendent. He fought for "his" park with great success for fifty-five years.

Anecdotes about "Uncle John" McLaren's single-minded devotion to the park are legion. When civic leaders asked him to suggest a suitable 90th birthday gift, he replied, "Ten thousand yards of good manure!" Manure, grass, trees, and water—and decades of patient labor—made Golden Gate Park what it is today.

The most impressive building in the park is certainly the delightful Victorian *Conservatory* on *John F. Kennedy Drive*. This building was ordered from New York by James Lick, the eccentric San Francisco millionaire and philanthropist. Lick, a great horticultural enthusiast, had originally intended to erect the conservatory on his San Jose farm, but on his death in 1876 the huge glass building was still in its packing crates. The Society of California Pioneers inherited the thirty-three tons of glass, which was in turn bought by twenty-seven wealthy citizens and presented to the Park Commissioners. When the conservatory was erected in 1879, it was one of the largest in America with its 15,000 square feet of floor space.

The building was partially destroyed by fire in 1883, but was rebuilt with funds contributed by Charles Crocker and others. Prior to the turn of the century, the conservatory was very much the focal point of the park, and even today its splendid quaintness and ever-changing outdoor floral displays are apt to be the first thing that captures the eye of a visitor.

The windmills at the beach end of the park are further examples of vigorous utilitarian architecture. The strong and steady westerly winds of the summer season and the presence of an apparently unlimited supply of fresh water beneath the sands suggested the use of Dutch windmills to solve Golden Gate Park's rapidly increasing water supply problem around 1900. The *North Windmill*, a handsome domed tower now rather forlorn looking without its huge sails, was constructed in 1902. It succeeded in pumping as much as 30,000 gallons per hour to an elevation 200 feet above sea level and two miles distant.

The success of this windmill suggested the construction of a second, at the southwest corner of the park. Largely built by funds donated by Samuel G. Murphy, it was named in his honor. At the time of its construction in 1905, the *Murphy Windmill* was the largest in the world, with its sails spreading 114 feet from tip to tip. These great sails were, until recently, a landmark on the Great Highway, though the windmill was equipped with an electric pump in 1927.

The popular *Japanese Tea Garden* is one of the relics of the California "Midwinter International Exposition" of 1893–4. The one hundred sixty acres of the fair grounds occupied the general position of the complex of large buildings—the Academy of Sciences and M. H. deYoung Memorial Museum—that now stand toward the east end of the park, and the fair itself was promoted at about the time that the eastern half of the park had really taken shape.

The Japanese Tea Garden was the brainchild of George T. Marsh, San Francisco's leading importer of oriental artifacts and one of the promoters of the Exposition. From 1910 through 1942 the family of Makoto Hagiwara lived in the garden and cared for it—a tenure sufficiently long to have been instrumental in maintaining and improving upon the original concept.

The Murphy windmill—in 1905 the world's largest

Golden Gate Park's eye-catching conservatory (left)

The entrance gate and tea house date from the Midwinter Fair. The two-story building that houses the gift shop has been extensively modernized. As the garden exists today, it is a Victorian interpretation of a Japanese garden, and a delightful one.

Two quite attractive Romanesque buildings constructed of rough sandstone are found near the eastern entrances of the park. The older, the *"Children's House"* at the children's playground off *South Drive*, was a gift of the estate of Senator William Sharon, erstwhile "King of the Com-

stock." It was built in 1885 from designs of Percy and Hamilton, with William Hammond Hall serving as consultant engineer.

The second impressive example of the Romanesque in Golden Gate Park is the headquarters building, *McLaren Lodge*, on *John F. Kennedy Drive* just off Stanyan Street. Designed by Edward R. Swain in the manner of the great H. H. Richardson, this building was erected in 1896 as a residence for John McLaren as well as a Park Commission headquarters. Now the entire building (and a modern

The Park's Romanesque "Children's House", below and in detail at left, was built in 1885 as a bequest of Senator William Sharon

The Japanese Tea Garden — relic of the 1893 midwinter fair

140

annex to the rear as well) is occupied as a Park Department headquarters. With its red tiled roof, with its unsurfaced sandstone walls heavily cloaked with ivy, the lodge provides a peculiarly elegant and appropriate administration building for the San Francisco park system.

The original landscape of the Sunset District and its subsequent development as a residential area rather parallels that of the Richmond, but at a later date. The first substantial development in the Sunset occurred around Ninth and Tenth Avenues from Lincoln Way southward a few blocks. A second, and more colorful, development sprang up in the sand dunes near the sea. Some built cottages, either for permanent residence or for weekend use, while others converted ancient horse-cars and cable cars (which had been condemned to the boneyard created by the traction companies at the foot of Lincoln Way) into exotic dwellings.

Two interesting old structures in the Sunset are found on Tenth Avenue. At *1348 Tenth Avenue* is the first firehouse in the Sunset, a Victorian shingle with bell towers, built in 1899. Abandoned in 1962, the old quarters of Engine Company 22 appear to be in such poor shape that the building may well be torn down before long, rather than being snapped up by one of the growing corps of old firehouse aficionados.

One of the earliest examples of the development of the Sunset is the charming Victorian house (with its hint of a Queen Anne tower) at *1546 Tenth Avenue* built in 1898. No doubt a good part of the character of this house stems from its being built on a double lot, which permitted the trees and other plantings which make it stand out.

A real suburban hideaway in the Sunset is the old Trocadero Inn, built well before the turn of the century by George M. Green. Now a part of *Sigmund Stern Grove, Nineteenth Avenue* and *Sloat Boulevard*, the flamboyant Queen Anne roadhouse, with its jigsawn crests, profusion of finials, patterned shingles, brackets, latticed arches, gables and dormers, is said to have been restored under the direction of Bernard Maybeck around 1930.

In the late 1890's and the early years of this century, the Trocadero was famous as a resort of political *bon vivants*, among them political boss Abe Ruef. The resort and its grounds later passed into the hands of Mrs. Sigmund Stern, who gave it to the city for recreational and cultural purposes. As one area in the grounds provided a natural amphitheater, Mrs. Stern and other music-loving citizens in 1938 formed a Sigmund Stern Grove Festival Committee for the purpose of bringing free concerts, ballet, opera, and drama to San Franciscans. The continuing midsummer festivals have been a great success (fog permitting), and have played to audiences as large as 10,000.

Of particular architectural notes is the rambling beach

1348 Tenth Avenue (top) was built in 1899 and served as The Sunset District's first firehouse. 1984 Great Highway, now a church, was built in 1905 by a San Francisco fire chief

cottage at *1984 Great Highway,* now occupied by the Eighth Church of Christ Scientist. This house was built in 1905 by Chief Engineer Dennis T. Sullivan of the San Francisco Fire Department.

In 1922 the home was bought by Fire Chief Thomas R. Murphy. The church group bought the building in 1947, and has modified the interior to suit its needs. The roof, which shows Sullivan practiced what he preached, is still the original asbestos shingle—a durable and fireproof material.

Presidio Heights contains a remarkably large number of handsome houses. In this small area—two dozen or so blocks, bounded by Presidio Avenue and Arguello Boulevard on the east and west, Pacific Avenue and Sacramento Street on the north and south—are a great many buildings that would be worthy of special mention were they in some other parts of the city.

"On the wall," the low wall bounding the southern edge of the Presidio between Presidio Avenue and Arguello Boulevard is one of the proudest addresses in San Francisco. The 3200 and 3300 blocks on Pacific Avenue are of particular interest, as they are largely built up with brown-shingled houses of timeless elegance and simplicity. The warmth of these houses overlooking the cypress-wooded Presidio seems almost invariably to impress the visitor with the idea of an informal yet dignified way of life: rubbed redwood paneling, cozy fireplaces, good conversation.

The north side of the 3200 block is particularly eye-catching and "San Franciscan." Here five shingled houses step down the hill from the Presidio gate, each house narrower than the one above as the Presidio wall squeezes in toward Pacific, finally pinching out to a sharp point at Walnut Street.

The 3300 block of Pacific Avenue as it looked when the fine old brown shingle houses were first built there in the early 1900's

The first house in the row, *1 Presidio Avenue,* is architecturally different than the rest of the group. Supported by a first story of brick, the upper two floors overhanging the first, it bulks larger than the other houses in the row. The interior has been extensively remodeled by an owner who is himself an architect, and in a manner in keeping with the nature of the house and its location.

The next two houses, *3232 and 3234 Pacific Avenue,* were built in 1902, at the same time as 1 Presidio. This pair was designed by architect Ernest Coxhead, who here adapted the Georgian theme to the native frame-and-shingle style. Bruce Porter, well-known San Francisco artist, writer and critic, is thought to have contributed heavily to the design of the houses, one of which was built for his brother-in-law, Julian Waybur, the other for himself.

In the Waybur house (3232) the interior staircase and its landings are employed for a most unusual external decorative effect, the form of the stairs being carried right through the Palladian window above the elaborate doorway.

In Porter's own house (3234) one finds the same plain front with the same simple but elegant window pattern highlighted by an imaginative central decorative device, in this case two pairs of Corinthian pilasters and a pattern of narrow windows that is artfully repeated at the entrance level and in the central third-floor window. A number of new ideas were incorporated into this house when it was built: floor-to-ceiling "picture" windows, all built-in wardrobes, and what may have been the first roof garden in San Francisco.

The last pair of houses in the row, *3236 and 3240 Pacific Avenue,* is a response to an unusual challenge: the lot that they were built on in 1900 is 194 feet long on the Presidio frontage—but only 16½ feet wide at its upper end and a

The 3200 block of Pacific today when an address "on the wall" has become one of the proudest in San Francisco

3232 Pacific Avenue, a handsome shingle version of the Georgian theme, was designed and built in 1902 by architect Ernest Coxhead

very sharp point at the lower end. Hence the intriguing pattern of roof lines and overhanging bays. The lower house steps down through four levels. The rear of the house is suspended over the Presidio wall; the lower end tapers to a tiny deck overlooking the Presidio.

Directly across the street from the wedge-shaped row on Pacific are three more unusually handsome shingled houses. At the corner, *3203 Pacific Avenue*, is the house designed and built in 1902 by E. T. Sheppard, a retired diplomat, as a wedding present to his daughter. The engagement was broken and Sheppard sold the house to

the Porters, who commissioned Willis Polk to enlarge and remodel it. Polk moved the entrance around to the Pacific Avenue side, jacked up the house and added a full story underneath—and otherwise completely remade it.

The resulting three-story house has floor-to-ceiling windows and two decks, one of them off the dining room. The front door is particularly noteworthy, with its broken pediment and urn-shaped finial over which is placed a small arched window with its own balustrade, wrought iron grill, and pediment.

Bernard Maybeck, the most resourceful of the Bay

Another Coxhead design — 3234 Pacific (left)
Some typical Maybeck touches — 3233 Pacific (below)
Willis Polk's subtle handiwork — 3203 Pacific (lower left)

The restrained Period style mansion on the next page was built in 1917 at 50 Laurel Street for Frank B. King

145

This faithfully-executed replica of Le Petit Trianon at Versailles was built for the Marcus Koshlands in 1902 at 3800 Washington
Intricate carved redwood decorations on the Roos house (left) at 3500 Jackson are the "signature" of architect Bernard Maybeck

Area's residential architects and the unsurpassed master in the handling of shingled houses and decorative detailing, designed the house at *3233 Pacific Avenue* built for Samuel Goslinsky in 1909. In some respects this house resembles a country house shipped in pieces from France. But more properly it is a pure Maybeck romance.

The accompanying photograph shows details of the entrance (which has a roof separate from that of the house), the handsome Gothic windows, the lovely gutter drain, the bold cornice setting off the rich but repetitious texture of the shingles. The main house behind the entrance is three stories, and has a steeply-pitched, hipped roof with the cornice line broken in a most unusual way.

Next to the Goslinsky house, at *3235 Pacific Avenue*, is another unusual shingled house, designed by William Knowles. This house is still occupied by the original owner, who recalls that he bought the lot on an impulse one day in 1908. He and his wife had been taking the air along the path by the Presidio wall when they saw a man in a kiosk near the top of the hill hawking the lots along the south side of Pacific Avenue. He reached in his pocket and found that all he had was a twenty-dollar gold piece—which sufficed for a down payment.

The English-country-church appearance of the house was not inspired by the theological tastes of the owner. It was a functional matter: his wife wanted a high ceiling

and a balcony in their living room. Hence the "cathedral" ceiling in the living room, the "steeple" over the library, which, with its balcony, gives a choir-loft effect to the interior. Ernest Coxhead designed and built wrought-iron-and-glass doors entering the library. In back of the house is a particularly charming garden.

The 3300 block of Pacific Avenue has a number of handsome brown shingled homes which we must here overlook as they tend to repeat the theme of the distinguished 3200 block. Turning from Pacific Avenue to Laurel Street, one finds at the corner of Laurel and Jackson one of the most elegant of the very large houses that give Jackson Street its distinctive character.

The graceful house at *50 Laurel Street* was designed in 1917 for Frank B. King by the firm of Bakewell and Brown, architects of San Francisco City Hall. This fine example of restrained Period style is as impressive as any home in Presidio Heights.

A Jackson Street mansion that combines grace, grandeur and warmth is the Roos home at *3500 Jackson*. The incomparable Maybeck achieved this *tour de force* in 1909, when merchant Leon Roos and his nineteen-year-old bride set out for a honeymoon in Europe, leaving the architect with a commission but no nagging supervision. The result was an exuberantly free interpretation of the old English half-timbered style with Gothic overtones. The Gothic

One of the most elaborately decorated houses in Presidio Heights is 3340 Washington Street (above and right), built in 1912 for a prominent French resident, John Andrew Bergerot

influence is seen in the carved quatrefoils supporting the cornice, and the geometric tracery of the balustrade to the left of the entrance. Maybeck's interest in decorative carving is attributable to his father, a professional wood carver, and themes shown in the carvings of the Roos house run through much of his work.

Maybeck often employed heavy decorative woodwork in the form of large projecting beams, elaborate brackets, heavy cornices, and such, and the surest indication of his mastery of the technique was that this essentially decorative work usually did not appear to be merely "tacked on."

The interior of the house is finished in Maybeck's favorite rubbed redwood. There are the usual, functional Maybeck touches—a picture window that hinges so that both sides can be cleaned from inside the house and folding doors as room dividers.

While the young Rooses went to Europe and came back to move into a Maybeck masterpiece, Mr. and Mrs. Marcus S. Koshland had earlier returned from the grand tour eager to duplicate a palace they had spotted at Versailles.

Thus in 1902, at *3800 Washington Street*, there arose a replica of *Le Petit Trianon*. The advantage of a stock design became apparent during the course of construction, for when the architect fell ill, Mrs. Koshland was able to supervise completion of the job with the help of an interior decorator.

It must be said that the Koshlands put their palace to full use. The grand housewarming in 1904 was a Marie Antoinette costume ball conducted (after the power failed) by candlelight. Mrs. Koshland patronized the arts, taking a leading role in the launching of both the Symphony and the Opera companies.

A Period Baroque elaborated into an architectural rarity is the house at *3340 Washington Street*, built for John Andrew Bergerot, a prominent member of San Francisco's French community, in 1912. Four different patterns of consoles support the cornices, and the volute pattern of the Ionic pilasters on the first floor is not only repeated in the consoles, but also in the framing of the arched windows of the second floor and the dormers of the Mansard roof, and again in the arches of the dormers. Urns have been openhandedly distributed over every available flat spot; dentils appear under the line of each cornice; rinceaux are strung in the spaces between the consoles on the first floor. Altogether the house comes off very well.

Around the corner and a block-and-a-half to the north at *21–23 Presidio Avenue* is a double house so restrained that one may be surprised to note that it, too, has Ionic columns by the doorways, dentils under the cornice, and balusters that are slightly more ornate than those at 3340 Washington.

This house was originally built in 1900, but in 1915 was remodeled by Bruce and Robert Porter for their in-laws, the Tinning family. The exterior, with its mullioned bay windows carried up to form the balustrades of the low arched dormers, suggests an application of the English Regency style to San Francisco shingles.

Clay Street, from Presidio Avenue west, has a number of fine homes and many of more than ordinary distinction. At *3362 Clay Street* is a particularly attractive four-story, shingled Georgian Revival town house designed by Willis Polk in 1896 for Russell W. Osborn. At this time Polk had recently returned from a trip to England, where he had been much impressed by Georgian architecture.

The tall, narrow effect of 3362 Clay, with its windows arranged in a vertical line over the entrance, is further heightened by its neighbors, which have crowded forward from the original set-back. A bay with windows on two floors dominates the front, leading the eye upwards to a dormer topped by a heavy, segmented pediment. Originally the house had ornate copper downspouts, much like those of the Maybeck-designed house at 3233 Pacific.

The interior plan of the house centers around a three-

story rotunda; curving wall lines are carried into other rooms, leaving few right-angled corners. The Period ornamentation is consistent with the exterior appearance of the house, but not at all what one would expect if only the brown-shingle effect had caught the eye.

At *3555 Clay Street* there is a pleasant brown shingled house designed by Charles Rollo Peters, a famous San Francisco painter of his time who is best remembered for his romantic oils of the missions and Monterey Peninsula scenes by starlight. Peters built this house for his mother and sister and her husband in 1901, reserving a third-floor studio for his own use. Of special interest is the ornamental half-timbering above the front door, the panels between the first and second-floor windows and the Coxhead-type garden gate which swings on two square, shingled posts.

William Bliss demonstrated his taste for classical details

The distinctive group of large houses in the 3600 block of Clay Street (above) dates from 1895 and shows variations on Victorian, Georgian themes. 21–23 Presidio Avenue (right) is a double house done in Regency style

152

in the house built for E. J. Bowen at *3575 Clay Street* in 1907. This Period home had the benefit of subsequent remodeling under the direction of the architect and, more recently, landscaping by Thomas Church.

The 3600 block of Clay has a row of three handsome variations on Victorian and Georgian themes. The most insistently elegant of the trio is *3620 Clay Street*, with its perfectly balanced facade, its columns, pediments, and balustrades. This house was built after 1900, the other two in about 1895. All three provide a pleasant and restful insight into the possibilities of Colonial and Baroque detail.

On the edge of Presidio Heights, at the corner of *Arguello Boulevard* and *Lake Street*, is *Saint John's Presbyterian Church*, a distinguished Gothic shingled structure built in 1906. Its founding pastor was Reverend William Anderson Scott.

153

SAN MATEO COUNTY

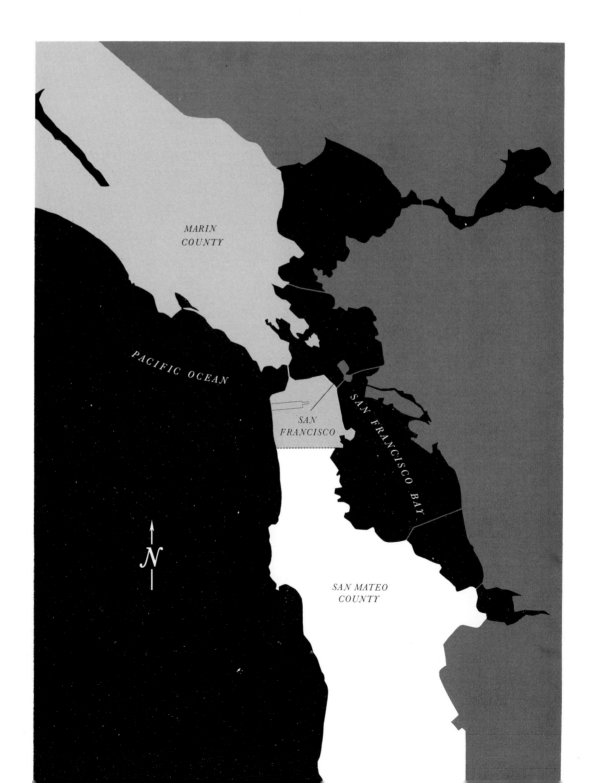

If any suburban area of San Francisco seemed destined for rapid growth, it was the country south of the city. No appreciable geographic barriers stood in the way of direct communication with San Francisco—certainly nothing to compare with the bay that separated the city from the fast-growing counties to the north and east. The climate was grand, the topography east of the coast mountains an attractive landscape of hills, valleys, and plains.

Originally a collection of such large Mexican land grants as Rancho San Pedro to the northwest (8926 acres) and Rancho San Mateo to the southeast (6438 acres), the region was part of the first San Francisco County, which extended from the Golden Gate to San Francisquito Creek, the present boundary between San Mateo and Santa Clara Counties. The political and social disorders that inspired San Francisco's Vigilance Committee of 1856 also inspired the Consolidation Act of the same year, a device contrived to shrink San Francisco County and gain a more easily-controlled government.

The Act also created San Mateo County, almost as an afterthought, and for a time at least the county became a refuge for crooked politicians and other highbinders exiled from the city. That these exiles did not significantly corrupt the government of the new county is probably a reflection of the fact that in 1856 there simply wasn't much around to corrupt.

The stupendous wealth that the Gold Rush brought to a number of San Franciscans brought with it an emotional need peculiar to Victorian America: the money had to be spent—gloriously, vigorously, and flamboyantly. The need gave rise to the creation of vast country estates south of San Francisco.

By the mid-1860's the county east of the mountains was occupied by landscaped estates, huge truck farms, and working ranches serviced by a few villages. In spite of the latter addition of a few solid, middle-class developments, this remained the essential character San Mateo County even after the arrival of the railroad.

A link between San Jose and San Francisco had been talked up as early as 1849, but it was not until 1860 that talk became reality. The San Francisco and San Jose Rail Road Company was formed, and on May 1, 1861, construction began. Even before the line was finished in 1864, optimistic speculators moved in—principally at Menlo Park, Redwood City, and San Mateo.

If the developers expected a growth spurt with the coming of the railroad, they were in for a disappointment. Even during the decades of the 1870's and 1880's, during which population boomed all over the Bay Area, San Mateo County just ambled along, and in the decade of 1890–1900, it gained only two thousand people.

There were two basic reasons for the county's sluggish performance. First, the peninsula's railroad was no commuter's delight, and second, the great farms and estates effectively blocked residential growth in all but a few minor areas. At the time of World War I, these factors had combined to limit the population of the County to something over 27,000.

By the end of the 1920's, however, the shape of the future was clear. This era saw San Mateo County's population double in less than ten years, a reflection in miniature of the first dramatic surge of America's population in the twentieth century. Slowly, the great estates of San Mateo county began to succumb to the rising tide of population, although many would hold out for another twenty years.

World War II, with its impetus to the growth of both industry and population, put the capstone on San Mateo County's suddenly-monumental development. In 1949 alone, 5900 residential building permits were issued in the county. For more than fifteen years such development has continued to eat into the few open areas left between the coastal mountains and San Francisco Bay, areas that once made San Mateo County an immense garden for the city of San Francisco.

Some pockets reminiscent of a more beauteous past do remain, but these are generally held by comparatively wealthy citizens capable of resisting the advance of progress; the rest has simply slipped away.

Only across the mountains on the Coastside is there a valid sense of the past of San Mateo County, and even here the march of progress is beginning to distort the landscape.

Let's take a look now at what is left.

Reminder of an elegant era.

155

MENLO/ATHERTON

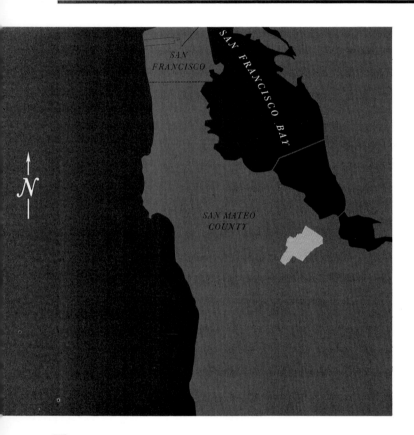

In the 1850's two young Irishmen fresh from Menlough on Lough Corrib, County Galway, arrived on the Peninsula. They settled on a 1700-acre tract, built adjoining houses, and over the entrance drive erected a three-arched gate which bore the legend, "Menlo Park."

The name they gave the tract remained, and was adopted by the San Francisco and San Jose railroad when it built a station across from their gate in 1863. A small village grew up around the station; agents and subdividers bought up the surrounding areas to be resold as villa lots or country estates. Within ten years these estates spread from the Stanford farm on the south to the Atherton estate on the north.

The Atherton estate was the summer home of the family of Faxon Dean Atherton, who had made a fortune in Chile and was one of the first City capitalists to find refuge from San Francisco's foggy summer climate in the sunny warmth of the Peninsula.

Other great estates were laid out by W. E. Barron, of the famous New Almaden Mine near San Jose, and Thomas H. Selby, owner of the west's biggest smelter and refinery and former mayor of San Francisco. James C. Flood's *Linden Towers* came in 1878. This breathtakingly irregular jig-saw villa was easily the most magnificent country establishment here, a fitting monument to a saloon-keeper who, with partner William O'Brien, had parlayed mining exchange tips into partnership in Virginia City's Big Bonanza.

Like most of the other towns on the eastern flank of San Mateo County, Menlo Park received its first impetus to growth (such as it was) from the completion of the San Francisco and San Jose railroad, and the oldest surviving station on the line (which became the Southern Pacific in 1868) is that at *1100 Merrill Street,* which was probably built around 1880.

The little wood, late-Victorian building includes such "gingerbread" touches as ornamental fish-scale shingling, shingled awnings over the windows, carved bracketing, Eastlake chalet-brace and decorative patterns set into the gables, and roof cresting and finials. Stick Style strips frame the openings; the window bay at the south end of the station once was the outlook of the "Ladies' Parlor," a horse-hair-cushioned and lace-curtained retreat in which distaff passengers awaited their trains in comfort.

At *1040 Noel Drive* is the former Mills house, a three-story wood mansion originally built about 1870 by T. Lemmen Meyer. The house was acquired by Edgar Mills, brother of the immensely wealthy Darius Ogden Mills, in the early 1880's and extensively revised then. During the First World War the Army leased it for an officers' club, and after the war the building was used as a hotel and later

Menlo Park Station, 1100 Merrill, dates from 1880

The Russian Orthodox Church, 1220 Crane Street, was once the Episcopal Church of the Holy Trinity

158

The gatehouse of the Timothy Hopkins estate (above) was once Holy Trinity Church's rectory

The huge Coleman mansion was built in 1882 for the nephew of one of the Comstock Bonanza kings but is now used as a private school

housed the Pacific Coast Military Academy, a boys' school. The twenty-one room mansion has survived all this well, and recently has served as a setting for receptions, meetings, and as a residence hotel for a few persons.

An engaging little wood, late-Victorian Gothic structure is the present Russian Orthodox Church, *1220 Crane Street.* Finished in 1886 for an Episcopal parish organized by Edward Engle Eyre, the church was called Church of the Holy Trinity and was originally located at Laurel Street and Encinal Avenue. Moved once in 1897, this structure was donated by the Trinity Church membership to the Russian Orthodox group and was moved again to its present site in 1947.

The rectory for the Church of the Holy Trinity in the years before the 1906 disaster was the gatehouse of the Timothy Hopkins estate, *439 Ravenswood Avenue.* This great estate, stretching from San Francisquito Creek to Ravenswood Avenue, between El Camino Real and Middlefield Road, was originally developed by W. E. Barron. In 1872 Milton S. Latham, railroad mogul, U.S. Senator and Governor of California, bought the estate. The main house burned in the course of remodeling—so in its place Latham built a larger establishment. This house was named Sherwood Hall by subsequent owner Timothy Hopkins.

The gatehouse appears to have been built about the

time of Latham's death, in 1883. The estate was purchased by Mark Hopkins for his adopted son, Timothy, who was his father's successor as treasurer of the Central Pacific-Southern Pacific system. In 1906 the main house was so damaged by the earthquake that the Hopkins family remodeled the gatehouse to serve as their Menlo Park quarters. A Mansard-roofed structure of quiet elegance, the Hopkins gatehouse is scheduled for eventual demolition. The land will be used as a park adjacent to the Menlo Park Civic Center.

The largest of the surviving country houses of the Menlo Park-Atherton area is the former Coleman mansion, *Peninsula Way* and *Berkeley Avenue.* A handsome building of Italianate design, with a few cast-iron ornamental details, the house was built in 1882 for James V. Coleman, a nephew of Bonanza King William O'Brien. Coleman's young wife, Carmelita Nuttall, died in 1885, apparently before the couple ever occupied the home. It is said that Coleman never set foot in the house, though he retained ownership of the property and regularly visited the estate; the house was put to little, if any, use for over thirty years.

In 1906, the Catholic Archdiocese of San Francisco bought the mansion for uses related to St. Patrick's Seminary; in 1925 the Peninsula School of Creative Education, the present occupants, took over the building. At one time

This Period mansion is now part of the Menlo School for Boys

condemned for classroom use, the building is now being renovated through the efforts of alumni and friends of the school.

The Church of the Nativity, 210 Oak Grove Avenue, is an excellent example of a wood Victorian Gothic church, with all the typical features: pier buttresses, lancet windows, hood molds, tower spire, finials and their knobby protuberances called crockets. Built in 1872, it was the first Catholic church in Menlo Park. The silver candlesticks and crucifix on the altar were brought by Mr. Denis Martin from Europe, and originally adorned the church that Martin built on his Searsville rancho in 1853.

Two Catholic educational institutions in Menlo are housed in quite distinguished structures designed by J. J. Devlin at the turn of the century. *St. Patrick's Seminary, Middlefield Road,* was built in 1898, damaged by the 1906 earthquake, and rebuilt under the architect's supervision in 1908. A somewhat more elegant Second-Empire structure by Devlin is the *Convent of the Sacred Heart, 1100 Valparaiso Street.* Its architectural relationship to St. Patrick's is immediately obvious, with the arched windows being carried along the second floor in both, and both having Mansard roofs and shallow dormers treated in somewhat the same fashion. The smooth brick walls of the Convent of the Sacred Heart produce a more powerful impression than the pilastered surface of St. Patrick's; also the treatment of the cornice, dormers, and roofline of the Convent is at once simpler and more elegant. Like St. Patrick's, the Convent was begun in 1898; the post-earthquake repairs and additions were supervised by the original architect.

Another school building in Menlo Park, *Douglass Hall* at the Menlo School for Boys, *Valparaiso Street,* is a fine example of post-1900 taste in private mansions. This classicized Baroque Period edifice was built in 1910 for Mrs. Theodore Payne, niece of William O'Brien of Comstock fame. Inventor Leon Douglass, a pioneer of underwater photography, acquired it later. Today the school uses the fifty-six-room country house as its administration building.

At *175 Fair Oaks Lane* in Atherton is a Period mansion of smaller scale but grand concept translated into Classical-Colonial architecture. It was built in 1895 for Mr. and Mrs. Perry Eyre just as styles in houses were changing from picturesque Victorian to domesticated Period interpretations.

The oldest house in the Menlo Park-Atherton area is the wood home at *25 Isabella Avenue,* built as a summer residence by Captain James W. Watkins, of the Pacific Mail Steamship Company, in 1860. Of Victorian Gothic style, this handsomely situated house was prefabricated in

Classical-Colonial mansion from 1895 at 175 Fair Oaks Lane

The Coryell carriage house was designed by Willis Polk after studying Mediterranean architecture in Spain at Coryell's expense

Captain Watkins' native Connecticut and originally erected on the site of the Atherton railroad station. Architecturally, it is a good example of a type very popular in mid-nineteenth-century America. Combining certain pleasant concessions to fashion with solid practicality, it is as desirable a residence today as when it was built over one hundred years ago.

Showing the still-strong influence of Georgian center-hall houses in plan, its detailing shows the development of Victorian Gothic; the pitch of the main gable and dormer gables is steep; hood moldings and brackets of the eaves have turned decidedly picturesque and non-classical; flattened arches of the porch are a Tudor variation of the pointed arch that characterized the Gothic style in general. Minor revisions and additions have not changed the overall character of the residence.

36 Middlefield Road has, on its porch, some of the crisp,

interlacing wood patterns and spooled embellishments that are associated with Gothic turned into Eastlake. Built prior to 1895 for Aron Doud, its picturesque shape is, however, obviously Queen Anne in overall effect—with the usual large corner tower of that style. Later owners have made few additions to the interior, leaving intact the numerous reception and service rooms on the main floor which were common to the later nineteenth century.

An attractive home at *57 Moulton Drive* is one of several former carriage houses belonging to extinct Atherton estates worthy of notice. This shingled structure was built in the 1880's for A. C. Bassett of the Southern Pacific Railroad; it was later owned by the Frank Moultons, during whose tenure the main house burned. The carriage house, with its octagonal tower, today makes a most handsome home—reasonable dimensions, an irregular plan of variety and charm, and informal atmosphere giving it a value

25 Isabella (above) came around the Horn from Connecticut
57 Moulton (left) was also a carriage house for a great estate

which the main house would have long since lost, had it survived. Thus, while some of the Peninsula's remaining great mansions carry about them the air of having seen better days, some of their former outbuildings are seeing their best days.

Another unusually attractive carriage house is the establishment at *45 Lloyden Drive*, built for Mr. Joseph R. Coryell who sent the architect, Willis Polk, to Spain to study Mediterranean architecture in detail before starting his design. Constructed shortly after the turn of the century, this Mediterranean-Mission-style structure of concrete, with its fixtures and tiles imported from Spain and Italy, was intended as a test run of Polk's services by Mr. Coryell.

If satisfied with the results of Polk's labors, Coryell, who then was occupying an older frame house on the property, intended to build a new main house in the style of the carriage house. However, before the subsidiary building

163

George Howard designed this adaptation of Le Petit Trianon in 1917 to grace the hilltop at 383 Walsh Rd. in Atherton.

was finished the old main house burned and the Coryells took up residence in the carriage house. Not long after, Coryell died. The carriage house was completed as a residence after his death and rooms intended for use as a family chapel and a private chapel for Mrs. Coryell were put to other uses by subsequent owners.

Among the oldest Menlo Park-Atherton mansions still in use as a private residence is the country house of Captain Charles Goodall, *151 Laurel Street*. The property was purchased by Goodall in 1885 from Peter Spreckels, who in turn had bought the land from Selim Woodworth, one of the most famous and respected merchants of Gold Rush San Francisco. It would appear that the three-story "annex" to the house dates from before 1895, though whether it goes back to Woodworth's time is questionable.

The house that Goodall built may be described as "Period-Colonial Revival"; the first-floor porch is a quite chaste Period Baroque, with paired Ionic columns and a symmetry which is simple but severe. The second floor flowers into the details of the nineteenth century Colonial Revival with Palladian windows, Adamesque garlands and

urns and with the towers of Queen Anne suggested in rounded bays. Deer and black swans once roamed the gardens around the mansion; much of the interior decor dates from the time of construction.

Another Atherton Colonial Revival residence built for Perry Eyre in the early 1890's, the residence at *85 Edwards Lane* naturally suggests comparison with the larger Colonial Revival house built on Fair Oaks Lane in Menlo Park. It is hard to avoid the conclusion that the more limited effort is equally successful. With its bold arch over the entrance, its semi-circular portico with plain Tuscan columns, and, more importantly, its straightforward, four-square appearance, punctuated with two-story Tuscan pilasters, this house seems appropriate to its suburban setting. It sums up Menlo Park and Atherton fifty or sixty years ago—an image of substantial, distinguished white frame houses scattered in park-like settings. It is the more unusual buildings and the great mansions that one naturally selects in surveying the area; but it is the houses like this that were more typical and gave Menlo Park and Atherton an air of solid affluence at the end of the century.

85 Edwards Lane (below)—Colonial Revival in the 1890's. The Church of the Nativity, 210 Oak Grove (right), was built in 1872

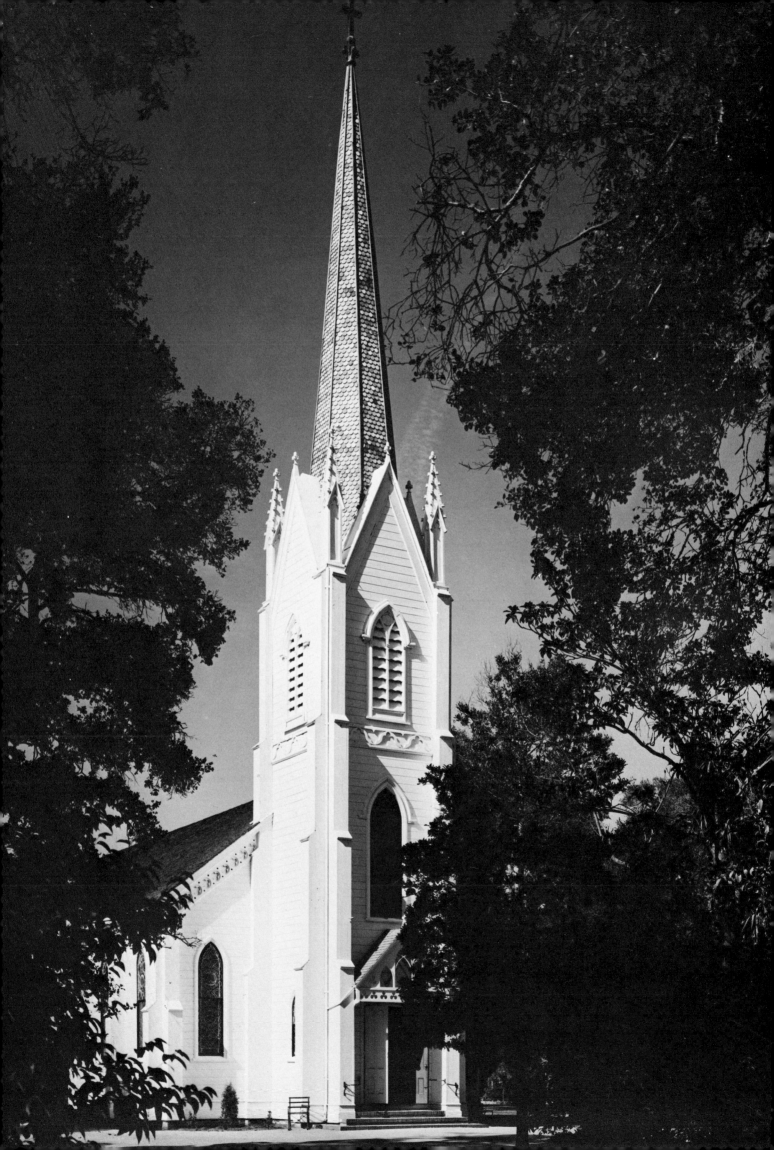

REDWOOD CITY
SAN CARLOS/BELMONT

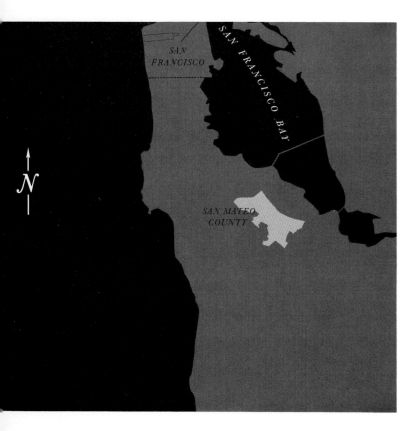

In startling contrast to the refined beginnings of Menlo Park and Atherton (and to most of the rest of the communities in eastern San Mateo County), Redwood City was born in 1850 as a miniature industrial complex and developed as such, with the gradual addition of residential housing that was emphatically middle—rather than upper—class, and has never made any bones about it.

When Dr. R. O. Tripp and his partners in the Woodside lumbering industry opened up a road from the Redwood country of the central valleys to the head of Redwood Creek, they inadvertently created Redwood City. In a short time, some one hundred and fifty people had clustered in a port that soon became the busiest south of

San Francisco. When San Mateo County was created in 1856, Redwood City became the county seat.

Redwood City was incorporated on March 27, 1868. Probably more than any other Peninsula town, the city benefited significantly from the arrival of the San Francisco and San Jose railroad, and by 1870 there were well over seven hundred people in the little port town. And by the turn of the century, its essential future as an industrial-residential area already was taking shape, if on a relatively minor scale.

Possibly the oldest house in Redwood City is at *90 Finger Avenue*. In 1852 Otto, August, and Theodore Finger settled on sixty-four acres bordering Cordilleras Creek. Their home was built in 1855 along "stripped" Victorian Gothic lines, a simple board-and-shingle farmhouse. In 1906, Otto's widow sold the house to Dr. Charles Boxton, a San Francisco Supervisor.

Nearly as old and far more interesting architecturally is the two-story wood Connor House, *627 Hamilton Street.* This proudly overt example of Victorian Gothic was built in 1860 by Benjamin G. Lathrop and was acquired in 1870 by General Patrick Edward Connor, an Irishman who had distinguished himself in the Mexican and Indian Wars, and had gained some local notoriety as the man credited with the death of Three-fingered Jack, bandit Joaquin Murietta's henchman. The nine-room house is an outstanding example of what is often called Carpenter's or Steamboat Gothic, with sharp, pointed gables and finials, bargeboards, and broad porch with octagonal pillars and flattened decorative arches.

The oldest commercial building in Redwood City is the Diller Building (which now houses the Quong Lee Laundry), *726 Main Street.* The building was constructed of brick in 1859 by J. V. Diller, who used it as a general merchandise store. The store was modified Classical Revival in character with quasi-Doric pilasters, a dentil course,

627 Hamilton, a Carpenter's Gothic marvel, around 1890

The lumber port of Redwood City in the Gold Rush days

and tall arched windows (now modified on the facade). The original veranda and iron shutters have been removed; and the bricks are now painted.

One of the earliest and most successful of Redwood City's industries was Frank's Tannery on *Bayshore Highway*. In 1872, Joseph Frank purchased the facilities of the Roney and Wentworth Tanneries, a complex of buildings constructed on pilings along Redwood Creek. This industry was a natural outgrowth of the availability of cowhide from local ranchers and tan oak from the hills. During its prime, the tannery had a production capacity of five hundred sides of sole leather daily, and its payroll was the county's largest outside the lumbering industry. The tannery ceased production in the 1950's and some of the old wood buildings were recently destroyed by fire.

The San Mateo County Courthouse, *Middlefield Road* and *Marshall Street*, is the third such structure to stand on this site donated to the county by the Arguello family in 1858.

The first was destroyed in the earthquake of 1868; the second was replaced by the present structure, built in 1904, and rebuilt after the earthquake of 1906 nearly leveled it. Constructed in Colusa sandstone in a Period Baroque style, the courthouse was designed by San Francisco architect Glen Allen. Easily the most impressive of its features is the large dome with stained-glass panels which somehow survived the earthquake. The interior is marked by a handsome rotunda and green marble Corinthian columns with gold capitals.

One of the most charming of Bernard Maybeck's designs, the wood and shingle home at *650 Edgewood Road*, was built for John A. Britton in 1912. The low lines and simplicity of this summer home foretell something of those modern ranch style houses so common today in suburban developments; but the grand sweep of the place with its deep, wide porch and second-story dormer give it a character all its own.

726 Main St. (above), shown here in 1908, was put up in 1859

Two turn-of-the-century views (below) of the San Carlos Station

For the most part, the cities of San Carlos and Belmont are creatures of the twentieth century, although their roots, like those of Redwood City, go back to the old Rancho de las Pulgas of the Arguello family.

San Carlos got its start, so to speak, when three men acquired varied sections of the Arguello grant: William Hull, a San Francisco brick man who established a brick-yard in the area in 1858; Senator Timothy Guy Phelps, who established a 3500-acre dairy farm in 1863; and Nathaniel Brittan, who granted a right of way through his section of land to the Southern Pacific, stipulating that a combination post office, depot, and telegraph office be built on his property.

Nathaniel Brittan was a world traveler, and a connois-seur of art. Sometime during the 1870's, he turned his eye to the development of his San Carlos land and the construction of an appropriate home to be called The Manor, now at *40 Pine Street.*

The mansion was constructed of wood, stucco and shin-gles, and featured such late-Victorian embellishments as richly-carved window pediments, brackets, and finials. The roof tiles were imported from France. The rest of Brittan's estate had its own color, which included an iron gate that opened and closed automatically, a bear pit, an aviary and a flock of peacocks, a tea house, stables and a mill.

This magnificent Redwood City summer home (above) at 650 Edgewood Road was designed in 1912 by architect Bernard Maybeck and shows the type of house from which the low-lying ranch style house of today got its inspiration. Nathaniel Brittan, a pioneer San Carlos landowner, built the Party House (left) at 125 Dale Avenue in 1872 so that he could entertain his cronies without disturbing Mrs. Brittan in the main house some distance away. The octagonal, steeply-gabled structure remains a delight to the eye to this day

The Manor (far left), at 40
Pine Street in San Carlos, was
Nathaniel Brittan's main house.
Like the Party House, it was
constructed in the early 1870's.
Belmont's Ralston Hall (left)
remains one of the Peninsula's
great mansions. Built in the
1860's, its eighty rooms
contain every luxurious detail
which Ralston could devise

Most of these innovations have long since disappeared, but among them was the Party House, which can still be seen at *125 Dale Avenue*. Brittan was a bon vivant, and to spare his home and family the more destructive effects of party-giving he built a house in 1872 which suited those needs. Possibly it was Mrs. Brittan who insisted on such a house, particularly after one traumatic night of revelry when, it is said, she was forced to fire a shotgun over the heads of Brittan's riotous cronies to get their attention.

At any rate, the Party House was built considerably removed from the main house. Admirably suited to its purposes, the place was built of durable redwood and contained a gaming room which offered billiards and other gentlemanly diversions. Architecturally, the house is a delight, with its steep gables, octagonal design, windowed cupola and great brick chimneys.

Built on land deeded by Brittan and of equal interest architecturally, the San Carlos Railroad Station, *El Camino Real* and *San Carlos Avenue*, is an excellent example of Romanesque Revival, a vogue of the late nineteenth century. It was constructed in 1888 of rusticated local sandstone and wood by Captain Nicholas Smith who acquired the cut stone blocks from newly completed Stanford University. It was damaged by the 'quake in 1906 but rebuilt in the original form. The structure has been used in the past as a church, post office, library, and currently houses the San Carlos Chamber of Commerce.

A typical example of upper-middle-class Peninsula domiciles of the turn-of-the-century is the shingle house at *540 Elm Street*. The three-story home was built about 1890 for John Valentine Clark, an auditor for the Southern Pacific and San Carlos' first tax collector and assessor. Architecturally, the house is marked by the high pitch of its gabled roof, the arches of the second-story porch, and the three-sided window bays of the lower stories, providing a slight hint of the Queen Anne tower so dear to late-Victorian hearts.

The development of Belmont was as gradual as that of San Carlos. In 1856, the town consisted mainly of the fourteen-acre estate of Count Leonetto Cipriani, and a combination road house, inn, and post office called Angelo's Corners.

For years one of Belmont's few citizens was one of the most famous men in California, William Chapman Ralston. By 1864, when he bought Count Cipriani's land and home, Ralston already had made his mark on California's economy and history, and he immediately proceeded to make his mark on Belmont as well. He employed John P. Gaynor to entirely revise and enlarge the modest house which Count Cipriani had begun.

Ralston Hall's interior has been restored to its original glory

Gaynor later designed Ralston's Palace Hotel in San Francisco, and many features in the four-story wood house, now Ralston Hall, *Ralston* and *Notre Dame Avenues*, were copied in the hotel. The main floor of Ralston Hall contained a foyer called "Half Moon" (from its curved doors) filled with exotic plants, a front drawing room, inner drawing room, banquet hall, ballroom, library, billiard room, music room, and sun parlor. The doors between these rooms were designed without thresholds; the etched and cut glass doors themselves could be raised out of sight or slid into the walls, opening up the entire ground floor for entertainment or dancing. An outstanding feature of the central foyer was a second-story opera box with silver-plated railings from which Mr. and Mrs. Ralston could view festivities.

Ralston had spent considerable time in his youth on Mississippi riverboats; there are hints of this past throughout the more-than-eighty-room mansion in the great wheel-like chandeliers and the doors that swing both in and out, covered with conventionalized flower designs found on many of the old floating palaces of Mississippi and Sacramento River fame.

The workmanship in the mansion is astonishing. The floors are parquet—walnut, maple and mahogany laid in different patterns for each room and fitted with such intricacy that hardly a crack can be found. Square-tipped wrought iron nails were forged and counter-sunk in the flooring and the holes plugged with matching wood. The door panels and knobs are all of silver from the Comstock Lode; the glass in the house was imported from France and Italy and hand-etched or cut; the painted paneling is covered with nine coats of enamel.

Ralston himself designed the intricate system of louvres and lattice work visible under the roof which provides for the constant circulation of fresh air—an obvious necessity, given the size of the parties and balls Ralston was accustomed to hold. For its daring spaciousness and many technical excellences, this house ranks as one of the greatest of its time in the United States.

After Ralston's death in 1875, William Sharon, his longtime partner, acquired Ralston Hall and it continued to be a center of Peninsula social life. Later, the great place became a girls' seminary, then a mental hospital. After twelve years in this capacity, it stood empty until 1922, when the Sisters of Notre Dame de Namur took it over for use as a college.

The Sisters attacked the ten-year accumulation of dust and dirt and somehow brought the old building to a semblance of its former magnificence. Through the years the interior of Ralston Hall has gradually been restored and refurbished until it stands today much as it was during the great days of the Bonanza Kings.

BURLINGAME/SAN MATEO HILLSBOROUGH

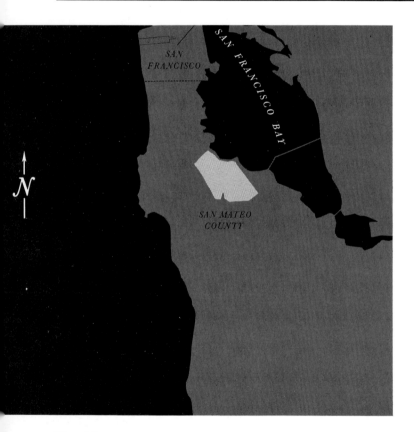

Mexican Governor Pio Pico granted 6438 acres of Peninsula land in 1846 to Cayetano Arenas, who called his acquisition Rancho San Mateo. Arenas held the land until well after the American occupation of California, but finally sold out in the early 1850's to William Davis Merry Howard, a pioneer capitalist.

After his death in 1856, Howard's property was parceled out to various individuals, including members of his wife's family, the Poetts, who subsequently played a large part in the area's development. Some legitimate growth followed the advent of the San Francisco and San Jose railroad in 1863, when an embryonic business district mushroomed around the railroad station.

Otherwise, development until well after the turn of the century tended to be advanced mainly by the creation of large estates by wealthy San Franciscans, who saw in the rolling green land of the San Mateo the essence of the gracious life.

Incorporation of the city of San Mateo was delayed until 1894, but the air of expansive living which had characterized the area could not long resist the twentieth century. Today, the principal legacy from that gracious past is found in the names of streets and parks—while acres of more modest homes creep over the lands of Rancho San Mateo.

John Parrott, the financier who in 1852 constructed the first substantial business building in San Francisco, built a summer home in San Mateo in 1868 near the area now known as Baywood. The home itself, unlike those of many of Parrott's peers, was comparatively unremarkable, but its gatehouse, which can be seen today at *87 Crystal Springs Road*, stands as one of the more delightful Victorians, with its Greek Revival detailing and embellishments.

Built on a cruciform plan, with octagonal rooms, the gatehouse departs from the Greek Revival in the suggestion of a Gothic arch beneath the eaves, in the rather romantic brackets supporting the cornice, and in the equally romantic handling of the quoining. An amusing relic of the days when the gatehouse was an important adjunct of a great estate is the little sentry box that once flanked the main driveway, but now, with the mansion and grounds long since departed, functions as a poolhouse.

Saint Matthew's Episcopal Church, Baldwin Avenue and *El Camino Real*, was designed by Willis Polk in 1909. Rebuilt on the site of the original church, which was erected in 1865 and destroyed by the 1906 earthquake, the present structure is nothing like its predecessor. Polk abandoned the Victorian character of the original church completely; his design is executed in a more purist English Gothic manner. The structure owes much of its elegance to this purity of design and to a sensitive use of material. Constructed with the earthquake still fresh in memory, the framework is of steel.

The essential simplicity of Polk's design was amply illustrated in 1957; the church was split laterally and its western section moved out thirty feet (to permit installation of one hundred and sixty additional pew seats) without noticeably altering its lines. Both this church and the original one were built on land donated by the heirs of William D. M. Howard and constructed of stone from his quarry on Crystal Springs Road. A crypt in the chapel of the church, marked by a marble obelisk, commemorates the connection with the Howard family.

A delightful representative of the Victorian Gothic in wood is the house at *45 South Delaware Street* built by William Sands in the 1860's. Its simple pointed lines have been enhanced by bargeboard decorations beneath the gables and "lacework" beneath the horizontal eaves of the steeply-pitched roof.

The fish-scale shingles and carved brackets under the eaves of the wood house at *218 Tilton Avenue* are typical of about 1880 or 1885. Interwoven scrolls of leaf forms in a kind of bargeboard under each gable, open spooling along the porch top, and the deeply carved fan design in one gable give an airy flavor of Eastlake Oriental intricacy. Stick Style strips at the corners and around windows emphasize a date in the 1880's. Originally a residence, the building serves as the office of United Voluntary Services.

In 1886, Anson Burlingame, U.S. Minister to China, visited San Francisco and was entertained by William Ralston at his estate in Belmont. While there, Burlingame was persuaded to purchase 1000 acres of W. D. M. Howard's Rancho San Mateo, and Ralston immediately suggested naming a town after the celebrity. A town was duly surveyed and placed on the maps of the region, but until 1893, Burlingame remained only that — a name on the map.

That year a group of prominent San Francisco sportsmen bought land in the area and built the Burlingame Country Club. For the convenience of club members, a railroad station on the San Francisco and San Jose line was constructed as well. The group then settled back to enjoy their rustic retreat.

To their horror, the very exclusiveness they fostered proved an irresistible magnet to others. A village grew up in the vicinity of the railroad station, and the earthquake of 1906 sent hundreds more into the area in search of new homes. In 1908, the village incorporated as the city of Burlingame in order to avoid annexation by San Mateo — and promptly began appropriating territory itself, even threatening annexation of the country club property. Club members quickly incorporated their own city before they could be devoured by Burlingame. And so Hillsborough was born in 1910.

45 South Delaware Street (top) was built in the 1860's and is a typical example of Victorian Gothic use of carved embellishment. 218 Tilton Avenue (above) dates from the mid-1880's and is similarly decorated with elaborate carving on its exterior

177

Hillsborough was quite deliberately planned as a "non-city." Its boundaries extended from the western edges of the cities of San Mateo and Burlingame to the Spring Valley Water Company's land at the top of the hill to the west. There were to be no sidewalks, no patterned street systems, and no business or commercial enterprises. The lot-size restrictions and building regulations have been so effectively enforced that the area has managed to resist the intrusions of citification ever since. The elegance of a past golden age can still be found in its quiet, winding streets and imposing homes.

The influence of the Mission Revival may be seen in the *Burlingame Depot, California Drive* and *Burlingame Avenue,* built by the Burlingame Country Club members in 1894. The architect was George Howard, whose family originally owned the land. Mission Revival flourished in the 1890's largely through the influence of the writer and editor, Charles F. Lummis.

The Burlingame Depot is one of the more successful examples of the attempt to superimpose the charm of the crumbling missions on functional, modern buildings. Curvilinear cornices in the mission church manner crown each facade, and poles protrude from the building in imitation of the primitive roof construction of Spanish colonial buildings. The roof tiles were salvaged from the ruins of the old mission hospice in San Mateo and the Mission San Antonio de Padua built in 1771 near King City.

Long a Peninsula landmark, *La Dolphine, 1760 Manor*

Rosecourt (previous page) was built in 1913 for the George T. Camerons. Carolands (below), a 92-room chateau, was jinxed from its beginning in 1913

Drive, is a formal French mansion suggested by Marie Antoinette's *Le Petit Trianon.* This three-story stone mansion was designed by Lewis Hobart and built in 1914 for George Newhall, Sr. The house was unoccupied from Newhall's death in 1929 until 1940, but has since passed through many owners. It currently occupies three and one half acres with formal gardens, hedge-bordered walks, and rows of European sycamores. Its three stories house twenty-one rooms, five master bedrooms, four marble-lined baths, and hand-carved marble fireplaces in the main rooms. Marble continues rampant in the floors and in a carved staircase with wrought-iron railing that leads from the entrance hall to the second floor.

Similar in scope and in many of its features to La Dolphine is *Uplands, 400 Uplands Drive.* The land for this estate was purchased from the heirs of William D. M. Howard by Charles Templeton Crocker, son of the California railroad pioneer. After moving the four-story home that was on the property when he bought it, Crocker commissioned Willis Polk to build him something more to his taste.

The Polk design of 1913 is along neo-Classic, Renaissance palace lines and, being constructed of steel, concrete, and brick, is one of the most solidly built grand mansions of the Peninsula. Although not quite so huge as some of its contemporaries, Uplands was specifically designed to give the impression of great size. In 1956, the massive structure was acquired from the Crocker family for the Crystal Springs School for Girls.

The house that C. Templeton Crocker moved from the Uplands property found its final resting place at *401 El Cerrito Avenue.* Getting it there was no simple matter. The original building was designed in 1878 as a four-story, thirty-six-room Swiss chalet, dark brown in color and 35 by 135 feet in size. Crocker told Charles T. Lindgren, a local contractor, that the house would be his if he could somehow move it off the Uplands property and across San Mateo Creek without destroying any trees. How he did it was related in the June, 1916, issue of *Popular Mechanics:*

"After placing heavy wooden needles under the mansion, it was jacked up. In passing over depressions it was raised by means of beams and cribs as much as fifty feet above the ground. About 200 eight-inch rollers were used in moving it along, horses furnishing the power. In going down an incline of one and a half inches to the foot, cables were required to hold it back. In order that it might be carried over a creek, a thirty-foot bridge of cribs was constructed. At the end of the first two months the crew of 18 men had moved the structure 350 yards."

Shortly after completion of its journey the chalet caught fire, losing two of its four stories. It was then plastered and the roof tiled. The house was further remodeled when it passed into the hands of William Randolph Hearst, and the dark brown Swiss chalet has become a white colonial residence, complete with porticoes and colonnades.

One of the most ambitious and ultimately ill-fated ventures into the realm of home building is typified by *Carolands, 565 Remillard Drive*. This stupendous dream house was the creation of Harriet Pullman, daughter of George M. Pullman of parlor car fame who left her his immense fortune. Miss Pullman had married Francis J. Carolan of San Francisco in 1892, and almost immediately the couple moved to the Peninsula, accumulating by 1912 a large expanse of land near the Burlingame Country Club. Their holdings included a thirty-room home, numerous outbuildings, an outlet on the Bay, a race track, and a polo field, the whole being christened Crossways Farm.

But Harriet Pullman Carolan wanted something more commensurate with her incredible fortune. In 1913 she purchased 554 additional acres, commissioned the French firm of E. Saint-Saens to design a French chateau, and hired landscape architect Achilles Duchene to plan the garden. Construction began in 1913 and ended in 1915 — although the mansion was never fully completed.

The chateau finally comprised some 1,000,000 cubic feet of space in ninety-two rooms, two of them imported bodily from France and the rest very careful copies. Equally awesome was the estate itself. Not only did it have two huge terraces, orchards, and gardens including some 32,000 trees and shrubs, but its own internal water system. There was a tea house, a picnic ground with a bandstand, statues scattered here and there, and many sculptured ornaments, the most impressive of which was the Temple of Love copied after that at the Palace of Versailles.

The Carolans moved into this manse in 1915 and soon discovered that all was not green in Eden. For one thing, the charming French windows rattled cheerfully in the stiff Pacific wind, and that same wind came whistling down the delightful (and expensive) French chimneys to scatter ashes with democratic impartiality. For another, the elegant French plumbing set up a gurgling roar which could be heard from every room in the place.

Not even so determined a Francophile as Mrs. Carolan could endure the great chateau for long. After seven months, she closed the place and moved East, while her husband retired to the old Crossways Farm. She did not again attempt to live in Carolands until the late twenties, when she returned with a new husband. And once again she gave it up, removed the furniture and put the entire property up for sale.

The land itself was subdivided and much of it sold over the years, but the huge chateau remained unoccupied, sitting in stark and neglected magnificence until 1950, when it was purchased by its new owner, who began the

La Dolphine was suggested by Versailles' Le Petit Trianon

245 El Cerrito Avenue (next page)

painstaking task of refurnishing and refurbishing this monumental house.

Less traumatic in history and far more successful in design is *Strawberry Hill* on *Redington Road*. In 1910, Joseph D. Grant, then president of the Burlingame Country Club, built a shooting box on this site, and then began additions in concrete and steel that transformed the box into a Period residence. Designed by Lewis Hobart, as are so many of these Peninsula houses, it was at first called "Villa Rose" from its color. The house is notable for its simple lines, the rooftop statuary and delicate iron filigree balconies, and gardens planned by Hobart, and for the paneling and carving throughout the interior.

Another handsome Hobart design, at *815 Eucalyptus Avenue*, was built in 1913 for George T. Cameron, a young millionaire who later served for thirty years as publisher of the San Francisco Chronicle. This home, *Rosecourt*, is distinguished by its simple eighteenth-century lines. The pink concrete exterior is topped by a classicizing cornice

891 Crystal Springs Road, Hillsborough. Designed by Bliss and Faville, this Mediterranean style house was built in 1914–17 for Count Christian de Guigne. A graceful metal spiral stairway leads to the patio.

360 Poett Road (below) was built for the Richard Tobins in 1907 and is a charming shingle version of a Norman chateau

183

The Uplands (previous page)
designed in 1913 by Willis Polk
for C. Templeton Crocker,
is now a girls' school

Strawberry Hill was designed by Lewis Hobart in Period style. 207 El Cerrito (below) is a 1905 mansion with Tudor overtones

and low plinths; the interior includes several rooms imported from France.

The designs of George Howard also proliferated in the Hillsborough area. One representative example is at *245 El Cerrito Avenue.* This Period residence, built near the end of the last century for Mrs. George Shreve, includes a heavy wood entrance door, leaded windows, and Corinthian composite columns which form a shallow portico beneath a facade balustrade.

Another Howard design, at *2155 Parkside Avenue,* is very much like Le Petit Trianon. Built in 1915–1917 for George T. Marys, U.S. Ambassador to Russia, in classicizing French Baroque style, the house is marked by long colonnaded porches, pilaster-framed arched windows, and a balustraded entrance stairway—done in the Baroque manner.

Two homes closely attuned to their sylvan settings are *207 El Cerrito Avenue* and *360 Poett Road.* The first, built about 1905 for the Robert Hookers by George Howard, shows his mastery of the half-timbered form. The massive rectangle of the house, like some medieval manse, is broken by a dramatically salient bay to one side of a distinctly Tudor entrance. The house at *360 Poett Road,* built for Mr. and Mrs. Richard Tobin in 1907, is a charming shingle version of a Norman chateau. Two wings project from a central tower-keep; the sharp character of the medieval prototype is here softened by treillage, a formal lily pool, and verdant lawns.

A French Baroque house at 2155 Parkside Avenue, Hillsborough

WOODSIDE

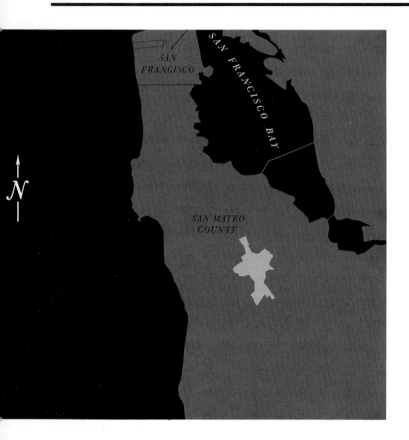

Logging of the great Coast Redwoods in the hills and mountains around the Central Valley had been commonplace during both the Spanish and Mexican periods, and the discovery of gold in California in 1848 soon brought the business to new heights.

M. A. Parkhurst and Charles Ellis shrewdly noted the high prices building materials could command in the swelling young city of San Francisco in the early months of the Gold Rush and determined to take advantage of the fact. They were joined in the enterprise by Dr. Robert O. Tripp, a dentist who had been disillusioned by the gouging tactics of his colleagues in San Francisco and thoroughly disgusted with the whole business of gold-seeking when he fell into the Sacramento River on his way to the diggings.

The partners came to an agreement with three San Francisco builders to supply the materials for much of the wharf construction of the early 1850's. Logging boomed. By 1859 the Woodside area claimed eight sawmills and three shingle mills with the combined capacity of 56,000 board feet of lumber per day. As the industry grew, so grew the town. Soon Woodside possessed two schools, a post office, a library, and direct stage service to San Francisco.

The capacity of the redwood country could not long sustain such a level of production, and during the latter years of the century the industry waned to such an extent that the area became renowned more for its rural attractions than its lumbering. Woodside's rustic charms brought the wealthy in increasing numbers over the years, until the entire valley took on the characteristics of such communities as Hillsborough and Atherton. The idyllic peace of the Woodside area has been stubbornly maintained to this day.

The oldest building in San Mateo County is probably the Charles Brown Adobe (Hooper Adobe), *2000 Portola Valley Road*. Charles Brown jumped ship in San Francisco Bay in 1833 and spent several years rambling about Mexican California as a soldier, lumberman and landowner. At some period between 1839 and 1846, Brown built his adobe and remained in the area until 1849. In 1852, Colonel Jack Hays, San Francisco County Sheriff and a former Texas Ranger, purchased the ranch. Some years later it passed into the hands of E. W. Burr, Mayor of San Francisco, who in turn sold it to lumberman-banker John A. Hooper in 1883. Much of the ranch property has since remained in the Hooper family.

The adobe is in remarkably good repair, its external appearance unchanged through the years. An excellent

The Charles Brown Adobe, 2000 Portola Valley Road, was built between 1839 and 1846 and is San Mateo County's oldest house

example of the so-called Monterey Colonial style, the squared adobe living space is completely surrounded by a veranda with heavy, cut timbers supporting the overhang of a tile roof. Because of its historical significance, the adobe is on the National Trust's list of buildings worth preserving.

Shortly after becoming involved in the logging operations which eventually gave birth to Woodside, Dr. Robert O. Tripp saw that someone was going to have to supply the rapidly growing little community. To this end he built the *Woodside Store, Tripp* and *Woodside Roads*, in 1854. Not only did he sell food and hardware items to the residents of the area, he also pulled their teeth, distributed their mail, and for the next fifty-odd years was the community's leader. The store has since been converted to a museum by the County of San Mateo, containing Dr. Tripp's meticulously kept ledgers and papers, a counter, post office, and assorted bins, equipment, and items representative of the era in which he functioned.

Dr. Tripp's home is across the street from the store at *3301 Tripp Road*. This is actually the second Tripp home, the first having been constructed sometime in the 1850's. The present structure is a simple two-story white frame house made conspicuous by its lack of ornamentation.

The single extravagance the Doctor seems to have allowed himself was the stylish double door with glass inserts.

The *Woodside Community Church, 3154 Woodside Road*, is Victorian Gothic in design, in keeping with its essentially ecclesiastical style. Built with volunteer labor in 1891, and seating one hundred worshippers, it is altogether typical of small town churches of the latter nineteenth century, but with characteristics all its own. The building's general plan is traditional, with such generic Gothic features as a steeply pitched roof, the pointed window over the foyer, and the bell tower with sharp, spired roof. The little church is faced with horizontal siding and has vertical cornerboards. An added feature is a sloping extension of the facade, perhaps to suggest the pier buttresses of earlier Victorian Gothic churches.

La Questa Vineyard was established in the 1880's by Emmett H. Rixford with vines imported from France. It became the best known San Mateo County vineyard and even survived Prohibition. The two-story winery, *240 La Questa Road*, was constructed by a Swiss mason of stones dug from the fields when the vineyard was laid out. Its beautifully-worked walls are eighteen inches thick. The building has been converted to an unusual residence by its architect-owner without substantially altering its lines.

189

Coffee King James Folger's massive Woodside home (previous page) was the perfect example of Edwardian splendor when it was built in 1905. Seldom have horses been so luxuriously housed as were those who enjoyed residence in James Folger's stables (above)

Of importance in Woodside's architectural history is the *Byrne-Shine House* on *Canada Road* built by Michael Byrne in 1882, twenty-five years after he arrived in Woodside. It uses refined late-Victorian Gothic details, but this is the practical, comfortable home of a successful farm owner. The board siding and the broad front veranda, supported by slender pillars and brackets, are commonplace in homes of this type; but three sharply-angled dormers with diamond-shaped windows give the home an exceptional air of grace. The house has been well maintained; the Shine family, present owners and descendants of Mrs. Byrne, have filled it with memorabilia reminiscent of the Victorian era.

Few establishments more impressively typify Woodside's transition from logging to genteel country living than the Folger house and stables at *3860 Woodside Road*. James A. Folger, "Coffee King" of San Francisco, was among the first of the very rich to move to Woodside's rural serenity. In 1905, he commissioned Arthur Brown, Jr. to design and build a house and barn for him in the town.

The four-story wood and stucco fantasy that resulted is a perfect illustration of Edwardian splendor. The impressive ground floor entryway has a porte-cochere, with balustrade leading to a second-floor balcony; the two upper stories are topped by a deep cornice, on brackets and interrupted at its crest with broken pediment and finial in the Baroque manner. The central section is flanked by two large wings—each lined with windows, each with its own balustraded balcony—terminating in tall pierced chimneys. A broad porch and balcony look out over the gardens behind the house.

The stables, half a mile west of the main house, are somewhat less complicated but no less impressive. Basically, they are similar in design to the house, including a deep roof with dormers and ground-floor arcades which approximate the porches and porte-cochere of the house. The interior features a cobblestone floor, mahogany paneling, and pink marble baseboards; seldom have horses been so luxuriously housed.

Vinegrove, 400 Kings Mountain Road, was constructed for Charles Josselyn with an interesting combination of stone, concrete and redwood in 1906—finished just in time for the earthquake, which damaged it enough to require architect Clarence Tantau to design and supervise the repairs. The home is in the shape of an inverted "U" with a colonnade of Ionic pillars spanning the open space at the front. Large redwood brackets support a deeply overhanging roof, and segmental pediments,

192

Vinegrove was badly damaged by the earthquake of 1906. Its original architect, Clarence Tantau, supervised the necessary repairs

broken in Baroque style, top the French doors at the end of each wing's facade. Also on the Vinegrove property is the original carriage house and barn, a handsome and straightforward structure of redwood board distinguished by two cupolas. Obviously this was never intended to be more than a place to house horses, hay and carriages; yet it strongly resembles some northern European medieval architecture.

Selah Chamberlain joined the exodus to Woodside in 1912, and commissioned Bakewell and Brown to design the house at *2889 Woodside Road.* The two-story wood and stucco home was styled in a shallow "U" shape of classicizing Baroque style; wings housing a dormitory and a solarium were added later. The landscaping around the home has always been outstanding; the present formal gardens were laid out in 1930 by the younger Frederick Law Olmsted.

One of the most remarkable structures to be seen in the Woodside area is the Gatehouse of Willow Brook Farm, *451 Portola Valley Road,* built in 1915 by Herbert Edward Law, a manufacturer of proprietary medicines and later President of the Western Steel Corporation.

His gatehouse might be described as Early Romanesque Castle Revival. The two-story house is constructed en-

tirely of assorted fieldstone, with entry gained through a castle "keep" pierced at intervals by narrow windows. A conical "dunce-cap" of a roof tops this formidable keep, and a weather vane sits like an afterthought on its peak.

William B. Bourn, President of the Spring Valley Water Company and inheritor of the great Empire Mine of Grass Valley, created in his estate, *Filoli,* on *Canada Road,* near Edgewood one of the most triumphantly sumptuous of all the Peninsula's great houses. It was built in 1916 from a Willis Polk design, styled after the Provincial Georgian architecture most often seen in the Tidewater area of Virginia. The mansion (whose odd name is an acronym contrived from the three things Bourn considered most important: Fidelity, Love, and Life) contains some 18,000 square feet of living space in its two stories. It is constructed of red brick with a white dentil course at the tiled roofline and a row of windows set in round arches on the main floor.

The main house is surrounded by sixteen acres of gardens, terraces, and orchards laid out in an elegant formal framework by Bruce Porter and Cheseley Bonestell; this landscaping is diverse yet superbly integrated, comprising cutting beds, vegetable rows, small fruit and other orchard areas, wildflower plantings, vines and collections of specimen plantings—all part of a sensitive Italian-French-

193

The Woodside Community Church (far left) was built in 1891. Sixteen acres of formal landscaping surround Filoli (left and bottom), a huge Georgian mansion built by Willis Polk. The gatehouse (below) of Willow Brook Farm is an architectural curio

The Woodside Store (left and below) was built in 1854 to serve the loggers who started the town. Today it is a museum. The Shine House (above) is an example of Victorian Gothic

based system of parterres, terraces, lawns and pools. Miss Isabelle Worn supervised the gardens and plantings to their present perfection.

Like Ralston's mansion at Belmont, Filoli stands as an impressive model of the architecture peculiar to the age of conspicuous consumption, when a man's home was expected to reflect his station in life.

What is particularly compelling about the architectural heritage of Woodside and the other communities of the Central Valley, however, is the fact that in its varieties of time and style, it provides a yardstick to the region's history—from the vigorous practicality of the lumbering years to the untrammeled self-expression of the pre-and post-Edwardian Age. The Central Valley is nearly unique in this respect; there is a superbly integrated line of remaining architecture that traces the pattern of changing life-styles through the years—the architecture of one era has been supplanted but not destroyed by the architecture that follows it.

COASTSIDE

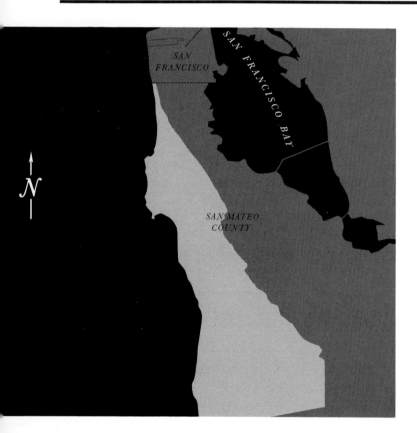

For the greater part of its existence, the Coastside of western San Mateo County has enjoyed a splendid isolation from the clamoring progress to the north and east. For years, it was effectively cut off geographically from the centers of government and commerce, and even when roads were built, it retained a spiritual isolation that marks it to this day.

Extending from San Pedro Point in the north to Ano Nuevo Point on the south, the Coastside is a narrow plain jammed between the Pacific and coastal mountains that make up in jumbled confusion what they lack in height. It is rolling, uneven country, sliced by arroyos and watered by a score of creeks cutting their way through the red earth to the sea. It has the appearance of an old land, an air of the primordial; wind and sea have altered it more than man.

The land was tramped by the Spanish explorer Don Gaspar de Portola in 1769, and later used by San Francisco's Mission Dolores to grow grain and raise cattle. After the Mexican government confiscated mission lands in the 1830's, the Coastside was parceled out in the form of grants, and until well after the American acquisition of California, it was populated principally by Mexican rancheros.

Slowly, much of the land fell into American hands, but its use was not significantly altered. It was still largely farms and ranches, quiet, unfilled, a relic of California's pastoral beginnings. The Coastside was too harsh and elemental, too often whipped by wind and blanketed in fog to appeal to the wealthy San Franciscans who had flocked to San Mateo County's eastern flank.

Pacifica has long since developed into a suburban community distinguishable from countless others chiefly because it is situated on a landscape of rugged dimensions, dominated by cliffs which crumble picturesquely into the sea. But it does contain two structures whose design, purpose and history are completely removed from that of their neighbors.

The first of these is *The Castle, 900 Mirador Terrace,* a building which qualified for a number of years as one of the most notorious on the Peninsula. It was built in 1908 by H. H. McCloskey; its crenelated masonry walls and towers made it something of a showplace until McCloskey's death just prior to the 1920's. It later became an abortion mill, and shortly thereafter, a distribution center for bootleg liquor and a stylish speakeasy. It is situated on a bluff overlooking the sea, which facilitated the transfer of liquor brought in under cover of darkness by rumrunners and hoisted into the Castle by ropes and winches.

During World War II the Castle was occupied by the

Coast Guard, and after that fell into disuse. It recently has been purchased and refurbished by an antique collector, who has filled its fourteen rooms with various relics of the eighteenth and nineteenth centuries.

The *Sanchez Adobe, Linda Mar Boulevard* and *Adobe Drive*, was constructed between 1842 and 1846 by Don Francisco Sanchez, *alcalde* (mayor) of a scruffy little village called Yerba Buena (later, San Francisco) and owner of a land grant comprising some acres in the San Pedro Valley. The two-story adobe was finished in 1846, the year the American flag was raised in Yerba Buena's Portsmouth Square.

Sanchez retreated to his new home in the San Pedro Valley and gave considerable thought to resisting the American invasion. Eventually he thought better of it and made his peace with the conquerors.

In 1852 Sanchez' claim to the San Pedro Valley grant was declared legitimate by the U.S. Courts, and until his death in 1862 the Sanchez adobe continued its role as the center of life in the San Pedro Valley. The adobe then changed hands a number of times, finally coming into the possession of General Edward Kirkpatrick in 1879. The County of San Mateo later purchased the adobe, and it was made an Historical Monument and restored in 1953. Today, it functions as a museum and is one of the few surviving examples of architecture from the Mexican period in the state.

The Montara Light Station on the *Coast Highway*, one mile south of Montara, was constructed by the U.S. Lighthouse Service in 1887. Its squat metal tower houses a light which can be seen from seventeen miles. The tower and the keeper's wood house behind it can only be called "lighthouse architecture"; the stern white practicality of these structures is reminiscent of those seen on the New England Coast. Now operated by the U.S. Coast Guard, the Montara Light Station is open to the public seven days a week, from 1:00 to 4:00 p.m.

Farther south on the Coast Highway another white brick tower looms over the pounding surf at Pigeon Point, casting its warning light eighteen miles to sea. Once called Whale Point, it was renamed when the clipper *Carrier Pigeon* was wrecked on the offshore rocks in 1853. The British ship *Hellespont* met a similar fate in 1866, and to avert further disaster *the Pigeon Point Lighthouse* was constructed in 1872. The bronze-mounted, multi-faceted lens of polished glass was originally operated by a weight which hung in the center of the tower and was wound like a grandfather clock. The lens was imported from France by way of Cape Hatteras, where it aided naval operations during the Civil War. The lighthouse is open to the public on Saturdays, Sundays, and Holidays from 1:00 to 4:00 p.m.

Half Moon Bay is San Mateo County's oldest town. Its first house, an adobe, was built in 1840 by a San Francisco Presidio soldier, Candelario Miramontes. In time a village clustered in the area, called San Benito by the Mexicans and Spanishtown by the few Americans who knew it existed. The settlement remained unchanged by the Gold Rush; access over Pedro Mountain was very difficult, and until 1853 it was no more than seven adobe houses occupied by some seventy people, including resident Indians. In 1853 the first Americans came over the mountains to settle, buying pieces of the Miramontes grant for farming purposes and eventually changing the name to Half Moon Bay.

Among the first American settlers were the Johnston brothers, James, Thomas, William, and John, who purchased the southern portion of the Miramontes grant and

The Castle, at Pacifica, was once a hangout for bootleggers

199

The Sanchez Adobe was built around 1846 by San Francisco's Mexican mayor. The Montara Light (right) was put up in 1887

introduced the first eastern cattle to the coast region. The *James Johnston home* at *Higgins Road* and *Main Street* was built of redwood timbers floated up the coast from mills in Santa Cruz. Constructed in 1853 or early 1854, the home was the first American house in the area, an example of New England saltbox, standing today in the middle of a cleared field – a deserted shell waiting to be razed for the construction of a civic center.

In less melancholy condition is the house of *William Johnston* at *Higgins Road* and *Main Street*. William built this home shortly after his brother's; it is essentially a Victorian Colonial, not of pure Georgian style. Attractive features of the home, now a residence for farm help, include the wood supports under the eaves, the original shutters and the off-center doorway. (Placement of a two-story wing next to the low entrance-utility wing reveals a provincial, nineteenth-century modification of Georgian formality.) It is noteworthy that the house was constructed entirely with wooden pegs rather than with nails.

At *546 Purisima Street* is a simple Victorian Gothic home of wood, built in the latter half of the nineteenth century. It possesses sharp lines and is marked by an intricate lace bargeboard under the gables' eaves and arched Gothic (lancet) windows in each of the gables.

Seven miles south of the town of Half Moon Bay is the *Tunis District School* at *Lobitos Creek Cut-off*. This simple wood structure is one of the two surviving one-room, one-teacher schools in San Mateo County. The present building was constructed about 1889 on the site of the original schoolhouse, erected in 1866. The little cupola for the school bell is especially nostalgic. At the rear is the "teacherage" which housed the faculty and was partially constructed from the original 1866 schoolhouse.

The valley of San Gregorio Creek contained some of the finest farms on the Coastside and the little town of San Gregorio was born of their various needs in 1854. In later years the town was a favorite base of hunters and fishermen. *The San Gregorio House* on *Stage Road* was built primarily for these sportsmen, but also was used as a way station by cattle drivers of the region. Constructed of wood in the 1850's, its main architectural feature is the full-length balcony on the second floor front. Eventually it became known as the Palmer and Bell Hotel, and today it stands empty.

In May, 1847, Eli Moore and his family left Missouri to make the rigorous trek across the Sierra, the first group of settlers to make that crossing after the ill-fated Donner party. The Moores traveled on to the coast, stopping in the vicinity of Santa Cruz, then moving north to the lush Pescadero Valley where they purchased a large section of the Gonzales grant, Rancho El Pescadero, in 1853.

Other settlers joined the Moore family, and a prosperous little farming community developed in the 1850's. From the 1860's to the turn of the century, Pescadero was the leading coast resort in San Mateo County; today Pescadero remains essentially the village it must have been in 1890, quiet, compact and untouched.

Issac Graham, a relative of Daniel Boone, was one of the earliest settlers. His house, built in 1851, still stands on *White House Creek Road*. For many years the white, two-story wood house was a comforting landmark to passing mariners, but it has since become obscured by surrounding eucalyptus trees.

Alexander Moore, Eli Moore's son, constructed a house at *Pescadero Creek Road* which was instrumental in setting the general architectural tone of the community. The fourteen room wood home was built along simple late-Greek Revival-early-Victorian lines in 1853. The timbers were brought by ox cart from Santa Cruz. Its porch (here L-shaped) with split pilasters, vaguely classical in character, appears throughout Pescadero with endless variation, giving the town the air of a Maine fishing village. The Braddock Weeks home on *Pescadero Creek Road* carries on the traditions set by the Moore house. It was built in 1856 along the same practical line for Weeks; but here the split pilasters become more Victorian, and the roofline has brackets.

Isaac Steele's home was built in 1863 near the *Cabrillo Highway*. The white, simple frame house contains twelve rooms; while it possesses no truly distinctive architectural style, it does—despite later nineteenth and twentieth-century revisions—suggest rural New England. Named "Green Oaks" by Steele, the house continues in use as a country home.

More formally reminiscent of Georgian New England is the house of Isaac's brother, R. E. Steele on *Cascade Ranch, Cabrillo Highway*. The wood house is enhanced by an encompassing porch with second-story balcony; balustrade and pillars assert a classical tradition. George, the third Steele brother, built his home on the *Ano Nuevo Ranch, Cabrillo Highway*. It is a simple, uncompromising saltbox. Like the others, the home was built in the early 1860's.

The William Ramsey house, also on *Cabrillo Highway*, was partially a gift from the sea. The main section was built in 1868 by Ramsey; the kitchen addition was built in 1898 with timbers retrieved from the wreck of the ship *Columbia* off the rocky coast. Of modest Victorian fashion in wood, the interior of the house appears today much as it did in 1895. On the exterior, quoins reiterate an eighteenth-century theme; split pilasters on the side porch and panelled doors suggest the mid-nineteenth century.

Split pilasters and a paneled door are again seen in the Elias Shaw home *on North Street*. It was built about 1875 by

546 Purisima, in Half Moon Bay, has a fine lace bargeboard

Split pilasters hold up the porch of the 1875 Elias Shaw House in Pescadero (above).
The San Gregorio House (below), now empty, was built to serve hunters and fishermen

This typical Pescadero house (seen here from the side and front) is located on Pescadero Creek Road. It was built in 1856 and is a bit more Victorian than its neighbors as seen by its elaborate pilasters and the brackets below its roofline

Shaw, a former miner, and remains an outstanding example of wood architecture common to this town. The Van Allen house on *North Street* is also in this architectural group and shares its characteristics. It dates from 1875.

Pescadero's Catholic community erected *Saint Anthony's Catholic Church on North Street* in 1870. Its fashion is late Greek Revival moving into the Italianate—with a tall, square tower, rose window and high spire, marked by four dormer windows with finials that echo Victorian Gothic ideas. Over the center door is a pediment on consoles; at the building's corners are tall pilasters.

The Pescadero Community Church on *San Gregorio Street* is slightly older than St. Anthony's—having been constructed in 1868. This unabashed late-Greek-Revival church with tall arched windows is dominated by a massive tower and spire. It is further distinguished by wood siding that has been carefully grooved to simulate stone, with its corners quoined. Characteristic of late Greek Revival is the roofline which ends in an entablature section to give the impression of a broken pediment. The "eared" circle above the main door and peculiar pointed, bracketed spire suggest Italianate-Victorian Gothic details.

From Ano Nuevo Point north to Half Moon Bay, the touch of the twentieth century has been light; this is still a serene island in time. In and north of Half Moon Bay, change has been far more dramatic, as the tracts of suburban homes creep south from Pacifica.

The Coastside—together with Marin North and West— still offers some of the last open land left in the Bay Area, one of the last chances to enjoy some sense of a quieter past amid farms and fields, cliffs and wild arroyos, where the wind carries with it the smell of the sea.

The Alexander Moore House in Pescadero was built in 1853 and set the general architectural tone of the community

Top: The Pescadero Community Church is probably the oldest Protestant church in the county

Bottom left: Saint Anthony's Church, Pescadero

Bottom right: Half Moon Bay's Community Church shows a touch of Victorian Gothic in its window and door moldings. The wing to the left was once a station for the old Coast Railroad

MARIN COUNTY

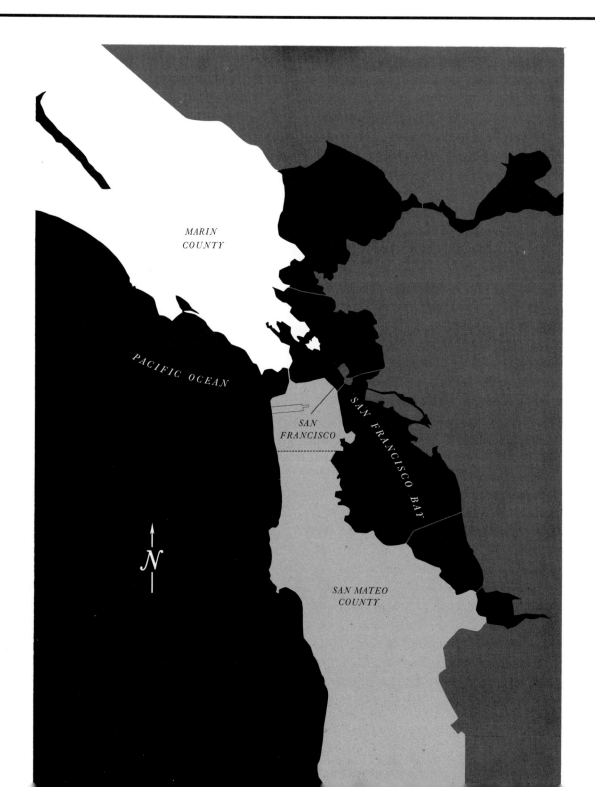

MARIN
COUNTY

PACIFIC OCEAN

SAN
FRANCISCO

SAN FRANCISCO BAY

N

SAN MATEO
COUNTY

From the suburban tracts of Corte Madera to the windswept resorts of Tomales Bay, Marin County is a remarkable collection of diversities. Its topography is complex and various, including a jumbled maze of hills and valleys, flat farmland, sea cliffs, and one bona fide mountain. It is a commuter's haven and a developer's dream, but it is also one of the few areas in the Bay Region that has not irretrievably succumbed to the raging demands of progress.

It harbors beach towns, artists colonies, bedroom communities, residential enclaves of the well-to-do, at least one legitimate slum, farm villages, Muir Woods National Monument, Point Reyes National Seashore, two State Parks, Hamilton Air Force Base, and San Quentin State Prison.

The population of the region reflects similar complexities, but displays one generally uniform trait: an unabashed fondness for Marin County. The average Marinite—newcomer or oldtimer—is quite convinced that his part of the country is unique.

The attitude is part of a venerable tradition. Ever since the first great commuter boom of the late nineteenth century, those who came to live in Marin County were looking for something different than those who settled on the Peninsula or in the East Bay.

Perhaps what that difference was can best be seen in the kinds of houses the people built and the places in which they built them. They were not rich men's houses, for the most part (the very rich generally chose the Peninsula); yet they possessed one predominant characteristic that distinguished them from the average just as clearly as grandeur: an uncommon regard for environment, be it forest, field, or seaside.

While the southern portion of the county particularly has been a hotbed of residential development, it has usually been accomplished with taste. Rather than spreading over the landscape and obscuring it, houses have been snuggled into its bosom—jammed into narrow canyons crowded with redwoods and manzanita, hidden among oaks, junipers and magnolias, perched illogically on innumerable slopes and ridges, or built so close to the water that they might as well have been landlocked houseboats. Some of them, in fact, were.

Everywhere, the vegetation has been encouraged to flourish. Emigrants to Marin did not arrive with conquest in mind; they cleared no forests and leveled no mountains—or at least relatively few until today. Theirs was a mutually agreeable compromise with nature based on an affection that has marked the county ever since.

There is some irony in the fact that it was the outright exploitation of natural resources that gave birth to the first extensive railroad system in Marin County—which in turn made it possible for commuters to embrace the wonders of nature. The North Pacific Coast Railroad, incorporated in 1871, was designed to run from Sausalito to Tomales. The inspiration for its founding was a hope that the lumber companies operating in the redwood forests on the Russian River would find the railroad more convenient than the steamers that loaded lumber from various "dogholes" on the coastline.

That realization never came to pass with the success the railroad's founders had hoped for, but after the road was completed in July of 1874, the true significance of it could be seen in the rapid rise of towns strung along the line between Sausalito and San Rafael like beads on a bracelet—among them Almonte, Corte Madera, Larkspur, Kentfield, Ross, and San Anselmo.

Encouraged by the sudden ease of transportation, commuters discovered the marvels of Marin and settled it with astonishing speed. They were given a choice of railroads in 1884, when the San Francisco and North Pacific opened a broad-gauge line from Tiburon to San Rafael.

Competition between the two lines was such that the patrons of each developed partisan feelings fierce enough to end friendships. At the same time, customers felt free to criticize their own. As Gilbert H. Kneiss writes in *Redwood Railways*, the only good thing one longtime patron of the N. P. C. could say about it was, "No matter how drunk a man might be when he boarded one of its trains, he was sure to be sober by the time he got off."

The N. P. C. was electrified in 1903 and renamed the North Shore Railroad. It functioned in independent style for several years until both it and the San Francisco and North Pacific were absorbed in the merger that created the Northwestern Pacific. Finally, the electric interurban system itself was junked in 1941, done in by the Golden Gate Bridge and the automobile.

Time and circumstance have not yet completely altered Marin County and its inhabitants. To those who call it home, Marin still is the closest thing to earthly perfection since Adam and Eve took a backward glance at the Garden of Eden.

SAUSALITO

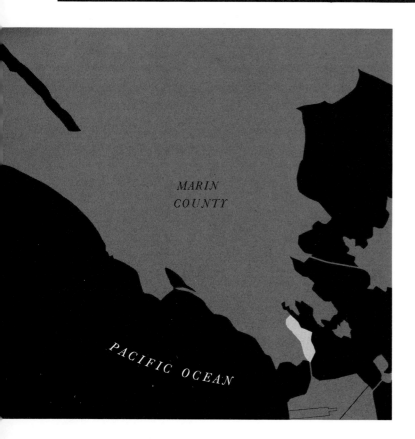

a shipping point for the crops grown in the surrounding area and a way station for vessels in need of wood and water.

The first important boost to Sausalito's growth came with the purchase of one thousand acres of the Rancho in 1869 by the Sausalito Land and Ferry Company. The company established a ferry line from San Francisco to the town, laid out numerous lots, and contrived the beginning of a water system.

This confidence was vindicated when the North Pacific Coast Railroad opened for business in 1874. Shops for the narrow-gauge line were established in Sausalito, and a healthy influx of families followed. Yet another boost to the town came when the North Pacific leased the ferry line and installed its own modern boat. Building progressed at a pace unmatched in the city's history, and until 1941 Sausalito was the major railhead and ferry landing for the streams of commuters between San Francisco and southern Marin County.

The San Francisco Yacht Club moved to Sausalito in 1878, which established the town as one of the major recreational boating centers in the Bay Area, an industry that—along with the tourist trade—has been largely responsible for sustaining the town since the railroad's demise.

In recent years, Sausalito has capitalized on one of its least tangible characteristics—its heritage as a haven for artists, writers and Bohemians in general. This particular aspect of its character has been well-established ever since poet Daniel O'Connell walked the city's hills in the late 1880's.

Sausalito is a blend of seaport, yachting center, tourist attraction and artist colony—a cheerful conglomerate that easily makes it the most distinctive community in Marin County.

The *Gardner House, Cazneau* and *Girard Avenues*, is the

S ausalito's first settler of any note was John Reed, who came in 1826, hoping to obtain the grant to Rancho Saucelito, a matter of nearly twenty thousand acres. He accepted, instead, a grant to Rancho Corte de Madera del Presidio across the hills in what would later become Mill Valley, and the Saucelito grant went to William A. Richardson, a former British mariner who took possession in 1838.

Over the next several years a tiny English-speaking colony collected in the area, but not even the American acquisition of California and the Gold Rush of 1849–1852 could lift the settlement out of the doldrums. Until 1869, the town was little more than what it had always been—

oldest Sausalito home still standing as designed, with its Victorian Gothic barge-boarded eaveline and delicate split porch pilasters. In overall character, this modest frame residence suggests California houses of the 1850's. It was built in 1869 by James Gardner on a lot purchased from the Sausalito Land and Ferry Company.

Gardner had come west in 1849 and mined on the Feather and Yuba Rivers. He prospered, and became a Senator from Yuba and Sierra counties and later a customs house broker in San Francisco. He invested heavily in San Francisco real estate and eventually settled in Sausalito, where he remained until his death in 1899. From its construction in 1869 until 1962, the house was occupied by only three families; in 1962 it was acquired by William M. Roth, an ardent devotee of historic buildings.

The *Valhalla, 201 Bridgeway*, had a comparatively lively history even before being taken over and refurbished by its present owner, Sally Stanford. Built sometime in the 1870's, the boxlike frame building served for many years as a small German beer garden patronized by fishermen and occasional visitors from across the Bay. During Prohibition, it was a speakeasy and, according to local rumor, the outlaw "Pretty Boy" Floyd tended bar here while a fugitive from justice.

The three-story *Tyrell Cottage, 47 Miller Lane*, was built in the early 1870's as a carriage house, probably for the Frank M. Bowens' home on Santa Rosa Avenue. Period characteristics appear in the flat hood-molded paired windows under the gables and in the modillions of these gables' eaves. The building was modified in 1880 to serve as a residence and most recently restored in 1955. This solid frame structure possesses the strength of simplicity; its clean white lines were not cluttered with an excess of ornamentation—as befitted a utilitarian carriage house.

Moved and modified occasionally during its life, the three-story Victorian house at *323 Pine Street* still retains much of its charm. Constructed in 1871, it was purchased three years later by Vicomte Gaston Pierre Domergue, a wine merchant from France, who altered the house to his own taste and moved it one block to the water's edge. Once again, in 1930, it was moved to its present site to make way for Bridgeway Boulevard. The shutters, gingerbread trim, and covered porches, were removed and the original redwood shiplap was shingled. It is still the home of the Domergue family.

Hazel Mount, 86 San Carlos Avenue, was built in 1871 as one of the few early estates in Sausalito. The San Francisco Yacht Club's Captain William Harrison, one of the area's first settlers, was the owner. He surrounded his mansion with extensive English gardens, which emphasized the native oaks and hazel bushes. The present owner of the house—which still serves as a residence—added a Japanese garden about 1950, designed by Nako Sakurai, of the Japanese Imperial Palace staff. There was a well on this property large enough to provide water for the whole town in the late nineteenth century.

Less ambitious than Hazel Mount is the two-story frame house at *639 Main Street*, built in 1874 by a carpenter

The charming Gardner House in Sausalito was built in 1869 and is virtually unchanged today after a century of life

Hazel Mount, one of Sausalito's earliest formal estates, once provided enough water from its well for the whole town

named Griswold, who knew what he was doing in terms of construction. Part Victorian Gothic, part French Provincial, and part sheer inventiveness, the home is distinguished by a villa tower and the exotic, gazebo-like latticed entrance. Altogether, it can be called the ultimate in "Carpenter's Gothic."

Christ Episcopal Church, Santa Rosa and *San Carlos Avenues*, is a Victorian Gothic frame building with shingled exterior. The main structure, with its pointed windows and buttressed shingle tower and belfry of Gothic inclinations, was in use in 1882. Guild Hall was added in 1889, and Memorial Porch in 1912. The fine bell was a gift of the Sausalito Land and Ferry Company; as a tacit recognition of the company's importance to the town, the bell did double duty as fog bell on the company's wharf. It was also the town's fire bell.

The shingled cottage called *Laurel Lodge, 41 Cazneau Avenue*, was erected, according to legend, "on a party" for James W. Coleman some time in 1886. Coleman loaned the cottage to poet Daniel O'Connell, who lived here with his family until his death in 1899. O'Connell was a Bohemian of considerable style, and lived with his wife and children in a tent on the beach until James Coleman provided him the house on the hill—which became known as "O'Connell Glen." It was an age in which the term "Bohemian" was not necessarily one of disrespect, and the pudgy O'Connell was one of Sausalito's most illustrious and fondly-remembered citizens.

A good example of late nineteenth century "Victorian Eclectic" is the *Fiedler House, 141 Bulkley Avenue*. The basic

style of the two-story home, built in the late 1890's, is irregularly Victorian. The somewhat-classicized columned and pedimented front porch anticipates the Period Revivals of the turn of the century. A fine Queen Anne tower with fish-scale shingles is tacked on almost as an afterthought. Altogether, the house illustrates the lighthearted enthusiasms of an era untroubled by inconsistency.

A far more consistent and equally distinctive home is the *Schuller House, 603 Main Street*. This two-storied confection was built in 1899 by a carpenter with a predilection for carving, reflected most attractively in the charming en-

639 Main, built in 1874, blends several architectural styles

212

trance porch and front door. Of what might be called American chalet style, the house features leaded glass and peaked, carved dormers on the gambrel roof, as well as shingle siding. Much of the decorative detail harks back to Eastlake motifs; but the shingles unify the ensemble.

Tank houses were once a relatively common sight in various towns west of the Mississippi; there are few of these delightful blends of the practical and the residential now left, and one of them, appropriately enough, is in Sausalito at *140 Bulkley Avenue*. This house was built around 1900 using a water-tank on the property of the old Geneva Hotel. After the transformation, it became a carriage house for a Mr. Hanify, who also bought the bowling alley of the Hotel and turned it into a cottage; Hanify obviously was a man of imagination. After his death, the tank-and-carriage-house was enlarged and converted into a three-story home.

The two story house at Turney and Bonita Streets was built for Adolph Silva, a turn-of-the-century local politician and barrister who was involved with the Craven-Fair case in 1900. A certain "Mrs. Craven" claimed secret marriage to the deceased Senator and Bonanza King, James G. Fair, in hopes of obtaining a share in his large estate. Silva achieved local prominence in his alignment with the Fair family who ultimately defeated Mrs. Craven's claims. After the trial, Silva bought half an acre of Sausalito land and erected this square Colonial Revival mansion-unique in style to Sausalito, although similar to many such homes in Oakland. Silva left Sausalito, and during the housing shortage of World War One, the big house was converted into four apartments.

Ondine Restaurant, 558 Bridgeway, is a relic of Sausalito's yachting past. The San Francisco Yacht Club, one of the oldest in the United States, was originally formed in 1869, and had its headquarters in a little shack on the "Long Bridge" that spanned Mission Bay in San Francisco. The club failed when it exhausted its entire treasury in promoting one glorious clambake in Marin in 1871. It was revived in 1873 and moved to the Ondine site in 1878.

The original San Francisco Yacht Club building at the Ondine site is said to have been a converted livery stable. When this building burned in 1897, it was rebuilt as the two-story structure that stands today. The club much later moved to its present location at the head of Belvedere Cove. The building stood more-or-less vacant through the 1930's and 1940's. In the late 1950's the superb location was again put to good use, with the conversion of the building into a two story lounge restaurant.

This mansion at Turney and Bonita Streets is one of a kind

141 Bulkley—late nineteenth century "Victorian Eclectic"

213

*Two views of Christ Episcopal Church as it looks today and
a view of it before the turn of the century when its
fine old bell also warned Sausalitans of fog and fire*

214

BELVEDERE/TIBURON

MARIN
COUNTY

PACIFIC OCEAN

"Belvedere, beautiful Belvedere," wrote Helen Bingham in her turn-of-the-century book *In Tamal Land,* " . . . who could view this thickly wooded hillside with its charming villas without exclaiming Beautiful!"

Back in the days when Helen Bingham was rhapsodizing Belvedere's beauties, its lagoon was not obstructed by man-made peninsulas and the island itself was comparatively uncrowded. Until 1888, in fact, the island had but one resident, a goat farmer by the name of Israel Kashow, who did battle with the heirs of John Reed over the ownership of the island.

Kashow claimed that Belvedere was in fact an island and his by squatter's rights; the heirs claimed that it was a bulbous peninsula and therefore part of Rancho Corte

Madera del Presidio—and theirs. The controversy was solved by Kashow's death, and the island-peninsula was purchased by the Belvedere Land Company in 1890.

The company laid out streets and planted eucalyptus and pine trees to mingle with the few scrub oaks indigenous to the island. By the turn of the century, there were less than a hundred homes on the island, including the large estate of Gordon Blanding at the end of Golden Gate Avenue.

The Union Fish Company was located on the Richardson Bay side of the island; here, cod from the chill waters off Alaska were processed and packed. When codfishing fell on hard times, a few of the fishery buildings became guest houses and studios for artists. They have since been replaced by new homes on West Shore Road.

The Tiburon Peninsula simply languished as the southernmost extension of John Reed's Rancho (and was called, in fact, Little Reed Ranch) until Dr. Benjamin Lyford tried during the latter years of the nineteenth century to develop the southeastern flank of the peninsula into a model community devoted to health and all the Christian virtues.

Less utopian in purpose were the designs of Colonel Peter Donahue's San Francisco and North Pacific Railway, which in 1884 chose Tiburon as a rail terminus and landing for its San Francisco ferries. Sites for the company's shops, depot and store were carved out of the peninsula's southwestern face, and by 1900 the community was a thriving little commercial complex. The nature of the place was softened somewhat by the presence of the Corinthian Yacht Club at the southeastern tip of Corinthian Island, but otherwise it displayed all the qualities of haphazard development typical of one-industry towns.

Its heavily commercial background left Tiburon susceptible to the blandishments of the twentieth century, and it has accepted progress in a more-or-less normal suburban fashion. Belvedere, on the other hand, has been blessed by her geography and sustained by a genteel heritage. It has translated progress into something beyond the ordinary, particularly in the comparatively recent lagoon complex. The island and the lagoon have remained a kind of spiritual city-state—a charming perpetuation of Helen Bingham's breathless assessment of long ago.

In the late 1880's, some of the first homes in Belvedere were "arks," house-boats used by boatmen as permanent dwellings and by yachtsmen as weekend moorings. Around the turn of the century, as Belvedere grew into a summer colony, the arks became more elaborate in style and construction—and amenities, being supplied with water and fresh groceries by local merchants who rowed out to offer their wares. Around 1910, many arks were pulled out and beached along Corte Madera Creek where they are still being rented; but not until 1946 was the last ark towed to shore.

In a row of several of its "sister ships" grounded on Beach Road, the ark at *27 Beach Road* typifies the later house-boats. One enters directly into the living-room, then down a hall that divides the two bedrooms from the roomy galley. The covered decks on either side are connected by a narrow covered walkway along the sides. The structure rests on a scow-bottom and one has only to lift a trap door to peer into the bilges.

One of the earliest of Belvedere's permanent homes was *Landfall, 296 Beach Road.* This shingle, two-story house was built in 1891 as a summer weekend home for Mr. and Mrs. Frederick Winthrop Bridge. Below the house was a dock that served as the stop for a commuting ferry, the *Marin,* which plied between Sausalito and Belvedere for more than thirty years. One of the most noteworthy features of this house is its charming "rainbow," barn-like roof. This aspect of the house has remained substantially

This ark at 27 Beach Road once proudly rode Belvedere's lagoon

unchanged through the years, although a succession of owners have added to the place, remodeled the interior, and revised the landscape.

The house at *460 Bella Vista* perches as formally on the hillside as Landfall nestles casually into it below. It was built in 1892 when its Queen Anne style was in vogue. What could have been a too narrow and tall facade, emphasized by two-story high Ionic columns, is relieved by the balustrade around the upper floor. There is a wealth of detail: the Adamesque frieze under the tower eaves, the pediment embellished with an oval design, even the wooden keystones enhancing the narrow basement windows.

In 1900, Gordon Blanding purchased nearly the entire southern tip of Belvedere, including several homes already occupied. Blanding retained some of these buildings for an estate, forming a complex of houses, stables, and gardens which dominated the crest of Golden Gate Avenue in his time. The main house at *440 Golden Gate* still stands, an enduring, two-story example of turn-of-the-century style; the carriage house, now at *333 Belvedere Avenue,* is a well-preserved example of shingle architecture.

Four other residences on the former Blanding Estate include the gardener's house, *343 Belvedere,* the boat house, *50 Rowley Circle,* the *"Organ House," 433 Golden Gate Avenue* and a Mediterranean villa designed by Julia Morgan, *450 Belvedere Avenue.* The "Organ House," a three-story brick and half-timbered structure, was originally built in the 1890's; there is evidence (particularly in the distinctive interior) that it was reworked by Willis Polk about 1906. The house received its name during this reworking: a wing, with concert room, was built to accommodate one of the largest privately-owned organs in existence at the time. The organ has been retained by succeeding owners.

Golden Gate Avenue is distinctive for more than the story of the Blanding Estate. In the short span of years before and after 1900 a series of uncommonly attractive and enduring homes were built, and each has been continuously occupied and well-preserved. One is located at *316 Golden Gate Avenue.* This three-story shingle home is an example of what might be termed a "Belvedere box" house. Built between 1905 and 1910, the house possesses the charm of simplicity—that kind of beauty that stems from a blend of the purely utilitarian and an intelligent use of environment.

Designed by architect Albert Farr in 1904, the three-story house at *334 Golden Gate Avenue* is a redwood variation on medieval English themes. Several features suggest Tudor influence, particularly the multi-gabled roof, the attractive half-timbered facade, and the mullioned and muntined windows. An unusual feature is the flat-roofed dormer neatly inserted into a corner of the roofline.

Certainly one of the most aesthetically satisfying homes on Belvedere is the former Valentine Rey home at *428 Golden Gate Avenue.* Built in 1893 (and perhaps the fourth house constructed on the island), the residence was the result of an especially happy collaboration between artist, Mrs. Valentine Rey, and architect, Willis Polk. Their concern was to make the house a work of art. A central light-well became the heart of the structure; and the house surrounding it was constructed of hand-sized and carved redwood—a standard practice of the time.

Not at all standard, however, are the strong Mediterranean qualities that the designers incorporated—revealed in the use of arches, tiled fireplaces, tiled roof, and stucco as the exterior material. The interior of the house is marked by spaciousness, most dramatically illustrated by the second-story family room—in reality an attic space—in which exposed redwood beams, redwood paneling, and a simple stone fireplace are used to great advantage. Overall, the design of the house is a perfect balance, its elegant lines giving it a character that is forever contemporary.

When Colonel Peter Donahue's San Francisco and North Pacific Railway selected Tiburon as its terminus in 1884, a number of frame houses were put up for the shop workers at a cost of between five hundred and one thousand dollars apiece, mostly on *Mar West* and *Esperanza Streets.*

A representative sample of these vintage 1880 houses still can be seen—a group of modest frame houses that doubtless are more appreciated for their charm today than they were by those who lived in them eighty years ago.

Saint Hilary's Roman Catholic Church was built on a hilltop in 1888 near *Esperanza* and *Alemany Streets.* The only way to get to it was via a narrow, redwood boardwalk that climbed up to the windswept crest of the hill—and once there, the parishioner was greeted by an unheated church exposed to miniature gales of arctic frigidity. In 1954, the parish was provided with a new church, and the old structure was saved by the Belvedere-Tiburon Landmarks Society, which bought and refurbished it as an historical monument. Today, it is officially known as Old Saint Hilary's Landmark and Museum.

At *2036 Paradise Drive* stands an unusual medieval tower, the last remnant of a dream called Lyford's Hygeia. The dreamer was Dr. Benjamin Lyford, who had come to San Francisco to practice medicine in 1866 and become a Marin landowner through his 1872 marriage to Hilarita Reed, daughter of John Reed and heiress to a large portion of Reed's estate. In 1876, Lyford and his wife retired to Strawberry Point and developed the Eagle Dairy, utilizing Jersey cows and "great kindness"—as Lyford put it—for the production of superior milk.

Landfall (upper left) was built in 1891 and is one of Belvedere's first permanent homes. A year later an elegant Queen Anne house (left) was built on the hillside at 460 Bella Vista. In 1893 Willis Polk designed the magnificent carved wood interior of 428 Golden Gate Avenue (above) The Blanding house (right) has long been Southern Belvedere's best known, most enduring landmark

218

Lyford eventually came up with one of those utopian fantasies so common to the nineteenth century: a community dedicated to his concept of the good, the true, and the healthy life. He called this vision Hygeia, after the goddess of health, and began a wall (never finished) that was to extend around his extensive property at the southern end of the Tiburon Peninsula. He also built a gate and tower on Paradise Drive and began selling Hygeian lots to carefully-screened buyers who were forbidden such unhygienic antics as smoking, or publicly drinking.

Some lots were sold, but Hygeia never did become the Garden of Eden. Perhaps the interdiction against kissing on the property had something to do with its failure. At any rate, the vision did serve one useful purpose: the carefully-contoured streets that Lyford laid out in the early 1890's formed the basis for modern Tiburon's street system in this area. Beyond that, the stone tower is all that remains.

Standing solitary and splendid on the far southeastern portion of Tiburon Peninsula are the buildings of the impressive *Keil Estate* at *Keil Cove*. These thirty-eight acres were purchased from Benjamin Lyford by Hugo D. Keil, and a handsome carriage house was built in 1898. Slightly later came a small house on the fresh water lagoon here; finally, an imposing Colonial Revival two-story main house was erected. It is said that cartridges were imbedded in the walls of the house during its construction — the theory being that if the house ever caught fire the cartridges would explode, thereby warning the occupants of danger. The unlikely system was never utilized.

Certainly the most interesting house on the Tiburon Peninsula is the *Lyford (Dickey) Mansion* at Roger's Beach *(376 Tiburon Boulevard)*. During the years in which Benjamin Lyford operated the Eagle Dairy on Strawberry Point, this house (built in 1874) was his home, and it remained in his possession until his death in 1906. In 1957, it was barged across Richardson Bay, restored by architect John Lord King and dedicated to the memory of Donald R. Dickey, naturalist and zoologist; today, it serves as headquarters and study center for the National Audubon Society, Marin Chapter.

The small Victorian frame house, two stories high plus tower, possesses two rooms on the first floor and four rooms and a hallway on the second floor. Basically simple, it nevertheless is given a compelling dollhouse charm by the Mansard roof, scalloped shingles, handsome trim, crestings and finials. The interior is marked by a mahogany stairway, occasional gilded trim (some doors and sashes are said to have been milled in England), and etched glass skylights — a feature particularly common to the 1870's. It stands today as a cheerful reminder of a more delicate past.

This Victorian gem (left), which now houses Marin's Audubon Society, was once the home of Dr. Benjamin Lyford, one of Tiburon's early residents

Old St. Hilary's Landmark and Museum was Tiburon's first Catholic Church

221

MILL VALLEY

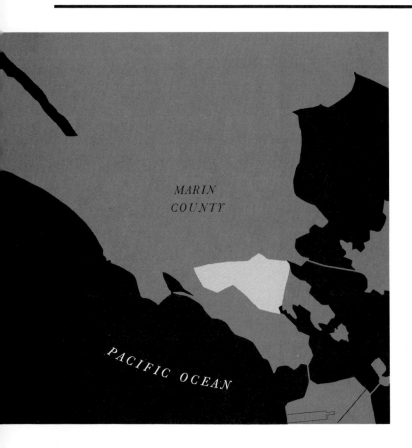

MARIN COUNTY

PACIFIC OCEAN

Sausalito and Tiburon, for all their obvious differences, were much alike in at least one aspect: both were largely unplanned communities that, like Topsy, just grew. Mill Valley, in contrast, was superbly laid out from the beginning. It was carefully designed to take full advantage of its environment, and if in Mill Valley the typical Marin County love affair with nature seems to have been raised to the level of a grand passion, the effect was quite deliberate.

Mill Valley developed on land that once was part of Rancho Corte Madera del Presidio, granted to John Reed in 1834—a grant that rambled from Corte Madera Creek to the Tiburon Peninsula and north to a marsh on the edge of Point San Quentin. To supply redwood lumber to the Presidio of San Francisco, Reed had two dams and a sawmill erected on Cascade Creek (near the center of the present town). Adjoining the Reed ranch was William Richardson's 19,000 acre Rancho Sausalito. Samuel Throckmorton became its administrator in 1855. A decade after Richardson's death, Throckmorton sold 4,000 acres of Lime Point and Sausalito, but was forced to mortgage the remaining 15,000 acres to the San Francisco Savings Union. In 1887, after Throckmorton's death, the company foreclosed. A farsighted group of San Franciscans, affiliated with the Savings Union and headed by Joseph G. Eastland, then organized the Tamalpais Land and Dairy Company. They hired a recently-arrived Dublin engineer, Michael M. O'Shaughnessy, to survey and plat the Throckmorton land, and the resulting town was dubbed Eastland.

Recognizing the importance of the railroad to the development of southern Marin, the Tamalpais Land and Dairy Company next constructed a one and three-quarter mile spur line south from Eastland to the North Pacific Coast Railroad at Almonte.

Having covered all the bases, the company threw the land open for public auction on May 30, 1890. Three thousand people gathered around an auctioneer's stand in the middle of the redwoods, and purchased lots at an average price of one thousand dollars an acre. The company's investment was vindicated to the tune of more than three hundred thousand dollars. While many of the new owners intended to develop their lots only for summer use, the presence of easy transportation also encouraged permanent settlement.

Unimpressed with the name of Eastland, the town's settlers voted later that same year to change its name to Mill Valley, after the mill erected in the 1830's by John Reed. Mill Valley it remained to those who lived there—although the postmark of Eastland hung on until 1904.

The town's next significant period of growth occurred after 1903, when the faster, more efficient electric trains replaced the steam cars. Commuting time between San Francisco and Mill Valley was so decreased (it took but nine or ten minutes to travel from the ferry landing in Sausalito to the station in Mill Valley) that the town inevitably became a commuters' haven.

But Mill Valley clings with admirable stubbornness to its quiet beginnings. It is still a small town, shaded and comparatively serene. Its streets are narrow and unobtrusive, its character that of a village where it is still possible to hear dogs barking and children calling to one another.

In a small city park just a few steps removed from the downtown center of Mill Valley is an effective reminder of the town's beginnings. *John Reed's Sawmill* on *West Blithedale Avenue*, built in 1836, was purchased and restored by the city in 1959, and has since become a State Landmark.

Another such reminder exists within the home at *205 West Blithedale Avenue*. Legend has it that a group of Mexican hunters built a small adobe shelter in what is now Blithedale Canyon sometime in 1833. The Blithedale Hotel, a popular health resort of the 1880's, used the old adobe as a cooling shed for milk, and later as a billiard room. Three walls of this adobe, each twelve by twenty-two feet, have survived; they now form the dining room walls of the house.

One of the first homes in the Mill Valley of 1890 was *The Maples*, on the hill behind *352 Miller*. It was built by Jacob Gardner, who came west in 1868 and managed Samuel Throckmorton's ranch holdings. The hipped roof and straightforward symmetry may be traceable to Gardner's Massachusetts background, although the double

The Arches, built about 1890, takes its name from the wide, arched upper-story veranda which provides a fine view of the valley

veranda is distinctly southern. Surface details suggest the style of the 1880's.

The Arches, 95 Magee Avenue, suggests a kind of individualistic house that was to become more common in the higher, craggier sections of the town. Lovell White, director of the Tamalpais Land and Dairy Company, hunted and fished in the area for years, and had this impressive, three-story hilltop home constructed about 1890. The house takes its name from the wide, arched, upper-story veranda that surrounds it and provides an awesome view of the valley below. Its predominantly late-Victorian character is climaxed with an octagonal Queen Anne Tower.

Burlwood, the three-story Tudor mansion at *565 Throckmorton Avenue,* was built in 1891 for Joseph Eastland and derived its odd name from the redwood burls used for paneling throughout the interior. Two gabled wings project forward from a broad, half-timbered facade, and the stained-glass and leaded windows heighten its English appearance.

A small variant of the main house exists in the *"Bluebird House"* on the same property; it was used as a combination schoolhouse-playhouse by the Eastland children. Their "playground" included the wooded hillside and Corte Madera Creek, which edged the property at the bottom of a long, terraced path.

Burlwood later became a private club; in the 1940's, the American Mercantile Association acquired it as a recreational resort for its employees. A bowling alley on the lower floor remains as a vestige of this particular period of Burlwood's history, although it now is a private residence again.

Michael M. O'Shaughnessy, who surveyed Mill Valley for the Tamalpais Land and Dairy Company, reserved a

This remarkable house at 15 Tamalpais Avenue was built in 1893 in the shape of a ferryboat by its owner, Alonzo Coffin

2 El Capitan is one of Architect Willis Polk's few Marin houses

lot for himself and his family at *60 Summit Avenue*. The home he built there is a lovely example of what might be called Victorian Rambler, a collection of wings and gables, porches and balconies. O'Shaughnessy went on to some fame as the engineer of San Francisco's Hetch Hetchy Reservoir in later years.

A number of lots sold at the 1890 auction which created Mill Valley were bought for summer homes by large San Francisco families. Several of the homes they built remain today along the banks of Corte Madera Creek. One of the most pleasant is *Redwood Lodge, 160 Corte Madera Avenue*.

It was built in 1891 for George E. Billings, a San Francisco shipping commissioner, who moved his family here permanently after the earthquake of 1906 (as did a number of Mill Valley's equally cautious summer residents). The redwood beams and paneling of this large, shingled house give it an air of early modern informality and simplicity—and typify houses obviously built as antidotes to the restrictions of city living.

Uncommonly compatible with its environment is the massive, redwood-shingled "cottage" at *167 Lovell Avenue*. Carefully designed to fit into its landscape with a minimum of aesthetic discord, this house, apparently built before 1895, admirably represents the use of unadorned redwood for its intrinsic beauty and durability—a trend that reached its apogee in the work of Bernard Maybeck, who also favored the varied roof forms seen here.

In an old photograph of the town, the *"Steamboat House," 15 Tamalpais Avenue*, sits on a denuded hillside like a stranded ferryboat. The illusion was no accident. Built in 1893, the house (then called "Vineyard Haven") was designed by its owner, Alonzo Coffin, and its architect, Emil Jahn, in the shape of a ferryboat, with a gallery encircling it and a rounded end presented to the view. Coffin owned a pattern shop in San Francisco that precut and milled the kind of gingerbread embellishments used by Victorian builders, and he added some of them to his own home.

One of the oddest and most delightful little railroads in California was the Mill Valley & Mount Tamalpais Scenic Railway, dubbed the "Crookedest Railroad in the World." Its slightly over eight miles of track wound in convoluted fashion up to the summit of Mount Tamalpais, and boasted no less than two hundred and fifty-six curves.

The line was constructed in 1896, despite the loudly-voiced dismay of many Mill Valley residents, who objected to this desecration of their beloved mountain. Dismay or no, the little railroad was an unqualified success and a great tourist attraction. Automobile roads and heavy fire damage had an adverse effect on the Crookedest Railroad, and in 1930 its track was torn up—to the loudly-voiced dismay of many Mill Valley residents, who objected to this desecration of their beloved mountain.

The only structure remaining from the happy days of the railroad is the *Inn* at *West Point*, originally called West Point Tavern, where the timid could fortify themselves for the ride down. At the railway's demise, the Marin Municipal Water Department purchased the old inn and leased it to a caretaker; profit was so minimal, however, that plans were made to tear it down. Various hiking clubs came to the rescue, forming the West Point Club to purchase and operate the inn, a shingled affair with massive masonry chimneys. Present facilities include seven sleeping rooms, four rustic cabins, and one honeymoon cottage.

The Outdoor Art Club, One West Blithedale Avenue, is evidence of Mill Valley's persistent interest in nature. The Club itself came into being at a public meeting on August 2, 1902. It was Mill Valley's first women's improvement association, and was born of concern over the destruction of trees and wildflowers.

Architect Harvey Klyce designed all his houses for relaxed family living and a perfect example is his own redwood shingle residence which he built in 1900 at 501 Throckmorton Ave.

225

The Club selected a site and chose architect Bernard Maybeck to design a clubhouse thoroughly in keeping with its surroundings and representative of the organization's aims and objectives. The shingled building was completed in 1905. One entire wall of the main wing is of glass panels that open out to a wide terrace. The indoor-outdoor compatibility is further emphasized by four heavy interior trusses, which project through the steeply pitched roof and are joined at right angles by four wall beams that push through the eaves.

Another notable recognition of the relationship between structure and environment can be seen at *501 Throckmorton Avenue*. The architect, Harvey Klyce, built large, comfortable houses designed for relaxed family living, with a direct utilization of the out-of-doors. One of the best examples of his work is this Throckmorton Avenue home—designed as his own residence in 1900. Redwood shingles cover the entire house, which has a massive appearance softened by the arched lines of the porches and the handsome carriage entrance that passes under the right wing. Wide, covered porches span both back and front, and "eyebrow" dormer windows break the lines of the large, sloping roof.

Much more formal in design and purpose is the *Ralston L. White Memorial Retreat, Two El Capitan Avenue*. Designed by Willis Polk, the stately house was built for the son of Lovell White around 1912. It is one of the few Marin mansions that attempted to match the splendor of Peninsula mansions of the day. As always, Polk paid great attention to the interior: this sixteen-room house includes inviting alcoves, a hand-carved mantlepiece with lion's head, and a fine, carved balustrade.

The elegant Outdoor Art Club was completed in 1905 by Bernard Maybeck and demonstrates the architect's ability to blend his buildings into natural backgrounds.
The trusses projected through the roof to meet the beams thrust through the eaves are a typical Maybeck touch

226

KENTFIELD/SAN ANSELMO/ROSS

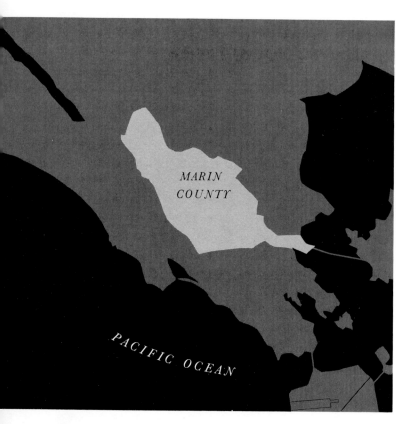

MARIN COUNTY

PACIFIC OCEAN

from which the North Pacific Coast Railroad sent a line east to San Rafael in the 1870's. Like branches from a tree, Ross and Kentfield to the south and Fairfax to the north grew in linear fashion as population funneled into the central valleys of Marin attracted by the railroad and by the efforts of such developers as San Rafael's William T. Coleman.

People came either as summer vacationers or as permanent, commuting residents; and, like the inhabitants of Mill Valley, they built their homes to comply with the demands of nature. Long before the turn of the century, the bucolic essence of the region was well-established; and by 1902, it satisfied as well as any area in southern Marin the evaluation of Charles Keeler in his *San Francisco and Thereabouts:* "A half-hour's ride on the ferry takes the suburbanite from San Francisco to his home. There he may enjoy nature, forgetting the cares of business and the stress and strain of the city, calmed . . . and enlarged in spirit."

Enlargement, of one kind or another, has continued and brought with it its own kind of stress and strain — altering sometimes beyond recognition the charm of the past. Yet the bulldozer has so far been relatively kind to these towns of the central valleys.

The area now occupied by Kentfield and Ross was once a portion of Rancho Punta de Quentin owned by Benjamin R. Buckelew, editor and publisher of *The Californian*, a newspaper of San Francisco's Gold Rush era. In 1852, Buckelew sold twenty acres of the Rancho to the State of California for the establishment of San Quentin State Prison. The rest of Rancho de Punta Quentin was purchased by importer-exporter James Ross in 1859; he established a wharf called Ross Landing and operated a fleet of boats for the transport of hay, wood, and bricks. A relic of this maritime past can be seen at *882 College Avenue, Kentfield,* a small, ramshackle building at least a century old.

Linked by the northwestward-curving Sir Francis Drake Boulevard, Kentfield, Ross, San Anselmo and Fairfax flow one into the other through narrow, wooded valleys north of Mount Tamalpais in such fashion that it is difficult to tell where one ends and another begins. Nor is the distinction particularly important; all four are as similar in character as they are in geography, each handsomely and sometimes impressively fulfilling the residential dreams of the thousands who flocked northward to escape the confines of big-city existence.

Like most of the towns in southern Marin, these were children of the railroad. San Anselmo, which developed first, was in fact for a number of years called the "Junction" for the simple reason that it developed around the point

The pressures of high living forced James Ross to sell off much of his land to early Ross pioneers. One of these was William Murray who, together with Patrick King, purchased a large section of the Ross land for purposes of farming and erected the two-story frame house at *9 Murray Lane, Larkspur,* in 1869.

The home is similar in structure and style to the Gardner house in Sausalito (also dated 1869). In both buildings, Victorian touches can be seen in the split pilasters supporting the front porch and a bargeboard edging the second-story eave line. The second story of the Murray house is said to have been added to the original five-room house in 1884; if so, the bargeboard was moved up at that time, as it is not typical of the 1880's. The simple frame house has remained in the Murray family ever since.

In the 1870's, Murray sold a section of his holdings to Albert Kent, who utilized it as a large estate, constructing the three-story home at *200 Woodland Road, Kentfield,* in 1872. Originally Victorian in style, the house was extensively remodeled along more Colonial and Classical lines in 1916 by Bliss and Faville, San Francisco architects. For well over seventy years, the great manor house (23,000 square feet of space, including basement and attic) was the center of the Kent Estate. In 1936, much of this land was subdivided into Kent Woodlands. The house and grounds served a number of social and civic functions through the years, however, most notably during the annual Grape Festival.

The massive residence called *Quisiana* (The Home of Happy People), *131 Laurel Grove Avenue* was built as a part of the Bach Estate in 1900 on the site of a house that had burned in 1880. The Bach family was provided with thirty-one rooms and 16,600 square feet of living space. The carpenters who built the huge, brooding place, a pseudo-Tudor, late Queen Anne house with "port-hole" balcony balustrades, lived in tents on the grounds until the home was finished.

The handsomely-functional, octagonal building that is now an office for the *Marin Art and Garden Center,* on *Sir Francis Drake Boulevard* across from *Lagunitas Road, Ross* was built in 1865 as a carriage house for Sunnyside, the Worn family estate on the old Ross property. The land was later sold to the Kittle family and then to its present owners. There is a superb eighty-five-year-old magnolia tree on the property.

The impressive three-story house at *34 Shady Lane, Ross* may date, in part, from 1865. However, it is usually dated 1874—a year more consonant with its size and style. This outstanding example of a Victorian villa (probably built for Clinton Jones) has a characteristic off-center tower and a very irregular floor plan. Some of the exterior details suggest work of the 1880's.

The frame house at *73 Winship, Ross,* definitely is of 1880's vintage, and may have been built as early as 1883 in its original form; it was then the residence of the owner and developer of the Barber Tract, one of the first real estate developments in Ross Valley. A domed Queen Anne tower and curious "eyed" dormers in a shingled roof that slopes down in an odd fashion to cover the front porch give the place something of a Near-Eastern appearance. In its present form, the house must date to the 1890's: the classicizing columns of the porch and modillioned cornice suggest the reappearance of Georgian details and the revival of interest in Period architecture common to the time.

Like the home at 73 Winship, the two-story redwood house at *One Garden Avenue* was built as a residence (and possibly an advertisement) by the developer of Ross Valley's Winship Park Tract. The first growth of redwoods in a grove owned by the Winship family provided the lumber for it in 1888. Very steeply-pitched roofs, extensive shingling, and the charming carved ornamentation in the angles between eaves give this remarkable house something of the aspect of a Swiss chalet—a part of the Eastlake phase of late-Victorian design. The rear portion of the house was added in the 1890's.

The octagonal Marin Art and Garden Center office in Ross was built in 1865 as a carriage house for the Worn estate, Sunnyside

The redwood shingle home at *Upper Road* and *Glenwood, Ross* reveals a use of material and environment that suggests the work of Bernard Maybeck or Harvey Klyce. This three-story home was designed by architect John White and constructed in 1896. It sports steeply-pitched roofs and an unusually tall brick chimney.

Another design of the popular White exists up the hill and to the left on *Upper Road*. Built in 1900, it was purported to be one of the first examples of the modular system in Marin (the modular system employs the use of some part of a structure or measurement of a person to determine the developed dimensions of the entire building). This long, three-story home is enhanced by half-timbering and by the Gothic lines of the dormers and porch. Its vast bay window and long balconies relate the house to its setting throughout.

One of Bernard Maybeck's many successful Marin homes is on *Winding Way* near *Canyon Road, Ross.* Built in the "West Coast Shingle Style" (in which Maybeck did some

This half-timbered house on Upper Road in Ross was built in 1900 and is believed to be one of Marin's first modular homes

of his best work), the redwood house was designed and built in 1905 for J. H. Hopps. Called *Grey Oaks,* it lives up to its pastoral image most successfully, blending into the landscape until it is nearly hidden from view—a camouflage only partially undermined by the sharp, white trim that gives the house a distinctive charm.

An effective use of half-timbering and other late Medieval details can be seen in *St. Anselm's Catholic Church, Shady Lane* and *Bolinas Avenue.* The frame and stucco church, designed by Frank Shay, was completed in 1907. One of its most remarkable features is the octagonal-roofed corner tower to one side of the entrance—a device reminiscent of the Marin Art and Garden Center building.

The San Francisco Theological Seminary, Bolinas Avenue and *Richmond,* broods over San Anselmo like a turreted relic from some misty Medieval past. Designed on a high knoll by Wright and Sanders, and completed in 1897, this seminary has been a graduate theological school for the Presbyterian Church for more than seventy years. One of the first buildings completed was *Montgomery Hall* (1892). Of native California stone, Montgomery Hall is Richardson triumphant, with ideas appropriated from different Medieval eras—particularly in the looming, windowed tower with battlements. This great tower was damaged somewhat by the earthquake of 1906, when several stones were shaken loose and plunged through the roof of the building.

The older buildings on the grounds have recently been meticulously restored, and the entire complex was greatly enhanced by the landscaping efforts of William Penn Mott, then Park Supervisor for the city of Oakland, who used characteristic plantings of the Holy Land.

The Carrigan House, 96 Park Drive, San Anselmo, was built in 1893 as a redwood-and-stucco adaptation of a Georgian country house. With only six fireplaces for heating, the huge place gained a reputation as the coldest house in Marin County. Andrew Carrigan and his wife moved out after only two years, and except for a short occupation by Andrew's brother, none of the Carrigans lived in the house again. Since 1963—its heating problems solved—the house has been carefully restored.

The three-story redwood-shingled home at *14 Entrata, San Anselmo,* was designed by Bernard Maybeck and built by his brother-in-law Mark White in 1905 and 1906. This design is among the best of Maybeck's Marin efforts. Both reflective of and complementary to its environment, the home is a masterwork of integral planning and construction.

The home at *15 Prospect, San Anselmo,* was designed by Julia Morgan in 1908. The low-pitched roofline belies the two stories it mantles; wood siding and textured brick steps leading to the front entrance give a rustic air, yet maintain the home's functional simplicity.

These Maybeck and Morgan houses, both comparatively modest residences of the twentieth-century's first decade, combined inventive variations on modern ideas with much of the cheerful picturesqueness of the preceding century—but with great practical success. They provide an unequalled insight into the evolution of the twentieth-century California house, particularly the Marin version.

The so-called *"Igloo House," 100 Alder Avenue,* was designed by San Francisco architect Maxwell Bugbee for George Breck in 1910. Simple yet elegant in line, the house has shingle siding of cedar, not redwood—something of a departure in itself—and the structure stands on a solid stone foundation. The Brecks once traveled to Alaska and brought back some interior innovations inspired by Eskimo life. Among these were a "step-down" conversation pit and a fireplace constructed in the center of the living room—features common today but revolutionary sixty years ago.

The house on Fairfax's *Smith Ranch, Sir Francis Drake Boulevard,* at *Glen Road,* was built in the 1890's by John Roy, whose holdings once extended from the middle of present-day Fairfax to the site of Woodacre. This cheerful, graceful, and internally consistent two-story home is of simple frame construction; the style is a late Eastlake fantasy in combination with Queen Anne, most markedly seen in the corner tower at the front. The later-Victorian patterned and painted shingles of the gable ends provide a nice contrast to the more neutral early-modern shingles seen in the homes of southern Marin's central valleys.

Grey Oaks, in Ross, is one of Maybeck's masterpieces in stone and redwood shingle

The San Francisco Theological Seminary in San Anselmo

Octagonal bell tower of St. Anselm's Church, (left) and 96 Park Drive, San Anselmo, once known as Marin's coldest house

SAN RAFAEL

MARIN COUNTY

PACIFIC OCEAN

however, was the presence of the Russian Orthodox community at Fort Ross.

The timing was not good. Five years after the mission's founding, Mexico won independence from Spain, and eleven years later the revolutionary government junked the mission system entirely with the Secularization Act of 1833. In 1844, some 22,000 acres of Mission San Rafael's land were granted by the Mexican government to Timothy Murphy, a long-time foreign resident of California.

Murphy was appointed *alcalde* of the tiny village that had clustered around the mission buildings, and after the American acquisition of California in 1846, the settlement took on the outlines of a town. Regrettably, the old mission buildings provided construction materials for home-hungry Yankees, and most were completely dismantled by the 1850's—by which time San Rafael had become a bustling little farming community with a short stage road to a steamboat and ferry connection at San Quentin Point.

The railroad did the rest. In March of 1870, the stage connection with San Quentin Point was replaced by the little San Rafael and San Quentin Railroad; when it hooked up with the more progressive North Pacific Coast Railroad in 1874 it helped make San Rafael the transportation, and later the commercial, center of Marin County.

Possibly the most historically important house in San Rafael stands at *1130 Mission Street.* Originally a simple frame house, built perhaps about 1852, it was purchased as a summer home in 1866 by William T. Coleman, a leading light of San Francisco's Vigilance Committee of 1856. It was neither the first nor the last of Coleman's real estate investments in the San Rafael area.

His "Coleman Tract" was one of the county's first subdivisions. Coleman hired William Hammond Hall, a landscape engineer and first superintendent of Golden Gate Park, to divide the tract into acre and half-acre lots, and to design a street system that followed the contours of the

If the railroad was the father of Marin County, then San Rafael must be considered its mother. Here the seeds of growth planted by the developing railroad found their first and most significant fruition, and the town has since been the institutional and civic hub around which the communities of the entire county have revolved.

The genesis of the town took place in 1817, when Franciscan Father Vicente Sarria founded Mission San Rafael Arcangel. The immediate inspiration for the establishment of the mission was the fact that this little valley north of San Francisco provided a climate suitable for the preservation of the health of the Father's Indian wards, who were not doing too well in the fog-ridden environs of San Francisco. No minor consideration behind the mission,

1130 Mission is probably San Rafael's most important house

land. A similar Coleman-owned development was the Baltimore Tract near Larkspur; other investments included the San Rafael Hotel, built in 1885, and the dam which formed Lake Lagunitas, source of San Rafael's water supply.

Coleman refurbished this house considerably and added a conservatory and some ten thousand trees in a twelve-acre nursery on the property. Edward McCarthy, who served several terms as Mayor of San Rafael, later lived in this large, comfortable house. Today it is divided into apartments.

The former Boyd house, *Maple Lawn, 1312 Mission Street,* was also probably built in the 1850's. Ira Cook, and his nephew Seth Cook, purchased and enlarged it in 1871. The house was inherited by Ira's daughter, Louise Cook Arner, whose husband, John Franklin Boyd, so improved the residence that it came to be known as the Boyd House. In the 1890's the Boyd Gardens gained a statewide reputation for the cultivation of nearly every known kind of fruit tree.

The two-story frame house was later modified by Boyd's daughter, Louise, a famous explorer. The lower floor still has the large porches so essential to the Victorian version of the good life, but only the interior truly suggests any of the building's original Victorian character. It is now owned by the San Rafael Elks Club.

Ira Cook added a wooden guest house to his property in 1879; today, it houses the *Marin County Historical Society Museum* at *1125 B Street,* where it was moved in 1924. This intricate charmer is an outstanding example of the self-conscious ornamentation so common to the Victorian period. Bargeboards, shaped to repeat the arched curve of second-story windows, are attached to the undersides of the gables. The vertical siding on the second floor is repeated at the base of the slanted bay window to contrast with the horizontal siding used on the first floor. Slender,

square wooden pillars support the veranda roof, just below a row of toothlike shingles. In 1907, the Boyds presented the house and a portion of their property to San Rafael as a park in memory of two young sons.

St. Paul's Episcopal Church, 1123 Court Street, has retained its appeal in spite of changes through the years. Originally built in 1869, at the southwest corner of Fourth and E Streets, as a spired, shingled Victorian Gothic church, it was enlarged considerably in 1894 and finally moved to its present location in 1923—with spire removed and shingles replaced by stucco. The interior, of finished California redwood and oiled and varnished Oregon white pine, has remained intact.

Once St. Paul's parish hall, the *Louise Boyd Natural Science Museum, 76 Albert Park Lane,* was moved with the

Maple Lawn was built in the 1850's but later greatly modified

church in 1923, then brought to its present location by the San Rafael Optimist Club in 1954. It retains many gentle Gothic features, including the bargeboard and lancet windows shaded by a hooded gable. The bargeboard here is not unlike that on the Ira Cook guest house; perhaps both structures were by the same builder.

In 1873, a German rice planter, William Lichtenberg, was appointed consul in San Francisco by his government. Like a number of such officials, Lichtenberg stayed in California. His home at *201 Locust Avenue,* built in 1875 and enlarged in 1886, is a rather special example of what might be called German Victorian Gothic—particularly with the great Queen Anne medievalizing romantic tower added in 1886 by William Curlett, an architect renowned for such details. The interior has a two-story hall lined with redwood and a stained-glass window lighting the stairway.

The three-story *M. J. O'Connor mansion* on *Fifth Ave.* and *Cottage Ave.* was a show place of early San Rafael. It was

This example of the Victorian era's love of ornamentation was built in 1879 and now houses Marin County's Historical Museum

A. W. Foster gave this home to San Rafael Military Academy

could. The San Rafael Board of Supervisors, recognizing the civic demands of the rapidly growing town, had the handsome *San Rafael Court House* (now the County Court House) erected in 1872, on *Fourth Street*. The building was designed with a fine Corinthian portico on a modified Italianate-detailed, Baroque-shaped structure of brick, stone and stucco. A non-traditional cupola that gave light to the broad interior staircase was later removed. The building is now scheduled for destruction.

On Upper Fourth Street, the only facade not yet completely modernized is that of the *Burchard Hotel* at *1330 Fourth Street*, with its Mansard roof and tall narrow windows decorated with triangular and rounded pediments on consoles. In the middle of the next block, at *1222 Fourth Street*, was the Central Hotel, now a store. If one walks through the original side entrance, however, the interior echoes the days of 1859, when the hotel was built by convict labor and sported an Italianate facade.

Across the street, the structure at *1225 Fourth Street* has retained its false front with corniced windows and bracketed cornice, although the pillared porch overhanging the sidewalk is gone. On its left, at *1221 Fourth*

built (1870) in a very formal Italianate quasi-villa form; some exterior trim has since been removed, but brackets and a few other details suggest the original. In 1892, A. W. Foster purchased the house and presented it to the Mount Tamalpais Military Academy (now known as the San Rafael Military Academy) and the O'Connor mansion is called Foster Hall.

Timothy Murphy's old adobe served as San Rafael's first court house. When it began to disintegrate in the 1860's, early residents calmly pilfered what lumber they

The handsome San Rafael Court House was built in 1872, later became the County Court House but is now slated for demolition

Street, stands the store—now stripped of all decoration—once owned by New Orleans merchant Camille Grosjean, who opened the county's first general store in 1872.

Gordon's Opera House, at *1333 Fourth Street*, was built in the early 1880's by Lipton Gordon for the presentation of vaudeville delights and community entertainments. In 1885 when Dr. Tagliaferro, San Quentin's first physician, died, he rested in state for three days in this elaborately-ornamented auditorium. And on June 5, 1891, San Rafael High School held its first graduation program here. Today it houses apartments over a downstairs store. The old fireplaces have been walled up, but the stairs still rise in wide grandeur.

The large wood Victorian house at *1408 Mission Street* was built in 1879 on property that once belonged to James Walker, president of the North Pacific Coast Railroad. In 1907, the house and land were sold to Robert Dollar—whose monogram was once seen on steamers all over the world. Dollar named the place *Falkirk* (for his place of birth in Scotland) and lived there until his death in 1932. Falkirk blossoms with gables, dormers, slanted and rounded bays and porches.

Another fine late-Victorian frame house, designed for John Sheehy by the San Francisco architect, Thomas J. Welsh, and built within the old Coleman Tract in 1885, stands today in weather-beaten dignity at *820 Mission Street*. A pillared porch surrounds the house, although the roof's balustrade is now gone. Bays are integral to the design, and the modified-Italianate ornamental detail can be compared with many similar wood houses of the 1880's in San Francisco.

One of the most impressive structures in all Marin County is the *Dominican Convent, 1520 Grand Avenue*. This four-story, towered and gabled Victorian institution was built in 1889 as a new home for the Dominican Sisters, formerly of Monterey and Benicia. The convent was constructed entirely of redwood, on a ten-acre plot bought from W. T. Coleman; it is a nearly perfect example of that Victorian tendency to make wood do the work of stone—and the later-Victorian use of Italianate formality, with hints of the baroque and anticipation of classicism.

Meadowlands on *Palm Avenue* and *Olive Street* was built in the early 1880's for Michael H. de Young, co-founder of the *San Francisco Chronicle,* and served as the family's summer home for over thirty years. In 1918, the Dominican Sisters purchased it for a student residence hall, and it is so used today. The brown-shingled building is of the Downing cottage type of the mid-nineteenth century. A great Dutch door opens into the entrance hall with its high-mantled stone fireplace. The hall is low-ceilinged, paneled with dark wood and has a dignity which is heightened by its graceful flight of wide stairs.

William Babcock, a shipping man and owner of the E. K.

Fourth Street and the Burchard Hotel as they looked about 1905

Wood Lumber Company in San Rafael, built a residence in the Magnolia Valley portion of Coleman's Tract in 1887. The Dominican Convent now uses this as a kindergarten and college residence. This multi-gabled building has many Georgian (Colonial Revival) accents: in the Palladian windows under the peak of the gables, the entrance porch columns supporting a frieze of carved garlands, and the small cornice modillions.

After Babcock died, his widow moved to *16 Culloden Park*. This house, which she named *Villa Giulia*, was built from designs of Maxwell Bugbee in the Coleman Tract in 1906–1907. The house illustrates a transition from the nineteenth-century use of materials to assume unnatural shapes and textures to a more natural acceptance of their own qualities. The upper parts of the house are wood Queen Anne with details of Colonial Revival, while the heavy stone foundation, with arched entrance, still shows the influence of Richardson.

Arthur Brown, Jr. designed the formal "Mediterranean" house at *55 Montecito* in 1910 for Truxton Beale, son of Edward Fitzgerald Beale, the Navy Lieutenant who played a large part in the American conquest of California. Brown, who designed numerous large homes and public buildings elsewhere in California, here displayed that facility for Period elegance which brought him much fame.

Another Period structure, the *San Rafael Improvement*

The Burchard Hotel on Fourth Street as it appears today shorn of some of its original exterior decoration but otherwise in good shape

236

Club, Fifth Avenue at *H Street,* was originally an exhibit at the Panama Pacific International Exposition of 1915. It was built inside another building—and thus had no roof when it was floated across the Bay on a barge to take its place in the ambitious Santa Venetia development just north of San Rafael. The planners of this community hoped to make it a second Venice of the West similar to the relatively successful enterprise of the day in Southern California. Streets were laid out and canals dredged, but the idea never quite caught on. Almost all that remains of the project are a few foundations standing next to mud-filled canals—and the Improvement Club, now in San Rafael and supplied with a roof.

The massive brown shingled house at *121 Knight Drive,* with its early-modern grouped windows and earth-hugging quality, was built in 1914 as the summer residence of Erskine Baker McNear, son of John A. McNear, who had purchased 2500 acres of what is now known as McNear's Point in 1868, one of the few great estates in Marin.

In 1882, John McNear leased one of his bayshore coves to a group of Chinese fleeing persecution in San Francisco. One of the two known shrimp beds in San Francisco Bay was just off their cove, and the settlement soon became the thriving fishing village of *China Camp.* Unhappily, the Chinese used nets to catch shrimp, and when the State seeded San Pablo Bay with bass in 1910, net fishing was banned. The camp floundered in desultory fashion for the next fifty years; today, it faces extinction at the hands of developers.

1408 Mission (top) was the home of Captain Robert Dollar. Meadowlands (below) is a Downing cottage of the 1880's

The magnificent old Dominican Convent was constructed of redwood and finished in 1889

237

MARIN: NORTH AND WEST

MARIN COUNTY

PACIFIC OCEAN

The country which comprises the northern and western portions of Marin County is a ragged rectangle of land bounded by rough lines drawn from the flatlands of Novato northwest over a jumble of hills to the ranchlands and dairy farms of Tomales, southwest across the fingerlike spread of Tomales Bay to the cliffs and salt marshes of Point Reyes National Seashore, southeast down the narrow valley of Bolinas Ridge to the resorts of Stinson Beach, and back across the mountains northeast to Novato.

With the exception of Novato, a bustling, eminently twentieth-century city periodically rattled by thunderous jets from nearby Hamilton Air Force Base, the touch of man on Marin North and West has been comparatively

light. Not until 1776, in fact, were the almost anonymous Indian tribes of northern Marin disturbed from their presumably idyllic existence. In that year, two young Spanish soldiers were sent across the bay from Yerba Buena on an exploring foray.

They came upon an Indian village called Olompali, composed principally of scattered wickiups. The representatives of Spain, in a friendly gesture which antedated the activities of the Peace Corps by nearly 200 years, taught the Indians the rudiments of brick-making. It was the beginning of an uncommonly pacific history of Spanish-Mexican and Indian relations. It culminated eventually in the awarding of probably the only land grant ever received by a California Indian—the Olompali Rancho given to Camilo Ynitia in 1843.

The essentially unhurried atmosphere of Marin North and West survived the coming of the Americans. Ranching and truck farming became the principal industries in the valleys of the central mountains; these were supplemented along the coastal areas by fishing and clamming. Until the narrow gauge North Pacific Coast Railroad crossed the mountains to Tomales in 1875, dairy and truck products of the northern country were shipped by sea from little ports in and around Bodega and Tomales Bay.

The railroad cut into coastal shipping, but the North Pacific Coast had troubles of its own, most of them caused by the uncertain roadbeds. One locomotive of the early days ended its journey wheels up in Tomales Bay, and at least one southern Marin newspaper grimly advised passengers to take along plenty of food, for the trip between Sausalito and Tomales had a tendency to be longer than advertised.

The narrow gauge ended its career in 1933. Unlike its effect on southern Marin, the changes it brought to Marin North and West were hardly revolutionary. The towns remained small—most of them serving as shipping and shopping centers for the ranches, dairies, and truck farms which surrounded them.

Olema, for a time, functioned as a center for sportsmen, and possessed nine saloons, a hotel, and a racetrack. Across the hill in Tocalema, the Tocalema Inn served as a prohibition-years hangout for various San Francisco political leaders. Other sports practiced in the regions in and around Tomales Bay included hunting, fishing and boating (all of which continue popular); Inverness near the southern tip of the Bay has always been an accepted spot for summer residency. These are exceptions, however, for the general tone of life in this section of Marin has been dictated by the seasonal demands of agriculture.

Development, then, has so far been nominal and leisurely, and while it is possible to predict with reluctant certainty a more complicated future, the present of Marin

north and west is not too far removed from the simplicities of a casual past.

On *U. S. 101* just south of Novato stands *St. Vincent's School,* the oldest school in Marin County. It was founded around 1853 by St. Vincent's Seminary to serve as an orphanage for homeless Catholic boys. The site was donated by Timothy Murphy, who owned most of the land originally held by Mission San Rafael. Most of the buildings are in a generic "Spanish style" (stucco with tile roofs). The local church's architecture is a more elegant twentieth-century variant of later-eighteenth-century Mexican design related to the Churrigueresque revival of B. G. Goodhue at the San Diego Fair of 1915.

The *Dixie School* stands on the west side of Highway 101 not far from St. Vincent's. Its site was donated in 1862 by James Miller, owner of Las Gallinas ranch, who wanted

St. Vincent's Church is an elegant variant of 18th Century design.

a school for his son to attend. This building served as the principal school of the district until its "retirement," when it became the district's administrative offices. It is now used as a maintenance center for the district—having remained in constant use for more than 100 years. Its solid frame-and-siding construction and modest Italianate style has remained essentially unaltered since it was built.

The *Reichart Villa, 716 Lamont Avenue,* is one of Novato's oldest homes. A wood country house with veranda, it was built sometime in the 1870's by Theodore Reichart, a San Francisco businessman who commuted to his Marin home via the old San Francisco and North Pacific Railway. Reichart once served as Surveyor General for the State of California. A later owner, Lord Pounding, remittance man and gentleman farmer, added the stable which combined plain Italianate with a scrolled pseudo-barge board in the roofs' gable end and a carved horse's head over its entrance.

A two-story Victorian frame home which stands on the Rancho Pacheco, *5495 Redwood Highway,* was built in 1881. The land itself has an older history. It was given to Ignacio Pacheco, Mexican soldier and San Rafael's first *alcalde,* by Mexican Governor Juan Bautista Alvarado in 1838—a grant of some 6660 acres. Pacheco had five sons and one daughter, among whom the land was divided at the time of the old soldier's death. Gumesindo Pacheco, one of the sons, built the house at Rancho Pacheco; and it has remained in the Pacheco family ever since.

The *DeLong house, 50 Rica Vista,* Novato, stands on the remainder of the Novato grant. In 1839, Governor Alvarado awarded 8870 acres of land to Fernando Feliz. The holdings changed hands a number of times, and were reduced in size, between 1839 and 1856; then they were acquired by Francis DeLong and Joseph B. Sweetser for a sale price of $35,000. DeLong and Sweetser developed the land with great efficiency, planting orchards and vineyards and raising cattle and horses. DeLong bought out Sweetser's holdings in 1879 and so expanded his operations that by the time of his death in 1886 the estate had an estimated worth of one million dollars.

DeLong's son, Frank, continued to operate the ranch. In 1888 he opened a subdivision which in time became the town of Novato. DeLong entered politics, and was elected

The DeLong House, 50 Rica Vista, in Novato stands on the remains of an old Mexican land grant and was built around 1870

to the State Senate. By 1893 he transferred the remainder of the ranch to the Novato Land Company.

Robert Hatch and Robert H. Trumbull rebuilt the property and substantially remodeled the house, into what might best be called Victorian and Colonial Revival. A most imposing feature is the full-front balustraded porch, complete with second-story balustraded balcony. Dormers in the roof add to the Georgian effect. Strip-corniced windows suggest the period when the house was originally built—1870. The older kitchen wing was a wood addition (1850) to Fernando Feliz' adobe (1838).

The sprawling 26-room *Burdell mansion* on *Highway 101* three miles north of Novato preserves within its walls portions of the original adobe built by the Olompali Indian village in 1776, after they had learned the brick-making trade from the two Spanish soldiers. The land on which the house stands has its own place in Marin's history. It was part of the Mexican land grant given to Camilo Ynitia in 1843; beneath its spreading oaks was fought the only "battle" of the Bear Flag Rebellion of 1846—a meaningless skirmish between the men of Lieutenant Henry L. Ford and a group of *Californios* which resulted in the death of one *Californio* and the wounding of several others.

Ynitia's land grant was given approval by the United States Land Commission in 1852, but the old Indian preferred the solid reality of gold coin and sold most of his ranch to James Black for $5200. Ynitia buried the gold in the nearby hills and refused to tell its location, which so infuriated his brother that he murdered Ynitia—to no purpose, it might be added, since nobody has ever been able to find the treasure.

James Black, a Scotsman who came to California in the late 1830's, had received a grant of land in 1835; by the time he added Camilo Ynitia's land to his own, he had become one of Marin County's richest men. He gave most of Rancho Olompali to his daughter, Mary, in 1863 when she married Dr. Galen Burdell. The property then became known as Rancho Burdell. The couple built their home here shortly after receiving the land and created Marin's first planned gardens on the property, with many of the trees and plants imported from the Orient.

The house was substantially rebuilt around World War I, incorporating within its walls the remains of the old adobe. It remained in the Burdell family until 1950, when it was sold to the University of San Francisco for use as a retreat. In 1964, USF sold the house and property to a group of San Francisco and Marin investors.

Nicasio's *Church of Our Lady of Loretto* has served Catholic residents since its construction in 1867. Nearly fifty years ago a tremendous windstorm blew the church off its foundations. When the storm was over the wood building was simply picked up and put back on its foundation, where its elegantly simple lines and superb preservation through the years have made the old church a favorite of weekend sightseers and Sunday painters.

The *Nicasio School* on *Petaluma Road* is one of Marin County's oldest school buildings, although no longer so used. Built in 1871, the little wooden school (now painted red and white) is easily one of the most charming examples of the Victorian architectural personality, marked especially by bracketed cornices, strip-corniced windows, and an engaging bell cupola on the roof. It is beautifully preserved as a weekend retreat by its present owner and has become an official historical landmark.

The stained and weather-beaten *Marshall Hotel, State Route 1*, Marshall, has served as a resort hotel ever since its construction in 1875. The present building, however, is only the half of the original structure which survived the earthquake of 1906. When the shaking ended that April morning, the hotel was floating in Tomales Bay. The owners had to cut the building in two to salvage even part of it and placed the surviving half on a new foun-

Rancho Pacheco, seen here front and rear, was built in 1881

241

dation, where it has remained—presenting its agreeable late-Victorian facade to the passing motorist.

Our Lady of the Assumption Church, State Route 1, Tomales, was built in 1860 and embellished with a number of Gothic features as interpreted by local carpenters, the most obvious of which are the lancet-arched windows, the pier buttresses on each side and the crenelated spire. The church has been uncommonly well-preserved through the years, as has been the rectory next door. Built somewhat later (probably in the 1870's), the rectory combines various decorative details and structural features in typically Victorian fashion.

Situated on a cliff some 296 feet above the restless sea is *Point Reyes Lighthouse,* on the westernmost point of Point Reyes National Seashore. The sixteen-sided iron light tower was built in 1870, and the lens—like that for many other such lighthouses—was imported from France. The light is powerful enough to be seen twenty-four miles at sea; during days and nights of fog, it is augmented by a massive fog horn embedded in a cliff notch one hundred feet below the light.

The lighthouse is under the supervision of the United States Coast Guard and is open to the public daily from 1:00 to 3:00 P.M. and on Sundays and holidays from 1:00 to 4:00 P.M. Branch roads lead to the historical marker on the spot where Sir Francis Drake landed in the summer of 1579; his chaplain here conducted the first Anglican services in America. The Point Reyes shore reminded Drake of the Dover Cliffs, and he called the area Nova Albion.

Point Reyes National Seashore was created in 1962—an irregular triangle of land linked to the mainland by a comparatively thin strip between the southern end of Tomales Bay and the northern end of Bolinas Lagoon. This land connection is along the line of the San Andreas fault, and the entire land mass of the National Seashore is consequently slipping northward but at a gratifyingly slow pace. A large portion of the triangle has been preserved for public use, and some twenty-six thousand acres are maintained under private ownership as a pastoral zone. It is a cool and windswept expanse of land—one of the few great open areas left in the San Francisco Bay Area.

The *Chamot House,* overlooking Tomales Bay in Inverness, stands as the last reminder of Auguste F. Chamot, who came to San Francisco and found love; went to Peking and found fame; and came to Inverness to find peace.

In 1895, Chamot married Annie McCarthy, the daughter of a prominent San Francisco real estate man. The Chamots, an adventurous couple, then went to Peking and opened a hotel. During the Boxer Rebellion of 1900, the Chamots saw to it that foreign residents, held more-or-less prisoner in the British legation, were kept supplied with food for seventy-eight days. The grateful governments of the captives awarded the Chamots various benefits, including the sum of $450,000 in gold.

In 1903 Auguste and Annie returned to California, had the massive three-storied home built on the hill in Inverness, and spent the next three years living in a lavish style that older residents of the town still recall in tones of awe. The house itself was impressive, with its tall grouped windows (an early modern feature) and heavy hipped roof. To this Chamot added his oriental treasures and an outdoor menagerie that included such domestic pets as a python and a panther. Chamot became something of a local character himself, given to such antics as attempting to sail his boat on Tomales Bay after drinking too much champagne.

It all ended suddenly on the morning of April 18, 1906, when the house was shaken into a shattered ruin. Chamot took what was left of his oriental treasures to New York for sale; he returned in 1907 with just enough money to rebuild the Inverness house, which he finally sold to Julia Hamilton Shafter in 1909. In 1908 Annie had divorced him, and in September of 1909 Chamot died—all but penniless.

Miss Shafter never lived in the big house after she purchased it, and it stood vacant for nearly forty years—fulfilling the universal need of children as the local haunted house. It has since been purchased, restored and refurbished for use as a summer and vacation home.

The Marshall Hotel was thrown into Tomales Bay by the '06 quak

Woodside, on the Stewart ranch at Olema, was built in 1864

The Oaks, in Olema, is a California manor house which stands in the serene setting of a meadow flanked by great trees, with a magnificent tree-lined entrance drive. The two-storied wood structure was built for Judge James M. Shafter in 1869 on land that was but a small part of the total eighty thousand acres of California land which the judge and his brother Oscar then owned. The judge was a successful San Francisco lawyer, an intimate of such figures as Leland Stanford, and reputedly drove the best horses in California. With a central hall plan, the house is an oasis

of cool serenity on hot summer afternoons. A pillared veranda surrounds two sides; a geometric interlaced balustrade above with a bracketed cornice at the roof are the few "style" touches on this fine old wood house.

Woodside, on the *Boyd Stewart ranch,* Olema, was built in 1864 by an Ohio farmer, Horatio Olds, who came to California with his family in the early 1850's. In 1856 he purchased 4400 acres of land near the southern tip of Tomales Bay from Don Rafael Garcia, and several years later contracted with two Nova Scotian carpenters for the construction of the two-story wood farmhouse. In 1870, Olds moved his family to Southern California, leaving his mother buried beneath a grove of eucalyptus trees—still standing—planted in her memory by Horatio's father.

The house changed hands several times between 1870 and 1923, when it and the ranch were taken over by Boyd Stewart. The Victorian house, marked by such vaguely Gothic features as the split pilasters supporting the front porch and the Italianate "eared" frames around windows, has been kept in good repair through the years.

What may well be the oldest home in northwest Marin County is the *Briones house,* off the *Olema-Bolinas Road* in Bolinas. In 1846 Gregorio Briones received the 8900-acre Baulines grant, which comprised all of present-day Bolinas. The first home on the property was a simple

The Oaks, in Olema, a California manor house was built in 1869 by Judge James M. Shafter, a wealthy lawyer and land baron

Our Lady of the Assumption Church in Tomales is remarkably well-preserved for a wooden structure put up in 1860

adobe dwelling which has long since disintegrated. In the late 1840's the family added the present structure, in the ranch style common to the Mexican period. The two-story redwood beam-and-board structure was built with Indian labor, and its original form included a second-story balcony, since removed. The old house, only slightly revised and renovated, has served as a home for owners of the property regularly since its construction.

Like the Briones house, two other Bolinas structures are illustrative of their time. The first of these is *Mary Magdalena Catholic Church, Olema-Bolinas Road.* Overlooking Bolinas' "old town" and the lagoon, the tidy little wood church with its hood-molded door and windows and bell cupola was built in 1877, solely from parish donations—although Gregory Briones had long before given land for the church and cemetery. Sunday Mass has been held in this building regularly since its construction.

Calvary Presbyterian Church, Brighton Avenue, Bolinas, was also built in 1877, on the property of William P. Pepper. In 1898, Pepper had the simple wood church, with large bell tower, moved from his property to its present location—picking the structure up whole and dollying it a mile down the rough country road and up and over Phinney's Hill. Both churches are modest, country variants of Victorian Gothic with a few other touches.

Near the sand, sun and surf which is such a delight to those who spend their weekends at Stinson Beach stands a home which is a quiet reminder that the sea is not always kind: the *Easkoot house* on *State Route 1.*

In 1876 Captain Alfred Derby Easkoot piloted his lumber schooner out the northern channel of the Golden Gate and began his routine run up the coast. The schooner went aground on partially-hidden Duxbury Reef—a sharp, rocky barrier that proceeded to break the captain's ship to pieces. It eventually washed ashore against the sandspit known today as Seadrift.

Captain Easkoot salvaged the ship's timbers (as well as her stairway), picked out a likely spot back from the beach against a protective knoll, and began building himself a two-story house.

This spot became known as Easkoot Beach (later changed to Stinson Beach), and the former sea captain entered the dairy business and served as the first Marin County Surveyor. The house has remained in much the same condition as it was when Captain Easkoot built it, aside from a pedimented porch and a marble fireplace, the latter severely cracked by the earthquake of 1906.

Marin North and West is still a country that possesses quality of landscape—variety, expanse, and that sense of timelessness all but lost in the rest of the country. Here the wind and the sea and the seasons carry on the dictates of unhampered nature. It is a country that provides insight into a past that may have had the qualities of an Eden.

Calvary Presbyterian Church in Bolinas has been use since 1877

APPENDIX

Presented here are approximately 2,000 buildings which add to the total impact of the West Bay's historic architecture.

SAN FRANCISCO

Abbey Street

23–27 and 37
(1875)
(1883)
In a cloistered location behind Mission Dolores, these neat pristine cottages represent simplified flat-front Italianate architecture.

Alta Street

25
(c. 1870)
This early Italianate house has a first floor modernization, which demonstrates how such a remodeling can affect the basic proportions of a house.

29 and 33
(c. 1880)
These residences, framing no. 31, once echoed their neighbor's architectural styling, although both are smaller in scale. Like 25, they have been extensively remodeled.

Alvarado Street

25–29
(c. 1892)
Records indicate an earlier well here as well as grazing horses and, later, an "Italian Ball Court." Today the gabled, matchboard farmhouse reminiscent of the 1870's remains quite unchanged.

28
(c. 1870)
Unadorned except for its hood molds and cornice, this Italianate cottage is a pure expression.

72–72A
(1874)
Perky pediments added over windows and door are features of this Italianate flat-front cottage. It is related in style to 28 although verticality is emphasized here.

443
(c. 1897)
A rounded shingle pattern in the gable which has leafy filigree in its apex (matching the frieze below) is distinctive here.

449
(c. 1898)
This Eastlake home's facade includes a lively mixture: floral chains, leafy filigrees, spindles, and diamond shingled pediment topped by a cartouche.

820
(c. 1902)
A standout among similar homes that are now modernized, this well-cared-for house has spindles, hanging finials, and angular columns at its entrance.

832
(c. 1898)
Another bright addition to the block, this delicate cottage has ornate bargeboard (ending in ball finials) outlining the roof.

869–9½, 873 and 877
(1898–99)
Heavy, ornate bargeboards overhang the waffle pediments on these three very similar cottages of Eastlake persuasion.

917
(c. 1906)
A free introduction of classical features is seen here. The lions' heads on the brackets of the portico and at the corners of the frieze are certainly not traditional.

921
(c. 1898)
Once part of a row of four homes, this house preserves its original details while the others have been altered. Its gable end is waffle-patterned with a sunburst in the apex, and heavy, studded bargeboard.

Arguello Boulevard

166
(c. 1903)
A steeply pitched gabled roof is the most striking element of this shingle house, designed by Neusen-Neusen.

182–84 186–88
(c. 1895)
The corner towers of these Queen Anne mirror twins face each other. The attractiveness of the buildings is enhanced by the fact that they are painted contrasting colors.

215–17
(c. 1897)
Fine Colonial Revival details are displayed on this shingle two-family residence.

Army Street

3623
(1889)
3627
(1886)
3635
(1889)
These Stick Style cottages stand out among the newer stucco buildings of this block. The house at 3635 is more ornate, with fishscale shingled semi-Mansard roof.

3728
(1902)
First Church of God and rectory were built for the German Methodist Church (using the old fellowship hall, built in 1860 as a nucleus). This wood Gothic structure houses its original German organ (imported 1902). The adjacent rectory is a shingle house unadorned except for the heavy hood-mold portico on elaborate brackets.

3754
(1888)
This pure Stick Style home with semi-Mansard roof presents a vivid contrast to its adjacent twin.

3755
(c. 1904)
This house is an example of the row homes of the turn-of-the-century. The gable contains checker-board apex, shiplap shingles and an awning-shaped base of diamond shingles.

3826–28 and 3840
(1887)
Two Stick Style homes with Eastlake embellishments were once part of a row of at least five. But the others have now had asbestos and aluminum siding added. The bay pediment and semi-Mansard roof have been removed from 3826–28.

3839, 3845, 3859, 3863 and 3867
(1888–89)
A fascinating aspect of these Stick Style row cottages is the porticos' hood molds which become part of the bays, which are topped by pediments in front of semi-Mansard roofs. Most outstanding are the friezes of jigsaw shamrocks and flowers.

3943
(c. 1897)
Built in basic Stick Style, this cottage has the spindles of Eastlake and false front of Italianate.

3975–77
(c. 1896)
This is an ornate example of Stick Style. The garage and stucco base are incompatible, but the scrolled pediments with finials are still lovely.

3992
(c. 1878)
Crisp bargeboard overwhelms the facade of this bright cottage. A unique broken spindle effect has been achieved over the doorway.

4177
(c. 1891)
This cottage with Eastlake features has a gable that is crowned with a sunburst, which is repeated in an unusual recessed triangular panel above the side window.

Ashton Avenue

71
(prior to 1906)
Hidden by foliage and a high picket fence, this brown shingle gabled cottage has retained its isolated rural air.

Austin Street

337–41
(c.1875)
Here is an appealing Stick — at its plainest — with even the single windows above the entrance doors omitted. The elongated brackets on the bay window are the only mild extravagance.

437–39–41–43
(1903)
One very unusual device has been used on this version of Classic Revival: the second floor

is supported on a series of free standing columns recessed into corners of the first floor.

401 Baker Street

Baker Street

401
(c. 1891)
Gedatsu Church of America. Unusually large and heavily ornamented in the spirit of the times, this former residence has two Queen Anne corner towers, each expressing individuality in shape, size and culmination.

1403–05–07
(1878)
This group of attached one-story bracketed cottages is treated as one unit and connected to the corner grocery store. They all conform to the flat-front Italianate style.

1510 and 1526–28
(1881 and 1886)
These two flat-front bracketed Italianates are compatible, although 1510 is one-story and 1526–28 is two.

1527
(early 1890's)
There is a squared corner bay on this Stick Style building, whose glass front on the Baker Street

ground floor is a modern addition.

1600
(1895)
Unusual wood carvings over the door and window frames contrast with the asbestos shingling that has been added to this house.

1605–07
(1890)
The Eastlake-Queen Anne feeling of the time has been incorporated into this shingle house.

1609
(1889)
A balustrade over the entrance and medallions are decorative on this two-story Stick Style house.

1611
(1881)
White paint picks out the brackets, window framing and other details on this one-story Stick-Italianate.

1613
(c. 1880)
The last in this row of four houses is a one-story flat-front Italianate with the traditional pedimented windows and doorway.

1705 and 1707
(1885)
These are probably two of the best one-story Stick Style houses in the city. They demonstrate an inter-mixture of neo-Classic forms with Stick Style motifs.

1709
(1887)
A false gable towers over the bay of this Stick Style house which, like its neighbors at 1705 and 1707, was built by H. Geilfuss.

1710–12
(1889)
Although the roofline on this one-story Stick Style double house is on the same level, one of the houses is lower to conform to the hill.

1716
(1889)
The pediments, frieze, and bracketed cornice on this Stick Style building are all elaborately worked.

1718–24 and 1730–32
(1888)
Although closely related in their Stick Style, 1718–24 is almost double the width of 1730–32. A center entrance surmounted by a balustrade leads to 1718–24.

1818 and 1824
(1886 and 1878)
Both of these Italianates were originally owned by the Roberts family (Roberts Grocery Store) and were moved from California Street in 1903–04. The detailing on 1824 is simpler and lighter.

1902 1905 1906 1907 1909
(1882)
Apparently all built by William F. Lewis, father of writer Oscar Lewis, (along with 1809–17 and 1810–16 Lyon), these present an attractive series of Italianate one-story cottages. All have been maintained with care and integrity.

1911–11A
(1883)
The cornice frieze on this Stick Style house is worthy of notice in this interesting block.

2038
(c. 1885–90)
Heavily-scaled Eastlake details almost weigh down this small, well-painted, delightful cottage.

2106–08
(1890)
An attractive carved flower motif is seen on small, well-defined areas of this Stick Style house.

2109
(1896)
This shingled English cottage has shallow square bays placed unevenly on two sides. The small portico suggests Colonial Revival.

2111–15
(1893)
Rounded and slanted bays, richly varied surface decoration, and a trellis effect appear on this Queen Anne-Eastlake house.

2550
(1910)
Designed by John Bakewell of Bakewell and Brown, this shingle home's details are Colonial Revival. The side entrance door is extra narrow because of the width of the lot.

Balboa Street

900
(1911)
This home with its free adaption of Classic Revival is similar in concept to 2400 Fulton, the two probably being the only ones of their types in the Richmond.

2300
(1914)
Pacific Gas & Electric Co. — Station K. This massive rectangular structure (with no fenestration) would have been severe had not its surfaces been relieved by corner rustications, and a leaf filigree design beneath the cornices.

Bartlett Street

113, 113½, 115, 115½
(1890)
Bright paint highlights the sunbursts with curling rays, the fluted pilasters, the elongated brackets and the large checkerboard panels of this house.

117,
117A,
119,
119A
(1893)

The same exaggerated brackets seen in 113 appear in this house. The slanted bays are elaborate with fluted colonnettes of a most unusual angular style—narrowing into spindle couplets at the top.

145–47
(c. 1893)

Moved from an earlier location on Mission Street, this house probably dates from the early 1880's. A meld of Stick, Italianate, and Victorian Gothic Styles, it has unique gull-wing brackets coupled at the wide gable.

203–3½
(1876)

This Italianate is amazing in that it has a balanced facade with central double entrances, one above the other, each with a separate wooden staircase.

255–57
(1871)

This thoroughly fine very early Italianate home has quoins and squeezed pediments on a flat facade.

259–61–
63
(1877)

This house is side by side with 255–57 so that they appear to be one long building. It is an Italianate also but the three-unit dwelling is composed of three slanted bay tiers and three separate entrances.

279–81
(c. 1894)

Exemplifying Stick-Eastlake, this ornate facade features a massing of carved elements under a heavy false gable and semi-Mansard roof.

318 and
320
(1875)

A small aluminum frame window on 320 is the only apparent alteration on either of these Stick Style mirror twins. The unusually wide bays and unusually low cornices give interesting proportions.

335 and
339
*(c. 1875–
1880)*

The only apparent differences between these two Stick cottages are the addition of a garage to 339 and the shape of their roofs—semi-Mansard on 339 and flat on 335.

373–75
(c. 1870)

Handsomely proportioned, this large Italianate presents the traditional limited decorative elements of that style—balustraded portico, cornices, hood molds and pediment.

432
(1875)

Executed in the flat-front Italianate style, this diminutive cottage is truly dwarfed by taller, newer neighbors.

476–78
(c. 1870)

Although not attaining true Italianate verticality, this flat front duplex possesses grandeur in its balanced facade and wide portico, where one original transom is etched with a vase of flowers.

494–96
(1870's)

This quite square, one-story house is very basic in concept—the hood molds and the cornice offer relief to the flat facade.

513
(c. 1870's)

The delicately handled flat-front facade is truly fine on this Italianate. The pediments are triangular on the second story, rounded on the first.

Battery Street

431–47
(c. 1907)

Once the Jones-Thierbach Coffee Co., this sizable brick building has recently been modernized and refurbished to accommodate offices.

750
(c. 1867)

Stiefvater Bldg. A photograph dated 1867 shows the high round arches of this former wine warehouse. Solidly constructed of brick (partially-faced with cement), with foundations of stones which had served as ship ballast, the building served as a wholesale bakery supply house for many years.

Bay Street

734
(c. 1865)

Concealed from the street by 736 Bay, this is a clapboard cottage with an outside stairway leading to the upper floor. The house was originally located at Leavenworth and Bay Streets and was moved in the 1880's.

736
(c. 1877)

The Hansen family, which had bought 734, also acquired this house in the 1880's. The cottage is of simple design, its false front being relieved by two porches connected by exterior stairways.

740
(c. 1879)

A small wooden house, this has been expanded nevertheless from its original three rooms to the present five.

830–32
(c. 1889)

The exterior of this false-front Italianate house has been virtually unchanged since its construction. Its decorative features include a bracketed cornice and arched pediments (both over

the windows and the recessed doorway).

844
(c. 1884)

The later addition of shutters has slightly altered the facade of this simple false-front house, the second attractive Italianate in the block.

Beaver Street

22
(c. 1882)

The window treatment of this Italianate is unusual in that some are framed in Tudor-like arches with delicate filigree ornaments while others are surmounted by pediments on consoles. The house still has its barn in the rear.

Belvedere Street

601
(c. 1870)

(4701 Seventeenth Street). Formerly a church, this structure has been converted to a residence, the nave serving as a living room and the choir loft as a bedroom.

Bemis Street

276
(c. 1880)

Moved from the Holly Park area in 1951, this simple Italianate cottage has been embellished with gilded eagles, medallions, paneled door, and sunburst arch, salvaged from demolished old homes.

Blackstone Court

30
(1885)

In 1947 this shingle cottage was moved from its original site where it faced Greenwich to its present location. This house was on the property of Charles Abraham, a nurseryman, along with a water tower, windmill, five green houses and a conservatory.

Broad Street

32
(c. 1900)

Saint Michael's Church and Rectory. With grace and simplicity, this Gothic frame church gives rise to a gabled roof and square bell tower with cupola, decorated with lancet windows and arches. A. Hughes designed the adjacent rectory in a Colonial Revival style.

117
(1896)

Firehouse for Engine Company #33. This Classic Revival frame firehouse was one of the last in San Francisco to be motorized. The careful balance of the facade is broken — attractively — by an alarm tower that contains windows shaped like semi-circles.

Broadway

908
(1912)
The Church of Our Lady of Guadalupe. Built on the site of the original 1880 church, this building is an attenuated interpretation of Medieval, Hispanic, and Roman Baroque. Architects were Frank T. Shea and John Loftquist. The church was planned primarily for the Spanish population.

1023
(c. 1907)
In 1919 sculptor Byron S. Johnson purchased 1023; later he installed the second-story French doors, which originally hung in a ballroom at the Panama-Pacific Exposition. In 1924 Johnson built a studio to the rear of the property (1021).

1027–29–
31
(1907)
Deep eaves and a square second-story bay call attention to the upper floor of this simplified shingle house.

1033
(c. 1907)
This small Period home was designed by Miss Williams, an architect, and Miss Lillian Palmer, a noted brass worker.

1067–69
(1909)
Friends and admirers of Ina D. Coolbrith, "The Poetess of the Pacific," had this house built for her. She requested that her house be similar to that next door at 1073–75.

1073–75
(c. 1909)
This three-story shingle apartment building is set on a brick foundation. It has dormers above the square bays.

1615
(1897–
1904)
Saint Brigid's Church. In 1896 H. A. Minton designed this church (built of granite blocks that once served as curb stones). Damaged in 1906, it was quickly repaired, and in 1965 a steeple of lead with copper sheeting was added.

1787
(1875)
An Italianate of handsome proportions, this house holds its own in the midst of larger, newer buildings.

1804
(1885)
An oeil de boeuf window in the gable is unusual in this Stick Style house. It is said to have been built by the Mormons.

1804 Broadway

1812
(1892)
Behind a hedged front garden, this black shingle house displays a very notable shingled gable end.

1879
(1882)
The bay does not reach to the second story of this Italianate. It is crowned instead with a balustrade matching that over the entrance.

2000
(1886)
A very controlled Queen Anne, this fine house has a paneled living room, imported black walnut in the library and stairway, and large enclosed English garden to the west.

2126
(1895)
Well-handled Colonial Revival details are manifested on this straightforward shingle house.

2151
(c. 1920)
The brick work (set in a basically stucco building) and two-story Corinthian pilasters are part of this mansion's handsome look. It now serves as residence and offices for the Consul General of Italy.

2201
(1914)
A balconied arcade with arches establishes the character of this brick house, designed by Albert Landsburgh. Inside, a charming European "gilded cage" elevator serves the four floors.

2249
(1917)
James Miller designed this Georgian Revival brick house for John A. Hooper, president of the First National Bank. The interior has wainscoting of Port Orford cedar.

2307
(c. 1892)
Situated on a prominent lot, this large Queen Anne cannot help but be impressive. Besides a marvelous array of Queen Anne embellishments (towers, stained glass window, gables), it has a hand-carved frieze added by Julia Morgan.

2398
(c. 1898–
1900)
Set on a solid sandstone foundation, this house asserts itself as an impressive mixture of Colonial Revival and Queen Anne (especially the modified corner towers).

2536
(1898)
Standing originally on the north side of Pacific Avenue near Scott, this shingle house was moved in 1905 to its Broadway site. A third floor was added in the form of a Mansard roof.

2714
(1900)
The noteworthy living room of this scholarly Georgian Revival brick house was brought from England and completely reassembled.

2750
(1903)
This shingle home's fine Classic Revival first-story window is barely visible behind a white brick wall.

2801
(1900)
Willis Polk designed this impressive wood Colonial Revival house, which is reached by twin flights of curving stairs. Pairs of monumental two-story Corinthian columns flank the entrance.

2880
(1913)
Designed by Willis Polk for Albert Ehrman, this stone and reinforced concrete house was inspired by Italian Renaissance "palazzos." It has a courtyard and elaborate interior paneling.

2898
(1899)
This beautifully proportioned, exquisitely detailed Dutch Colonial brick house was Walter Bliss' first commission; it was built for his own family. The house not only has white marble trim, but massive concrete foundations and piers set into rock. When one of the towering chimneys toppled in the 1906 earthquake, all of the chimneys were removed as a precaution.

2960
(1913)
Designed by Willis Polk for S. L. Naphtaly, this is a stucco adaptation of Spanish city architecture. It is built around the traditional central courtyard.

Broderick Street

One and One A
(1886)
A corner lot allows side bays on this nicely maintained Stick Style two-family residence.

26
(1889)
The addition of a garage and brick steps in front have not detracted from this Eastlake home's interesting decorative values — such as fishscale shingling and a garlanded fresco.

1705
(1883)
Hinkel built this Italianate with its fine Corinthian columned portico. Its shingles were probably a later addition.

1709, 1713, and 1719-19½
(1883)
These Italianates, also built by Hinkel, are very similar to each other and to 1705 — except that these have not been shingled.

2111 and 2113
(1889)
These two Stick Style houses have nearly identical details, although the difference in the color of paint disguises the similarity.

2201
(1889)
This modified Stick Style house is the first in a block that contains especially well preserved houses of the 1880's.

2203
(1885)
A redwood Stick Style cottage with Eastlake detailing, this is the twin of 2207 (1883), which has been lived in by five generations of one family.

2205
(1883)
Built as a reverse twin of 2203 and 2207, this house has been extensively reworked so that it now includes Colonial Revival detailing.

2213
(1885)
A semi-Mansard roof and more controlled surfaces distinguish this Stick Style cottage from others on the block.

Bryant Street

2636
(c. 1890)
Reminiscent of an earlier period is this Italianate residence. The double windows which flank the central entrance are arched and surmounted by squeezed pediments.

2648
(c. 1889)
Nicely set off by trees and gardens is this Geilfuss-designed Stick-Eastlake residence. The former carriage house to the rear is architecturally interesting in itself.

Buchanan Street

602 through 626
(1876)
These six straightforward Italianates (or, three sets of double houses) give a harmonious look to this block of Buchanan.

708-10 and 724-28
(1885)
Here are two pairs of Stick Style flats, but 708-10 has an unusual balustrade and frieze between the two stories.

906-16
(1876)
A double stairway leads to the triple columned entrance of this commanding Italianate building, which consists of four apartments.

1126-28
(1895)
Floriated friezes give an interesting texture to this Eastlake house, which also has a unique triangular window over the entranceway.

1130-34
(1885)
A wrought iron fence lends character to this Stick Style house, whose moderate amount of ornamentation anticipates Eastlake.

1701-17
(c. 1880)
This commercial building illustrates how the Stick Style could be used to best advantage in large structures, where the repetition of a basic design concept strengthens the overall effect.

1720-22 and 1724-26
(1884)
A first floor modernization almost obscures the fine Italianate at 1720-22. The house next door at 1724-26 is similar in its decorative values although it has reached Stick Style.

1721-23 and 1725-27
(1876)
The basic vertical lines (the essence of Stick Style buildings) have been slightly modified on 1725-27 by the balustrade which reaches from the portico to the bay. 1721-23 has, on the other hand, elaborately incised panels on its Stick bay and portico.

1735-35A, 1739 and 1743
(1876)
Opposite the Stick houses, these three detached houses form an impressive row of pure Italianates.

1852 and 1868
(1881)
Corinthian-columned porticos and pediments provide the outstanding decorative elements on these similar Italianate houses.

1931-33-35-37
(1888)
This Stick-Eastlake richly detailed double house is impressive on its block.

1954-56-58
(1871)
The bay is wider in relation to the overall width of this Italianate house than is usual.

1962-64
(1876)
Given the expanse of a corner lot, this large pristine Italianate enjoys the luxury of a side as well as front bay.

2016 and 2018
(c. 1885)
These two Stick Style houses form an attractive pair, although the portico with broken pediment and Corinthian columns is much more impressive on 2016. A restored "gaslight" is in the front garden of 2018.

2139-41
(1880)
This finely detailed Italianate was the setting for many lavish parties when it was owned by Federico Barreda, Minister Plenipotentiary from Spain and Peru to the Court of Saint James and the United States. After 1904 Willis Polk married the Barreda's daughter, Christine Barreda Moore, and Polk proceeded to remodel the house, making it into two flats. The upper flat was used by Madame Barreda and her daughter, while the Polks lived in the lower.

2439
(1895)
The architect of this brick Colonial Revival house was considered eccentric for using such a simple, subtle style — out of fashion at that time.

2457
(c. 1890)
Carved spandrels and a deep frieze add interest to this restrained Queen Anne, which exploits its corner site beautifully.

2620
(1889)
Built by Hinkel, this gabled residence is distinguished by a squared corner tower. Decoration is limited to the shingles and fret work.

2655
(1891)
Elaborate Eastlake detailing has been carefully designed and executed by the prolific builder Hinkel on this predominantly Queen Anne house.

Buena Vista East

153
(c. 1895)
A number of architectural motifs are included in this house: a Palladian window, cartouche, balustrades, and Doric columns and pilasters.

Buena Vista Terrace

70
(1884)
The strength of this Stick Style home lies in the three-story column of square bays. It was built by the Delano brothers for the Delano family.

99
(c. 1893)
Although this Eastlake one-family dwelling has been converted into flats, there has been no change to the exterior of the house. It still has the elaborately carved gable and fishscale shingling.

Buena Vista West

615
(1906)
A remarkable projecting Gothic central section thrusts dramatically upward breaking the line of the steeply pitched, interestingly surfaced roof on this shingle residence.

Bush Street

530
(1916)
Pacific Gas & Electric Co., Substation R. Great Western Power Company of California built 530 Bush as a steam generating plant. Its facade is composed primarily of two expansive arched windows set in brick and concrete.

645
(1911)
It is the top floor that is of interest on this apartment house: arched windows set within larger arches are secured by prominent keystones.

1195
(1915)
Saint Francis Hospital Nurses' Residence. Originally the Florence Ward Hospital, this brick building was purchased by Saint Francis Hospital in 1923 and until the late 30's was known as Central Medical Building.

1636
(1867)
Set behind a small front garden with a fine large tree, this well proportioned Italianate is of the flat-front variety.

1663
(c. 1880)
Hinkel built this semi-Mansarded Italianate.

1669–71–73
(1879)
A small bay window is superimposed above the entrance porch instead of the Italianate's usual single window.

1677
(1890)
The top story of this Stick Style building is clearly differentiated by a flared water table and by a shingle finish.

1710 and 1712
(1875)
The remodeling of the garden gate of 1710 illustrates a conscientious effort to do the job properly. There is a delightful architectural "ruffle" achieved by the series of arched pediments over the second-story windows on these virtually identical Italianates.

1814–16, 1818–20, 1822–24, 1826–28
(c. 1870's)
This row of four presents a style basically Italianate (bays and roof cornices), but the entrance porches and squeezed pediments of windows above the entrances are surely Stick, looking as if they were added later.

1901–03
(c. 1875)
Opulent, large-scale and vigorous details of the Second Empire appear above the ground floor on this Italianate building.

1909
(1876)
The main entrance of this Italianate double house has been very successfully remodeled for the building's present use as a church.

2033 and 2035
(1887)
Infusions of Stick Style elements are seen on these late Italianate mirror twins, which have unusually large bays.

2043
(1884)
A boldly scaled, especially good cornice with widely spaced brackets dominates the facade of this flat-front Italianate.

2055 through 2099
(c. 1904)
This half block of Classic Revival apartments gives an animated and vigorous look to the street. Although they are essentially similar, the buildings do deviate in their roof treatments and in their decorative details, 2055 being the most elaborately decorated.

2070
(1876)
The traditionally fine detailing of the Italianate style is seen on this well-proportioned house.

2100
(1883)
This Stick Style house shows the unique way in which the second floor is projected entirely over the first floor bay window, which has been modernized.

2104
(1883)
Matching serrated pattern friezes are seen over all openings on this Stick Style house, whose decorative elements are unusually consistent.

2107
(1874)
An exceptionally fine stained glass window on the front door is the highlight of this Italianate house.

2215–17
(1890)
Nearly the entire front of this Queen Anne is occupied by a full height slanted bay, which extends beyond the main roof and becomes a hexagonal spire containing a dormer.

2254
(1870)
This flat-front Italianate cottage displays a paneled frieze between the double brackets of the roof cornice.

2257–59
(1870)
A spool frieze and pierced quadrant brackets add interest to the porch of this Italianate cottage.

2570–72
(1871)
Except for the necessary brackets, there is literally no ornamentation on this Italianate double house.

2797
(1895)
Garlands in the frieze add charm to this corner building, which with 2800 Bush and 1527 and 1600 Baker forms a powerful architectural expression at the intersection of Bush and Baker.

2800
(1889)
Sideways steps rise to the second story across the front of this Italianate structure with rounded corner bay.

2809
(1883)
A deeply recessed center entrance breaks the flat front of this Italianate cottage, which has squeezed pediments over all the openings.

2832
(1895)
The gabled end of this Eastlake cottage is decorated with fishscale shingles and small drop finials.

2838 and 2840
(1883–4)
Although these Italianate one-story houses were both built by D. C. McGraw as apparent twins, 2840 has been stripped of some of its ornamentation.

2862
(1886)
The lean-to shed roof over the porch of this busy Stick-East-

2900 *(1892)*	Some Colonial Revival details have crept into this intricate late Queen Anne.
2905 *(c. 1885)*	The three gable ends of this Stick-Eastlake cottage have unusual stucco work illustrating the interest in the rustic associated with more extreme examples of Queen Anne.
2908–10 *(1884)*	A unique interpretation of San Francisco Italianate is seen in this symmetrical, square-plan house with hipped roof and veranda across the ground floor front.
2909 *(1878)*	The window above this Italianate's entrance porch is trimmed with heavy hood molding and a vase-like cartouche at the center.
2911 *(1885)*	Various patterns of boarding decorate the wall areas of this Stick-Eastlake cottage. The cantilevered bay has an independent shed roof.
2913–15 *(1883)*	Incised panels are above the segmental arched heads on all the openings of this finely-detailed Italianate.
2945–47 *(1885)*	This is a two-story version of 2911, except for a variation in the bay window, which has an independent flat roof and small brackets.

lake matches the similar intermediate roof of the bay.

850 Cabrillo Street

Cabrillo Street

850 *(1908)*	Park Presidio Baptist Church. Frederick Boese designed this wood Gothic church for the Zion Lutheran congregation. In 1950 when the Lutherans sold the building, it was moved two blocks to its present location.

Calhoun Terrace

9 *(c. 1854)*	The open verandas and romanticized Victorian Gothic bargeboards of this unusual house are consistent with the date.

9 Calhoun Terrace

California Street

90 *(1910)*	Originally owned by A. B. Spreckels, this building became the home of the Rolph Navigation and Coal Company. The classic granite building has beautifully proportioned Ionic colonnades on both open facades.
240–42 *(1909)*	Whimsical in an area of towering high rises is this two-story metal and glass structure. Its delicate bronze facade culminates in a pie-crust cornice.
350 *(1909)*	Clegg Building. Although it has had another floor added, this building has maintained its Classic Revival character. Originally there were three more Doric columns in the center of the facade.
1551– 53–53½, 1555A– 57– 59 and	These three wooden buildings are remarkable because of the female figures that support the balustrades. Number 1561–65 is even more notable with

1561– 63–65 *(c. 1909)*	two amorettos perched in front of the third floor bays.
2018 *(1886)*	The unusually elaborate detailing on this very late Italianate conforms to the Stick-Eastlake style. It is the first in an important group.
2020 *(1882)*	Built for importer Frederick Wieland, this house is similar to its Italianate neighbor, 2018 California, except for the probable later addition of shingles.
2022 *(c. 1885)*	This house is said to have been built for Judge Morrison, who used the top floor to house his extensive library. The hardware is dated 1876; however the richly detailed facade suggests a later date.
2026 *(1878)*	This Italianate house has unique rounded-glass bays that anticipate the Queen Anne. The window framing on the window above the portico is exceptionally fine.
2115 *(1890's)*	A few Classic Revival details have intruded on this late Queen Anne, a strong version of the side-hall row house type. The finely-detailed broad bay is garnished with pilasters, mullions, and two decorated friezes.
2129 *(1874)*	Carved diamond and checkerboard patterns and a witch's hat roof differentiate this eccentric Italianate from its kin.
2145–49, 2151, 2159 and 2165 *(1882)*	These four row houses present a cohesive group although their details are varied. The three at 2151, 2159 and 2165 are very late Italianate while 2145–49 is a version of Stick Style.
2174 *(1876)*	Elements of both the Italianate and Classic Revival are evidenced on this house. The third floor could conceivably be a later addition.
2175 and 2187 *(1879)*	Intricate intermediate cornices are the most prominent feature of these two mirror twin Italianates.
2186 *(1880's)*	A center pediment dominates the wide space between the two tiers of bays on this immense Italianate apartment house, which includes twenty-six units.

2226
(1885)
Built by Hinkel, this house is essentially Italianate with Period detailing. It has a portico that almost overwhelms the facade.

2271-73
(1903)
This Classic Revival set of flats has been handled with utmost freedom. Virtually the entire front is two tiers of semi-circular bays, a portion of one being an entrance porch.

2309 and
2311
(1876)
These two Italianate houses—proffering some Second Empire details—are virtually identical.

2332
(1885)
A dormer window pierces the gable end of this shingle house which is set on a brick base.

2338
(1875)
Dr. Edward R. Taylor—at one time Mayor of San Francisco—lived for a time in this forthright Italianate.

2344
(1885)
This Italianate is simpler in concept than 2338 although their Corinthian-columned porticos are virtually identical.

2366
(1879)
The addition of a garage detracts from this Italianate. The multi-paned windows are probably also later additions.

2370
(1882)
The unusually deep cornice is of interest on this Stick-Eastlake house.

2383
(1881)
Exceptionally fine raked eaves are seen on this Stick-Eastlake house, which also has elongated brackets (merging into the strips) and chalet bracing.

2557
(1878)
A Thomas Church garden is hidden in back of this Italianate, notable for its one-story bay topped by a balustrade (with pierced panels and ball finials).

2591
(1877)
The balustraded, one-story bay on this Italianate is very like that at 2557 California.

2678
(c. 1892)
Mixed Period details on this robust house are dominated by a pediment broken by an arch and centered over the bay window.

2733
(1886)
This Stick-Eastlake has wonderfully intricate detailing, especially the bracketing of the bay window's main pediment.

2912
(c. 1880)
This impressive Italianate may have been built by contractor M. J. Kelly. The apparently original iron fence enhances the house which is set on a double lot.

2914
(1883)
Predominately Stick Style, this residence is enhanced by quoins, a holdover from the Italianate, and low pediments over the second-story windows.

2915
A and B
(1892)
The dramatic gable (containing a blank, arched opening and tiny semi-circular balcony with metal railing) illustrates the artistry and virtuosity of the carpenters of this period.

2970
(c. 1880)
Now housing the Filipino Community of San Francisco, this residence is late Stick with a richly ornamented, yet orderly exterior.

3083
(1884)
Here the bracketed roofline is thrust slightly higher than is usual in such Stick Style houses.

3091-93
(1895)
A Romanesque doorway and fishscale shingling are among the vigorous Queen Anne elements of this house.

Capital Street

14
(c. 1890)
A chain link fence is all that separates the late nineteenth century from the present on Capital Street, for the freeway runs right beside this finial-topped Stick Victorian, one of the first farmhouses in the area.

Capp Street

437
(1887)
This one-story house has a finely detailed cornice, pedimented front window, and tiny entrance with balustrade above.

717
through
765
(1889-94)
Nine of this row were built in 1889, the other four in 1894. These predominantly Eastlake houses have undergone varying degrees of alteration.

Carl Street

199
Standing on part of what was

(1900)
once a dairy farm, this impressive Queen Anne house has been impeccably maintained. The only addition to the original building is an outside stairway, built in 1963.

Caselli Avenue

58-58A
(c. 1885)
This severe Stick Style cottage is now dwarfed by taller surrounding buildings. A Victorian vintage iron fence adds an appropriate touch.

191
(1896)
This house features a slanted dormer bay unfolding into a beautiful gable where a large shell is centered in leafy filigree.

199
(1896)
The gables of this house contain ornate pediments, the smallest of which hoods a festooned bay, and has a unique apex filled with alternating panels of minute vertical and horizontal striae.

306
(1898)
The springs of Joost Water Works serviced this house and neighboring ones until about 1930. Notable on this Stick Style home are squeezed pediments with large ball flowers at the flattened apexes.

312
(1894)
A jigsaw and gingerbread masterpiece, this gabled Stick-Eastlake features a circular and eyelet scallop theme. It has pediments filled with carving in every available space.

318 and
360
(1898)
Unique to the Mission District, these magnificent Queen Anne shingle homes were built by a wealthy contractor, who never lived to complete a third house like them. They display gabled roofs and slender corner towers with cupolas and finials.

Castro Street

162
(1885)
The usual vertical thrust of the Italianate Style is evidenced on this house.

480-98
(c. 1880)
This corner structure has always housed a row of shops with living quarters above. Above the shops are two facades with six beautifully-trimmed Stick Style bays, five of which have pediments.

521–25
(c. 1880)
Built as a two-family Stick Style home and raised above a new store in 1910, this graceful structure retains its strip detail and Italianate squeezed pediments under a semi-Mansard roof.

602–04
(c. 1883)
A lovely border of scallops containing incised fleur de lys and stained glass window panes distinguish this graceful Stick Style home.

668
(1884)
Numerous graceful carved swirls and pediments that culminate in two squares draw attention to this Stick Style home.

709
(1897)
A rare example of Queen Anne remaining in the Mission, this house was built by Fernando Nelson, contractor and builder, who himself lived in it until 1904–5. A store was probably located in the ground floor now converted into six garages.

711–13–15
(1897)
Displaying the imagination of builder Fernando Nelson, this structure features tall tiers of slanted and triangular bays. Three identical doors with Eastlake detailing are seen through the ball-fringed portico arch.

712
(1894)
Designed by Charles L. Hinkel, this home is distinguished by its wide paneled door with diamond-shaped window detail, friezes of richly embossed scroll, and leaded, stained glass window panes.

725, 727–29 and 733
(1898)
Fernando Nelson, who is known for exact duplication in the construction of his homes, was responsible for these three restored Stick-Eastlake homes. One of Nelson's trademarks used here is the doorway panel that is a series of cut-out circles.

740 and 746
(1892)
In a row of five majestic Stick-Eastlake homes, built by Charles L. Hinkel, these remain as good examples of his ornate jigsaw detailing. The Hinkel home at 740 is particularly distinguished by lavish use of spindles.

753
(1903)
This gabled wooden home, built on the site of an old cattle ranch, has rounded corner bay tiers. The entranceway is distinguished by a rounded arch that flows into square pillars.

865–65A, 869, 875 and 879
(1892)
Of this colorfully painted row of Eastlake gabled homes, two retain their graceful spindles and balustrades at the upper and lower porches.

1614, 1616, 1618
(1892)
A row typical of the style of Fernando Nelson, these Stick Style homes are identical in all respects save one: the middle house has a false parapet and gable.

1631
(c. 1880's)
The original iron fence and wooden newel post at one end add charm to this Stick Style home, as does the decorative old door.

Chattanooga Street

104
(1892)
This Stick-Eastlake house's carved wood detailing (garlands, a sunburst) is highlighted by white paint against brown background.

106
(1887)
Built in Stick Style with elaborate stair balustrades and ball-newel posts, this house is partially hidden by a terraced garden, trees, and hedges.

116
(1872)
The narrow, vertical forms of the Italianate are evident on this house. A side port hole window is unique.

118
(c. 1885)
Considerable vertical detailing is apparent on this flat-front Italianate, which is set in a lovely garden.

193–95 and 197–99
(1890)
Built essentially as Stick-Eastlake mirror twins, these homes feature porticos and second-story porches at the front and and side, where lattice work forms pretty arches.

227–29
(c. 1893)
This majestic white house displays small, intricate medallions and nobs on the squared bay tier and on the Eastlake portico, where convoluted, crossed jigsaw pieces form support brackets.

228–30
(c. 1885)
Tall and slender, this Stick Style house is noted for its decorative balustrades, at the steps and above the portico.

280–80A
(1876)
The balanced facade features slanted bay consoles flanking the simple squeezed portico of this Italianate.

283–5
(c. 1892)
Built in Stick-Eastlake Style, this house retains every original detail. It has been flatteringly painted.

288
(c. 1887)
Beneath a semi-Mansard roof, this little Stick Style house rambles back in tiers, behind a squared bay console, where heavy pilasters stand out in white.

291–91A
(c. 1890)
Original balustrades, newel posts, and portico screw pillars lead up to a weathered facade, where squeezed pediments, sunburst panels, and etched, stained glass are featured.

Chenery Street

32
(c. 1880)
This impeccable flat-front Italianate cottage originally had a rear stable for two horses and two cows. The house has had a new slab door added.

246
(1877)
The simplicity and age of this Italianate cottage make it stand out amid newer, busier homes.

830
(1906)
This cottage is notable for a facade entirely shingled in various patterns, with a row of semi-circular shingles carried across to form a portico border of tiny arches and fringe points.

Cherry Street

15
(1913)
The exterior of this multi-gabled house is of red brick with white grouting. Designed by Houghton Sawyer, the house now serves as the residence of the Consul General of Belgium.

145
(1916)
Hermann Barth designed this house, a copy of a Dutch Colonial home in Salem, Massachusetts. It has a gambrel roof, shuttered windows and a large Palladian window commanding the facade.

237–39 and 249
(1903)
(And 3902 Clay Street). All three of these houses are attractive individual interpretations of Shingle Style. The property of the houses was once one parcel, which was divided up into unequal-sized lots.

Chestnut Street

273
(c. 1910)
(One Whiting Place). This residence is set off from those around it and has extremely large, terraced formal gardens extending from the house to the street.

Chula Lane

75–77
(1872)
The white trim on the barn-red facade highlights the simplicity of this flat-front Italianate.

81–3
(c. 1898)
This frame house was built over a well which is reputed to have served Mission Dolores and suggests simplicity of a farm house in the 1860's. It has a singular wide semi-Mansarded portico, a slanted corner bay, and mutules.

Church Street

120
(1892–93)
Unique in its neighborhood, this Eastlake cottage has an ornately floreate frieze, above which the gable end is filled in with fishscale shingles and a waffle design.

152
(1905–07)
Saint Francis Lutheran Church. This is one of the few churches in America made possible by the generosity of a Queen – the Queen of Denmark contributed 500 kroner toward its foundation. The brick Gothic building was a seamen's congregation, known as Saint Ansgar.

542–46
(1886)
Built for Chauncey B. Williams, a successful street contractor, this majestic Stick Style mansion is simple but elegant. It occupies a spacious corner lot, permitting a full view of the large garden behind the original, graceful iron fence.

924
(1885)
A new stucco retaining wall and garage do not impair the striking appointments of this Italianate, high on a hill.

1005A
(1905)
This Romeo and Juliet apartment building was given a paint scheme that successfully picks out the panels, window frames, and balustrades of the open central stairway.

1026
(c. 1878)
A Stick Style hilltop home, this was constructed of redwood and square nails. Especially notable are the floreate scroll panels, the Ionic pilasters, and the ornate round-arched portico.

1036–38
(1884)
Above a beautiful, high terraced garden enclosed by a Victorian vintage iron fence, this Stick Style home is distinguished by its eyelet scallop fringe and the Eastlake treatment of its portico and window frames.

1117–19
(1889)
This imposing, shingled Stick-Eastlake home features an ornate gable end, supported by large latticed brackets the height of the second story, a decorative round-arched portico, and a lacy iron fence.

1171
(c. 1870's)
Italianate detailing is seen on the flat facade beneath the false parapet of this house. The old iron fence has been retained.

1408–10
(c. 1870's)
The quoins, pediments and beautiful paneled doors add distinction to this flat-front Italianate.

1500–02
(1887)
Originally a store with dwelling and "wire goods factory" above, this structure is noteworthy today for its Stick Style detailing at the second story – especially the Corinthian pilasters.

1542–44
(1887)
A frieze of large, delicately-incised flowers with a lacy jigsaw border is the major detailing on the Stick Style second story of this building. The original hitching post still stands at the curb.

1700–02
(c. 1880's)
The Stick second story is delicately detailed beneath the original shingled semi-Mansard roof of this house, distinguished for having continuous ownership by one family.

1746–48
(1889)
(202 Day Street). A polygonal corner bay and two squared bays adorn the decorative Stick second story, crowning a conventional business facility.

1854 and 1858
(c. 1880's)
These semi-Mansarded Stick Style twin houses graphically illustrate how the imaginative use of colorful decor on one facade can transform and distinguish it from its twin.

Clay Street

937–49
(c. 1909)
The refinements of this simple brick structure hark back to the Italianate period.

1329
(1908)
This shingle and stucco house was originally built as a four-family dwelling. It is half-timbered with casement windows and a steeply pitched roof with an elaboration of the bargeboard.

1433
(1909)
This half-timbered apartment building was one of the first carefully designed buildings built in the area after the 1906 fire. Inside is a magnificent balustraded staircase.

1433 Clay Street

2422
(1879)
Reputed to have been built by Hinkel, this basic Italianate house is not typical of his style.

2442–44–46
(1904)
A Queen Anne tower is surmounted by an unusual onion-shaped dome on this house; the motifs are repeated on the bay window.

2472
(1889)
The treatment of the portico, brackets, and gable end suggest the introduction of Eastlake in the Stick Style of this Hinkel house.

2503
(c. 1871)
The present owners have restored this Italianate house (with Federal style doorway) to preserve the original flavor.

2524, 2530 and 2536
(1874)
These three detached Italianates were undoubtedly originally one-of-a-kind. The two at 2530 and 2536 retain nearly all their original features while 2524 has had its cornice and portico altered.

258

2586
(1874)
This house presents a good example of later shingles on an Italianate house; also notable is the circular light in the front door, possibly added later.

2767
(1890)
An exuberant use of Period detailing—particularly on the dominating gable end—is seen in this house.

2773, 2775 and 2781
(1890)
All three of these houses were built by D. F. McGraw, who used vigorous and varied Period detailing.

2807
(1885)
The effect of double roofs is particularly noteworthy on this Stick Style cottage. The use of wooden steps adds further charm to the house.

2812
(1886)
A straightforward interpretation of the Stick Style is seen on this house.

2822
(1886)
The gable over the bay window is more richly varied than is usual in this Stick Style residence.

2824
(1886)
This was possibly built as a reverse twin to 2822 Clay. A garland motif under the cornice is a decorative addition.

2900
(1880)
An unusually broad first floor square-end bay window exploits the corner site on which this impressive Stick Style residence stands.

2947
(1883)
Small-scaled ornamentation enhances this Italianate cottage whose narrow recessed doorway is reached by stairs with original wood bannisters.

2965
(1880)
The lovely window heads on this house seem Italianate while the balustrade, shutters, and vertical siding (in the gable and under the eaves) appear to be later additions.

2990
(1891)
Here is another Hinkel free adaptation of the Queen Anne with Period details added.

3073–75
(1883)
This house is distinguished by the all-over intricate low-relief surface decorations.

3100
(1897)
An exuberant use of Queen Anne details and form is manifested in this large corner house.

3201
(1899)
First this was a one-family residence; then during the 1930's a "Party House"; and later a rooming house. The Colonial Revival residence has been tastefully reconverted into a single-family dwelling.

3329
(1880's)
An especially well-kept Stick Style house, this still has its original stained glass windows, front door, and brass trimmings.

3346
(c. 1880)
This Stick Style house was the first on its side of the block. The strips have been nicely handled.

3522
(1899)
A second-story, squared-off bay window of carved wood is an unusual feature of this shingle house.

3581
(1909)
Built for Mrs. E. J. Bowen to complement her residence next door to the east (see main text), this home has often been attributed to Willis Polk, although it was actually designed by Bliss and Faville.

3595
(1910)
This four-story, stucco apartment building was built in the Mission Revival style. The many bays of the corner building make a lively, vigorous exterior.

3766
(1907)
Period decorative touches have been used on this wooden house, which has had a modern garage added at the basement level.

3891
(c. 1890)
The tower of this Queen Anne residence originally faced the corner of Clay and Cherry. In 1909, the building was moved east to the next lot so that now the tower partially confronts the blank side of the corner building.

3905
(1898)
This large, twin-gabled shingle home was the center of a neighborhood controversy in 1964 when it was leased and occupied by Synanon, a group rehabilitating narcotics addicts.

3933
(1908)
This shingle home was first owned by Rabbi Neito, a much-revered member of the Jewish community.

Clayton Street

955
(1904)
This Bay Area Shingle gabled apartment house was built in the tradition of Maybeck and Julia Morgan.

Clement Street

301–05
(1897)
On the floreate bargeboard this wood building's identity is clearly carved out: Richmond Hall. The Hall has always been the center of many neighborhood activities.

Clinton Park

226, 232 and 236
(c. 1878)
These stately Italianate Style homes have lovely etched or stained glass transoms. They are several of a Stick and Italianate group hidden from major thoroughfares in Clinton Park's 200 block.

244
(c. 1884)
The more richly carved surfaces of this Italianate house (quoins, ornate Corinthian pipe-stem colonnettes, and window framings) indicate its later date.

252–54
(1884)
Ornate little modillions at the bay and portico cornices are distinguishing on an otherwise disciplined Stick Style house.

258
(c. 1883)
Built in Italianate Style (and moved to this location after the 1906 disaster), this bright house displays Corinthian pipe-stem colonnettes with fluted bases.

Clipper Street

19–21
(1879)
Beautiful paneled doors carved with wreaths are an addition to this simplified Stick Style house.

23–25
(1879)
Nicely detailed pediments appear on this flat-front Italianate.

38
(c. 1880's)
Beneath a semi-Mansard roof of original fishscale shingles, this hillside house features Stick Style appointments.

59
(1883)
Once surrounded by flower and vegetable gardens, this Stick Style cottage has ornate, rather uncommon, Eastlake support brackets and a beautiful iron fence of the Victorian era.

119 and 121
(1883)
Once boasting a fine wine cellar and large garden fountain, these twin homes represent the unadulterated Italianate Style, with simple detailing and false parapets.

153 and 159 (c. 1886)
Another pair of twin Italianate cottages, these attain some vertical interest with their squeezed pediments.

171–73 (1887)
This Stick Style home is notable for its original door, carved with a wreath and window escutcheon, and squeezed pediments.

184, 184A (1887)
Behind a storefront ground floor section looms this Stick Style corner house which has a stunning paneled, spindled Corinthian portico beneath an original fishscale shingled, semi-Mansard roof.

205 through 225 (1888–90)
Build as a row of nine by Frederick C. Kleebauer, carpenter and contractor, these Stick Style semi-Mansarded cottages, though somewhat altered, are still interesting. Many in the row have graceful original stair balustrades with ball-finial newel posts.

325 (c. 1892)
Continuously owned by one family, this Stick-Eastlake cottage boasts unique spool brackets and a checkerboard bay pediment.

355 (1889)
Spool brackets and intensive vertical detailing are displayed on this semi-Mansarded Stick Style cottage.

517 (c. 1891)
Built amid large vegetable gardens, this Stick Style semi-Mansarded cottage has exquisite incised Pennsylvania-Dutch panels and vertical detailing which recall the era of skilled wood carving.

522–24 (1883–84)
Built on a large lot, with a well which served neighbors during the 1906 disaster, this simple, petite Stick Style cottage is shaded by tall pines.

526–28 (1891–92)
This Stick-Eastlake house is notable for its hobnail, waffle pediment, classical mutules, and portico.

Collingwood Street

36–38 (1887)
Of particular note on this Stick Style house, whose adjacent twin has been remodeled, are the angular, squeezed pediments with squared apexes.

76 (1908)
Simplicity and charm mark this little gabled house, which is enhanced by a beautiful side yard, tall palm, and ivy-covered iron fence. It was built for Mayor Patrick H. McCarthy, whose former home was used as a nucleus.

197–99 (c. 1891)
(4134 Nineteenth Street). This Stick Style corner home has a heavy concentration of Eastlake detailing, not a piece of which has been removed or altered. Even a little side gate (where the sunburst theme is reiterated) remains.

252 (1889)
Eyelet scallop fringes and a heavy Eastlake chalet gable end enhance this home which has front and side bay tiers.

284 and 290 (1886–7)
John A. Swenson, carpenter and builder who lived at 284 himself, built both of these lovely one-story Stick cottages. They are almost identical, although Mr. Swenson unleashed his creativity on the differing roof treatments and elaborately-carved friezes.

Columbus Avenue

253–55 (1913)
This building, which curves around a corner, has a notable pedimented doorway that leads to a narrow marble staircase. On the second floor there are Palladian windows set off by pilasters.

Commercial Street

604 (c. 1851)
Modernization conceals the fact that this is probably one of the oldest buildings in San Francisco. Presumably, the building was severely damaged in the 1906 fire but portions date from the 1850's. Recent remodeling has covered the groined vault ceiling, the building's most outstanding feature.

608 (1877)
The first United States Mint in the West, which opened April 3, 1854, occupied this site. The building was razed in 1874 and the new four-story Sub-Treasury filled the lot. The building was dynamited in 1906 to slow the fire's progress but the massive lower walls and basement vaults remained standing and are the basis for the present building.

Commonwealth Avenue

51 (1906–7)
The Armenian Apostolic Church of Saint Gregory. J. C. Jordan had this stucco Spanish Style home built on the street named after one in his native Boston. In 1957 the home was bought by the Armenian Apostolic Church.

70 (1906)
Prominent features of this Shingle Style house include grand bays on two sides of the home, a triple lancet window in front and a delightful dormer with balcony.

Cook Street

46 (c. 1870)
George J. Smith, a director of the Odd Fellows, planted his estate with many trees which he obtained from the cemetery. Today all that remains on his property is a one-story Italianate home and carriage house.

137–39 (1880's)
The only two-story Italianate in this block of mixed styles, this is an unadorned interpretation of that style.

156–60 (1894–95)
Fishscale shingling and an interrelationship of gables are the decorative features of this basically Eastlake house.

164 (1890)
Perhaps the most notable of the small homes on this block, this cottage has ornate bargeboard with a pendant finial and stained glass edging on the windows.

184 (1885)
An example of a stark flat-front Italianate, this cottage is one of a pair. Its roofed portico is perhaps a later addition.

Corbett Street

189–91 (c. 1875)
Originally this Stick Style house stood near the present entrance to the Twin Peaks Tunnel but was moved to Corbett around 1914 when the tunnel was built.

236 (c. 1882)
This small, flat-front Italianate cottage was constructed almost entirely of redwood. The well-maintained house has had a lean-to addition on one side.

238
(c. 1885)
Like its neighbor at 236, this is a flat-front Italianate cottage, also well-maintained and with a pleasant front garden.

Cumberland Street

96–98
(c. 1885)
(635 Dolores Street). A vast gambrel roof adds a Dutch Colonial dimension to this building. The gable ends formed by the roof are filled in with shingle patterns.

Day Street

27
(1880's)
Built in Stick Style, this trim semi-Mansarded cottage is interestingly painted to display its detailing.

39–41
(1891)
Ground level treatment here offers an interesting comparison with this Stick Style home's almost twin at #27.

187
(c. 1886)
A tannery on this property burned in 1912, but the little Stick Style cottage (so similar to 27 and 39–41) remains.

207
(1885)
This beautifully-detailed Stick Style residence has a false-parapeted semi-Mansard roof. The pedimented portico is very narrow, and the squared bay console rests on angular pillars.

228
(c. 1892)
Unusual sawtooth and square shingles on the upper frieze and gables highlight this Stick-Eastlake cottage. Lovely finials, with both pendant and projectile sections, call further attention to the gables.

248
(1891)
Gold sunbursts in the squeezed pediments and friezes of square medallions with central nobs accented in gold add character to yet another Stick Style cottage.

Delgado Place

18–20
(1910)
There used to be a spring running down the hill where quaint Delgado Place is now located. One of the handful of buildings on this alley is this simple building with bracketed cornice.

Delmar Street

124
The arch and composite col-

umns of the portico are repeated in the window of this cottage, whose surface ripples with fishscale shingles.

124 Delmar Street

Diamond Street

67–69
(c. 1890)
This house was originally across the street, and when threatened by construction of the Twin Peaks Tunnel, it was moved to this location. It is a shingled Queen Anne with Colonial Revival features.

70
(c. 1886)
Panels of overlapping circle medallions, elongated brackets and a hood of circular shingles on the bay are noteworthy on this Stick Style cottage.

80
(c. 1890)
This Stick Style residence retains its folded false gable but has had a cement block base, garage, and brick steps added.

232–34
(c. 1890)
White trim paint emphasizes the tidy details of this delicate Stick Style cottage, which is very well maintained.

244–246A
(c. 1891)
Particularly interesting on this Stick Style residence are the squeezed pediments with sunbursts over medallions, which surmount bays and portico.

306
(1890)
This Stick Style home has a particularly handsome paneled and stained front door. Fluted composite columns and pilasters are painted white as is the garland over the entrance.

372
(c. 1894)
This delicate Stick-Eastlake cottage has a richly-carved pediment, featuring a theme of jigsaw eyelet scallops, diamonds, and circles.

838–40
(1894)
An example of Stick-Eastlake, this was once part of a row of four, the others now being stripped of ornamentation. Circle and diamond medallions decorate the hood mold over the portico and the false gable.

940 and 946
(c. 1894)
Built by S. A. Born, these houses are similar although not identical, 946 being larger in scale. Both have lattice work at the bay corners with spindles and hanging finials incorporated in the portico arches.

1007–09
(1892)
Notable Eastlake features are seen in this Stick residence constructed by builder Fernando Nelson. This home was once a twin to 1001, which has been altered considerably.

1143
(1890)
An unusual feature of this Stick Style cottage is the bay's pediment, which is squared off and filled in with jigsaw work.

1607
(1901)
The only concession to ornamentation on this minute cottage is in the form of the shingles (fishscale and sawtooth), which cover the entire facade.

2629
(1898)
On this hillside house there is an arch at the portico that contains floreate cartouches. A Palladian window in the gable end suggests the introduction of Colonial (or Classic) Revival.

Divisadero Street

99
(c. 1905)
Southern Pacific architect Dakin and builder S. A. Born were responsible for this awesome brick Georgian-Colonial residence.

1045
(1902)
A witch's hat (conical shape) roof on the tower and a soaring gable end give verticality to this Queen Anne house.

1911 through 1915½
(1888)
This block of identical buildings — with non-aligned floor levels — illustrates the adaptability of the vertical Stick Style to various residential uses: flats,

1934
(1884)
The bold Eastlake hood over the door of this Stick Style cottage relates nicely to the cornice brackets.

2101
(1877)
Similar in form and situation to 2900 Clay, this house displays delicate Italianate details.

2110 and 2116
(1891)
The exceptionally large bays culminate in turreted independent roofs that contain false dormers on these mirror twins.

2131
(1883)
The juxtaposition of turret gabled bay windows and exaggerated pediments distinguish this delightful one-story residence.

2131 Divisadero Street

2195
(1877)
On this Italianate house the lower cornice extends full width across the facade; in fact, it dominates all other features.

2197
(1877)
This well-preserved Italianate house is certainly closely related to 2195, yet here the portico is allowed to be an independent entity.

2203
(1877)
Another disciplined interpretation of Italianate, this house has details that deviate only slightly from those of 2197.

2221
(1877)
Although the interior of this Italianate has been extensively remodeled, the exterior has been changed only by the addition of a brick wall, a garage and single dwelling and apartments.

single-pane glass windows.

2229 and 2231
(1874)
Julia Morgan bought these two Italianate houses both of which she remodeled—she even went so far as to remove the second story of 2229. Miss Morgan moved into the one-story house herself and turned over the two-story residence to her staff. Eventually though she moved into the lower floor of 2231.

2229 Divisadero Street

2300
(c. 1900)
Two-story slanted bays and pedimented dormers imposed on a gambrel-roofed shingled apartment distinguish this house.

2310-12
(1908)
These nicely-detailed shingle flats—especially the carved door frame and brackets—are harmonious with the corner apartments.

2505
(1899)
This forthright red brick block includes elements of Georgian Revival. It is part of a brick group that moves around the corner to Pacific.

2710
(1893)
Many old trees and shrubs nearly obscure this free translation of Queen Anne-Eastlake. Unusual features are the entrance porch, with its Gothic arches and tracery, and the intersecting gable ends and chimneys.

Dolores Street

263-65
(1892)
Most notable in this Period residence are the two large decorative shells, containing lovely sculpted cameo heads. Unusual too is the modified bay with a minimal square window.

655
(1916)
Second Church of Christ Scientist. During construction of this Classic Revival stucco church, designed by W. H. Crim, Jr., a local steel strike halted all work, but the steel plants reopened and the church was completed as scheduled, a fact which the congregation attributes to their prayers.

760-62
(1889)
The amazing vertical strips on this Stick Style house are painted white in brilliant contrast to the brown facade. They give a powerful vertical expression to the house.

770
(1905)
This remarkable house rises from a cement and brick retaining wall. The entrance portico and Palladian window above it certainly are Colonial Revival, while the corner tower culminating in a metal cupola (now rain-washed and rusted), is assuredly Queen Anne.

846-48
(c. 1892)
Richly carved with medallions and covered with sawtooth and ship-lap shingles, this house has a unique decorative device (resembling a cylinder), which protrudes beneath the cornice.

890
(c. 1876)
This Italianate cottage, wedged between two newer, taller structures, features a concentration of detailing at the portico, where heavy split pilasters support a hood mold above a ribbed archway.

1010
(1875)
Once nearly covered by ivy, sheltered by palms, and part of a group of three, this Italianate now stands in solitary splendor. A graceful old iron fence and gate on a stone wall still set off the property.

1037-39
(c. 1887)
Built as a private residence but converted to two flats by 1910, this ornate Stick-Eastlake house is trimmed with strips, flowers, and a sunburst-filled gable end.

1074-76
(1885)
This Stick-Eastlake house (with elaborate portico and chalet gable) still has the original carriage house in the rear. Second-story additions were made later.

1080-82
(c. 1880)
Wooden stairs lead to a simple double entrance on this Italianate, originally located on Van Ness Avenue but moved here

after the fire. The house is behind a garden, separated from the street by an iron fence on a stone wall.

1202
(1909)
It is hard to imagine that this Queen Anne house (with its profusion of gables, bays, shingled areas, stained glass windows, and corner polygonal tower) grew out of a one-room shack, built before 1879. Charles Katz bought the property in 1879 and waited until 1909 to construct this house, which incorporates the earlier modest dwelling.

1204
(c. 1892)
Built with an interesting combination of Eastlake detailing (in the balustrades, portico columns and spindles) and Classical mutules at the cornice, this house has an unusual trapezoidal bay above the portico.

1275–77
(c. 1903)
The gable end of this house is filled with fishscale shingles, a sunburst in its apex, while pretty spindles are decorative below.

1285–87
(c. 1870)
Elaborate stairs with nice balustrades make their way to the second-story entrance on this flat-front Italianate.

1289
(c. 1883)
A shed roof protects a porch on one side of this cottage, while a large pediment over the bay breaks into the roof.

1434–36 and 1438–38A
(c. 1880)
These two Italianate cottages are essentially similar. However, 1434–36 has squeezed pediment hoods on the windows and door as well as over the front and sides of the bays, while 1438 has a shed roof for the door.

1503–03A and 1511
(1892)
Essentially twins, these two Stick Style houses were built by J. M. Cumerford. Both are notable for their Eastlake porticos with spindles, round jigsaw arches, and angular columns. A semi-Mansard roof crowns 1511, while 1503–03A is flat-topped.

1573–75 and 1579–81
(1887–89)
Again almost Stick Style twins, these have a few differences in their details, particularly the absence of a balustrade over the entranceway of 1579–81.

Dorland Street

216–16½
(1890)
Incised carving adds a decorative effect to the vertical strips on this Stick Style house.

231–33
(1892)
A very late Stick Style house, this structure is important on its short street. Incised brackets and strips as well as rows of medallions have been highlighted by the paint job.

Douglass Street

178
(1888)
This Stick Style cottage boasts hoods, incised panels, and semi-fluted pilasters as well as a frieze of strips.

180–180A
(1890)
Unusually shaped, this Stick Style residence has a semi-Mansarded tiered roof. An interesting stairway leads to its handsome Period door.

183
(1885)
This Stick cottage is noteworthy for its unusual bay trim: crossed wooden bars shaped like batons, square medallions, and elaborate brackets with rows of studs.

187
(c. 1880)
Windows surmounted by delicately-incised panels and hoods are of interest on this flat-front Italianate. Shutters with cut-outs blend with the decor but appear to be a later addition.

210
(c. 1885)
This simple, unique chalet-type house has vertical siding in the gable end into which second-story windows intrude.

219
(1893)
Intricate jigsaw detailing makes a very animated facade on this Stick Style cottage.

559
(1894)
A lovely paneled front door, waffle patterning in the gable end, and a portico with spindles and sunburst highlight this house.

706
(c. 1893)
Eastlake decorative devices are seen on the floreate frieze, latticed balustrade and angular columns of this house. The diamond shingles are repeated in the gable end.

710
(1892)
Built by Jonathan Anderson, this Stick Style cottage has an especially narrow bay with tree branches carved in its panels.

808 and 810
(c. 1891–92)
Shingled, sloping hoods protect the bays and windows while squeezed pediments have been added to the doors on these Stick Style cottages.

818
(c. 1891)
Detailing reminiscent of the Pelton-Eastlake Styles is evident on this sprightly cottage whose strips are well developed.

874–76
(c. 1891)
This simple Stick Style residence has side stairs and an entrance on the second floor that may result from alteration but blend in due to new paint.

Duncan Street

143
(1885)
The white trim on this Italianate cottage picks out the brackets and moldings handsomely.

151–53A
(c. 1887)
Around 1965 this Italianate was beautifully restored. Considering some of the decor had fallen off, this was quite a feat. The powerful intermediate cornice that extends across the house dominates the facade in a unique manner.

162
(c. 1886)
Smartly remodeled into flats, this is a Stick Style building with elongated brackets supporting the pediments and cornice.

169–71
(c. 1888)
Built as a horse barn, this building was later moved to the present location and converted to a residence. Its charming facade in a Stick-Chalet Style features a rare, timbered pediment gable overhanging the old arched hayloft window.

311
(c. 1884)
This Italianate cottage is of interest because of its original fishscale-shingled semi-Mansard roof and carefully painted white detailing.

Eddy Street

395
(1908)
Above the store level on the first floor, this hotel building has two stories of attractively patterned brick work.

969
(1899)
This modified version of Classic Revival is now used as a parsonage by Saint Paulus Lutheran Church.

Edward Street

One
(1870's)
This cottage is said to have been the caretaker's lodge for the Odd Fellows Cemetery. When the cemetery was removed, the small frame house was moved a short distance to its present location.

Eighteenth Street

3250
(1887–1888)
Saint Charles School. Notable here is the central tower of the Italian Villa style as well as the delicate squeezed pediments over the many windows on both floors. The building was used for church services until 1894.

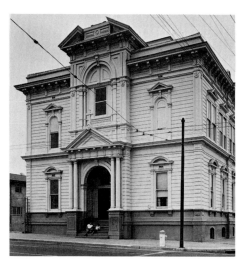

3250 – Eighteenth Street

3827
(c. 1886)
This Stick-Eastlake cottage has Corinthian colonnettes and a tricky frieze as decorative elements.

3883–85
(c. 1892)
The spiky Eastlake gable and portico and the exaggerated white strips and pilasters are of interest on this Stick Style house.

3887
(c. 1880)
This Italianate house with its simple rounded squeezed pediment over the entrance is approached by simple wood stairs.

4311
(c. 1898)
Pediments filled with circular medallions, fluted pilasters, and slim strips give vertical interest to this chaste cottage which is an elaboration of the flat-front Italianate.

4427
(c. 1912)
This post-fire cottage exemplifies a more modern treatment of nineteenth century jigsaw trim styles in its startling pediment designs over a delicate diamond-point fringe.

4521
(c. 1877)
Originally surrounded by a dairy ranch and serviced by a well from 1877 to 1892, this one-story cottage has been imaginatively painted to enhance the Italianate detailing. The only vestige of its former use is the deep lot on which it sits.

4600–02
(1892)
This large corner house is in the Queen Anne style with Italianate and classical highlights beneath a gabled roof. Notable are its octagonal corner tower with cupola and multi-shaped bays richly adorned with wreaths and festoons, Ionic pilasters and columns, mutules and modillions, and floreate scroll. It is enclosed by a lovely iron gate and fence.

4745
(c. 1913)
This picturesque cottage, bright yellow, with white detailing and picket fence, features a wide, wavy jigsaw bargeboard decorating a peaked roof, adding Victorian Gothic flavor.

Eleventh Avenue

327
(1885)
This trim one-story Stick Style cottage holds its own quite well in its neighborhood, where it is one of a kind.

Elizabeth Street

42–44
(c. 1876)
This Italianate cottage was remodeled in 1902 to accommodate a second family, probably on the ground level.

57
(1887)
The strip detailing is important on this semi-Mansarded Stick Style house.

315–17
(c. 1890)
Also Stick Style, this starkly simple house features many vertically-ribbed wooden pieces.

325
(c. 1887)
Beautifully-incised squeezed pediments and wide fluted pilasters point gracefully to a diamond-shingled semi-Mansard roof on this Stick Style residence.

375
(c. 1875)
This tiny flat-front Italianate cottage (behind a beautiful garden and iron fence) is the only unaltered old home in the block.

408
(c. 1892)
Built in the Stick Style, this home features inverted fleur-de-lys and snow flake medallions among its rich trimmings.

430–432
(1890)
A theme of circular and scalloped detailing dramatizes this Stick Style house, which is framed by a lacy old iron fence and gate.

557–59
(1886)
This Stick house is particularly noteworthy for its delicately incised panels, fleur-de-lys in the pediment over the broad portico, and sunburst in the frieze.

565–67
(c. 1891)
Simple and white, this Stick Style house has panels of slanted strips.

583
(c. 1889)
This unadorned Italianate flat-front cottage features split pilasters and shallow hood molds.

608
(1891)
A robust Stick-Eastlake, this house once had a bluing factory in the basement. It has the original carved door and double sawtooth shingles in the gables and the frieze.

727–29
(c. 1875)
This minute flat-front Italianate was once part of a small cabbage farm. It has been given new iron railings on the front stairs.

731–33
(1896)
Eastlake decoration is seen in the spooled, narrow portico and the serrated border at the eaves of this house.

780, 782, and 788
(1893)
(1892)
(1892)
A row of cottages all believed built by O. W. Carlson, these have slanted bays, porticos and pediments that differ only slightly. As a group, they are notable for spindles and spokes, fishscale and diamond-shingled pediments, elaborate scrolls, and numerous finials.

832–34
(1903)
The gabled end of this cottage is filled with decorative shingle patterns above a delicate spindled portico arch. The original iron fence adds a nostalgic touch.

Ellington Avenue

400
(1912)
The original character of this Queen Anne has been preserved with integrity. The only house of its vintage left in the area, it occupies a prominent place on a corner lot.

Elsie Street

336
(c. 1900)
This simple farm house, set in a well-maintained garden, looks as if it really belongs on the San Mateo coast. From its lot next to

a reservoir, the home commands a fine view of Twin Peaks.

Euclid Avenue

620
(1919)
A heavy cornice and a giant order of Corinthian pilasters (two stories high) dominate the exterior of this wood house.

Eureka Street

84–84½
(1890)
This Stick Style house is most notable for its fancy portico which has fishscales recessed in the pediment, spokes, and scallop border.

118–20 and 122–24
(c. 1895)
Representing a blend of Eastlake and Queen Anne, these two rather ornate homes are almost mirror twins and are notable for rounded archways of Romanesque flavor. Both also have shingles and elaborate friezes, making busy surface patterns.

158–60
(c. 1875)
An unusual third-story, square observation tower in the center of the roof makes this Italianate home most striking.

188
(c. 1895)
Unique on this Stick Style cottage are the new wooden stairs and rails, replicas of the originals.

282 and 286
(c. 1893)
These two essentially identical Stick-Eastlake residences have narrow bay tiers, decorative pediments, "chalet" gables, and many areas of concentrated carved wooden pieces, all typical of the other homes built by Fernando Nelson.

328
(1898)
The second-story shutters would appear to be later additions to this house. A mixture of styles, it moves from an Italianate first-story bay to Queen Anne shingles that work their way half way down the second story.

329
(c. 1892)
The square panels above and below the windows and the stair railing are painted a bright green on this Stick Style cottage.

462–64
(c. 1896)
The second-story windows of this amazing residence recall the early Italianate rounded windows with squeezed pediments. These tall, well-detailed windows differ from those of the entire lower section,

obviously altered, which is simpler, newer and smaller in scale.

468
(1903)
This charming cottage (with sharp gabled roof and finials at the sides) lends simplicity and color to its street.

572
(c. 1896)
Elaborate finials piercing the pediments and an unusual front door distinguish this Stick Style cottage.

Evans Avenue

1305–07–09
(1878)
Strikingly simple, this wood building has the fine dimensions of many flat-front Italianates.

1369
(1880–82)
The flat front of this home is relieved by pediments over the windows on the first floor, cornices over those on the second. It is close in concept to 1305–07–09.

Fair Oaks Street

31
(1888)
Framed by a colorful garden, this Queen Anne shingled home features a large corner tower, an array of fishscale and shiplap shingles, and a gabled portico with lattice-filled spandrels.

68
(1888)
Stick-Eastlake moving into Queen Anne emerges as the style of this house, originally owned by Fortunatus D. Traveler. On one side of the facade, a square second-story bay (its surface broken by sawtooth shingles, a waffle-designed frieze and brackets emerging from strips) rests on a slanted first-story bay.

68 Fair oaks Street

108–08A
(1891)
This is a beautifully restored and maintained Stick Style dwelling.

200–02
(1886)
The surface of this double Stick Style residence has bays, doorways, pediments, balustrade, and modillions.

210
(c. 1889)
The balanced facade on this center hall, late Stick Style house reiterates the plan seen at 200–02 Fair Oaks.

212
(1873)
The original carriage house (now converted into a home) remains to the rear of this Italianate, whose facade is of the controlled, flat-front variety.

214–16
(1870's)
This Stick Style house and 212 present two of the oldest, best preserved houses in the area. The two houses are complementary, although this residence has more mass and verticality.

223–25
(c. 1883)
The original barn of this Stick Style house has been converted to a garage now. An unusual feature of the house is the small, three-leafed clover carved above each window.

260
(1870)
With a style and elegance now rare in the Mission district, this house—once a single family home—serves today as an apartment building. Behind a rose-filled garden and a wealth of bougainvillea, the extra-wide bay and balustraded portico still command attention.

435
(1888)
This Stick Style home is adorned with iron cresting above the portico, festoons, eyelet scallops, squeezed pediments, and fluted pilasters.

455
(1890)
Holy Innocents Episcopal Church. Built as a mission chapel of Saint John the Evangelist Church, the rear section of this Gothic shingled structure (with gabled roof and bell tower, lancet and ogee arches) is now partially hidden by a matching lower entrance section added around 1913.

463
(1878)
This Stick Style home features both a squared bay tier and a slender slanted bay above the portico balustrade. Unique embossed panels and arches are

265

filled with ball flowers and acanthus leaves.

464
(1886)
Built in Stick Style, this house displays iron cresting, a tiny row of brackets at the cornice, flattened pediments, and a festooned frieze.

Fell Street

261
(1910)
(162 Hickory Street). Church of the Advent of Christ the King. This is one of the oldest Episcopal parishes in the city, having been founded in 1858. The present stucco building is Spanish in style with a tiled roof and beamed ceiling.

501
(1876)
This Italianate structure takes advantage of its corner lot with a dramatic and lovely corner bay.

501 Fell Street

507 and
511
(1872–74)
John Winkel, who originally owned 501 Fell, was also the first owner of these two harmonious residences. The refinement of details on these homes is Italianate.

Fifteenth Street

1957–59
(c. 1880)
The garage for this handsome Stick Style house was once a store. The new slat fence above the garage has been styled to complement the vertical strips on the house.

2005
(c. 1903)
Saint Nicholas Cathedral. Originally constructed as Saint Luke's German Evangelical Church, this small wood building was acquired by the Russian Orthodox Church in the early 1960's.

A shiny blue onion-shaped cupola—holding a gold cross—was added to the exterior, a contrast to the essentially Gothic structure.

2149
(c. 1891)
This restrained flat-fronted Italianate residence must be older than its date implies.

2340
(c. 1880)
The Eastlake decoration of the gable on this house is repeated in the pediment of the portico.

Fifth Avenue

45
(1905–06)
The first of three particularly interesting shingled houses—at once similar and yet quite different—this one has giant pilasters and a mullioned main window.

49
(1904)
A pattern of strong timbers appears in the street gable of this house, the second of the group.

55
(1902)
Originally built as a two-story cottage occupying half of the present lot, this house was extensively remodeled by Edgar Mathews in 1905.

Filbert Street

226
(c. 1863)
This unadorned frame cottage adds to the charm of the Filbert Street steps.

381–83
(1868)
A very plain false front is seen on this extremely simple cottage.

566
(1907)
This prefabricated shingle house was sent from Holland as a wedding gift for the first owners. The asymmetrical design of the house stems from the irregular gable roof.

666
(1912 design)
The Church of Saints Peter and Paul. Charles Fantoni was commissioned to design the church, which reflects the forms and lines of Italian ecclesiastical architecture. Its construction took ten years.

727–29
(1906)
Presently used as a warehouse, this plain (except for its molding) building was originally a stable.

1100–12
(c. 1906–07)
Like several others on Russian Hill, this large brown shingled apartment building is prominently situated and, therefore, a focal point of the area although

it is architecturally restrained.

1138–40
(1907)
This house is known by the name, "Alta Cottage," because it was built for Dr. Howard M. Engle to replace the cottage which had first been occupied by the proprietor of the *Alta California*. When new apartments blocked the view, Dr. Engle had the Dutch Colonial house raised a story and moved back on its lot.

1154
(1908)
Once a cottage, this has been converted into a delightful townhouse. It is located in back of 1156–58 Filbert.

1156–58
(1908)
This is typical of many of the multiple-unit buildings of its period. It has squared and rounded bays as well as a flat, corniced roof.

1160–62
(1908)
Like 1154, this delightful house is set in back of 1156–58 Filbert. It consists of two flats with arched windows and iron balconies.

1164–66
(1908)
Now flats, this was built as a single-family home and during World War II was turned into a rooming house. Apparently the shingle building was moved from the front to the rear of its property.

1906–08
(1891)
A rosette frieze and a carved pediment over the entrance are of interest on these Stick Style flats.

**1978,
1980 and
1982**
(c. 1878)
A strong rhythm is created in these three one-story row houses by the repeated gables. It is accentuated by the pierced bargeboards and the many finials.

2285–87
(1882)
This corner building offers a good example of utilitarian San Francisco architecture. The projecting Queen Anne bays create a strong rhythm.

2582
(1908)
This brown shingle English cottage with leaded windows has a large well-planted side garden. The new owner has built a high shingled wall behind the old iron fence.

Fillmore Street

2358–60
(2489–91 Washington Street).

(c. 1882) Representative of Queen Anne commercial buildings of the 1890's is this handsomely-detailed structure. Delicately-framed blind windows enhance large gables; a frieze of laurel wreath panels adds unity to the building.

2501
(1901) Calvary Presbyterian Church. The cornerstone for this structure was laid on July 4, 1901, and it was dedicated in 1904. The building presents a rather attenuated version of Classic Revival, built on a cruciform plan.

2525
(1883) This towering Stick Style house has rare arched window heads. Its bay is surmounted by a large projecting Eastlake gable.

2527
(1885) Fishscale shingling on the gable ends marks this Stick-Eastlake house which later had a garage added.

2529
(c. 1885) The detailing on this Stick house refers back to Italianate rather than forward to Eastlake, like its neighbors.

2609
(1883) After the fire this Stick Style house was used as a quality tailor shop. Carefully restored by the present owners, they once found a note under the front door saying:

"O little black house
You have character
God bless you standing next to
    that big apartment building.
Carry on!"

2935–37
(1905) Over-scaled and exaggerated Baroque details make a very animated facade on this unusual house.

First and Brannan Streets

(c. 1868) Oriental Warehouse. Probably built to coincide with the beginning of the Pacific Mail Steamship Company's China line to Hong Kong and Japan, this powerful brick structure is owned by the Southern Pacific Company.

Folsom Street

2533
(c. 1885) Harking back to the days when it was part of a farm is this Stick Style house, which is more rambling than is traditional with that style.

3340
(c. 1880) Originally an unadorned one-story farm house, this structure was given a second story prior to 1906 (with trim, hood molds, strips and brackets) and a third story above the cornice in 1930 (when the trim was removed).

Ford Street

26–28
(1888) A wooden stairway ascends to the second story of this two-story Stick Style residence, whose roof is tiered back.

32
(c. 1890) An extraordinary verticality is achieved in this one-story Stick-Eastlake by the towering false gable end, which is pierced by a finial rising from a console.

61–63
and 67
(1885) Side-by-side, these Stick Style houses display delicately incised panels and false semi-Mansard roofs.

Forty-seventh Avenue

806
(c. 1878) Presently a residence, this was originally the Golden Gate Lifesaving Station and was located in the Coast Guard compound at the northwest corner of Golden Gate Park. It was moved to its present location around World War I and changed slightly. It is reminiscent of Pelton-design residences, forerunners of the Eastlake Style.

1468 Forty-seventh Avenue

1468
(late 1890's) This well-kept shingle house is one of the few Queen Annes in the Sunset. It has attractive shingle patterns and a witch's cap turret.

Fourteenth Street

888–98
(c. 1885– This Stick Style building was designed and built especially

90) for the Stelling brothers, Charles and John, proprietors of the Stelling Brothers' Markets. The focus of the building is a highly unusual stellar-styled corner bay, shaped like half of a six-pointed star.

Francisco Street

769–71
(1899) An exuberance of carved detailing makes a lively facade on this Eastlake set of flats.

807
(late 1880's) Possibly this now-three-story shingle house was once only one-story. Joseph Esherick did the extensive remodeling of the house, including the addition of the "sky room" and the raising of ceilings.

864
(1912) This distinguished pink stucco house is frequently said to be a Maybeck, although John Galen Howard and Mark H. White were listed on the building permit as the architects.

898
(1914) This Tudor Gothic half-timbered residence was built for sculptor Haig Patigian. The house—a pure Period essay—is interestingly compared with the half-timbered effects that Maybeck produced at 3500 Jackson Street.

Franklin Street

714–16
(c. 1869) The bay of this relatively unadorned Italianate house is supported by unique columns.

736–38
(1876) The facade of this flat-front Italianate is broken up by more doors and windows (some pedimented) than is usual.

1355
(1905) Century Club of California. A private home—the core of the present building—was purchased by the club in 1904 and remodeled extensively. It was used for two years after the 1906 earthquake by the State Supreme Court. Then in 1914 the Classic Revival building was remodeled by Julia Morgan.

1700
(1915) First Church of Christ Scientist. Edgar Mathews executed this church in a Northern Italian Romanesque style with a cruciform plan and vari-colored brick walls and tile roof. The

fence panels are beautifully made of cast metal.

1901
(1900)
Golden Gate Church. A Baroque feeling has crept into the decorative touches of this massive Classic Revival house.

1945
(1877)
The Georgian touches that were added to this Queen Anne in a 1910 remodeling dominate the house.

2003
(1891)
A nice frieze adds a diversion to this large Stick-Eastlake house. This is the only other Victorian in the block with the eminent Queen Anne at 2007 Franklin (see Main Text).

Frederick Street

109
(1890)
Widow Mary A. Fritz entered the real estate field in 1885 and almost immediately saw the possibilities of Ashbury Heights. She had built for herself this lively Queen Anne house.

117
(c. 1901)
This residence combines the simplicity of the West Coast Shingle Style (the size and shape of the windows) with the more ornate Queen Anne (the corner tower).

Fulton Street

628 through 642
(1870's)
The usual Italianate bays on this row of attached uniform houses are crowned in an unusual manner by triangular pediments, which are surmounted by a continuous roof into which are incorporated rounded pediments.

651 through 673
(1905)
The bays, projecting cornices, and rounded pediments of this later row of houses derive from the Italianate.

858-64
(1880)
Holy Virgin Community of San Francisco. The Russian Orthodox Church bought this building in 1930, and it has continued to serve as their cathedral even after the erection of the Holy Virgin Cathedral on Geary in 1965. The shingle building, whose facade has been stuccoed, has a double roof and Gothic lancet windows.

881-83-85-87
(c. 1878)
Impressive three-story bays dominate the facade of this double house which has finely detailed balustrades, cornices and strips (foretelling Stick Style).

893-95-97-99
(c. 1880)
On the same block appears another noble Italianate double house. This one has only two stories but is also well detailed.

1124
(c. 1895)
This distinctive building, which is a residence for Roman Catholic priests, has a rounded corner that gives the effect of a bay and unusual wrought iron balconies at the second and third floors.

1201
(1896)
There is a small amount of Tudor half-timbering on this stucco home, whose most noteworthy feature is the steeply pitched roof with peaks culminating in finials.

2400
(c. 1904)
R. A. Vance of the Vance Lumber Company family of Eureka was the designer and owner of this home. He imported wood for the house from all over the world, including mahogany paneling from India.

2400 Fulton Street

6000
(1896)
"The Claremont" (as this building was known) had a reputation as a roadhouse and "French Casino", a resort in the tradition of the old Cliff House.

Geary Street

495
(1915)
Clift Hotel. Lawyer Frederick Clift had MacDonald and Applegarth design this hotel to accommodate visitors to the Panama-Pacific Exposition. In 1928 the hotel was expanded by New Yorkers Schultz and Weaver.

650
(1917)
Islam Temple. Adding a lavish dash of style to the downtown area is this Moorish romance, designed by Shriner T. Patterson Ross.

659 Geary Street

860
(1914)
This stucco apartment building, designed by Dunn and Kearns, is distinctive because of its Moorish design and intricate detailing. It relates in kind to 650.

Geary Boulevard

1109-21
(1869)
Above the street level shops in this frame building are windows that are of especially handsome Italianate proportions.

2250 and 2256
(1870)
The only houses of their vintage left in this neighborhood, these two frame homes seem to support each other in their modern environment. On the porch at 2250 is a Fireman's Insurance Plaque, one of the few original plaques remaining in the city.

4420
(1914-17)
Star of the Sea Church. The present stucco building is typical of eclectic ecclesiastical architecture. It replaced a simple, wooden church serving as the first Senior Catholic Church of the Richmond.

Golden Gate Avenue

133
(1900)
Saint Boniface Church. This Rhineland Romanesque church was designed by Brother Wewer and constructed under the supervision of Brother Idelfonse Lettert. It is built of pressed stone and reinforced steel.

760
(1887)
This small Stick Style building demonstrates a fine integration of a first-floor store and second-floor residence.

1400, 1402, 1404, 1406,
These Stick-Eastlake houses are distinguished by their interesting conical roofs over the bays. However, their importance rests

1408,
1410
and 1412
(c. 1884)

on their continued existence as a row of consistent design, even though some have had asbestos shingling added.

1482
(1876)

Notable on this Italianate house is finely detailed ornamentation, including quoining and unusual bracketing on the portico and intermediate cornice.

1503
(1875)

This well-restored Italianate has a handsome portico with Corinthian columns supporting a balustrade to which has been added an eagle.

1513,
1515,
1519,
1525,
1527,
1529
and 1531
(1875)

This exceptional row of false-parapeted Italianate residences is notable for the filigree work in the panels over the windows. Several additional residences are contained within the row but have been altered.

1671–73
(1894)

A fanciful, intricately-carved arcade has been stuck on this basically simple wood structure. The whole is surmounted by a pavilion.

2034
(c. 1885)

This recently-restored Italianate residence may signal the beginning of restoration for an entire block. The second story is thought to have been added as much as twenty years after the house was built.

Golden Gate Park

North American Hall (south of John F. Kennedy Drive)
(1916)

Lewis Hobart designed this neo-Classic building, the oldest of the Academy of Science buildings in the Park and one of the first museums to use realistic settings.

Temple of Music (south of John F. Kennedy Drive)
(1899)

Terminating the grand tree-shaded concourse is this outsized Italian Renaissance orchestra shell, a gift of Claus Spreckels, and designed by James and Merritt Reid.

Gold Mine Drive

30
(1890's)

A real stand-out in the Diamond Heights area is this barn-red Eastlake house. Once this structure served as a roadhouse, and many a dairy farmer stopped there on his way home.

Gough Street

1703,
1705,
and 1709
(1875)

These three distinguished Italianates which are remarkable in that they are so close to downtown, are well-maintained, and are more practical in size for single-family dwellings than are most Victorians.

1707
(1885)

The simple Classic Revival style of this house breaks the Italianate harmony established by 1703, 1705 and 1709. Still the house adds to the importance of the block.

2000
(1885)

A merry conglomeration of roof shapes appears on this nevertheless subdued Queen Anne house.

2004
(1889)

A full flowering of Queen Anne exuberance exists here: fishscale shingling, carved spandrels and gabled ends, turrets, gables, balconies and cut-outs.

2312
(1875)

This dignified Italianate is beautifully maintained and carefully painted so that its brackets and window frames are emphasized.

2414,
2418,
2420
and 2424
(1895)

These Hinkel-built houses exemplify the proliferation of Stick-Eastlake details and the richly-varied surface areas that he liked.

2461
(1904)

Howard White designed this house for the John Mailliard family; it represents a straightforward, solid expression of the Shingle Style.

2523
(1891)

A witch's hat turret (almost obscured) and curious bargeboard add character to this shingled Queen Anne.

2525–27
(1890)

This house's jazzed-up pediments and spandrels result from the intrusion of Eastlake into Stick Style.

Grant Avenue

250
(1909)

Albert Pissis designed this Beaux Arts building to house Raphael Weill's White House department store. This is the largest of the former White House complex of four buildings now

remodeled to accommodate specialty stores.

400–14
(1913)

Hankow Tassel Building. The first building in its block to have been rebuilt after the fire, this structure is of Oriental persuasion with a tiled blue and gold Chinese roof.

855–67
(c. 1907)

This severe brick building with shops on the first floor and rooms above is said to be on the site of the first slipper shop in Chinatown.

1123
(1912)

Corinthian pilasters and a decorative cornice add interest to this building, more neo-Classic than Chinese.

Great Highway

1626
(1906)

The front of this shingle building sports a wide three-story bay, calculated to give the upper floors a sweeping view of the beach and ocean.

Green Street

678
(1912)

Fugazi Building. A cousin of the richly-surfaced Custom House, this Italianate Baroque building was designed by Zanolini. J. F. Fugazi had this building constructed as an Italian community center.

743
(1908)

Located in a neighborhood of simple row houses, this Queen Anne home draws attention.

745–51
(1908)

This apartment has remained in the same family since it was built to the design of a Yugoslavian architect. The architect was inspired to incorporate certain touches reminiscent of homes in his native land.

852
(1907)

This trim, impeccable house was built on charred timbers used before the fire to support a considerably larger home.

982
(1878)

The south side of this simplified Italianate was scorched in 1906. This side was shingled, but the present owner has restored the siding—a reversal of the usual trend.

1111
through

The surprise of this apartment complex is the circular entrance

1133
(1909)
courtyard replete with trees, bushes and flowers. The building offers an assortment of bays, carved balconies and gabled roofs.

1122–24–26
(1897 and 1916)
This building consists of a two-story flat, probably the original residence; another flat above, built later; and one lower apartment. The stark look of this stucco building is softened by French balconied windows.

1132–34
(1912)
Brass fixtures on the mahogany doors add to the entranceway's attractiveness on this stucco building. Twin gables sit atop the slanted bays, adding a vertical interest to the building.

1135–37–39
(1909)
Perched atop a towering retaining wall this shingle and half-timbered building consists of three two-story row houses. The entrance path leads through a garden setting to four shingled cottages in the rear, 1139 A, B, C and D Green.

1136–38–40
(1911)
The front doors of these flats are reached by a partially-enclosed stairway with Roman arch and wooden balustrade. Two sets of squared bays lead to the bracketed roof line.

1140 A
(1902)
A wooden balustrade graces the entranceway of this home which complements its neighbor on Green. A garden has been added atop the roof.

1152–54
(1909)
(30 Delgado Place). A third story and gabled roof edged with bargeboard were added to what was originally a two-story shingle residence.

1175–77–79
(1909)
A vertical thrust is evident in these flats, which have two groups of slanted bays that lead upward to the dentil molding at the roof line.

1328
(1918)
A version of Parisian Baroque Revival, this house has the rusticated bottom story, iron balconies and ornamentation that derive from that style. Its cornice is more robust than might be expected.

1629 and 1635
(1917)
Lovely scrollwork from the 1915 Exposition is seen inside these Bay Area Shingle houses. They

were designed by Elizabeth Austin who placed them in a garden setting.

1665 and 1667
(c. 1879)
Old and rare (for this area) redwood trees set off these two houses built on the Burr property, which once ran down the hill from Vallejo. There is almost an Oriental illusion to the sweep of the portico's roof on 1667.

1713
(1890)
Diamond shingling, a frieze and spoolwork make engaging patterns on this Stick-Eastlake house, built by contractor George M. Salsbury.

1715
(1894)
An even later Stick-Eastlake than 1713, this one has decorative elements that have become more playful.

1717 and 1719
(1888)
The interest in this Stick Style pair lies at the roof line, where friezes, scalloped shingles and cut-out gable ends mix.

1748
(1902)
This is an unadorned yet distinguished shingled building (now flats) that has been completely modernized inside. It overlooks Allyne Park.

1761–63
(1890)
This Stick Style house once made an appearance in *House and Garden Remodeling Guide* (Fall-Winter, 1964).

1767–69
(1889)
This house has the same scale as 1761–63 but differing details. This has small-paned windows, balustrade above the entranceway and semi-Mansard roof, which the other did not have.

1800–02
(1884)
Except for its brackets and dentil courses, this Italianate is truly basic and unadorned.

1806–10
(1885)
Handsome window frames and a Corinthian-columned portico highlight this Stick Style house, built by contractor-architect William Wharff.

1900
(1885)
Crisp decorative details are seen on this Stick Style corner house, now converted to flats.

2421
(1893)
The brothers Coxhead designed this dramatically simple, shingled house for themselves. It is an excellent example of the Cox-

heads' ability to make a home comfortable and spacious, and to integrate the out-of-doors with the interior.

2423
(1892)
The Coxheads built this English cottage for their friend, James F. McGauley, next door to their home. The house has been remodeled by Francis McCarthy, who fortunately maintained the home's charm—a result of the use of half-timbering, leaded windows, brick work and a rippled roof.

2508
(1901)
Edgar Mathews designed this half-timbered house, an especially good example of its style. It relates to his houses at 2415 and 2421 Pierce.

2801
(1905)
A truly outstanding shingle Colonial Revival house, this residence is also fortunate in being set in a profusion of trees and shrubs.

2829
(1870's)
Two capped wells remain on the property of this cottage—one of the first farm-houses in Cow Hollow. There have been a few changes to the pristine red house with hooded windows. For instance, what is now the middle window was once the front door reached by a boardwalk.

Greenwich Street

631
(1907)
Within sixty days after the fire, this cottage was built as one of the first "emergency houses" with timber salvaged from old ships. The house has remained in the same family.

659
(c. 1907)
This wooden house was moved to its present location in 1912. A colorful garden extends from the street to the polished white marble stairs leading to the elevated entrance.

1324, 1326–28 and 1330
(1870's)
These were three of five houses reputedly built by a shipmaster who brought to San Francisco a cargo of Honduras mahogany which was then used in these cottages. The cottage at 1330 and its parent house on the street are now rather plain shingled structures; 1324 has an elaborate diamond shingle pattern. All have been renovated and remodeled.

270

1331
(1907)
Gardner Dailey remodeled this house in 1935, using as a prototype the London Bloomsbury house. Of interest is the metal bas relief fire insurance plaque on the facade. In former days this connoted membership in a fire insurance company and meant a fire company would protect the house.

1342–44
(c. 1875)
Originally a one-story cottage on Larkin Street, this shingled Italianate house found new life after the fire when it was moved to its present location and given a second story.

1356
(c. 1906)
Large cracks in the cellar floor lead the present owners to speculate that this very simple, shingle home survived the earthquake. William Wooster remodeled the interior.

1753–55
(1870's)
In 1900 this early Villa house was moved from a previous location at the corner of Octavia. The especially excellent window frames and open-work balustrades add character to the large house.

1919–33
(1890)
This row of two double late Stick Style houses presents an effectively unified picture.

**2371,
2377 and
2379**
(1875)
These three attached one-story, flat-front Italianates form a handsome, yet exceedingly simple group.

2845
(c. 1885–90)
Apparently the upper story of this house (with fanciful Moorish type carvings centered around a sun) was once a beach cottage. In 1888 this house was combined with another cottage by raising the house and inserting the cottage underneath.

2845 Greenwich Street

Grove Street

503–05
(1885)
Ornate decoration, which includes gold medallions, highlights this Stick-Eastlake house which has been well-maintained.

537
(c. 1880)
The paint scheme highlights the floriated frieze, the gable end with its fan carving and other Eastlake decorative devices on this small house. The original stable still stands to the rear of the home.

**636,
640–44,
648–50**
(c. 1872)
These three Italianates form a unit, although 640–44, being three stories to the others' two stories, dominates.

814
(1882)
One of four unusually well-preserved houses in this block, this residence basically adheres to the grace of the Italianate style.

823
(c. 1890)
This residence is visible from the street although behind 825–27. A central squared bay on the second floor acts as a portico for the entrance below which has unusually handsome front doors. Other windows have pediments of varying widths, balancing the facade.

824
(1886)
Stick additions have been applied to this basically Italianate structure, which is one of the important houses in this block.

825–27
(c. 1877)
Built by John Hinkel, this elaborate Italianate residence was constructed to take advantage of its once-larger lot as witnessed by the large bay on its east side.

834
(c. 1874)
Built for Philip Stephen Fay, this was the first house on the block and was once surrounded by a deer park. The house is a classic example of the Italianate enriched with details drawn from the Renaissance Mannerist styles.

957
(1890)
Arched windows and carved finial-topped gables are interestingly juxtaposed on this small Stick-Eastlake house.

Guerrero Street

102
(c. 1883)
This slender, graceful Italianate home has wide, ornate bays which are especially lovely at the first story. The colonettes and window frames are all extensively embellished.

104–14
(c. 1910)
This late Period six-unit dwelling has a balanced facade with classical mutules and porticos.

226
(1906)
When this Sheet Metal Workers' Union Hall was built, Mayor McCarthy was quoted as saying it was "the most beautiful union hall in existence". Perhaps he was referring to the lacy balustrade that frames a central monument from which rises an eagle atop a globe.

801–05
(c. 1870)
The Italianate details (quoins, pediments, Corinthian columns on the portico) have been treated with care on this house.

811–13
(c. 1877)
Incised panels and a carved balustrade above the portico add to the ornamentation of this Italianate.

827
(1880's)
A lively, crowded exterior is presented by this early Queen Anne house. Fishscale and hobnail shingles, horizontal siding, clustered vertical strips, richly-carved panels and stucco segments all help to enliven the facade.

845
(1871)
Although this house is bordered by the same stone wall as 827, it is strikingly different architecturally, for this residence is of simple flat-front Italianate design.

862
(c. 1883)
The elaborate, carved panels of vertical strips and studded diamond medallions trimming the portico distinguish this Italianate house.

863
(c. 1872)
The original door and iron fence enhance the charm of this Italianate cottage.

900–02
(c. 1895)
Built as the family home of rancher-dairyman John D. Daly, this Queen Anne house has a corner tower, a rich array of bays, floreate friezes and ship-

271

lap and fishscale shingles. Directly behind, Mr. Daly built a small Colonial Revival house.

906
(c. 1882)
The original wooden double doors (with beautifully-carved panels and stained glass transom) greet one at the top of a great flight of stairs on this Stick Style house.

915–17
(1879)
The striking feature of this Italianate house is the long frieze of jigsaw ogee arches above the high arch and short composite columns of the Romanesque portico (surely added later).

948
(1878)
A slab stucco apartment crowds this distinguished Italianate, which is set back from the street on a knoll. The portico shows an intrusion of Stick Style, for it is composed of angular columns supporting a hood mold.

964–66–68
(c. 1890)
A lovely frieze of scallops, strips and dentils and diamond-shingled hoods over the bays (the first-story one extending across the portico) are distinctive on this Stick Style double house.

986
(1883)
This small, delightful house stands as testimony to the skill of Charles Geddes, who designed the home for his family. He skillfully blended details of Stick Style—its basic design—with Victorian Gothic ones.

988–90
(c. 1895)
A fanciful version of late Stick-Eastlake merging with Queen Anne, this house presents a towering cupola above a row of colonnettes, above the pedimented cornice, above the frieze of waffle design.

1056–58
(c. 1889)
A simple but fine Stick Style duplex, this has carved diamond medallions in the panels over the windows.

1074
(1895)
Mission United Presbyterian Church (formerly Stewart Memorial Presbyterian Church). This large grey shingled church combines Victorian Gothic and Romanesque styles under a steep gabled roof. The entrance is a heavy round arch, with ogee-like frame, and the major windows have high round arches though the largest ones have lancet-shaped hoods.

1076
(c. 1887)
Most unusual window and door treatment is seen on this predominately Italianate (slightly Gothic) one-story house. A stained glass transom is above the door while the rounded windows of the front bay are surmounted by more such transoms.

1169 and 1177
(c. 1881–1882)
These two slender flat-front Italianates, painted contrasting colors of barn-red and blue-gray, have retained their dignity.

1180–82
(c. 1884)
The balanced facade on this Italianate double house contains a finely-worked portico, whose entablature contains friezes with dentils and cartouches.

1233–37
(c. 1889)
This towering house encompasses the late, ornate Stick Style with Eastlake detailing, especially in the waffle pediment.

1241–1241A and B
(c. 1887)
On this Stick Style house there are floral panels unique to the Mission District. Some have heavily embossed ball flowers and leaves; others have acanthus shells and budding clovers.

1286
(1894)
A number of Queen Anne features come to fruition in this pink home with its elaborately-carved surfaces, small, rounded balustrade above the entrance, and finial-topped tower.

1317–19
(c. 1889)
This Stick-Eastlake house is notable for its heavy bargeboard and finial-topped portico pediment.

1320
(c. 1880)
Although unusually wide, this Italianate has the traditional quoins, hood molds and ribbed consoles.

1325
(1886)
Captain A. Dodd, a master mariner, brought the lumber for this house to San Francisco on his own ship. It is Stick Style with many well-handled strips, panels, and pediments.

1335
(1918)
Built on a steel sub-structure, this elaborate building does not relate specifically to one style but contains features of Classic Revival, Baroque and neo-Renaissance.

1413, 1415–17
(c. 1894)
Striking ornamentation is evident on these Stick-Eastlakes, built by Fernando Nelson. Interestingly, on 1415–17 (a double house) the portico is topped by a windowless, quiet stretch between the bays.

1558–60
(c. 1890)
Basically Stick Style with an infusion of Eastlake and Romanesque touches, this house has rounded arches at the portico, whose rhythm is reiterated in the frieze.

Haight Street

37–47, 49–59, 61–65
(c. 1875)
In a block giving way to commerce, this row of three identical double Italianate apartment houses maintains its architectural integrity. Each building gives the effect of being a double house with two side-by-side entrances.

121
(1877)
This Stick Style house was erected by the Trustees of the San Francisco Theological Seminary, belonged to the Communist Party during World War II, then was bought by the Baptist Church and is now used as the Fellowship Bible Institute.

588
(1884)
An exuberance of detail is played across the top two floors of this Stick Style house. A grocery store takes up the ground floor.

588 Haight Street

Hancock Street

129
(1877)
Knox, Kosovitz and Narrin remodeled the interior of this Italianate in the mid-1960's so

272

beautifully that it was featured in *House Beautiful.*

142
(1880)
This low, pristine Italianate cottage is now nestled between taller, newer, bolder buildings.

173–75
(1898)
An interesting intersection of the gable end with the conical tower is seen on this Queen Anne. It has a lively surface treatment with friezes and fish scale shingles.

Hartford Street

45
(c. 1901)
A proliferation of pilasters, a floriated frieze and a "spider web" arched doorway of Queen Anne derivation are seen on this house, built by Fernando Nelson.

164
(c. 1890)
An astonishingly busy facade has been given this small house built by Louis Landler. Consoles, strips and filled pediments, and three layers of cornices add to the activity.

177
(1888)
The Eastlake portico and gable end are decorative elements of this cottage's facade.

219
(1882)
The most elaborate feature of this simple late Italianate-Stick cottage is the entrance portico. Beneath the shingle hood is a frieze of spindles above jigsaw panels.

251
(c. 1891)
This house was built by Louis Landler. The same type of treatment of consoles (becoming strips), pediments, and tiered cornices is seen here as on 164.

253–55
(1890)
Again built by Louis Landler, this house incorporates features of the Stick and Eastlake styles. The blend of fishscale and sawtooth shingles on the facade provides added interest.

257 and 259
(1890)
These two similar, though not identical, homes were also built by Louis Landler and have detailing similar to 253–55 (above). The row of three shows the effect of variable detailing on the basic theme.

Hayes Street

615–19–21
These three Italianate houses are actually one continuous building. A strong rhythm is established by the bays, balustrades and cornices.

1027
(1891)
High above a concrete stairway is this towering Queen Anne, whose vast gable end almost obscures the corner tower.

1045
(1877)
This Italianate has few embellishments. It is set above a concrete retaining wall and overlooks Alamo Square.

Henry Street

15–17
(c. 1889)
The original doors, stairs and balustrades (with stubby finials) are still part of this Stick Style house.

73
(1893)
This one-story house is Stick-Eastlake with Queen Anne-Stick overtones. A pediment-gable (almost hiding a semi-Mansard roof) pulls the square bay and porch into a unit.

156
(1888)
A striking little Stick Style house, this has a facade highlighted by black paint picking out the decorative details.

158–60–62
(1882)
An abundance of Eastlake details suggests a date about a decade later. Quite startling is the horseshoe pendant at the apex of the gable.

178–80
(c. 1897)
This beautifully painted house sports an elaborate floreate frieze, pediment with sawtooth shingles, and Ionic columns and pilasters.

191, 193–95 and 197–99
(c. 1892)
An unusual cupola, corner tower, and Eastlake chalet gables make this house of interest.

209
(c. 1906)
Recently restored, this attractive house retains its shell medallions, composite pilasters and octagonal shingles in the pediment.

Hermann Street

220 and 222–24
(c. 1878)
Almost identical, these Stick Style mirror twins have unusual ornamental detailing, particularly over the central windows in the squared bay tiers.

230 and 232–34½
(c. 1872)
The imposing house at 232 is perhaps the only of its kind in San Francisco. The central portion of this Italianate is seemingly projected from the remainder of the residence which forms wings on either side. The restrained Stick Style of 230 is complementary.

337
(c. 1887)
In this Stick Style cottage, windows are framed in Tudor-like arches, the theme being repeated in the portico, which is surmounted by cresting.

Hill Street

16–16A
(c. 1883)
Built in the slender Italianate style, this house has concentrated portico, window, and cornice detailing.

22–22½ 24–24½
(1878)
These Italianate twins, enclosed by their original iron fences, are not noticeably affected by newer side entrances.

25 and 35
(1885) and (1880)
Behind graceful old iron fences and separated by a tree-shaded garden, these identically painted homes offer a study in two early styles. That at 25 depicts Stick Style with lavish Italianate details, while 35 is a cottage of pure Italianate persuasion.

34
(1880)
Strips of Stick Style appear here. This house is a lovely interpretation of the Italianate. The lacy balustrade with urn finials adds distinction to its portico.

49
(1881–82)
A Stick Style home, this is most notable for its panels delicately incised with Pennsylvania-Dutch swirls and patterns. The original iron fence, gates, and posts add to the attractiveness.

59–61
(1882)
Spacious and regal, this Stick Style home has heavy, squeezed pediments with squared apexes.

69–75
(c. 1887)
This extremely large Stick mansion was altered in 1920 to form a side entrance for multiple units. It still is very impressive, with because the more modern section being recessed behind the portico.

77–79
(1883)
Many finely incised panels add elegance to the facade of this Stick Style house.

83,
91-93
(1883)

Virtually twins, these two Stick homes have squeezed pediments (over the second level squared bays) filled with delicate Pennsylvania-Dutch filigree.

87-89
(1883)

This unusual Stick Style home is between two others, which it resembles. It is notable because it was either altered or was created with an extremely wide squared bay at the second level.

543 and
544
(1889)
and
(1890)

From an original group of eight similar houses built by Isaac Anderson, only these two Stick-Eastlake homes remain unchanged. Strikingly elaborate wooden ornamentation adorns the bay tiers, their pediment hoods, and angular porticos.

Hoffman Avenue

20
(c. 1897)

High graceful stairs (with original newel posts and balustrades) and an ornate waffle pediment decorate this home.

119
(c. 1880's)

This impressive flat-front semi-Mansarded cottage with Italianate detailing does not attain the true verticality of Italianate.

121
(c. 1898)

Built in a semi-Mansarded Italianate derivative style (with one slanted bay), this house still has its old picket fence and tall, shading trees.

Homestead Street

55
(c. 1892)

Although recessed and lowered, this cottage is unique on a street of newer or remodeled houses. Its shingled, stripped and carved surfaces are well under control.

Hyde Street

1005
(1915)

Edward E. Young designed this corner apartment house with its rounded bays and cornice richly decorated with leaf brackets, bands of egg-and-dart motif and dentil molding.

1200
(1908)

The Chinese Seventh Day Adventist Church is now housed in this pristine Greek Revival building. It has the Ionic columned portico that would be expected with that style.

1255
(1908)

Now the Chinese Southern Baptist Church, this building was designed by H. T. Starbuck for the Third Baptist Church. A massive tower and Tudor arched windows dominate the building.

1317
(1909)

This attractive apartment house, still in the family of the original owners, was designed and built by E. H. Denke. The half-timbering has been contained on the square bays.

1255 Hyde Street

1317 Hyde Street

1401-
03-05
(1908)

The striking feature of this apartment is the dome topping the corner bays. It is said that corner bays fell from favor around this period because of the cost of curved glass.

1954-64
(1911)

An intricate use of a dentil course, egg-and-dart molding and a bracketed cornice give character to this apartment house with its four groupings of rounded bays.

2319-23

(1100 Lombard Street.) This

(1899-
1900)

stucco residence, often called the "Stevenson House," was built for the widow of Robert Louis Stevenson, perhaps to the designs of Willis Polk. Originally the house was two instead of four stories at the Hyde-Lombard corner and had the air of a Tudor-Baroque country manor rather than that of a Mediterranean villa as now.

2319-23 Hyde Street

2646-48,
2650-52
and
2654-56
(1902)

Here is a group of three houses with much carved ornamentation. The two at 2646-48 and 2654-56 have especially heavy carving on their central spandrels.

Ivy Street

416-18
(1889)

The plain flat-front on this house has certain Stick Style features such as strips at the corners, and certain Italianate features such as a bracketed cornice.

Jackson Street

400-02
(c. 1882)

(701 Sansome Street) This beautifully maintained rough brick structure provides a meaningful beginning to the 400 block of Jackson Street. Notable are the arched ground floor openings which are framed in white stone.

435-41
(1861)

Cast iron pilasters on the first floor and brick work on the second give a distinguished appearance to this building which once housed medical-dental offices. The hulls of two dismantled schooners were used in its construction.

470
(1866)

A wide variety of businesses has occupied this attractive brick building—a Chinese printing firm, a liquor warehouse and now decorators' shops.

1152
(1912)
Four Corinthian columns support the portico of this wood apartment house, designed as an eight-unit apartment house but looking more like a one-family residence.

1224
(1910)
The elaborate carved ornamentation on the rounded bays of this apartment house is of interest.

1231–33,
1235–37
and
1239–41
(c. 1909)
These three homes make a cohesive group. The center one was built for George C. Warren, for many years the drama critic of the *San Francisco Chronicle*. It has a low tile roof and clinker brick fringing the entranceway. The other two flanking it have steeply pitched gable roofs.

1535
(1913)
Chinese Community Church. This brick and cement building was originally a doctors' office building. It is marked by four giant order Ionic pilasters.

1659
(1881)
Moved to its present site in 1912, this Italianate residence was apparently originally located in the unburned area west of Van Ness. It is probably the only house of its kind left in the general Nob Hill area.

1659 Jackson Street

1819
(1889)
The frieze of the bay extends into a balustrade on this Queen Anne-Eastlake house.

1901
This monumental Classic Re-

vival mansion has had a number of uses: a residence, a school, a restaurant, a guest house and presently a retirement home. The interior detailing reflects the opulence of the era: carved moldings, damask walls, crystal chandeliers.

2020
(c. 1902)
This stately brick Classic Revival residence housed the offices of Union Trust Company of San Francisco and Wells Fargo-Nevada National Bank as well as the law offices of Heller, Powers and Ehrman for approximately a month following the 1906 fire and earthquake.

2020 Jackson Street

2232
(1873)
Small iron balconies do not appear original on this otherwise pristine flat-front Italianate.

2260
(c. 1895)
Interesting textural qualities exist within this home's gable end while Classic Revival details set off the doorway window units.

2434
(c. 1885)
The Eastlake chalet detailing on the portico and gable and the exaggerated verticality of this house give it distinction.

2441
(1891)
This striking Queen Anne (with a profusion of gables, balustrades, friezes and patterned shingles) is now used for Conard House, a halfway home for mental patients.

2811
(c. 1887–1891)
Perhaps it is the somber paint that makes this Queen Anne seem disciplined.

2891
(1889)
Brackets that become strips and nicely defined window areas are of interest on this Stick Style house.

2904
and
2930
(1890
Almost identical, these basically Stick houses have an infusion of Eastlake detailing. The house at 2930 has had a modern

and
1889)
garage added at street level.

2970
(1888)
The pedimented portico and bay work together to form a unified facade on this Stick Style house designed by William Lewis.

3065
(1918)
Katherine Delmar Burke School. Julia Morgan designed this building for Burke School. Generally of Spanish Revival stucco architecture, the tile-roofed school is built around a central patio.

3157
(1908)
Delightfully set amidst an abundance of foliage, this shingle house is approached by a private funicular.

3232
(1897)
The facade of this residence is dominated by a Colonial Revival portico and bracketed cornice.

3249
(1895)
This small wooden Queen Anne-Eastlake was at one time divided into five apartments. It was subsequently converted back to its original use as a single family dwelling.

3286–
88–90
(1908)
A pair of three-story squared bay windows, quoining and a dentiled cornice make this a distinctive building. Inside, the trim varies greatly from room to room, indicating the carpenters improvised as they went along.

3356 and
3362
(1898)
These mirror twins are joined by a party wall and common roof. The half-timbered exteriors of the two houses differ only in the stain of the wood.

3425
(1908–09)
Built by R. Schieve and Joseph Byrns, this distinguished shingled house is of English derivation. Its cantilevered second story with partially enclosed porch is dramatized by the double gables.

3430
(1916)
This home was built for a gentleman who wanted his home to resemble a Second Empire French townhouse. In 1944 the interior was altered considerably; the exterior, with its attractively patterned brick work, was left unchanged.

3675
(1901)
Engineer W. D. E. Blankenburg designed this stucco house for

his family. It is of Queen Anne persuasion (the conical roofed tower) with Classic Revival details.

3675 Jackson Street

3855
(1912)
William Hammond Hall, superintendent of Golden Gate Park, designed this stucco home for his wife. It was early split-level, having been built on five levels. There were a number of innovations for the time, such as air conditioning, an intercom system and an earthquake shelter.

Jersey Street

229
(c. 1891)
Built in Stick, semi-Mansarded Style, this house is notable for panels carved like tree branches and its heavy Eastlake waffle pediment.

255
(c. 1891)
Built with an upholstery and sheet metal works on the property, this unique Stick Style house has a wide porch flanked by narrow, squared bays.

261, 265,
271 and
283
(c. 1891)
These are the only unaltered homes in an original Stick Style row built by Nelson S. Hammerton. They are notable for their graceful, tall balustraded stairways.

349
(c. 1892)
Quantities of vertical stripping lead the eye upward on this Stick Style cottage. The squared bay, supported on heavy brackets, is capped by a semi-Mansarded hood which repeats the false parapet.

385–87
(c. 1893)
This two-story Stick house has a center entrance surmounted by a balustrade between squared bay tiers.

409
(c. 1875)
This flat-front Italianate residence has particularly fine squeezed pediments over the door and windows.

416
(c. 1891)
Festoons of fruit and leaves decorate this semi-Mansarded Stick Style house.

422, 426,
428
(c. 1891–92)
These semi-Mansarded Stick Style row cottages are noteworthy for high, sloping fishscale and diamond shingled hoods.

514
(c. 1892)
The stained glass-rimmed windows remain on this semi-Mansarded Stick Style cottage.

552–54
(c. 1896)
Greatly resembling 514, this Stick Style one-story home is the least altered in a row of several.

587, 593
and 595–97
(1895–96)
E. J. Plant built these three Eastlake cottages with gable roofs. 595–97 has a newer ground-level addition which has served as a store for many years.

Jones Street

1342
(1913)
This relatively small apartment house, which represents the work of Arthur Laib, uses his characteristic graceful multi-paned French windows.

1350
(1909)
This Georgian Revival brick townhouse, along with 1342, adds warmth and personality to a street dominated by large apartment houses. Restauranteur John Tait and actress Ina Claire are among those who have lived in the house.

1711
(1912)
Joseph Riffier, the original owner, is said to have drawn up plans for this brick house based on his former home in France.

1763–65
(1908)
(1101–11 Vallejo) This recently refurbished frame house is opposite the Vallejo Street ramp. Its details are indicative of its era: an arched entrance supported by columns and bracketed roof line.

1801–03
(1913)
On the northwest corner of Jones stands this three-story brown shingle building designed by Mastropasque. An interesting feature is the series of roofed squared bays at the second and third floors.

2230–34
(1907)
An outstanding "Romeo and Juliet" staircase graces the front of this three-story wood apartment house.

Jordan Avenue

71
(1907)
This home was built by Joseph R. Leonard, who constructed several homes in this area, including the twin to this at 57. A Queen Anne tower with a beehive-shaped dome is glimpsed through thick foliage.

Jordan Park

(1906 and thereafter)
South of California Street and east of Arguello Boulevard is this early-day development laid out on the streets of Commonwealth, Jordan, Euclid, Parker and Palm. Constructed on a cemetery, the area was named after the Jordan family, which bought the tract shortly after the earthquake.

Josiah Street

134
(prior to 1906)
Highly individual, this house sits way back on a large lot across whose front extends an unpainted wooden fence composed of handsome balusters. A fine stairway leads to the second story entrance of the house.

Juri Street

1–1A
(c. 1894)
2
(1887)
3 and 5
(c. 1894)
Louis Juri, owner of a large ranch here, sold some of his land for the San Francisco-San Jose Railroad in 1858 but retained this adjacent property. 1–1A is a unique, trapezoid, festooned Stick Style house. 2 has a chaste flat facade. 3 and 5 were once separate Stick Style mirror twins but now share a common portico and a lovely theme of pediments.

Kearny Street

527–29
(c. 1911)
This building, designed by Crim and Scott, is presently used as a hotel with stores on the first floor. It is a five-story building whose best feature is the series of Corinthian columns that rise to the fourth floor.

Kent Street

12
(1906)
This rustic, slant-roofed box was built by a contractor named de Martini. Sometime after 1943 the clapboard exterior was shingled and the famed sign—

Rusty's Fort MCMVI—was mysteriously hung on the front.

Laguna Street

Corner of Rose *(1883)* Thomas Welsh designed this barn, a simple rectangular structure, whose hayloft door and square louvered cupola (used for ventilation) are still intact.

1603–09 *(1871)* The notable "roof scope" of this old house is reminiscent of German and Dutch town roof shapes done in the sixteenth and seventeenth centuries; the hipped roof makes a good foil for these shapes.

1613–15–17 *(c. 1890)* Boldly scaled Stick details on this house include an independent gable that floats over the eaves above the main bay window.

1618 *(1878)* The pipestem colonnettes of this simple Italianate house are banded midway up the windows.

1622 *(1875)* Double windows substitute for the more usual bays on this flat-front Italianate which does achieve the usual verticality of that style.

1730–32 *(1877)* The center element of this Italianate's bay has been divided into two narrow windows (instead of the usual single window) thus emphasizing the vertical effect.

1735–39, 1743 and 1745 *(1891)* This triple Italianate house, along with the house-shop complex on the corner, makes effective street architecture. Together they comprise a substantially unchanged late Italinate half-block.

1747–49–51 *(1880's)* (1901 Bush Street) A seemingly effortless integration of the shop on the corner with the house behind has been achieved mainly by a careful alignment of the floor and roof levels and the continuation of the intermediate cornice of the house as a balustrade around the shop.

1802, 1804, 1806 and 1832 *(1877)* The "stepping-down-the-hill" of these nearly identical Italianate houses makes for a lively effect along the street.

1933 *(1874)* The center hall plan seen in this Italianate is unusual—especially for a one-story cottage.

2535 *(1902)* Dr. Florence Ward, one of the city's first female physicians, bought the large corner lot at Laguna and Broadway and commissioned Coxhead and Coxhead to design three houses as an income venture. This redwood shingle house is the only one remaining.

2808, 2810, 2812, 2814 and 2816 *(c. 1885)* Planned and constructed simultaneously by Robert Brotherton, this distinctive row of houses was built on speculation. Variation was achieved by the width of the lots and the number of stories: 2808 and 2816 (three stories) are on 25-foot lots, while the middle three (two stories) are on 18-foot lots. The houses have been tastefully maintained.

2819–21 *(1890)* The usual embellishments of the Italianate style are slightly exaggerated here—no doubt due to the late date.

3029–31 *(1884)* This tiny flat-front Italianate has had a wood wall added along the sidewalk. The windows, too, are no doubt later additions.

Lake Street

300 *(1902)* The Little Sisters of the Poor own this imposing brick building designed by Albert Pissis as a home for the aged. It leans toward Georgian Revival in style.

944 *(1907)* This gabled shingle house represents a style often seen on Lake Street. It is well-maintained and painted vivid red.

1000 *(1906)* This shingle gambrel-roofed house, like all the houses on the north side of Lake between Eighth and Funston Avenues, backs on Mountain Lake Park, campsite of De Anza in 1776.

Larkin Street

1560 *(1907)* (1595 Clay Street) This shingle and brick multi-bayed, multi-gabled apartment house has distinctively treated doorways.

1560 Larkin Street

2447–49 *(1907)* This building has undergone considerable remodeling. The new touches of the balustrade at the roof line (taken from the original porch), doorway and shuttered windows give a Colonial Revival look to the residence.

2565 *(1906)* The plans for this house were drawn up before the fire, but the house was not constructed until after. It is a shingle home whose simplicity is relieved by a dentiled cornice.

2601–03 *(1909)* Resembling a large shingle bungalow, this comfortable, rambling apartment house finds its principal ornamentation in the bracketed cornice.

2705 *(c. 1900)* This house and its two neighbors form an appealing group. Although the exterior of this house has been remodeled, the straightforward lines are much as they were originally.

2707
(c. 1903)
Owner-architect Joseph Esherick has remodeled the interior of this house. Outside, a lead and glass canopy over the door presents an interesting digression from the simple lines of the Bay Area Shingle house.

2709
(1903)
A free adaption of English Tudor is seen in this shingle house whose bottom story is stucco. An unusual roof facia projects over the front of the house.

Laurel Street

201
(1906)
This handsome example of Bay Area Shingle Style has a semi-Mansard roof, a feature not normally seen in this period.

312
(1880)
The exterior of this small Italianate home is covered with white shingles with corner boards. The recessed front door is especially narrow.

Leavenworth Street

1109
(c. 1908)
(In Acorn Alley) Corner pilasters and a hood mold over the door are distinguishing elements on this tiny wood one-story house.

1201–19
(1908–1909)
(1400–10 Sacramento Street) There is a rich display of bays, gables, carved decorative touches on this large frame apartment house.

1907
(1906)
This three-story brown shingle apartment building is set on a black brick foundation. The roof line is accentuated by a heavy bracketed cornice painted a contrasting white.

2366 Leavenworth Street

2366
(1908)
This simple house was built on the foundations of the present owner's grandparents' home. The house possesses a lovely Thomas Church garden, the focal points of which are two gazebos.

2434
(c. 1885)
Wisteria vines hide some of the details of this Stick-Eastlake house. The chalet implications of Eastlake are here reduced to a pattern under the main gable; a mixture of decorative details spills out below.

2502
(1885)
An unusual effect is achieved in this residence by the placement of a squared-off bay directly on a slanted one.

2504
(1884)
The lines of this brown shingled house are crisp and sharp. It is a good foil for 2502.

Leona Terrace

1323
(1908)
Built of lumber salvaged from buildings demolished after the fire in 1906, these two buildings on this tiny street are identical. They have simplified Classic Revival details especially manifested in the two-story-high Ionic pilasters.

Lexington Street

317–19
(1876)
This Italianate home is notable for its quoins and for its window arrangement, featuring one slanted bay console beneath a flat second story.

329, 333–35 and 337–39
(1877)
The original iron fences frame this row of three chaste, identical false-front Italianate houses.

330
(1876)
Framed by a picket fence and beautiful garden, this Italianate home features heavy, ribbed, squeezed pediments.

334, 338, 342
(1876)
This row of three identical Italianate homes is almost a duplicate of 329, 333–35 and 337–39.

351, 351A and 353–55
(c. 1883)
These delicately carved Italianate mirror twins are placed wall-to-wall to simulate a duplex.

359–61
(prior to 1899)
house's flat facade adorned only with hood molds on brackets.

367
(c. 1883)
Behind a pretty iron fence, gate and garden, this Italianate home features a first-story bay beneath a flat second story like 317–19.

376
(1876)
Here is still another unadorned Italianate but it is surrounded by newer or altered homes.

Liberty Street

15–17
(c. 1893)
The wooden ornamentation has an Eastlake flavor on this basically Stick Style house.

19–21 and 23–25
(c. 1877)
Both of these are Stick-Italianate homes with slanted bay tiers.

20–22 and 24–26
(c. 1879)
These Stick-Italianate mirror twins are notable. Both seem to have been built simultaneously, one perhaps as the owner's residence, the other for rental units.

27–29
(1894)
Easily the most elaborate of the row, this large, unusual residence is Queen Anne in character with quantities of Stick Style detailing. Particularly notable is the Romanesque arch at the portico surmounted by a giant pediment, which breaks into the balustrade above.

31–33
(c. 1892)
This Stick-Eastlake home has a false gable (above the bays) which creates the illusion of a tower. Fantastic panels of decorative wreaths, ovals, and arches are highlighted in white.

35–37
(1878)
This graceful Stick-Italianate residence has two identical entrances (one recessed, one in front) with unique lace-like balustrades above.

43–49
(1870)
Built for the family of Marshall Doane, merchant and contractor, this Italianate complex was originally a three-family dwelling. The family's residence was undoubtedly 45. A driveway on the east leads back to a tree-shaded area and structure which resembles an old carriage house.

44–46
(c. 1889)
A narrow squared bay tier and wide windows are seen on this

278

Stick Style house. A false semi-Mansard roof slopes down over the bays to squeeze the pediment.

50
(c. 1889)
This Period home has Stick detailing, including a squared bay tier. It also incorporates sawtooth shingles and a Tudor arched window left of the entrance.

58
(1876)
This balanced Italianate house has one slightly recessed bay tier and entrance. A Mansard-like roof overhangs the structure and forms broken pediment hoods above each bay tier.

70
(1871)
The balanced facade, central entrance (containing slender horse-shoe arched windows and etched transom) and three-story bay tiers of this house are unusual Italianate.

76
(1878)
The detailing has become a little heavier on this Italianate house — especially on the portico.

77–79
(1873)
The front and side slanted bay tiers of this house have round arched windows on the first floor, while those on the second are considerably different.

112–14
(c. 1870)
This Italianate house retains its beautiful fluted Corinthian pipe-stem colonnettes and graceful arched windows.

154–56
(c. 1871)
In bright splendor, this Italianate home features incised panels, accented in pale gray, on the white facade.

180
(c. 1871)
Built as a one-story residence, this Italianate had a matching second story added in 1895. It has an exquisite Eastlake portico, which would certainly be of the later date also.

219–21
(1886)
Stately and beautiful, this semi-Mansarded, Stick Style house towers on its hill. It has heavy ribbing above the windows.

241–43
(c. 1870's)
This tall Italianate house is almost hidden behind a high retaining wall. It once had an adjacent twin which has now been modified.

533–579
(1897–98)
There is a theatrical as well as literary background to this row of houses, built in an Eastlake style. "I Remember Mama" was filmed on this block, once part of a large dairy farm owned by author Peter B. Kyne.

546
(c. 1897)
The false gable end of this house contains a sunburst and a bargeboard of circle medallions supported by a central console.

572
(1897)
Built in late Stick-Eastlake Style, this house has an ornate double door.

Lincoln Way

1601–05
(1910)
The porticos of this four-unit apartment house are supported by Ionic columns while two-story Ionic pilasters delineate the corners.

Linden Street

305–11
(1908)
A floriated frieze and "Romeo and Juliet" center stairway adorn this four-unit frame apartment building.

433–39
(1885)
The second story of this Stick Style house dominates the structure, for the two square bays only appear at this level. They are connected by a balustrade and topped with gables.

Locust Street

123
(1909)
The dominant feature of this shingle house is a slanted, second-story bay window resting on a squared base of carved wood.

201
(1916)
Built in the tradition of Italian Renaissance, this large stucco house has a luxurious interior which includes a ballroom.

Lombard Street

950
(c. 1907)
Willis Polk designed this interesting shingled residence to replace an earlier one (destroyed in 1906) built for Seldon S. Wright, prominent San Francisco attorney and one-time supervisor.

1065
(1909)
This straightforward shingle house is said to have been a copy of 1075 Lombard. It is set in the middle of the block.

1075
(1907)
This comfortable shingled residence was rebuilt after the fire following the plans of the house that had previously stood on the property. To the rear stands the cottage at 1071.

1210–12
(c. 1898)
Now two flats, this building was once a single-family dwelling. Its shingles are a modernization and the entrance and window moldings were probably also a result of a remodeling.

1249–51
(c. 1878)
The central portion of this Italianate dates from 1878. The eastern wing was added slightly later and the fourth floor later still. During that addition the original cornice was removed.

1268
(1861)
This Italianate is now half below street level as a result of the grading of Lombard Street. Therefore, access is by means of a bridge. The shingling is probably a later addition.

Loraine Court

1
(1894)
San Francisco Memorial Columbarium. Here is the last vestige of the old Lone Mountain Cemetery. The building combines a classic interior with a Baroque exterior — the latter a product of reconstruction after the earthquake.

Lyon Street

124
(1891)
William H. Lillie designed a row of houses on Lyon for the Rountree brothers, well-known builders. Only this one has retained its original character. Lillie attempted to emulate characteristics of the Queen Anne by "incorporating bits of brick and gravel, variegated shingles, and several bay windows" into the design.

1405–07
(1888)
The richly profiled opening of the recessed porch brings distinction to this Stick Style residence. The squat Corinthian columns of the portico are especially expressive.

1652
(1885)
The entrance porch is recessed into the street facade of this one-story Italianate which is that style at its most restrained.

1722–24,
1726–28
(1888 and 1885)
Generally similar in appearance, these Stick Style buildings do have different window proportions, roof shapes and decor-

279

touches. The elongated brackets on the windows raise the cornices on 1726–28 so that it attains greater verticality.

1810, 1812, 1814 and 1816
(1882)
William F. Lewis built these early day tract houses with the aid of the Hinkels. They are all one-story Italianates with the exception of 1812 which was raised in 1890 so that an additional story could be slipped under. They still form an especially well-unified (and maintained) row.

2006, 2008 and 2010
(1901)
A row of sensitively cared for houses, 2006 and 2008 are shingle homes with little ornamentation and 2010 is a wood home with classical ornamentation.

2041
(1889)
Although no particular style is explicit in this house, it approximates the designation of Italian Villa (with leanings toward Queen Anne).

2116
(1893)
The original frame siding of this house, now slightly Colonial Revival in flavor, was replaced by shingles in a 1935–36 remodeling.

Maple Street

101
(1895)
The architectural style of this large shingled home can be best described as Queen Anne. A somewhat abbreviated tower dominates the home which is set on an impressive corner lot.

101 Maple Street

Market Street

65
(1916)
Southern Pacific Building. At one time, the railroad planned to use this site for a grand terminal to which trains would come from the Third and Townsend station. Instead this massive building, designed by Bliss and Faville, was constructed.

760
(1908)
Phelan Building. One of the city's illustrious flat-iron buildings, this structure is encased in stone veneer. It replaces an earlier Phelan Building which was destroyed by the fire of 1906.

785
(c. 1907)
Humboldt Bank Building. An elaborate dome crowns this neo-Renaissance building, designed by Meyer & O'Brien. At the time of the 1906 disaster it was under construction, but being completely destroyed, it had to be rebuilt from scratch.

835
(1896 and 1908)
The Emporium. Constructed for the Parrott estate, this Period landmark was designed by Albert Pissis and Joseph Moore. Merchants originally occupied the first two floors and the California Supreme Court the third floor.

901
(1908)
J. C. Penney. This building (on the site of the Windsor Hotel) is noted as being one of the first post-fire multi-story reinforced concrete buildings.

973–77
(c. 1908)
Wilson Building. The tiled Byzantine facade of this building survived the 1906 fire and was retained in the construction of the present building by architect Henry Schulze.

Mason Street

1200
(1907)
Cable Car Barn. Originally built in 1885–87 to house the cable cars, the substantial brick structure was reduced to rub-

1200 Mason Street

ble in 1906 but was rebuilt along similar lines. In 1967 the Public Utilities Commission sensitively refurbished the building no longer used for cable cars but now made open to the public.

1400–04
(1912)
These are two separate buildings but both follow precisely the same Classic Revival forms. They house the True Sunshine Mission (Episcopal Church in Chinatown).

1657–59
(1907)
There is a touch of Queen Anne in the rather abbreviated corner tower of this frame home.

1934–38
(1907)
The most notable feature of this set of flats is the arched doorway with wooden spokes that emanate from it. The plans for this building were drawn up by Cesare de Martini, contractor turned architect.

Masonic Avenue

1450
(c. 1891)
This predominantly Queen Anne residence recalls the Richardsonian style in the large entrance arches which are repeated on the second floor above the entrance.

McAllister Street

909–11, 917 and 921
(1880's)
These identical attached Italianates prove once again that a group has great forcefulness.

1341–43
(1901)
A gabled roof with bargeboard and a projecting wood second story above the brick first level give character to this house.

1463
(1880)
A square corner bay, a blind window and rounded pediments with carved cherubs on the bay and over the portico distinguish this Stick Style house.

2686
(c. 1888)
This modest frame house which was constructed with square nails dates back to a much earlier age than its neighbors. Its garage was once a stable.

Mendell Street

907
(1898)
This large Queen Anne mansion is architecturally unusual in this area.

Midway Street

16
(1893)

This plain red frame fisherman's house can be found behind a newer building. At the time the house was built, it was closer to the shore.

Mission Street

2875–79
(c. 1883)

The Stick Style detailing on the upper two floors is particularly striking in this highly commercial district. The ground floor still incorporates a store as it has for many years.

2901
(c. 1891)

This is a fine example of Stick Style street architecture.

Monterey Boulevard

230
(1899)

This little gabled house features front and side bays with ornate scroll friezes and jigsaw corner hoods.

Montgomery Street

1
(1908)

Crocker-Citizens National Bank. This Italian Renaissance building, designed by Willis Polk, has been extensively remodeled, including sheathing with terra cotta. The outstanding feature is the rotunda entrance supported by granite pillars.

460
(1907)

Sutro & Company. This neo-Classic building is constructed of granite. Massive pillars guard the entrance and the well-scaled roof line detailing includes a substantial stone balustrade with carved medallions and lions' heads.

716–20
(c. 1859)

Ship Building. This building was so named because a ship's hull—historically thought to be the *Georgian*—is incorporated in the building. Much of the original facade was covered during remodeling in 1954 and 1959.

814
(c. 1860's)

Presently used as a warehouse, this structure was originally built as the headquarters for the Society of California Pioneers with money left to the Society by James Lick. Of severe design, the brick building was rebuilt extensively in 1907.

1252–52A
(1876)

This simple shingle building was a one-family residence, later renovated into two apartments. An opening was broken through the facade for the second-story doorway, which does not line up with the off-centered first-floor door.

1254–56–58
(1865)

This Italianate building was once a one-story wooden cottage. However additions and renovations have altered that cottage until it has become a two-story, six-unit apartment.

1309–11 and 1313–15
(c. 1863)

Detailing is simple on these Italianates. It is confined to incised brackets and simple pediments over windows and doors. Modernizations—particularly doors—have been added.

1405
(c. 1870)

The only substantially unaltered building in a row, this is also an early Italianate. Behind this building—and the ones on either side—are three cottages which are probably much older.

Murray Street

450
(c. 1884)

(301 Richland Avenue) This residence, predominantly Stick, once sat on a far greater piece of property and was serviced by both well and windmill. Particularly unusual is the square corner tower surmounted by a Mansard-type roof.

Natoma Street

149
(1908)

This brick firehouse was built as headquarters for the Underwriter's Fire Patrol. The structure (which still incorporates the fire pole) has been beautifully restored for use as an office building.

New Montgomery Street

55
(1912)

The Sharon Building. Built by the Sharon Estate, this brick and concrete structure was designed by George Kelham.

72–78
(1914)

The Call Building. Built by the Sharon Estate Company for the *San Francisco Call*, this building became the first home of the merged *San Francisco Call-Bulletin* in 1929. It was designed by the Reid brothers.

Nineteenth Street

1243
(c. 1900)

This Queen Anne home, believed to have been assembled by ship carpenters, was constructed with three thicknesses for the walls: vertical, horizontal and diagonal. It was designed by Albert Danielson, whose son is the present owner.

3928–30
(c. 1884)

Italianate detailing of the flat second-story facade of this house contrasts with the heavier Stick Style below, where awning-type hoods adorn the portico and squared bay.

3932–34
(c. 1891)

This chaste Stick Style house is accented with many squared medallions and fluted pilasters that lead to its semi-Mansard roof.

4018–20–22
(c. 1880)

Moved to this lot in 1915, this Stick Style house is most notable for its festoons and ornate balustrades above the composite portico; fluted pilasters draw attention to the heavy, angular pediment crowning the bay console.

4027–27A
(1877)

Graceful stair balustrades enrich this chaste semi-Mansarded Stick Style house, the first in a group of three.

4031
(1889)

Quoins and squeezed pediments add an Italianate flavor to this basically Stick Style house, which is reached by steep stairs.

4033
(c. 1897)

Built in the Stick-Eastlake style, this house has retained its original semi-Mansarded bay tower and roof.

4050–56
(1888)

(184–86 Hartford Street) This Stick Style dwelling appears to be two separate structures because of a deeply indented connecting wall. An Eastlake flavor is achieved from the busy friezes.

4051–53–55
(c. 1891)

(202 Hartford Street) On this corner Stick Style structure the bays are inset with long narrow double window panes. The frame foundation has been cut to resemble stones.

4057–59 and 4065–67
(1888–89)

These semi-Mansarded Stick Style mirror twins do have some differences in detailing—4065–67 having more involved Eastlake work.

4069
(c. 1886)
Especially notable in this Stick Style cottage are the railings leading to the entrance and the portico detailing, which includes an inverted finial.

4075
(1888)
Incised panels and hood molds are the decorative features of this tiny Italianate flat-front cottage.

4131–31B–31C
(c. 1883)
Now half hidden behind a stucco wall and garage, this Stick Style house nevertheless offers an array of details including heavily carved strips, panels, balustrade, squeezed pediment, and keystone medallions.

4135–37
(c. 1891)
This Stick Style house features unusual ornaments on its corner strips and portico. These ornaments resemble ball-shaped newel post heads.

4306–08
(c. 1894)
An Eastlake-type pediment hovers over the bays of this Stick Style house. Interesting interior detailing prevails.

4312
(c. 1894)
The bargeboard frames a high diamond-shingled pediment over the slanted bay on this cottage, while jigsaw corner hoods create an arch effect.

4431
(c. 1870's)
Originally this Stick Style cottage was located in the vicinity of Fifteenth and Castro Streets, but after a fire damaged the house, it was turned over to the firemen as "payment" for putting out the fire. After 1900, it was moved to its present location.

Nineteenth and Dolores Streets

(1908)
Ascension Lutheran Church. The Lutheran Church bought this Romanesque brick structure from the Mission Park Congregationalist Church in 1930. Although the exterior was left unchanged, the inside was appropriately remodeled.

Noe Street

344–46
(c. 1890)
An especially vertical Italianate, this house has side walls covered with wooden shingles.

437–39
Beautiful old doors, etched

(c. 1891)
transoms, and incised panels are of interest on this Stick Style house.

451–53
(1886)
(87–93 Ford Street) Once the focal point of a family complex, this Stick Style home today features delicate details highlighted in brown and white.

559
(1887)
The original iron fence still encloses this tiny, square house whose style hints very faintly of Colonial Revival.

560
(1885)
Originally on a large lot with stable and horses, this Stick Style home retains the aura of a secure homestead. It has a matching picket fence and gate.

591–93
(1864)
This elegantly simple matchboard home has a broken pediment at the gabled roof, Italianate quoins, and a heavily tree-shaded walkway. It is slightly hidden by an appropriately styled frame garage.

657
(c. 1890)
Set high on a hill in a terraced garden, this delicate false-front Italianate cottage presents a pretty picture.

822
(1900)
This rustic shingled house sits in a colorful garden whose wall is made with cobblestones from the street. This was one of the first houses on "Poppy Hill", so called because of the many wild poppies.

906, 912, 918, 924, and 942
(1905–06)
Complementing those houses in the 3800 block of Twenty-Second Street and also built by John Anderson, these row homes also display imposing cartouches and three types of ornate pediments.

1039
(c. 1889)
The only unchanged older house in its block, this Stick cottage still has the old wooden steps leading to the recessed doorway.

1051
(c. 1891)
(491 Elizabeth Street) An excellent example of Queen Anne (with Italianate and Eastlake features), this enormous house presents various shingle patterns (hob-nail, sawtooth, diamond and fishscale), carved friezes, an octagonal corner tower, and old matching wooden doors.

1071–71A
(c. 1891)
The cock's comb (or cresting) over the pediment on the bay and the intricately carved panels add to this Stick cottage's distinction.

1075–77
(c. 1888)
This Stick Style house is notable for its frieze, through which elongated brackets extend.

1082
(c. 1892)
Originally on a large lot with greenhouse and additional buildings, this richly appointed home manifests the semi-Mansard Stick Style, especially in its many panels of embossed flowers and flared, fluted pillars.

1104–06
(c. 1875)
This slender, pristine house features the flat facade of the Italianate. A unique incongruity exists at the second story, where one of three identical, ornamented, arched windows looms considerably larger than the others.

1189
(1891)
A decorative paneled door, original newel posts, iron fence, and carved gable ends are especially emphasized by the paint of this Eastlake-detailed home.

1190
(c. 1890)
This Stick Style house displays spindles on the porch portico. Its barn-carriage house offers carved decoration under the gable on the Twenty-Fifth Street side; the projecting fulcrum, used for lifting hay, remains.

1257
(c. 1892)
On this example of Stick-Eastlake (built by Fernando Nelson) the varied decorations have been handled neatly and carefully.

1607–17
(1911)
This three-story wood apartment building with "Romeo and Juliet" stairway has a balanced facade and decorative frieze.

1623–25
(c. 1880)
A very old iron fence stands before this simple, false-front Italianate.

North Point

501
(1907)
Cost Plus West. Formerly Joseph Musto Sons-Keenan Co., marble works, this handsome brick structure has recently been strikingly refurbished and remodeled to accommodate stores.

767
Fishscale shingles fill the gable

(1901) end and a floriated frieze crosses the facade of this wooden house.

Oak Street

307–11
(1870)
This three-story Italianate resembles a double house with one side more cramped than the other. The original iron fence still stands in front.

361
(1869)
The principal ornamentation of this house lies in the cartouches above the windows. Horizontal fins follow the roofline in the manner of Greek Revival.

375–77
(1885)
The paint on this Stick Style two-family residence emphasizes the precise details.

457
(1876)
This grand Italianate has arched windows, balustraded portico and strips that foretell the Stick Style.

461–63
(1885)
A profusion of exaggerated Eastlake decorative details make a busy facade on this house.

465–67
(1876)
The hood mold, pediments, quoins and bracketed cornice produce nice surface qualities on this flat-front Italianate.

471–73
(c. 1885)
The quoining and bracketed cornice on this Italianate carry out the lines established by 465–67.

729 Oak Street

472–74
(1871)
An Italianate double house, this has especially attractive doorway treatment with two arched openings contained within one hood mold.

729
(1896)
Inside this ornate home are many of the original embellishments: gas lights, marble washbasins, a pair of ten-foot-tall stained glass doors and a grand mahogany staircase.

985–99
(1904)
An unusually placed, medallion-shaped stained glass window—above the rounded corner bay—dominates the exterior of this three-story wood building.

990–96
(1891)
(410 Scott Street) Eccentric carved peaks top several of the squared bays of this dwelling, built by John Fisher, turn-of-the-century contractor. It and 985–99 together produce a dramatic effect at the corner of Oak and Scott.

1000–02–10
(1906)
(409–11 Scott Street) High conical towers and gables (with heavy cornices) make an animated profile on this apartment house, possibly two buildings remodeled into one.

1152
(1893)
Steamer #21 and Hook and Ladder #6 once were housed in this old fire house which saw active duty until three years ago. The hose tower presents alternating rows of fishscale and criss-cross shingles.

1153
(1885)
Some of the original decoration on this elaborate Stick Style home is gone. Originally

it stood on a large plot of land, surrounded by a wrought iron fence; now it has close neighbors and no fence. There is now a massive concrete stairway in front of the house, replacing the original wooden stairs.

Octavia Street

523–29
(c. 1885)
This Stick Style double house has a centered entrance with squared bay tiers on either side.

631–33 and 643–45
(1883)
Both of these almost-identical Stick Style houses have rather uncommon three-story bay tiers.

1701
(1875)
1802–04½ Bush Street. These two flat-front Italianates complement each other and are unified by their matching cornices.

1703
(1873)
This pristine Italianate now runs smack into the blank side wall of its newer neighbor.

1707
(c. 1880)
This large house illustrates the transition from Italianate to Stick Style. The north wing, more truly Stick, is perhaps a later addition.

1807
(1870's)
Built in the grand style, this Italianate house beautifully displays quoins, bracketed major and minor cornices and a balustrade above its portico.

1809
(1889)
Varied texture and ornamentation common to Queen Anne-Eastlake are seen on this house.

2521
(c. 1880–85)
The elements of this restrained Italianate house are especially well-controlled.

2619
(1885)
This well-maintained Stick Style house is a straightforward interpretation.

2711
(c. 1877)
Here is a cottage that is an excitingly different translation of Stick Style. A lattice-work gazebo is part of the entrance stairway. Its mood is echoed in the roof treatment, whereby a balustrade is topped by a finial. The home is further enhanced by carved panels and frieze.

2754
(1885)
Fantastic interior decor sets the mood of this Stick-Eastlake one-story house, the San Francisco home of stage designer Tony Duquette.

2942
(1875)
This somberly painted flat-front Italianate house has had brick front stairs added.

Olive Street

231
(c. 1875)
Although the shingles are surely a later addition, this Italianate manages to maintain a purity of line. Expecially interesting is the blind window on the side.

Ord Street

106
(c. 1885)
A commanding Stick structure, this was recently converted into a six-family building.

126–28
(c. 1894)
This Stick-Eastlake has a portico with squat Corinthian columns whose look is repeated in the pilasters.

140
(1870's)
This flat-front Italianate cottage, beautifully restored and painted to enhance the detailing of the brackets and moldings, has a formal front garden.

Pacific Avenue

298
(c. 1907)
Best known as the Old Ship Saloon, this substantial brick building recalls the Gold Rush when vessels were pulled up on the muddy San Francisco foreshores and used for commerce. It is considered to relate to the *Arkansas* which was beached nearby and converted to an English ale house in 1850.

315–19
(c. 1907)
This building—an excellent example of post-earthquake masonry construction—is unique in its demonstration of brickwork craft (pressed bricks instead of hard fired). New methods of construction were used on the building, which is set on a raft beneath the waterlevel.

440
(c. 1911)
Although possibly dating to 1878, this sensitively remodeled building is commonly thought to have been built after the fire. It subsequently served as a hotel and now houses an architectural firm.

574
(1907)
Architect Beverly Willis did extensive interior and minor exterior alterations on this building now used for offices. Formerly the building served as a boarding house and later as a hotel.

638–44
(1912)
Elaborate moldings over the windows and Corinthian pilasters are architectural pluses for this commercial three-story building.

1812–14
(1891)
This extraordinary Queen Anne with richly plastic facade was built for Isaac Liebes, president of H. Liebes and the Alaska Exploration Company. However for the past thirty years the home has been owned by Dr. and Mrs. Leon Kolb.

1942
(1869)
This house was built at the corner of Pacific and Gough for Rudolph Spreckels, who had it moved west in 1900 to make way for his mansion. The house was leased to the Theodore Roosevelt, Jrs., at one time, and Mrs. Roosevelt wrote about the house in her book *The Day Before Yesterday* as " . . . this little house. . . a dream of perfection".

1948
(1887)
The extension of the portico's cornice on this Stick Eastlake house engages the bay window and masks the transition from first floor angled bay to the second floor square bay.

2000
(1894)
Here is an amalgamation of Colonial-Classic Revival (the cornice, window trim, porch) and Queen Anne (the frieze, cartouche, conical roofed corner tower).

2015
(1894)
Willis Polk designed this Period residence. The overhangs of each story, molded brackets and grouped casements are specific expressions of Tudor Revival.

2019, 2021 and 2023
(1890)
These three row houses show Stick-Eastlake moving into Queen Anne. The latter two are identical, each one possessing a two-story corner tower superimposed on the main floor bay window.

2083
(1905)
Originally owned by John D. Spreckels, Jr., this predominantly Georgian Revival stucco house was used as a guest house

for his mansion next door.

2223
(1875)
Individual and complete cornices over the bay windows on each floor—in addition to the main cornice—are attractive elements of this Italianate.

2300
(1905)
This notable brick house—the first in a group of three—has two unique features: a recessed cartouche with hard-edge design set in the top floor and a central chimney connected to the parapet by scrolled buttresses.

2301
(1897)
Formerly a family home, now apartments, this house is a strict interpretation of Classic Revival. Of interest are the changing shapes of window pediments on each story.

2312
(1900)
An urbane townhouse, this house has Classic Revival details. It is the second brick house in the row.

2324
(1904)
The third distinguished brick house, this one varies from the others in that it is entered through the ground floor. Also, the top floor is set within the Mansard roof.

2405–07
(1886)
A decorative integration of second floor window heads with the frieze and cornice brackets appears on this late Italianate-early Stick Style house.

2418 and 2420
(1905 and 1902)
Lewis Gerstle bought the lots for these two houses for his two younger daughters and eventually saw that homes were built for them. Both houses are Classic Revival although 2418 is of brick with marble trim and 2420 is of stucco and wood.

2430
(c. 1910)
The large balustrade-topped bay is impressive on this brick and concrete house with green tile roof.

2440
(c. 1895)
Around 1930 Gardner Dailey modernized this large Classical Revival house which adds to the distinction of the block.

2505
(1889)
The consoles beneath the pediment on this house are the same design as those on 2507 and 2511, but the chevron pattern

284

and batten on the pediment is like 2509's.

2507
(1889)
This house is a duplicate of 2511. It has a small pediment superimposed on the gable end; the pediment is supported by consoles, matching those on the entrance porch.

2509
(1899)
Notable is the corner tower of this house on which there is a corbelling transition between the square corner base and the hexagonal shaft; all this is topped by a bell-domed roof.

2511
(1889)
Duplicate of 2507, this house like 2505 and 2507 Pacific and 2523 Steiner, was originally owned by James Stewart.

2513
(1890)
A simplified Queen Anne, this has a projecting pedimented gable end in which is contained a Palladian window — fairly common in late Queen Annes.

2517
(1884)
The date is very early for a clean-cut Classic-Colonial Revival house, so perhaps this house was remodeled. The matching main and raked cornices on the gable end have square brackets.

2519
(1892)
This simplified shingle version of Queen Anne has a conical domed semi-tower, intersected by a prominent gable end.

2523
(1903)
Similar to Willis Polk's 2015 Pacific, this house of his is also English in feeling. The finely scaled molding at the subtle projection of stuccoed upper floors over the brick ground floor and the independently roofed dormers are of special interest.

2676
(1881)
A grand Baroque facade scheme is seen on this stucco Classic Revival house whose date appears to be very early for this style.

2698
(1904)
Newsom and Newsom designed this Classic Revival stucco house which is completely harmonious with its neighbor at 2676. Here the heavy-membered cornice, quoins, and pedimented window suggest an Italian Renaissance derivation. The circular portico is particularly distinguished.

2739
(1894)
Known as the "Ellinwood House," this late Queen Anne-early Classic Revival mansion has an impressive rusticated masonry foundation wall necessitated by the location at the crest of a steep hill. The wall terminates down the Divisadero hill in a carriage house.

2800
(1899)
This corner house in a block of monumental brick mansions is Classic-Revival with Georgian Revival proportions and disposition of ornament. There is a consistent use of brick: for quoins, trim, retaining walls, walks and steps.

2810
(1910)
There is a vertical thrust to this brick house — basically Classic Revival — caused mainly by the towering gabled roof, broken by pedimented dormers, and the entrance in which an arched window surmounts the balustraded porch.

2820
(1912)
Miss Alice Griffith, founder of the Telegraph Hill Neighborhood Association, had Willis Polk design this grand house following the plan of an Italian palazzo. The materials used (stucco and tile), the arches, and the formal garden give a Mediterranean look to the house.

2830
(1910)
Orthodox Georgian Revival is seen in the rectangular block plan of this house, brick walls with painted trim, and roof hidden behind balustrade. The centrally located bay window is not Georgian Revival however.

2849
(1910)
Eugene Freeman designed this brick house for Joseph Peltier, a conductor on the old Pacific Avenue car line who, when he became wealthy, insisted on having an interior that was reminiscent of the old Palace Hotel.

2863
(1905)
Most of the detailing of this brick house is Classic-Georgian Revival although the arched entrance way is of Moorish extraction.

2889
(1890)
A handsome combination of Queen Anne with Classic (or Colonial) Revival, this shingled house is thought to have been designed by Arthur Brown, Jr. The entrance porch has been integrated with five surrounding windows into a single element by flat scrolled trim.

2889 Pacific Avenue

2950
(1907)
Architect Albert Farr designed this Cape Cod Colonial shingle house for the Edwin Newhalls, the design having apparently been Mrs. Newhall's idea.

3001
(1907)
There is a splendid array of broken pediments on this vine-covered brick Georgian Revival house, a design of Walter Bliss. The mansion currently houses the Consulate of the United Arab Republic.

3153
(1912)
Ernest Coxhead used a Prairie School approach on this stucco house in which modular bands of windows and intervening stucco spandrels are projected from the face of the building.

3196
(1891)
J. R. Wilson built this Colonial Revival house for his friend E. T. Sheppard, who owned much of the surrounding land. The symmetrical front is divided into three equal sections by the two-story (giant order) pilasters.

3198
(1890)
This Shingle Style house, also owned by the Sheppards, has a fascinating central section on which each story overhangs the lower one.

3255
(1910)
The facade interest of this substantial stucco house is concentrated on the expansive living room window with its Corinthian pilasters, iron railing, and dentil molding.

3277
(1913)
Willis Polk was commissioned by Mrs. Catherine Hooker to build this grand residence, patterned on palazzos she had seen in Italy. The tile roof, high arched

windows, and tall chimney of the stucco house all combine to give the effect of an Italian loggia.

3277 Pacific Avenue

3333 and
3343
(1902 and
1903)
These two almost identical shingle houses, plus a third at 3355 Pacific, were designed by Albert Farr. That at 3355 Pacific was torn down, and a new shingle home, which is harmonious with the remaining two, was built on its lot in the 1920's. The homes have slight variations in their window treatments and in certain details, such as the placement of the front doors.

3377
(c. 1908)
This shingle house has an interesting trapezoidal roof. It is a Julia Morgan design.

3515
(1911)
This brown-shingled home was completely remodeled in 1950 by Campbell and Wong, both inside and outside and from the top of its gambreled roof to its present Thomas Church garden.

Page Street

153–55
(1890)
The facade of this Stick Style house shows the Eastlake influence.

Palou Avenue

1552
(1895)
Probably built as a farmhouse, this residence shows a profusion of carved wooden decorative details, partly derived from the Eastlake tradition. The barn, whose ornamentation carries out the theme of the house, is still intact.

Pennsylvania Street

367
(1870's)
Restored with imagination, this frame house was apparently a pre-fab shipped around the

1552 Palou Avenue

Horn. In remodeling the house, its present owners found that it was put together with bolts and screws.

Pierce Street

809–11
(1894)
An especially ornate Queen Anne, this house has stained glass detailing in the windows, a turret, friezes, balustrades, and amazing carved decorative features (including pendant finials).

1016
(c. 1886)
N. J. Andreozzi, the owner-architect, built an elaboration of the basic Stick Style. The Corinthian columns of the portico, undersized pediments, and banded colonnettes differ from the usual statement of those components.

1016 Pierce Street

1026–28
(c. 1886)
This elaborately ornamented Stick-Eastlake house echoes the mood of 1016, although its surfaces are carved in dissimilar ways.

1900
(1886)
Unusual unification is seen in this Queen Anne due partly to the consistent use of similar consoles on all openings and on the porch and the containment of the surface patterns and molded decorations within well-defined areas.

1905–07
and 1911
(1881)
Although these two Italianates appear very similar, 1911 has a balustrade and 1905–07 has dentil courses and incised panels.

1918,
1922,
1928 and
1932
(1877)
A row of four identical Italianates, these all have crisp, small-scale panels, moldings, and brackets.

1923
(1881)
The corner boards of this Italianate—built by Hinkel—repeat the patterns established by the main elements of the house.

2123
(1888)
A small floriated frieze and an Eastlake portico (its pediment filled in with fine carving) are attractive elements of this Stick cottage.

2415
(1897)
Edgar Mathews designed this stucco and wood house (with a small amount of half-timbering) in a fashion advanced for its years.

2421
(1897)
Mathews was also responsible for this house, which he obviously designed in conjunction with 2415; together they form an attractive pair.

2652
(1905)
Pilasters divide the facade of this Classic Revival house into three sections, its center section being emphasized by an oeil de boeuf window.

2700 and
2720
(1906–
1907)
Jeremiah Dineen had these two houses built—2700 for himself, and 2720 for his sister-in-law. The Baroque style has manifested itself in 2700, while 2720 is a more simple structure with some Classic Revival detailings.

2701
(1904)
William Curlett designed this house for himself. It is a vigorous, generalized interpretation

of Tudor with some half-timbering, leaded windows, and a Romanesque entranceway.

Pine Street

301
(c. 1910)
Pacific Coast Stock Exchange. One of the few buildings in the downtown area that is only a single story, this Timothy Pflueger designed building was used as a sub-treasury until 1930. The Greek Revival exterior is marked by Doric columns and two monolithic statues by Robert Stackpole "symbolizing Mother Earth's fruitfulness and Man's inventive genius . . ."

1130–32
(1911)
Wooden bays are set in the stucco facade of this gabled four-story half-timbered apartment house.

1201
(1909)
An unusual, large pediment, with a triangular window inside, sits in a rectangular area above the doorway of this wood apartment building.

1250
(1919)
There is a plastic quality to the facade of this ornate building with its iron balconies, large rounded pediment, and slanted bays with moldings.

1837
(1890)
This very late Italianate has an especially unique feature: the pediment above the bay window contains a half-pagoda roof effect. Also, there is a hint of the villa type in the entrance set behind a deep porch in a pseudo tower.

1843
(1873)
Pretty fluting is seen on the lower half of the porch columns and pipestem colonnettes on this Italianate.

1855
(1876)
Although very similar to 1843, the trim on this Italianate is quite different; it has especially nice molded wood corbelling under the bay window.

1907
(1869)
The early Classic Revival facade of this house would appear to be a later addition. The first floor window heads have been raised by blank round arches with pediments above.

1911
(1880)
Transom-type attic windows have been set between the eaves brackets on this carefully-made Stick Style house.

1918
(1876)
Incised panels above the windows and frieze add interesting decorative values to this Italianate house.

1924
(1877)
This well-maintained Italianate is imposing in spite of the addition of a garage at the ground level.

2005–09
(1889)
The lines of this Stick-Eastlake are similar to 2011–13 although details are dissimilar. Modern windows have been added.

2011–13
(1890)
The engagement of this Stick-Eastlake's bay window by an extension of the porch is more convincing than most such attempts.

2016
(1877)
A very unique mixture: except for the rounded arched window heads, the entire upper half says Colonial Revival and the entire lower half Stick.

2017–21
(1890)
An interesting adaptation of the standard side hall row house facade has been extended here to three flats.

2018, 2020, and 2022
(1874)
Although not identical, these three Italianate houses present a row. Fishscale shingles have been added to the facade of 2020, and 2018 has had a large garage added.

2043–45
(1874)
This house displays an infusion of Stick Style into the Italianate.

2047–49
(1878)
Double, extra narrow bay windows are very handsome on this Italianate house.

2115–17–19
(1872)
Especially pronounced colonnettes that become brackets for intermediate cornices are of interest on this Stick Style house.

2121–23
(1883)
The lightly-scaled porch of this Stick double house is more arcade-like than porch-like, due perhaps to the tall, shallow shape.

2139–43
(1890)
Three full stories of two bay tiers are unusual features of this ornate Stick-Eastlake.

2208
(1877)
Fairly pure lines are displayed on this Italianate, which has been maintained with care.

2210
The frieze panels and window

(1875)
frames are outlined by paint on this miniature flat-front Italianate.

2231
(1872)
This truly simple clapboard house could have easily been built prior to 1872. It has the horizontal fins along the gable and corner boards associated with Greek Revival.

2237–39
(1871)
New doors have been added to this otherwise pristine Italianate two-family house.

2255–57
(1880)
Although it has slanted bays, this house is more Stick-Eastlake than Italianate. The bas-relief (small scale half-sunbursts) were made on the jigsaw, as were the quadrant, pierced brackets.

2256–58
(1880)
The proportions of this Italianate's detailing are especially heavy and give it a neo-Classic feeling.

2262–66
(1876)
A rare model, this flat-front Italianate is a double house with very narrow entrances at both corners.

2273–75
(1881)
This traditional Italianate has a full component of decorative details: pierced work balustrade, incised panels, and paneled frieze.

2279
(1882)
This flat-front Italianate has a window treatment and a cornice similar to those of 2262–66.

2283
(c. 1875)
A flat horizontal spandrel band clearly separates the basement story (shop) from the main floor (living quarters) on this Italianate.

2414–14½
(1890)
Very distinctive "folded ribbon" brackets are used throughout (on the cornice, portico and windows) on this Stick-Eastlake house.

2416
(1884)
The style of this house appears to be of two different periods. The roof cornice is correct Classic Revival while the segmental arched window with stained glass transoms and the open frieze above the porch appear to be Queen Anne.

2424
(c. 1895)
This Italianate sports quadrant-cornered trim over the window

and door heads (a new variation).

2426
(1889)
A remarkable cat-tail frieze of molded plaster is part of the rounded corner tower of this Queen Anne.

2428 and
2430
(1878)
These two handsome Italianates—with slight variations in trim—make an unusually fine grouping along with the building at 1900 Pierce, corner of Pine, and the row of four around the corner on Pierce.

2519–21–
21½
(c. 1880)
A nice array of strongly framed segmental arches appear on this Stick Style residence, while flat-top pediments are also used.

2590
(1885)
The designer of this Stick Style house (with Eastlake-Japanese effects) took advantage of the corner lot to add bays on the side. The front porch has especially fine Corinthian columns.

2609
(1876)
One of the refinements seen in this one-story Italianate is the careful alignment of the joints of the quoins and the wall boarding.

2673 and
2683
(1877)
A fascinating (and seemingly unaccountable) variation in floor levels exists in these otherwise identical Italianates.

2709
(1887)
This Stick Style house has a fine portico which contains a sunburst, a variation on Corinthian columns, and a shingled roof.

2714
(1886)
An interesting use of strips (modules) is seen on this Stick Style house; the strips terminate in strong, simple, elongated brackets.

2777
(1877)
The original wood railing is still part of this Italianate, whose bay is squeezed over next to the porch.

2811
(1883)
This Stick Style house was probably once part of a row of alternating twins.

2825
(1887)
This neat Stick Style cottage shows an ingenious use of incised, delicate panels.

2832
(1886)
A fine version of late Stick exaggeration, this house has elon-gated brackets on all the corners and even longer brackets on the main roof cornice.

2911
(c. 1885)
(1661–63 Scott Street) The upstairs corner diagonal bay has been so neatly joined to this Stick building that the complete window trim fits perfectly.

2932
(1888)
On this late Stick Style cottage the imaginative entablature has all the classic components, which have, however, been whimsically reproportioned.

3047–49
(1889)
The engaged porch-bay window element of this house modifies a symmetrical facade.

Pixley Street

113
(c. 1897)
A frame cottage with lacy bargeboard, this house—along with others on the street—stands where Frank Pixley's original house was.

245
(1885)
This simple flat-front Italianate cottage certainly harkens back to the farm days of Cow Hollow.

Plymouth Street

222
(c. 1898)
This structure is probably not duplicated in the city. It has a very involved interrelationship of planes and shapes and a complex roof design.

333–35
(c. 1890–97)
One of the few Victorians remaining in a changing neighborhood, this is a simple frame structure. The principal decoration lies in the patterning of wood in the gable and the pediment.

Point Lobos Avenue

Point Lobos Avenue

(1893–94)
The only building of note remaining in Sutro Heights, where once Aldolph Sutro's house stood, is this curious little kiosk. It was apparently used as a concession stand at the Mid-Winter Exposition of 1893–4 in Golden Gate Park and moved to its present location by Sutro.

Polk Street

602
(1912)
California Hall. Said to have been inspired by a castle in Heidelberg, this building may be described as Teutonic Baroque. The structure, designed by F. H. Meyer, was financed by the German-American Society.

602 Polk Street

2740
(c. 1884)
One of the few houses left standing east of Van Ness in 1906, this Stick Style home has few embellishments.

Pomona Street

43
(c. 1870)
The Samoan Church of LMS of San Francisco, Inc. Nothing is known of this building previous to its move to this site in 1929. The simplicity of its Italianate style suggests the 70's date.

Post and Mason Streets

(1913)
The First Congregational

Church. The original Gothic Congregational Church was destroyed by the 1906 fire. When the present neo-Classic building was begun Dr. Asked, the pastor believed, "A city's un-churched multitudes are more ready to go to, and more at ease in, a non-Gothic and non-eccle-siastical edifice".

Post Street

57
(1910)
Mechanics' Institute Building. Mechanics' Institute, one of the first educational institutions in California, dates back to 1854. Its present building, designed by Albert Pissis, was erected on the site of its 1866 building, destroyed in 1906.

250
(1865 and 1906)
Gump's. Founded in 1861 by Solomon Gump, this firm first sold mirrors for saloons. With architect Clinton Day and Japanese carpenters, A. Livingstone Gump undertook the extensive remodeling of this two-story building in 1906 to house Gump's Oriental treasures.

524
(1912)
The Olympic Club. The oldest amateur athletic club in the country—dating back to 1860—this club has produced many star athletes and teams. This is a brick-faced Period structure.

1362
(1876)
A superb combination of Italianate and Stick is seen in this house. There is fine granite detailing on the steps leading to the porch. In fact all the details have been carefully handled.

1400
(c.1885)
The later addition of a first floor store obstructs the view of this Stick Style house, whose strip trim has been partially removed.

1406–08
(1893)
A mixed style of Queen Anne and Stick is seen here. There is a unique arrangement in which a broad pediment above the cornice surmounts the centered entrance and one set of bay windows. Excluded from this is a semi-circular bay to the left.

1480–82
(1889)
A slanted second-story bay extends over the flat-fronted first floor on this Italianate house.

1484 Post Street

1484–86
(1874)
A flat-fronted Italianate, this house has handsomely executed windows: on the main floor they have squeezed arched pediments and on the top squeezed triangular pediments.

1600–06
(c.1910)
(1603–09½ Laguna Street) The notable "roof scape" of towers and gables is reminiscent of German and Dutch architecture of the sixteenth and seventeenth centuries. The Queen Anne corner tower is surmounted by an unusual cupola.

1624
(1876)
The hood moldings over the bay window sashes show up here due to the carefully-painted facade of this Italianate.

1760
(1882)
Mount Pilgrim Baptist Church. A fine effort to interpret Italian Romanesque in wood is expressed here. The vertical strip trim can be read here as flat buttresses following the historical style.

2148
(1888)
A busy treatment of the surface, including sawtooth shingles, appears on this Stick-Eastlake house.

2158–60, 2170 and 2174
(1885–1886)
These three houses are all different interpretations of Stick Style. The gable ends on 2158–60 and 2170 echo that of 2148.

2351–53
(1897)
The original wood stairway with balustrade still is part of this simplified Italianate.

2357 and 2361
These side-by-side flat-front Italianate cottages reinforce each other's strengths. There are nice decorative panels above and below the windows of 2357.

2479 and 2485
(1880)
The frieze, brackets and pierced work are busier than was common in the Italianate style on these mirror-twin cottages.

2507
(1889)
Flat pierced decoration within the pediments is a highlight of this prim Italianate cottage.

2515–19
(1891)
This Stick-Eastlake house is so late that even the strips are decorated. The independent gable roof of the bay window is lowered and aligned with a deep entablature of the main eaves.

2529–33
(1892)
Queen Anne in the form of garlands and molded decoration within the squeezed pediments is seen creeping into this late Stick Style house.

2556–58
(1871)
The symmetrical facade of this one-story Italianate is due to the center hall plan. The usual verticality of this style is not achieved here.

2600–02
(1885)
The architectural decorations have been strictly confined to the openings on this splendid Stick Style corner building.

2609, 2611, and 2613
(c.1882–84)
Although each of these Italianates is tiny, they all work together to form a strong group.

Powell Street

449
(1913)
Poetz Building. F. H. Meyer designed this brick building to house the old Press Club. The carved cutwork stone balustrade and arched windows at the third floor level are a pleasant surprise.

1022
(1916)
Heavy vines cover the facade of this brick apartment house, but one can glimpse the leaded windows at the entranceway.

1441
(1908)
Saint Francis Day Home. Charles J. Devlin designed this Classical Revival structure, which replaced a pre-fire Home. The facade is dominated by a central unit, in which the doorway is flanked by Ionic columns supporting a pediment.

Presidio Terrace

Across Arguello Boulevard, just west of Presidio Heights the Terrace has a private removed aura to it, being a great circle entered through an impressive pair of gates. Although the Terrace was laid out in 1905, most of the houses were not built until later.

3
(c.1905)
This horizontal, half-timbered home with octagonal tower complements its neighbor at 28 Presidio Terrace, although they are quite different in detail.

16
(1905)
A Bakewell and Brown design, this handsome house is atypical of San Francisco, more closely resembling a house of the eastern seaboard—even to the inclusion of a widow's walk.

16 Presidio Terrace

20
(1910)
Lewis Hobart was the architect for this stucco home, following a French Provincial style. Its steeply pitched, hipped roof is especially distinctive.

28
(1908–09)
Architect A. F. Whittlesey gave this house a Swiss chalet look, springing from the wood trim and cupola. More exotic touches include a patio with a rare bird aviary, two orchid houses and two rooms for tropical fish.

30
(1909)
Fernando Nelson, developer of Presidio Terrace, had this half-timbered rustic home built for himself.

34
(1915)
George Applegarth designed this concrete French Renaissance Revival house for stage star Pauline Fredericks. Its balanced facade is enriched with

30 Presidio Terrace

classicizing details, such as a frieze, dentil molding, and an Ionic-columed portico.

Prospect Avenue

34
(1870's)
The well-known painter, Samuel Marsten Brooks, had this small clapboard house built for his family. The house (which has been remodeled) stands on property almost the equivalent of four city lots.

Prosper Street

34
(1888)
Stairs with new iron railings lead to this one-story Stick cottage, which has elaborated strips.

40
(1892)
Although built later than its next door neighbor, this house was a replica of its neighbor at 34.

56–58
(1888)
The unique semi-Mansard roof of this Stick Style house culminates in a waffle-design cornice and cascades back in tiers, following the lines of the facade.

Randall Street

178
(c. 1895)
The frieze of fishscale shingles is repeated in the similarly shingled semi-Mansard roof on this cottage.

Russell Street

15–17
(1908)
Russell Street is a miniscule alley whose sidewalks are lined with redwood boxes filled with trees and violets. Carved garlands are the decorative feature of this Russell Street house.

29
(1906)
The wide roof overhang on this small shingle house gives it the look of a Swiss chalet.

40–42
(c. 1906)
Simply designed, this shingle building has a bracketed cornice and arched entranceway with pilasters.

51–53
(c. 1906)
This frame residence has decorative elements similar to 40–42 but with dentil moldings added.

Sacramento Street

568
(1913)
(569 Commercial Street) PG&E Sub-Station J. This power plant was built with one large room, forty-eight feet high, with ornamental iron stairways leading to balconies. Architect Frederick H. Meyer concentrated all exterior ornamentation in the massive doorway treatment. In the 1950's the building was converted into a night club.

920
(1907–08)
Cameron House is the better known name of the Presbyterian Mission House, one of the oldest service agencies in Chinatown. This building was constructed of clinker brick on a substructure of concrete and rubble after the fire; however, its history on the site dates back to the 1870's.

1182
(1906)
In August, 1967, this town house (as remodeled by Ted Moulton) presented an entirely new, exciting facade to view. Once a simple wooden residence, now this house is close to eighteenth century French in design.

1230
(1916)
Arthur Laib saw that the interior of this house was a masterpiece of workmanship. It has a myriad of impressive details: carved moldings, beveled glass French doors, graceful curving stairway and a massive fireplace in the dining room.

1242
(1916)
This French Baroque Revival apartment house typifies Arthur Laib's work. It has the slightly bowed, multipaned French windows with iron railings in front that Laib often used.

1266–68–70
(c. 1909)
This attractive set of flats was designed by architect Nathaniel Blaisdell, who gave this shingle

building a simple facade with squared-off bays and Doric columns at the entrance.

1359–65
(c. 1907)
Glass now encloses the graceful "Romeo and Juliet" stairway of this four-story wood apartment building.

1590
(1911)
Rounded bays alternate with slanted bays on this apartment house, and the whole is topped with a richly decorated cornice with a piecrust edge.

2055
(1895)
A Renaissance scheme has been scaled down on the facade of this house to domestic proportions. The wood residence (designed by E. J. Molera) is festooned with garlands and lavished with Corinthian pilasters and columns.

2151
(1881)
This florid adaption of the French Baroque Revival would seem to point to a date between 1900 and 1910 rather than in the '80's. Both the plan and facade of the stucco building are unique.

2212
(1895)
The first of a group of three houses that give a monumental look to this block, this Classic Revival house was designed by A. Page Brown.

2220–22
(c. 1886)
This second house is dominated by robust Queen Anne corner towers. Of note are the Gothic moldings and engaged finials over the porch and tower windows.

2224
(1900)
Nathaniel Blaisdell was the architect for this house of Classic Revival detailing. Nearly the entire street front of the residence is occupied by the single great window element.

2245
(1903)
The bay window on this house (divided into apartments now) is used uniquely as an entrance. The broken pediments, balustrade, and proportions all reflect Georgian Revival.

2395
(1911)
This sensitive adaptation of a Classic Revival facade follows the recipe of rusticated base, giant pilasters, and attic arcaded frieze. Built to house the Stanford Medical Library, it is now part of The Presbyterian Medical Center Complex.

2509
(1886)
Part of the appeal of this house—one of the most richly ornamented of the one-story Stick cottages—is the clear organization of ornament on its small scale.

2517
(1883)
The bay window of this Stick Style house is independently roofed with its own gable.

2519 and 2521
(1875)
The same builder undoubtedly put up these Italianates, whose variations occur at the entrances—one has a portico, one has a hood.

2530 and 2538–40
(1871)
Again these are closely related Italianates, but here the variations are more pronounced. The house at 2530 is wider, has decorated corner boards, and has fancier bosses over the windows.

2605
(1885)
This is one of a group of unique one-story Stick cottages. The cresting over the entrance door hood is unusual and the hood itself is detailed to match the cornice of the bay window.

2608
(1884)
This Italianate still has the original balustrades on the steps and brackets under the bay window.

2614
(1874)
The stained glass sash windows have been retained on this early Stick Style house. A glassed-in entrance porch over a garage has been added.

2619–21
(1886–89)
A remarkable paint design has highlighted the fine details of this Stick Style house. The entrance porch—nearly a separate entity—is a delightful little pavilion with horseshoe arches, pediment, and tiny balustrade.

2625–27
(1889)
Another Italianate row house (with Stick ornament), this one is adapted for upper and lower flats.

2657–59–61 and 2663–65–67
(c. 1900)
These buildings—mirror twins—present facades with lively surface treatment, which results from the bays, quoins, cornices and pilasters.

2671, 2675 and 2679
(1871)
Typical of 1870 row houses, these three Italianate dwellings are unified by the single facade and common floor levels. They present a fine kind of street architecture.

2691–93
(1894)
There is such a great amount of glass on the facade of this Queen Anne that there is hardly room for the usual low-relief ornamentation.

2780 and 2790
(1902)
Rounded bay windows left over from Queen Anne are mixed with Classic Revival details on these two pairs of flats.

2912
(1878)
This false-front cottage adheres to the late Italianate tradition. It has squeezed pediments over the windows and doors.

2920
(1886)
There is a hint of late Victorian Gothic in this house, set in a well-tended garden. The round arched window heads are unusual.

3397–99
(1895)
This Stick Style apartment building, which houses a decorator's shop on its first floor, has a five-sided corner bay, as well as the usual squared bays.

3487–99
(c. 1889)
This building presents a profusion of interesting details: slanted bays with blank front sections, a flattened tower verging on Queen Anne, and unusual shingling and carved decorative sections.

Saint Francis Wood

After the area west of Twin Peaks was made more accessible by the opening of the Twin Peaks Tunnel in 1912, Saint Francis Wood was conceived. Its design was executed by Frederick Law Olmsted and John Galen Howard. The Wood was one of the first tract subdivisions where design control was attempted with restrictions placed on architects in an effort to avoid repetitious "tract building" and with attempts to build attractive homes set in ample garden space. Howard designed the architectural features seen throughout the beautifully maintained area: the gateways, the fountains and pools, the Circle, and even the brick-patterned sidewalks.

San Benito Way

44, 50 and 58
(1913–
These houses were planned as a unit by Louis Mullgardt, who was employed by Mason-Mc-

14-15) Duffie Company to lay out the general style of all houses in Saint Francis Wood. However, only 44 (later used as the model home) was completed by Mullgardt, and Henry Gutterson finished the other two.

San Bruno Avenue

2380
(1880's) This large Italianate home now sits looking out forlornly upon the maze of freeways that criss-cross in front of its yard.

San Carlos Street

147-49
(1878) A theme of semi-fluted composite columns and pilasters is carried through on this Italianate, beautiful in its detail.

Sanchez Street

342-44
(c. 1891) This squared-off Stick Style house has detailing that is accented by three different paint colors. Ornate filigree panels over the upper-story windows are unusual.

406
(c. 1887) The facade of this Stick Style cottage is dominated by the pediment containing sunburst and circle medallions and surmounted by a finial.

**455-59,
461-65,
467-71,
473-77,
and 479-
83**
(1906) Originally all five of these apartments—each containing six units—had "Romeo and Juliet" stairways. However, two of the buildings have had their central stairs enclosed.

462
(c. 1885) This Italianate cottage is dressed up with triangular squeezed pediments over the windows and an arched squeezed pediment over the entrance.

491-99
(c. 1889) The ground floor of this Stick Style commercial building (with flats above) housed an early-day saloon which admitted women—if they used a separate entrance. The original loft and carriage house have been converted to garage space.

517-19
(c. 1894) The wide slanted bays and detailing at the entranceway are of the 90's, but the basic premise of this house is Italianate.

525-29
(c. 1893) Like 517-19 this house has a basic Italianate expression with the bay broadened and the details more Stick-Eastlake.

545
(c. 1889) This Stick Style house has been owned since construction by one family. Its tiny portico with Eastlake angularity fits tidily between the two bays.

576
(1885) A real beauty, this Stick Style semi-Mansarded home sits on a large tree-shaded lot. The bays and balustraded portico are lavishly carved.

775-77
(1904) The first residence on Sanchez Hill, this house is rustic and simple, fashioned of shingles and wood. Maple or redwood plank floors, ceilings, and beams adorn the interior.

919
(1885) Originally this handsome one-story Italianate house—then numbered 909—was part of a row of at least four similar dwellings. Today two have been altered. Another was pushed to the back of 925's lot in 1915 to make room for a newer residence.

950-52
(1891) Fishscale shingles cover one complete side of this corner house. A coach house complete with turret and weather vane remains in the rear.

968
(c. 1891) The detailing of this house is Stick-Eastlake (the bracing of the gables, the waffle-patterned frieze, and angular columned portico).

974
(c. 1891) Similar to its neighbor at 968, this cottage has a frieze composed of shiplap and sawtooth shingles and pendant finials at the apex of the gables.

1004
(c. 1891) The exterior color is most unusual in this Stick Style house: pilasters, pipestem colonettes, brackets, diamond medallions, squeezed arched pediments and window framings are all white against a green background.

1040
(c. 1896) The half-moon entranceway and sawtooth-shingled gable end of the embellishments make this cottage interesting.

1201-03
(1891) Built in Stick Style, this large corner house features concentrated Eastlake ornamentation at the eaves, portico, and support brackets.

1280
(c. 1889) The sawtooth shingles on the facade of this basically Stick Style cottage tell of the Queen Anne influence.

**1306,
1310,
1316,
and 1320**
(c. 1892) An excellent row of Stick-Eastlake essentially identical houses, these are notable for the intricate carving on their bays which have pediments containing sunbursts.

1374
(c. 1892) Notable features of this Stick Style house include the gracefully carved original stairs and balustrades and delicately incised panels.

1387
(c. 1890) A nice sawtooth-shingled semi-Mansard roof and a careful aligning of the windows with the cornice brackets are seen on this Stick Style cottage.

**1402,
1404,
and 1406**
*(c. 1891-
92)* Fernando Nelson built these three Stick-Eastlake cottages as part of a group of four. (The fourth is now changed by the addition of a new window.) The gables dominate with their waffle design and heavy carving.

**1557,
1561,
1569 and
1571**
(c. 1891) The simplicity of this row of semi-Mansarded Stick and Italianate cottages recalls the early 1880's, although the dates of water supply are later.

1566
(1889) This straightforward Stick Style cottage is typical of many older homes in the area and resembles 1560 and 1570 in particular.

1570
(1887) Delicate incised carving highlights this Stick Style house, but it is most notable for its original heavy paneled door with wreath, and the floreate framing around the oval window.

1604
(c. 1894) (and 401-03 Twenty-Ninth Street.) In the early days this Stick (Strip) Style building contained a saloon and grocery store as well as flats. The building makes attractive use of its corner site with its commanding corner bay.

1676
(1899) This very late Stick Style house has delicately incised and slightly slanted bays. The original paneled door, stairs, and balustrade are of interest.

1768
(c. 1891)

The paint picks out the neat details on this Stick Style cottage. The diamond-shingled hood still protects the bay.

1793
(c. 1887)

An array of squared panels, strips in the deep frieze, and variously-shaped squeezed pediments enliven the facade of this Stick Style cottage.

San Jose Avenue

200
(c. 1877)

This serene Italianate residence sits on a corner lot. A one-story bay on the side is garnished with an ornate balustrade.

210
(1878)

Built by John Greenwood for his family, this fine old Italianate house features marble fireplaces and marble corner washstands. The exterior is dramatized by quoins and a bold Corinthian portico with balustrade.

248 and 254
(1884)

Chalet bracing on the porticos and gables adds an Eastlake dimension to these basically Stick houses.

325–27
(1885)

This simplified Stick Style house has its detailing concentrated on the window framings.

330–340
(1876)

This Stick Style multiple dwelling has three-storied bays on the balanced facade, Eastlake detailing at the wide portico, and large tiers of wooden stairs with latticed balustrades.

380
(1884)

Built as one-story Italianate, this house had a matching flat-facaded second story added in 1911.

393–95
(c. 1875)

Though its adjacent twin has been changed, this house still manifests the straightforward Italianate look, with delicate window framings on the flat, balanced facade.

Sansome Street

One
(1910)

California Office, Crocker-Citizens National Bank. Albert Pissis designed this granite bank building in a Classic Roman style. In the lobby, walls and columns of travertine lead to a coffered ceiling.

310
(c. 1906–8)

Alaska Commercial Building. The architecture of this building, designed by Meyers & Ward, reflects the occupation of its original owners, who dealt in Alaskan products. Motifs include carved seals and polar bears, icicles and sea shells.

710
(1907)

The handsome simplicity of this buff-colored brick commercial structure — once used as a spice mill — has been retained.

712–14
(1897)

The arched ground floor windows and overall chaste effect make this building compatible with its neighbor at 710. This building once housed a mosaic works.

Scott Street

9 and 17
(1890)

Hinkel built these late Stick Style houses which are similar in some of their details, such as the pedimented porticos.

33–35 and 39–41
(1888)

These two Stick Style houses were both built by Hinkel. Changes have been made over the years.

79–81
(1888)

Some of the wood trim of this Stick-Eastlake house has been removed to ease upkeep, but there remains an impressive amount of ornateness.

93
(1890)

This Queen Anne house has a slim tower above the entranceway. The tower is broken by a cut-out for a recessed window.

95–97
(1891)

A towering Queen Anne house on a prominent corner location, this has now been converted into apartments.

301–03 and 305
(1886)

Hinkel built these Stick Style houses as well. The iron cresting over the portico on 301–03 gives that building a distinctive touch.

318½
(c. 1889)

Eastlake accessories (especially in the gable end and portico) appear on this basically Stick Style residence.

330
(c. 1895)

Moving ahead of 318½ into the Queen Anne, this house has a corner tower and gable pierced by an arched opening.

348–50
(1890)

Exceptional carving and intricate pediments and gables highlight this Italianate double house.

1810–12
(1883)

This Italianate double house has been especially well restored. Two nineteenth century gas lamps have been added in front.

1814–14½
(1875)

The gable end of this Stick Style cottage is filled with a carved waffle pattern and topped by a finial.

1853–55
(c. 1878)

The traditional simplicity of a flat-front Italianate is evidenced on this one-story double house. The doorway is very fine; it has rounded, aggressive pediments over the side-by-side narrow openings.

2030
(1888)

Familiar Italianate proportions and features (including iron cresting above the porch) are subtly transformed into Stick on this house.

2100
(1897)

All the Classical (Colonial) Revival elements have been decoratively adapted and interpreted in a late Queen Anne manner in this house.

2133
(1878)

The chief Italianate features of this one-story house remain: the bracketed cornice, hooded entrance, and bay trim.

2139–45
(1878)

The unusual organization of the Italianate elements in the facade of this house are due to a center hall plan.

2151
(1878)

The standard Italianate features appear in this house but with particularly rich details on the entrance porch.

2207
(1885)

Another one of Hinkel's Stick Style houses, this one is highlighted by various framed panels and a bracketed cornice, last vestiges of Italianate.

2305
(1888)

Only the semi-circular window heads remain from what would have been a Stick-Italianate facade on this house.

2509
(1898)

E. A. Mathews designed this English Cottage house in a

fashion popular at the time in England. George Livermore added a new wing in 1961, successfully carrying out the low eaves, half-timbering and casement windows of the older core house.

2650
(1889)
This early Georgian Revival home—brick, solid, four-square—presents two unique mannerisms: second-floor window heads that meet the entablature and exceedingly wide quoins.

2700
(1897)
Coxhead and Coxhead were the architects for this Classic Revival house rendered rather monumentally and impressively in stucco.

2710
(1893)
It would take somebody with the style and sophistication of Willis Polk to combine the disparate elements seen in this shingle house: a richly detailed Baroque door frame, a group of cottage casements, a dormer window, and large areas of uninterrupted wall and roof.

3016
(1884)
A delightful wood Greek Revival house, this is similar to a number on San Mateo's Coastside and Marin's northern area but unique in San Francisco.

Second Avenue

304
(c. 1892)
The bay window of this small Stick-Eastlake home has been modernized, but the rest of the house is original. It is one of a row of three.

317
(1890)
Sawtooth shingling and carved bargeboard pierced by a finial are of interest on this Eastlake cottage.

422
(1889)
This example of Victorian Gothic has the air of having anticipated being squeezed between two much larger buildings—but carries off the crush well.

Seventeenth Street

3639–41
(1874)
Built in very early Italianate splendor, this house features quoins, a balustrade with finials, and ornate composite colonnettes.

3650–52
(c. 1888)
The variously shaped windows are the interesting feature of

this Stick house. One is rounded, one is triangular and one is squared off at its apex.

3656
(c. 1875)
This beautiful quoined Italianate house replaced a predecessor built in 1869, at which time a stream meandered down through the area.

3763–65
(c. 1887)
A stairway leads to the second floor of this chaste Stick Style cottage. It once had a stable that housed four horses.

3773–75
(c. 1882)
The original stable and carriage house of this Italianate house have now been converted to a garage.

3859
(c. 1886)
This Stick Style cottage has highly decorated cornices with high brackets. A decorative overhanging protects its Period front door.

3863–65
(1886)
The most unusual feature of this Stick Style house is the little pointed, bracket-like medallion on each second-story pilaster.

3873–75
(c. 1889)
New doors have been added to this chaste Stick Style home which has squeezed pediments and panels of vertical strips accenting its height.

3883
(c. 1880's)
Balustrades on the wood stairs and fluted Corinthian columns draw attention to the semi-Mansard roof of this Italianate cottage.

4718
(c. 1908)
This Period residence is set back somewhat from the street. It contains a number of articles from older San Francisco homes which have been demolished.

4081
(1909)
The first in a vintage row of houses which were built on the property of a prosperous farmer, William Kennedy. This one has slanted bays in the correct Period styling.

4087
(1885)
Probably the most noteworthy of the group is this house which was built to house the Kennedy family after their original farmhouse was demolished. The cottage has been refurbished with its Victorian charm retained.

4093
The squared bays, balustrade

and semi-Mansard roof on this house follow the standard Stick Style quite faithfully.

4097–99
(1904)
This last house in the row shows a vestigial Queen Anne tower with pure Colonial Revival detailing.

Seventh Avenue

5
(1898)
An old stable is still standing in back of this shingle home, which enjoys a location next to the Presidio wall. This house introduces a block of exceptionally good shingle houses.

7
(1898)
In the early 1920's Louis Plank, for whom this house was built, was a neighborhood sight as he set off on weekends in his Locomobile to go gold mining. Fishscale shingling fills in the gable end of the home's roof.

15
(1905)
Compared to its neighbors, this home has a very vertical effect due mainly to its sweeping gable roof.

19
(1898)
In the late 1890's a Swedish sea captain sailed into San Francisco Bay, fell in love with the area and eventually built this home. Later, Hother Wismer, first violinist for the San Francisco Symphony, bought the four-room home. So that he could give musicales, he added a thirty-foot living room.

23
(1903)
The second-story off-center windows, which are carefully set into the roof, give a highly individual asymmetrical look to this shingle home.

27
(1905)
The second-story balcony with its fine balustrade is hardly visible through the heavily-vined facade of this shingle house.

37
(1899)
The redwood-paneled living room of this house was added in 1909. This room follows the Maybeck tradition, having a beamed ceiling and windows that look out upon the unusually large garden.

53–55
(1900)
A perfect balance is achieved on the facade of this gabled shingle house.

Seventh Street

700
(1905)
Constructed of solid brick and occupying a complete block, this warehouse is one of the few that survived the fire and earthquake unscathed.

Sharon Street

79
(1895)
A suggestion of Eastlake (especially in the portico) creeps into this Stick Style cottage. The original stairs and door grace the house.

Sharp Place

12
(1902)
An entranceway, enclosed with stained glass, is located on the south side of this house. The gable roof has curled corner brackets with dentil molding.

Shotwell Street

306
328–30,
334–36,
340–42,
346–48,
and 352
(c. 1879)
Here is an almost complete block of Victorian homes, around the corner from Saint Charles School. The structures are all Stick Style except 306, which has slanted bays, decorative cornice and gabled roof and was built in the 1880's.

522
(c. 1870)
A quiet witness to the past is this Italianate house, which lacks the verticality usual in that style.

648
(c. 1884)
This interesting false-front Italianate structure has a limited amount of detailing.

650–52
(c. 1899)
This Stick Style residence with semi-Mansard roof is notable for its identical pediment hoods over the lower bay and entrance.

658
(c. 1899)
This frame residence in Colonial Revival Style is heavily quoined and has a slanted bay on the lower floor.

651–57
661–63,
667–79
and
671–73
(c. 1895)
The flat-fronted Italianate house at 661–63 stands out in this row of essentially Stick Style buildings with assorted details.

682
(c. 1870)
Owned by the same family since its construction, this residence is centered on an uncommonly large lot. The uncomplicated design of the house is enhanced by fishscale shingles and shuttered windows.

1150–52
(c. 1875)
Window detailing is essential to the character of this flat-front Italianate. The lower floor windows are arched and capped by squeezed pediments.

1164
(c. 1899)
Designed and built by German architect-builder Robert Trost as his own residence, this Tudor house displays definite influences from the architecture of his native land.

Sixteenth Street

3150
(1908)
Engine #7 Firehouse. Under the Van Ness Ordinance this site was reserved for Fire Department purposes in 1867–68. This—the third structure on the site—was one of several "temporary" frame firehouses constructed after the quake. The Classic Revival building will either be demolished or sold when Engine Company #7 moves to Red Rock Hill.

3281
(1907)
Saint Matthew's Lutheran Church. The only church in the city offering complete services in both German and English, this green shingled Gothic structure displays lancet arches, turrets, and a beautiful rose window.

South Van Ness Avenue

1321
(c. 1884)
The details have been carefully handled on this fine Italianate.

Spofford Alley

39–49
(1907)
Kwang Yin Temple—a Buddhist temple—was once on this site. After the fire this brick building, which shows some Chinese influence, was built.

Spruce Street

100
(1909)
This brown shingled, multi-gabled house, had a third floor added by Hyman and Appleton in 1922.

Stanyan Street

1248
(c. 1903)
Recalling the 1890's, this residence has an unusual turreted Queen Anne corner tower surmounted by a finial. Only its architectural simplicity and the pitch of the roof suggest the later date.

Steiner Street

908
(1888)
The Corinthian pillars at the entrance and the commanding bracketed cornice of this house are of interest here.

1057
(1890)
This amazing Queen Anne has a broad facade which is composed of corner towers, a gable, a dormer, double-arched entranceway with balustrade above, a frieze, and unevenly spaced windows.

1823
(1881)
This handsomely-proportioned Italianate has quoining and prominent brackets at the cornice.

1827–29
(c. 1885)
Nice details—including quoins—appear on this Italianate house.

2030–30½
(1884)
A sculptural effect is achieved in the facade of this Italianate set of flats, which is adjacent to commercial properties on California Street.

2126
(1884)
A prominent portico and an unusual vertical use of boards under the eaves are interesting facets of this house's Stick Style architecture.

2148
(1876)
Details on this late Italianate-Stick Style house are so disciplined that the front almost becomes Classic Revival.

2150
(1877)
Meticulously-handled intermediate cornices are of interest on this Italianate house, which has had red brick steps and a garage added.

2204,
2206 and
2208
(1873)
A row of three outstanding Italianates, these were no doubt constructed by the same builder. Variations occur mainly in the entrance porches, although 2204 is now distinct from the others because of the addition of shingles and the loss of some window trim.

2231
(1874)
This trim flat-front Italianate has a roof that would appear to be newer than the house. A Thomas Church garden adds charm to the back and like the

2242
(1873)
others on the block, this house is enhanced by the street trees.

An exceptional restoration job has been accomplished on this Italianate. The facade had been stripped when the present owner bought the house. But he found cornices on a similar house that was being torn down and had a cabinetmaker cut them down to fit the exact scale of this house.

2251
(1874)
This very early Stick Style house is chaste and unadorned — almost unaware of that style's future.

2257-59
(1877)
The usual side-hall plan of a Stick Style house is here expanded on the extra-wide lot. The bay window is more generous and is topped with a cartouche.

2302
(1896)
This large house has a Classic Revival scheme (the giant order and impressive frieze) but the ornament and its disposition is late Queen Anne.

2310
(1876)
Well-proportioned and well-detailed Tudor Revival has been executed in shingle on this house.

2400 and
2402
(1900-
01)
Although quite different in materials and concept, these two houses were both done by Willis Polk. The house at 2400 is a gabled, shingled English-style house. The house at 2402 is a tall, narrow house with some half-timbering, leaded windows, convoluted colonettes and a whimsical, carved gable end.

2510
(1870)
The interior of this flat-front Italianate (now shingled) has been opened up and modernized. However, the staircase and fireplace, which originally came around the Horn are intact.

2523-25
(1889)
A wonderfully varied collection of Queen Anne forms, transitions and surface patterns (some of which were removed in a 1964 remodeling) exist on this house. Extensive molded plaster panels — rough cast — decorate the main frieze.

2640
(1899)
This house is so late Queen Anne that its details are Classic Revival. However, the two identical rotund corner towers are choice Queen Anne. Hints of the bungalow style to come are seen.

2744
(1900)
Although this shingle house is not true Queen Anne, its octagonal corner turret is. There are interesting overhangs at each floor level with brackets beneath.

2848
(1901)
Two notable features of this late Stick-Eastlake house are its patterned shingles (arranged in friezes) and the flattened pointed arches of its window heads on the first floor.

2850
(c. 1878)
A simplified and somewhat heavy-membered Italianate, this house has window trim with keystones and paneled lunettes that is unusual.

3009-11
(c. 1880)
A *Sports Illustrated* picture shows this house when it stood on the corner of Union and Steiner. In 1915, when the house was moved to make room for a grocery store, it was raised, and the present lower story added.

3009-11 Steiner Street

Stevenson Street

83
(1909)
"The California Farmer" now uses this small building, whose original purpose — a post office — can be guessed by the mail chutes.

Stockton Street

735
(1906)
Unique in this concrete neighborhood, this simple frame house is set amongst a group of trees just above the north entrance to the Stockton Tunnel.

925
(1916)
Chinese Presbyterian Church. The first mission organized by the Chinese was at this address. This present building is of Colonial Revival derivation.

1000
(1907)
Chinese Methodist Episcopal Mission. The first Chinese Boy Scout troop (Number Three) was organized in this building in 1914. The brick building has a definite Oriental character.

Sutter Street

250-52
(c. 1907)
This is one of three buildings which served for many years as the Sutter Street headquarters of the Goldberg Bowen grocery and delicatessen. Unusual here is the decorative iron work squares which frame the first three stories. Perhaps more remarkable though, is the heavily-flowered and elaborately-ornamented cornice.

640
(1916)
Metropolitan Club. Bliss and Faville gave a look of dignity to this building. Balconied and arched windows highlight the third floor; Corinthian columns rise the extent of the fourth and fifth floors.

1458
(1874)
A ground floor entrance leads to this simple Italianate, which has quoining and medallions.

1525
(1874)
Unusual dormer windows are of interest on this Italianate house, whose Eastlake-type details speak more of the 1890's than the 1870's.

1527
(c. 1875)
The fluted columns on the front porch of this Italianate are similar to those of 1525 Sutter.

1533
(1889)
(1544 Octavia Street). This prominent stucco corner house shows the influence of Queen

Anne styling based on the English revival of Tudor design elements.

1689
(1875)
This very rare example (probably one of the best) of a front wooden fence, which once was common on most San Francisco homes, stands before a standard version of Italianate.

1695
(1876)
The most outstanding feature of this flat-front Italianate is the very lovely cornice.

1740–42
(1884)
The balustrade over the entrance of this Stick Style house is almost hidden by a prominent portico.

1745–51
(1884)
Carefully-executed carved detailing is in evidence on this Stick Style double house.

1771 and 1773
(1881)
This handsome Italianate double house has a subtly-worked-out frieze and Corinthian-columned entranceway.

1783 and 1785
(1885)
Appearing to emulate the success of the duplex at 1771 and 1773, this is another double house – but one that follows the later Stick Style.

1809 and 1811
(1880)
Incised carving, pediments and bracketed cornices appear on this pair of Italianate row houses.

1813
(1876)
A ground-level store breaks the purity of line of this flat-front Italianate.

1815
(1878)
In *Annie's Captain*, author Kathryn Hulme wrote the story of her grandparents, Captain and Mrs. John Cavarly, the original owners of this beautifully-restored Italianate house. A plaque stating that the house was "built in 1878 by Captain John M. Cavarly" has been placed on the front of the home.

1890–92– 96–98
(1884)
The window framings and pediments on this Italianate building are very elaborate in the use of pipestem colonnettes and other moldings.

1942 and 1948
(1874)
A glassed-in front porch at 1942 distinguishes it from its near twin at 1948.

1955–59
The pediment in the eaves of

(1873)
this stucco building contains a handsomely-sculptured female face. The second-floor windows are nicely framed.

1961–63– 67–69
(1877–86)
Squeezed pediments – including rounded ones above the cornices – are used freely on this double Italianate. This building demonstrates how well street-floor commercial use and upper-floor residence use can be handled together.

1971–75 and 1985
(1876)
Again these Italianate buildings show the mixture of commercial and residential use.

2016–18
(1892)
This is one of the strongest statements of the Queen Anne row house in San Francisco because of the proportions of the various major architectural elements – the tower and the size and proportions of the front porch columns.

2057–59
(c. 1875)
Quoins, squeezed pediments, and restrained carving are seen on this early Stick Style building, whose windows are especially narrow.

2128–30
(1884)
Not easily classifiable, this house has an exuberant and playful display of varied ornamental devices: twisting colonnettes, balustrade, scalloped shingling, carved gable ends, carved spandrels and turret broken by soaring gables.

2207–09, through 2287–89– 91
(1886– 1891)
This row of nine Italianate and Stick Style flats is exceptional in that so many related styles in good condition are massed together.

2450–66
(1910)
Busy Baroque detailing can be seen on this building, now housing the Russian Center of San Francisco (formerly the German Turnverein Hall).

2496–98
(1890)
The many-angled corner bay of this Stick Style building is unique. More conventionally shaped, yet highly-decorated bays appear on two sides of the building.

2540–42– 44
(1884)
Small roofs with aggressive dentils surmount the three windows on the bay and the en-

tranceway of this Stick Style building.

2564
(c. 1890)
An exact duplicate of 2932 Pine Street is this one-story Stick Style cottage with floriated frieze.

2611, 2613 and 2615
(1877– 1879)
Although these three Stick Style flats form a row, the middle one has a different profile because of its false gable.

2619
(1888)
This small shingle Italianate with a prominent hood mold has been shingled (obviously later).

2621
(1885)
Similar in effect to 2619, this Stick Style house has an outside stairway leading to the second story.

2701–01½
(1889)
This large Stick Style building takes full advantage of its corner site with its square corner bay.

Taylor Street

1809
(1894)
Said to have replaced the Russian Hill Hotel, this finely maintained Queen Anne – with Stick framing – is a very solidly-built home, designed by William Mooser for Louis De Martini.

Tennessee Street

1104–06, 1108–10, 1112–14 and 1116–18
(1870's)
This row of four houses has been relatively unchanged since its construction. All four have well-defined Italiante falsefronts.

Tenth Avenue

1480
(c. 1902)
There are nice Colonial Revival details on this wood house. Of special note are the cornices, window framings and Palladian window in the gable end.

Tenth Street

165
(1890)
The trustees of James Lick's estate built this house, with its separate facilities for men and women, and hot and cold running water – a luxury at the time. Basically, the structure, with its two-foot walls, is unchanged – even though it has been used as a laundry since 1920.

Third and Market Streets

(1898)   Hearst Building. Built on the site of the Neucleus Hotel, this building previously housed the *San Francisco Examiner*. A. C. Schweinfurt designed the terra cotta building with decorative marble elements.

Third Street

86
(1906)   Mercantile Building. Originally known as the Aronson Building, the Mercantile Building is a steel and concrete structure. Owner Abraham Aronson was a Russian immigrant who bought the Stockton Street Synagogue in 1886.

Third and Townsend Streets

(1915)   Southern Pacific Railway Station. Constructed as a "temporary" station to handle visitors to the Panama-Pacific International Exposition, this station is considered one of San Francisco's most notable examples of the Mission Revival style.

Third and Townsend Streets

Thirtieth Street

409
(1892)   The base of the slanted bay on this house tapers to a point which is finished by an acorn pendant.

462
(1893)   The detailing between the semi-Mansard roof and window tops of this house is elaborately Stick. Here, panels under the eaves are in the "ball and stem" motif while below, elongated checkerboard panels surmount the windows.

Thirty-fourth Avenue

726
(1905)   Probably the smallest residence ever designed by Willis Polk, this home was built for newspaperman Charles Horn. The

unadorned brown shingle house stands in contrast to its stucco neighbors.

Thirty-ninth Avenue

539–41
(c. 1905)   At the time the earthquake hit, a bricklayer was working on the fireplace of this shingle home. He was killed on the spot, probably by falling bricks; the house, though, remained virtually intact.

Townsend Street

131–135
(c. 1907)   Charles Lee Tilden originally owned two buildings with a vacant lot in between. To make use of the lot he had a front wall built, using the sides of the other buildings as common walls. Presto: a new building.

310
(1907)   W. & J. Sloane built this handsome brick warehouse with its decorative cornice and shuttered windows. It is now used by the Julliard Fancy Food Company.

Treat Avenue

1200–02
(c. 1890)   This Stick-Eastlake building offers a busy facade with three bays overhung by chalet gables.

1204–06
(c. 1885)   Constructed by builder John McCarthy (as was 1200–02), this house is a pure version of the Stick Style.

Turk Street

751
(1875)   Panels decorated with garlands add interest to this Stick Style house which is well maintained.

763–67
(1889)   The unusual pattern of this Stick Style house's facade springs from the non-alignment of the two bays on the second floor with the one on the first floor.

770
(1868)   This example of Italianate style commands respect. It has especially fine window framing on the second floor.

773
(late 1880's)   The crowded ornate facade on this Stick-Eastlake house is crowned with an unusual tower.

1733–35   The balustraded porticos line-up

and
1739–41
(1884)   nicely on these Stick Style mirror twins.

1761
(1877)   A monumental Italianate, this was built as a three-family dwelling but is now used as the Triumph Church and Kingdom of God in Christ.

1825
(1895)   H. W. Cleaveland may have been the architect for this noble Queen Anne, conspicuous because of its great size and large lot. It has the usual tower, fish-scale shingles, carved work and dormers.

1844
(1875)   The fine detailing on this Italianate is heavier and more aggressive than was usual. The large house is set in a lovely garden.

Twentieth Avenue

450
(c. 1900)   This delicate, minute Victorian Gothic house has pediments filled in with sunbursts and a lacy bargeboard effect along the gabled roof.

Twentieth Street

3365
(1914)   This stucco Classic Revival church was built for the Emanuel Evangelical Church, founded in 1864. Now the church and convent belong to a Russian Orthodox order.

3441–47
(c. 1891)   (And 501–03 Capp Street). A superb articulation of the emerging Queen Anne style is seen on these buildings which form a

3441–47 Twenty-first Street

fine example of street architecture. A busy quality is achieved by the floriated surfaces, hobnail shingles, and procession of gables leading to a conical tower.

3549–51
(c. 1876)
This Italianate home is notable for the pretty leaf molds beneath the consoles and for the highly-polished natural wood front door.

3625
(c. 1888)
This two-story home has been beautifully painted to point up its Italianate detailing. Especially distinctive are the double front doors, and the tapered base of the bay tier culminating in a pendant finial.

3635
(1879)
The original barn, with hayhoisting pulley rod, recreates the nostalgic horse-and-buggy era around this semi-Mansarded Stick Style mansion whose surfaces are crowded with detailing.

3643
(1891)
This Italianate cottage has a semi-Mansard roof and a decorative arch which is repeated on the hood above the entrance.

3647
(late 1880's)
A semi-Mansard roof surmounts this Italianate cottage. The squeezed pediment above the bay matches one over the door.

3733–35
(c. 1880)
Vertical timbering under the ornamented eaves and panels of diagonal strips give an Eastlake flavor to this gabled Stick Style house.

3737–39
(1876)
A typical early Italianate, this has a bay console which tapers to a pointed base. It also has a fine balustraded portico.

3755
(1887)
This towering semi-Mansarded Italianate has lavish, distinguished detailing.

3763
(1880)
In semi-Mansarded Stick Style, this home retains its original interior and graceful vertical strip trim.

3765
(1876)
This tiny house has traditional Italianate detailing on its flat facade but also has Corinthian pilasters.

3769–71
(1871)
A most unusual post-and-lintel portico (with five small roof beams perpendicular to the lintel) bedecks this early, stark Italianate.

3851
(c. 1893)
At first glance this Classic Revival house—unique in its surroundings—appears to be of stucco rather than of frame construction. It has the refinements of quoins, dentils, and an Ionic-columned portico.

3919–21
(1890's)
A beautifully-ornate and unique house, this originally stood on Church Street, where Mission High School is now located. It was moved prior to 1906, along with the two houses that now flank it.

4021
(c. 1885)
The irregular facade of this Stick Style house is recessed in tiers. Pilasters and friezes of vertical strips lead the eye up to the semi-Mansard roof and hoods.

4141–43
(c. 1897)
Fernando Nelson built this Stick Style house with Eastlake-Chalet flavor in the gable above the steeply-slanted bay tier and in the portico.

4150
(c. 1891)
An Eastlake sunburst pediment surmounts this house's semi-Mansard roof, and this theme is repeated on a larger scale in the connected garage.

4160
(c. 1891)
This Eastlake-detailed cottage has an especially-interesting portico.

4325–27–29
(c. 1890)
Involved Eastlake gables and trim are seen in this house. The entrance is high above old stairs and balustrades.

4331–33
(c. 1890)
Complementary to 4325–27–29, this house also has Eastlake gables, trim and portico. It is enhanced by stained glass panes in every window.

Twenty-eighth Street

47 and 51
(c. 1890)
Floriated wooden trim decorates the facades of these twin Stick Style cottages.

183
(c. 1890)
There is intricate Stick Style detailing on this cottage.

219
(1889)
A flower petal motif is contained in the squeezed pediments over the windows and portico in this Period cottage.

232
(1888)
A rising sun motif enhances the squeezed pediments over the windows and squeezed arch over the portico in this essentially-Stick Style cottage.

235
(c. 1885)
This nicely-proportioned, late-Italianate cottage has been given a modern front door and stair rails.

254–56
(c. 1880's)
The gold facade of this Italianate displays an old paneled door with stained glass window, which is sheltered by a simplified portico.

260
(1897)
This Stick Style cottage's decor comes from the pediments, containing sunbursts, on spooled brackets.

313
(1892)
This Stick Style house was built for Charles C. W. Haun, owner of Haun and Co., artificial stone contractors, whose property included large side garden, driveway and rear building (#311). These all remain today. The rear building served once as a stable for horses but since 1901 has been a dwelling over a garage.

Twenty-fifth Avenue

1 and 2
(1909)
Frederick Knickerson designed this Spanish stucco house with tile roof, wrought iron balconies and walled-in front garden. In 1939 the cliff-edge home was made into a two-family residence.

Twenty-fifth Street

2501
(1917)
#37 Engine, #9 Truck Firehouse. Soon to be abandoned is this unique one-story Moorish-Romanesque firehouse. White stone has been used for decorative details against a brick background.

4036
(1891)
Surrounded by asbestos-shingled buildings, this Stick-Eastlake house has remained true to its style. Even the stained glass windows have been retained.

4078
(c. 1891)
The rising-sun design in the pediment is repeated in the squeezed pediments over the modern door and flat window on this Stick Style house.

Twenty-first Street

3233–35 These two examples of Stick-
(c. 1885) Strip Style architecture are re-
and lated although the Corinthian
3239–41 portico at 3239–41 is more
(c. 1885) elaborate.

3320 and Built by two captains for their
3324 families, these detached, quite
(c. 1877) grand Italianate residences are
almost identical.

3325 This tiny appealing Stick Style
(c. 1885) cottage is painted bright barn
red with matching picket fence.

3329–31 Intricate carved detail is con-
(c. 1883) centrated around windows and
on the composite pilasters and
colonnettes of this stately Italianate.

3333–35 Offering an interesting study
(c. 1890) in Period details, these Stick
and Style homes both have semi-
3339–41 Mansard roofs. 3333–35 is the
(c. 1876) more ornate, with festoons and
a heavy, shingled, gable end.

3343–45 A heavily-embellished Stick-
(c. 1885) Eastlake house, this has sweeping arches filled with cartouches.

3343–45 Twenty-first Street

3352–54 On this Stick Style residence
(1876) the portico is composed of semi-
fluted Corinthian columns
which support a frieze and a
rounded arch containing a floral
pattern.

3364 This especially fine flat-front
(1873) Italianate has traditional quoins
and arched pediments on con-
soles. An old gas lamp post with

hanging baskets of geraniums
brightens the front.

3367–69, These nearly identical Stick-
3371, and Eastlake Style homes, have
3375 highly-decorated gable ends.
(1885) Squared medallion friezes appear on the lower bays.

3567 Graceful Italianate detailing is
(1884) displayed on this petite Stick
Style cottage with semi-Mansard
red roof.

3650 This small essentially Stick
(c. 1883) house has a lovely pattern of
vertical siding with scalloped
border along the eaves. Bougainvillea partially covers the
simple squared bay.

3701 An old well on the property of
(1884) this house remains; its mineral
water, in fact, gave the area its
nickname of "Mineral Springs
Hill." A lovely garden surrounds
the unpretentious farm-type
house.

3733 A double stairway leads to the
(1885) subtle and pure Italianate
cottage painted a flattering
yellow paint.

3816–56 These gabled houses are remark-
(1903–04) able in that they form a row of
fifteen almost identical cottages,
built and designed by Isaac
Anderson, carpenter, architect
and builder. Several have had
aluminum siding or asbestos
shingles added; the row is, however, colorfully painted and well
maintained.

3833 Heavy ornate pediments at the
(1892) roof and portico unify this imposing Italianate residence. A
unique spiral colonette adorns
a seldom-seen triangular bay,
flanked by elongated brackets.

3837–39 Stick-Eastlake ornamentation is
(1893) seen on this small house. The
stair balustrades and newel posts
are especially heavy and ornate.

3845 The heaviness of this Stick
(1896) house is relieved by the use
of brackets, spindles, and balustrades. A squeezed pediment
caps the paneled front door
which contains a round window.

3859 This remarkable Stick-Eastlake
(1893) house has elaborate decorative

devices. These include a carved
square panel, friezes, and a
fascinating portico. This is composed of a "basket handle" arch
with jigsaw pieces filling the
spandrels.

Twenty-fourth Avenue

107 (125 El Camino del Mar). Diffi-
(1910) cult to see from Twenty-fourth
Avenue, this rambling, half-
timbered home is readily visible
from Lincoln Boulevard. It is
distinctive for its open porches
and hexagonal tower which
nestles between two wings.

107 Twenty-fourth Avenue

Twenty-fourth Street

3514 Some Stick detailing appears on
(1882) this essentially Italianate house
which has been nicely painted.

3515–19 Interesting squeezed pediments
(c. 1873) and the repeated use of "spool-
on-stick" motif highlight this
Stick Style house.

3900–02 (1082 Sanchez Street). The second
(c. 1893) Stick Style story of this multiple-
use building features heavy,
scroll-filled, squeezed pediments.

3968–70 The total facade of this Italian-
(1888) ate is covered with fishscale
shingles; otherwise the house is
basic Italianate.

4281 This immaculately restored and
(c. 1896) maintained home boasts a
slanted bay decorated with
chains of shells and cameo
faces. The center attic window
is a variation of the Palladian
Style.

4303 and These two were once identical
4305 in a row of three Stick Style
(c. 1891) cottages. They have sunbursts
on the doors and friezes of
diamond medallions with nobs

300

centered over the doors and windows.

4313
(c. 1892)
Eastlake embellishments on this house are exemplified by the portico pediment which sits on heavy carved consoles and contains a cross-timbered ornament.

4403 and 4405
(c. 1896)
This cottage boasts diamond and fishscale-shingled patterns on its slanted bays, which have broken pediment roofs. The gable ends at the bay corners form overhanging hoods with inverted finials.

4407
(1896)
This house has a most unusual wooden strip design around the oeil de boeuf dormer window.

Twenty-ninth Street

215 and 217
(1895)
These mirror-twin Stick Style residences were constructed so that they seem to be one building. The semi-Mansard roofs provide a unifying element.

328–28½
(1888)
Alternating rows of fishscale and diamond shingles on the recessed portion of the facade create a most unusual effect for this late Stick Style residence.

475
(1892)
Still standing in back of this Stick-Eastlake house is a red barn which is connected to a large tower. There is an extravagance of carved detailing which forms crenellated, waffle, and floriated patterns.

Twenty-second Street

3126
(1900–01)
Saint John's Evangelical Lutheran Church. The rose window on this frame and shingle Gothic church has carved wood instead of the usual stained glass.

3322–22A
(1875)
Built in pure Italianate style, this house is notable for its high, round-arched windows matching the portico archway. The home is framed by a delicate old iron fence.

3354–56
(c. 1884)
The remaining unaltered Stick Style member of original mirror twins, this house has considerable vertical detailing.

3378–80
(c. 1890)
This very elaborate Stick Style house is particularly important

for rosette-like crests, a splash of fishscale shingles, and six finials atop the semi-Mansard roof.

3385–89
(c. 1884)
A Romanesque portico leads to this Stick Style house. The elaborate friezes of festoons, wreaths, and floral scroll are outstanding.

3426–32, 3434–36 and 3438–40
(c. 1899)
This Italianate row is composed of two mirror twins and one double house. Their cornices (major and minor) and hood molds establish a rhythm and movement.

3573
(c. 1887)
B. J. Malone built this Stick Style house for his own family; it remained in the family until 1964. The Eastlake cottage has been beautifully maintained and provides an example of paint accentuating architectural features.

3704 and 3762
(1892)
These two houses are the only unaltered ones in a row. Their facades are alive with fanciful details including a number of pendant finials.

3741, 3745, 3749, 3753, 3759, 3763, 3767, 3773
(1897 and 1908)
These colorful members of an original row of Eastlake-detailed homes feature gabled roofs containing various ornamental patterns. Most fascinating are the carved vases at some of the second-floor corners.

3816
(1909–10)
Now successfully converted into a residence-studio by the present owners (both artists), this building originally functioned as the firehouse for Chemical Company #44. The stucco structure was executed in a Mission Revival style. Its tile roof remains as do the huge central arch and the tower at the rear.

3817, 3821, 3825, 3829–31, 3835, 3839, 3843, 3847, 3853, 3857, 3865, 3871
(1905–06)
The gable ends of these row homes are richly trimmed in three patterns, and are highlighted by large cartouches and flowering Grecian urns. They follow the pattern set by the row in the 3700 block. Like the other group of Eastlake houses, these were all built as single-family homes by builder John Anderson. Of the entire row, 3843 is the only house which has not been altered.

Twenty-seventh Street

232
(1888)
Nicely proportioned, this Stick Style cottage has well-defined surface areas. Two garages have been added at the ground level.

409
(c. 1892)
An unusual mixture of shingle patterns adds variety to this frame cottage as does the portico lattice work, which is repeated in the stair balustrades.

Twenty-sixth Street

3733, 3735, 3739, 3741, 3743
(1887)
Although all five cottages were built at the same time, their architectural styles vary from early to late Stick Style to Italianate. The row is unified by the use of identical architectural detailing—squeezed pediments over windows and doors, brackets under eaves, and delicate incised designs on panels.

3927
(c. 1889)
This extra-wide Stick Style cottage was once part of a vegetable and dairy farm.

4063
(1891)
An unusually-shingled, semi-Mansard hood runs the width of this Period cottage and protects the slanted bay and portico. It is surmounted by a similarly-shingled, bracketed false parapet.

Twenty-third Street

3035
(c. 1893)
This Period cottage incorporates elements of both Italianate and Stick-Eastlake styles.

3035 Twenty-third Street

301

3261
(1891–92) Trinity Presbyterian Church. The congregation of this Queen Anne church, designed by Percy and Hamilton, has recently merged with that of Stuart Memorial Presbyterian Church. The latter is used for worship while this building is used for a variety of community activities.

3326,
(c. 1877)
3330,
(c. 1886)
3336
(c. 1882) John Hinkel built these three row houses. The center house has a squared bay window in Stick Style, and is flanked by the other two Italianate homes. Vivid red paint adds to the character of 3326, now converted into the "Second Hand Rose Store".

3339–49
(1877) Gracing the corner of Bartlett and 23rd, this lovely Italianate building houses shops and living quarters. Large panels feature incised Pennsylvania-Dutch vines and buds, and ornate bracket couplets interrupt the fringe of pointed scallops.

3350-52
(1877) (180–82 Bartlett Street). Rambling and imposing, this Italianate corner residence has elaborate carving and quoins at six corners. It is not noticeably altered by the enclosure of the portico and the addition of a small room at one side.

3366–68
(c. 1895) This residence differs from usual plans in that the slanted bay tier is in the center and balanced by recessed flat walls.

3503–05
and
3507–09
(1892) (100 San Jose Avenue). These two immense Queen Anne-Eastlake homes are notable for their extremely decorative panels and friezes. 3507–09 has the illusion of a corner tower where a polygonal cupola emerges from the roof, while 3503–05 has a protruding square tower with a cupola interrupting the gable.

3552–58
(c. 1880) One of the most fascinating old buildings in the Mission District, this Italianate building has a facade alive with a procession of bays and polygonal turrets. These turrets (all ending in finials, broken by pediments, and rising from brackets and friezes) are not Italianate but rather harbingers of the Queen Anne.

3679–85
(c. 1880's) An important landmark in a block of more recent structures, this Italianate double residence presents a straightforward balanced facade.

3751
(c. 1890) Squared bays with stained glass panels are decorative on this Stick Style house.

3761
(c. 1889) The paint decor makes this cottage extremely attractive and points up its essentially Stick Style features.

3767
(c. 1889) This Stick Style semi-Mansarded cottage closely resembles its neighbors.

3771
(c. 1889) This Stick Style cottage is indeed very similar to 3761 and 3767. Its details are sharp and precise.

3933
(c. 1891) This trim, bright Stick Style cottage contrasts with its somber neighbor.

3968
(c. 1897) The conical tower of this interesting Queen Anne is barely visible from the street. The rich surface patterns of the facade derive partly from the fishscale and diamond shingles and partly from the floriated frieze.

3998
(c. 1892) This simple Stick Style house has a lovely arcade which develops from the extension at the bay's intermediate cornice.

4020–20A
(c. 1880) Beneath the semi-Mansard roof of this house, wavy ribbon designs fill the panels, while an individual triangular bay is wedged into a corner between the side wall and the recessed section.

4069–71
(c. 1889) The Eastlake decoration occurs in this house in the angular portico, the gables, and the carved sunburst panels.

4073–75,
4077–79
(c. 1891) These two Stick Style residences appear to have been mirror twins at one time, but 4077–79 no longer has a balustrade over the entry hood.

4200
(1892) Another Stick Style house designed by Fernando Nelson, this has an enclosed front porch on a stone base.

4225
(c. 1880) This gaily-decorated gold cottage displays a fishscale-shingled frieze and semi-Mansard roof.

4226
(1892) Built by Fernando Nelson, this single-story Stick Style cottage has a bay window crowned by a gable end on which there is lattice work and simple bargeboard.

4250
(c. 1886) A turreted coach house still stands behind this Queen Anne. The Queen Anne's roof forms cupolas above the octagonal corner tower and a simulated smaller tower.

4279,
4283,
4287,
4293
(c. 1890) As part of the false parapets, there are jaunty false gables ending in finials. These give a sharp precision to this row of homes.

4297–99
(1896) (703–05 Douglass Street). This corner Stick Style building has squared bays on the second floor. 4297–99 and 703 appear to be connected by stairways to 705 Douglass, a newer-looking structure but painted to match and apparently now part of the entire complex.

4452 and
4455
(c. 1897) Although across the street from each other, these Stick Style cottages are essentially twins. They are important because they alone are older in an area of newer homes.

Union Street

287 and
289
(c. 1850's) Now somewhat modernized, these two similar houses apparently date from the early '50's. Popular writer Charles Warren Stoddard is believed to have lived in 287, and it was in this house that Stoddard gave Robert Louis Stevenson a copy of his *South Sea Idylls*, thereby inspiring Stevenson's interest in that area.

293
(1860's) The stylistic simplicity of this one-story frame cottage makes it seem ageless. It complements its neighbors to the east, and also emphasizes the height of 291.

2506
(1899) The first in a row of four distinctive brown shingle houses, this version has Colonial Revival touches: a pilastered and pedimented entrance door frame and windows. The third floor dormer is a California touch.

2512
(1897)
Richly patterned fan lights that are used unconventionally, and a frieze of diamond-pattern shingles are a part of the delight of this house.

2516
(1896)
Great understanding of the shingled cottage tradition is shown in this house, designed by Maybeck and altered by John Funk in 1955. Effective are the shingled bargeboard and massive redwood log columns.

2518
(c. 1888)
Originally situated on Scott Street near Pacific, this simplified Period Revival house was moved to this location in 1895. The half-tipped roof of the front gable foretells its later use in bungalows.

2526
(1897)
This Dutch Colonial is a correct interpretation with gambrel roof and oeil de boeuf attic window—although no Hudson Valley Dutchman ever had a semi-circular first-floor bay.

2551
(1889)
There is good Eastlake spindle work on the gable end of this Stick Style house. But more novel is the horizontal molding marking the bottom of a non-existent frieze.

2590
(1899)
The steeply-pitched gables with heavily-molded bargeboards, slightly-rounded eaves and molded consoles are Tudor elements on this large shingle house.

Valencia Street

933, 945 and 953–55
(c. 1875–76)
These three are the best that remain of a once much longer row of Italianate residences. The balustrade has apparently been removed from the portico of 953–55; 933 and 945 have retained theirs.

956–68
(1878)
(3–5 Liberty Street). This immense Stick Style corner structure was built with large spindled arches between the ground-floor store fronts. Lavish ornamentation and most uncommon angular strips and colonnettes have been used.

1427
(1880's)
This handsome interpretation of late Italianate has been in the same family since 1898; it was then that dairyman John A.

Christen moved into this house and built the brick dairy depot (now idle) next door at 1423.

1447–49
(c. 1889)
This large Stick-Eastlake residence incorporates an interesting gable end with checkboard patterning.

1453
(c. 1881)
A crisp bargeboard enhances the gable of this cottage whose porch runs the full width of the house. Columns with simple leafy capitals run along the porch and support the overhanging roof.

1457–63
(c. 1885)
This Italianate double house has its entrances at opposite ends rather than grouped together at the center.

1458
(c. 1882–84)
No. 13 Engine Firehouse. The handsome Italianate building (basically brick) features a cast iron facade on which Corinthian pilasters on the first story and composite pilasters on the second set off the arched openings.

Vallejo Street

1001
(1906)
At the foot of the Vallejo Street steps is this enormous Period house built by R. G. Hanford. Apparently the mansion was unoccupied until 1913; then after it changed hands several times it was purchased by Paul Verdier in 1919. Since then it has been used as a Russian dancing school, Inter-America House and a USO during the second world war.

1075–77
(1908)
While the front of this frame residence dates from 1908, it is possible that an earlier cottage was incorporated into the rear of the house.

1255
(1907)
This stark white house is set far back from the street at the rear of a lovely garden.

1616
(1890)
The neat shingles may not be original, but the rest of this house is pure Queen Anne. Beautifully handled is the carefully casual intersection of gable, console and tower (with hexagonal spire).

1625
(1889)
The prominent pediment of this Stick Style house almost makes a separate tower out of the

the three-tiered bay window—perhaps builder Hinkel's intention.

1628
(1888)
A number of this house's Italianate details—actually quite late here—have been removed. Remaining are cartouches surmounting the richly-molded second-floor window trim. The house has a charming side porch.

1806
(1896)
This richly-ornamented Queen Anne and its neighbors at 1808 and 1814 offer a one-stop illustration of the bewildering variety of decorative devices employed in the late nineteenth century.

1808
(1904)
Only hints of the original style remain on this building, for it has been extensively remodeled. The wide entrance porch has a Romanesque arch while the bay windows have Classic Revival details.

1814
(1890)
There is some Stick mixed with Queen Anne on this house. Four different shingle patterns have been used plus assorted brackets and panels. The corner turret ends in a witch's hat.

1815
(1904)
This shingle house (whose irregular placement of windows and classical detailing make it distinctively charming) was designed by Joseph Mailliard, who had the plans approved by English architect John W. Corly.

1815 Vallejo Street

1827
(1904)
Tudor elements, simplified but correct, exist in this house: diamond-patterned windows, half-timbering and pointed arches at the entrance.

2053
The usual corner tower of the

(1895) Queen Anne style appears here as well as a second, shorter one above the doorway. Fishscale shingling and a floreate frieze add surface textures.

2065
(1891) This Queen Anne's portico is set behind an arcade—although this feature is overshadowed by the very prominent gable, which intersects the corner tower.

2090
(1919) A superb statement of Georgian Revival, with meticulous detailing, this brick house was designed by Clarence Tantau, who normally favored Spanish Colonial. A fine row of poplars screens the house from Buchanan Street.

2090 Vallejo Street

2100
(1911) Houghton Sawyer designed this house for Mrs. Adolph Spreckels, who planned the house for her mother. The stucco house—now covered with vines—is four-square and unassuming in its refinements.

2190
(1904) Edgar Mathews used that restrained San Francisco combination of dark shingles and dark red brick in this house, whose walks and garden walls are also brick.

2250
(1901) Opulence worthy of fine stone is seen in this Baroque Revival house built entirely of wood and plaster. Especially notable is the molded frieze—deep enough to incorporate the top floor windows.

2360
(1905) Again Baroque elements make for richly varied surface qualities on this wood and plaster house. The dormer window alone has consoles, pediment, and cartouche.

2375
(c. 1887) The heavy membering of the eaves and mullions indicates a late Italianate style on this shingle house, whose beautifully-handled entrance porch is assuredly of that persuasion.

2501
(1905) This Period shingle house has a number of gables (the trim of which forms pointed arches), which add great movement to the exterior. The home was built by J. A. Deneen for Mayor Eugene Schmitz.

2535
(1898) Redwood is the theme of this Jacobean house, designed by Oliver Everett. A redwood tree is the focus of the garden. Redwood shingles cover the exterior while redwood paneling is used on the interior.

2698
(1911) The bottom story of this Tudor Gothic Revival house is recessed under the second floor; the upper story has half-timbering so intricately patterned that it suggests paneling.

2727
(c. 1905) A steeply-pitched roof harbors a gable window, and below this two simply pedimented windows break the roof line on the upper floor of this house. Also notable is the richly-ornamented French door.

2732
(1899) This charmingly irregular shingle house is essentially Period although its shaped gable ends and leaded sashes suggest Tudor Revival.

2737
(c. 1903) Complementing its neighbor at 2727 is this shingle residence. Aside from its larger steeply-pitched roof, the most notable feature is the French window surmounted by an unusual pediment.

2858
(1901) The steep and deep gable, decorated bargeboard, and pointed arches of the first floor windows all suggest Tudor Revival as the style of this appealing shingle house, designed by Albert Farr.

2980
(1908) The low English Cottage style was used here by Edgar Mathews. As he so often did, Mathews in this house favored a "limited palette"—here unrelieved plaster walls and shingle roof.

2990
(1908) Walter Bliss produced here a simplified Italian Mediterranean house, its tile, hipped roof and prominent chimneys adding to this effect as do the stucco house and garden walls.

Valley Street

49–53
(c. 1892) An imposing three-story bay tier rises to the semi-Mansard, fishscale-shingle roof on this Stick Style house. The portico features ornate circular designs in the frieze and the balustrade.

175
(c. 1888) This little Stick Style cottage with semi-Mansard roof is of increased significance now, since the once-identical homes on either side have been altered.

221
(c. 1900) Saint Paul's Church and Rectory. The massive granite-faced Gothic edifice presents a large, round stained glass window, lancet arches, pier buttresses, and tall slender spires, unequal in height, with crocket-like projections forming vertical spines around each. The rectory, in neo-Classical style, features a Palladian window above the portico.

Van Ness Avenue

2134
(1909) Moses J. Lyon (once an associate of Polk) designed this building with a half-timbered facade above a brick base (probably using bricks salvaged from the fire).

2209
(1901) International Institute. Moses Lyon was the architect of this distinguished Classic Revival residence. The exterior is dominated by the two-story Ionic columns, surmounted by a Palladian window. Inside, opulent touches remain: a Gothic Revival reception hall, teak-finished dado paneling and hand-tooled Venetian leather in the dining room.

2256
(1908) Truly a unique building, this residence has a real vertical thrust to it. The asymmetrical front reaches its apex in a steeply pitched gable with finial.

2826
(c. 1875) This truly distinguished Italianate house was moved to its present site from the corner of Larkin and Broadway in 1903. It was built by 49'er Frank Tillman, whose daughter is the present occupant.

304

Vicksburg Street

2–14
(1874)
This colorful row of homes was constructed by P. F. Furguson who built 2–6 for himself. Charcoal gray 2–6 is the most regal, despite some alteration; its most striking feature is an ornate Classical portico. The others (also altered somewhat) are more conventional Stick-Italianates.

25
(c. 1887)
A novel version of Eastlake, this house has a folded-over roof encompassing part of the facade. A prominent waffle pattern is incorporated into the facade design.

69
(c. 1892)
On this home, Romanesque detailing is especially apparent in the frieze and portico. The very unusual rounded corner contains a bent glass window.

75
(c. 1891)
The Stick Style facade of this house is recessed in irregular sections, and it is crowned with tiers of hoods and semi-Mansard roofs.

132
(c. 1891)
This home's gabled roof includes sawtooth shingling and decorative bargeboard. A stable remains in the back.

133
(c. 1886)
Decorative squeezed pediments and carved panels forming a frieze are notable on this simple Italianate flat-front cottage.

140
(c. 1893)
This simple flat-front Italianate house (built with a small bedroom cottage in the rear) retains its original iron fence and gate in front.

160
(c. 1907)
Ionic fluted columns and a Palladian window show Colonial Revival influence on this house. The decoration is enriched by festoons of garlands, floreate medallions, and balustrades of lattice work.

308–10
(c. 1889)
An Eastlake chalet gable and a hood mold of scalloped shingles are part of the decoration of this late Stick Style house.

312
(c. 1888)
This Italianate flat-front cottage has well-handled details, especially in the window and door frames which work into the pediment.

Waller Street

883–85
(late 1880's)
An unusual column supports the two-story square bays on this Stick Style house.

Walnut Street

15
(1903)
Recent remodeling has once again made this wood and stucco home into a handsome structure, French in character.

100–112
(1903)
These two shingle buildings (each of four flats) are under one roof but separated by a common wall. The multi-gabled roof with overhanging eaves is typical of Edgar Mathews, the architect.

Washington Street

530
(c. 1860)
E.O.I. Building. Originally a warehouse, this yellow brick building is now used for offices. It is Italianate in style and has been carefully restored.

857
(c. 1907–08)
Window boxes on the second-floor level enhance this exceptional and powerful brick structure. Here, narrow windows are deeply recessed behind arched brick frames.

1380–82
(1908)
Clinker brick was used on the first floor of this two-story apartment building; stucco and wood create a half-timbered effect on the second floor.

1644
(1909)
This wooden three-story apartment building has rounded windows on its first floor while slanted bays appear above the intermediate cornice on the second and third floors.

2108
(c. 1875 – the core)
In 1925 the core of the present house was moved—complete with furniture—from its location by the Spreckels' wall to its present site. The house, now the Danish Consulate, was then completely remodeled by Lewis Hobart.

2150
(1915)
Senator James D. Phelan had this house built in time for the 1915 Exposition so that he could entertain the visiting celebrities. The tile-roofed brown brick house is Period Revival, built around a courtyard.

2447
(c. 1888)
Once flats which included doctors' offices, this is builder Hinkel's interpretation of the late Stick Style with heavy Eastlake detailing at the portico.

2465
(1878)
Simple detailing of this Italianate residence is painted white against a soft green background. Most eye-catching are the ornate capitals of the pillars and pilasters which support the prominent portico.

2506
(1889)
Two tile-roofed modern garages have been added to this correctly-detailed Italianate house.

2531
(1884)
A remarkable array of brackets, pediments, Corinthian columns and carved panels differentiates this Stick Style house as does its general profile—the non-alignment of bays. The house has been painted beautifully to highlight all its features.

2560
(1879)
A very impressive double house is this Italianate with Mansard roof and balanced facade, which includes two tiers of bays.

2561
(1885)
The entire surface of this Queen Anne is active with small-scale, low-relief patterning of various kinds. The circular corner tower is superimposed on an octagonal base.

2566
(1878)
An amazing-angled, enclosed porch and a gable end that merges with the corner bay give a curious expression to this Queen Anne, which is basically the typical sidehall row house.

2572
(1878)
Seldom seen are the well-shaped basement windows on this detailed Italianate house, whose moldings seem especially vigorous.

2958
(1886)
The arbitrary decorative surfacing of this house is Queen Anne; the neatly arranged areas and panels Stick. The facade is symmetrical except for a false gable to the left.

2999
(1887)
The simple window heads, hood molds, and cornice of the Italianate are seen in this frame commercial building, which has always played an important role in the neighborhood.

3021
(1890)
The German-American Bund occupied this house before World War II, holding meetings

in a cottage in the garden. The house itself is late Stick with strong hints of Queen Anne and Eastlake.

3024 and 3026 *(1886)* The fine scale of the elements of these identical cottages is late Italianate. On each house the squeezed pediments of the portico and window match perfectly.

3116–18 *(1889)* This Stick Style building presents a contrast with 3112 in that they are of two distinct fashions but built only ten years apart. Notable here are the four different shapes of pediments.

3600 *(1897–98)* Portrait stained glass windows on the Locust Street side are most unusual on this Queen Anne corner house.

3638 *(c. 1900)* This Bliss-designed house has some finely-executed Period details, among the most notable being the cartouche above the entrance and the oeil de boeuf window.

3638 Washington Street

3898 *(1909)* Patterson Ross was the architect for this home, built for a wealthy shipowner. The exterior has "ship lap" wood patterning and heavy, bracketed cornices.

3900 *(1912)* This brick house has a Mansard roof and classical details, such as the Doric columns at either side of the entrance and the broken pediment with finial above the entrance.

3955–57 *(1904)* Two balustrades—one above the entrance and one above the third floor—are attractive features of the facade of this Period residence.

Waverly Place

1–15 *(c. 1908)* First Chinese Baptist Church. In 1874 the American Home Baptist Mission Society sent some thirty men here to assist in the running of the Baptist mission and in 1888 a structure was built for the Society on this site. The present brick building continues as a center for the community.

30–38 *(1907 and 1912)* Rebuilt with many of the old bricks of its predecessor, this building adjoins the site of the oldest Chinese restaurant in the United States.

117–19A *(c. 1907)* Dentil courses and a bracketed cornice are decorative elements of this brick building that houses the Chinese newspaper, *The Times.*

143–45 *(1907)* Owned and partially used by the Wong Family Benevolent Association, this building is post-earthquake in style and detailing.

Webster Street

701 and 709–11 *(1891)* These similar houses—with their pediments and balustrades—serve to introduce an extraordinarily good block.

717–19–21–23 *(c. 1890)* Very unusual—and very attractive—squared-off double stairways dominate the front of this building (in effect a double set of flats).

725 *(1890's)* This house demonstrates Stick Style moving into Queen Anne. New brick stairs lead to the surprisingly plain entranceway.

735 and 737–39–41 *(c. 1877)* These almost-twin Italianates have quite correct detailing, especially on the lovely Corinthian-columned porticos.

1421–27 *(1885)* A double stairway leads to the handsome side-by-side porticos of this Stick Style double house, which is very well maintained.

1706–1710 *(1884)* The entrance porch of this very late Italianate (whose heavy membering is Stick) has been removed.

1717–19 *(1888)* The decoration on the window moldings and on the balustrade

that surmounts the double doorway is deftly controlled and very attractive on this basically Italianate double house.

1810 *(1877)* The slanted front doors of this Italianate are recent additions. Its twin next door has been stuccoed.

1814 *(c. 1870)* With the looks of an old farmhouse, this simple, handsome, detached house is rare in this part of the city which is given over to row houses.

1931–33 *(1891)* A vastly-inflated bay—with Palladian window—is one of the surprising features of this elaborate Classic Revival, built most unusually on the side-hall row house plan.

1940 *(1884)* The bay—more an extension of the front wing—presents a fine expanse of glass on this early Queen Anne.

1944 *(1879)* A complete finished side with bay window has been permitted on this Stick Style house because of its extra wide lot.

1955–55A *(1886)* Half of a Hinkel-built Italianate double house, this side has been allowed to retain its original splendor, while the other half has been altered.

2244 and 2252 *(1880)* The details on these two nearly identical houses are pure and classic Italianate. They are part of an especially notable block.

2315, 2317, 2319 and 2321 *(1878)* William Hollis, President of the Real Estate Associates, built this row of four Italianates. Fascinating minor variations exist—with numbers 2315 and 2319 being similar and numbers 2317 and 2321 similar.

2411 *(1914)* The original owner had this Baroque Revival building copied after one that struck her imagination on a trip to Paris. The recessed ground floor openings give an urbane effect.

2416 *(1892)* John Field was responsible for the careful restoration of this Stick-Queen Anne house—with its perky witch's hat roof dominating the facade.

2654–58
(1889)
Pierced patterning, fishscale shingling and sunbursts are decorative elements of this house. Overall, the house demonstrates Queen Anne intruding on Stick Style.

3027
(1875–85)
When this delightful frame cottage was rehabilitated some years ago, it was combined with another cottage to the rear. Bargeboard and dormer windows were added as well.

West Clay Park

52
(1912)
West Clay Park, which was developed beginning in the early 1910's, is not truly a park but rather a street that curves around off of Lake Street. The predominant builder of this area was S. A. Born Building Company, whose staff designed this shingle home, with its gently-sloping, gabled roof and leaded glass windows.

Whiting Place

2
(1912–13)
Formerly the house for a larger piece of property, this residence had an entrance on Chestnut Street until about 1930 when the change in the street grade left the bottom entrance step high off the ground.

Wilmot Street

16–18
(c. 1878)
The door hood of this flat-front Italianate is a deeper version of the window cornices.

Wood Street

73–75
(c. 1870)
This traditional Italianate residence is unique in its area. It has an attractive cottage in back at 67.

Presidio

Funston Avenue, south of the dispensary

(1873)
Behind unbroken stretches of lawn and old palms sit these thirteen frame duplex houses, forming an impressive row of modest "Army Gothic" Victorians.

Kobbe Avenue, between Ralston and Upton Avenues

(1915)
Officers' Family Quarters. Set in spacious gardens, this brick Georgian Revival house is entered through a handsome portico supported by Ionic columns.

Lincoln Boulevard and Anza Avenue

(1900)
Bank and Post Office. This brick building seems safe behind the barred windows, which remind one that the building originally served as the Presidio Guard House.

Lincoln Boulevard

Near Park Boulevard
(1902)
Religious Activity Center. This frame building stands alone on a hilltop near the Golden Gate Bridge approach. Its entire facade is lined with simple columns that support a second-story porch.

Moraga Avenue at Funston Avenue
(1904)
Pershing Hall (Building #S-42). Named in honor of General John Joseph "Black Jack" Pershing of World War I fame, this brick Georgian Revival building was originally used as a bachelor officers' quarters. Outstanding are the first and second floor porches of the wings.

Moraga Near Mesa Street

(1873)
Our Lady's Chapel. The Presidio's Catholic Chapel was built on the site of the original Spanish chapel of 1776. It was completely renovated and re-dedicated in 1952, and now resembles a miniature New England village church.

Sheridan Avenue and Anza Street

(1845 or 1847)
Ammunition Storage Building. This pristine stone powder house is said to have been built of materials salvaged from Spanish and Mexican structures. The building is only twenty-three by twenty-eight feet, but has walls three feet thick.

Sheridan Avenue at Ord Street

(1891)
Post Chaplain's Quarters. A simple frame Army Victorian, this building was originally

used as a home for an enlisted man's family.

Fort Mason

Franklin Street near MacArthur Avenue

(1891)
Building #231. This single-family Victorian frame house is one of a row of pre-1900 Army residences.

Franklin Street Near Funston Avenue

(1891)
Building #238. Another one-family Victorian frame house within the harmonious Franklin Street group, this house has a rock foundation, gabled roof and fishscale shingling.

N.C.O. Quarters #12

(1864)
Building #232. The cost of this clapboard residence was $750. It has changed little since its construction.

N.C.O. Quarters #13

(1878)
Building #234. This simple frame house was built for one family for a modest $875.

W.O. and N.C.O. Quarters #14

(1864)
Buildings #235A, B and C. Built to house four families, this Army Victorian cost $2,000. It has been changed little.

Franklin Street near MacArthur Avenue at Funston Street

N.C.O. Quarters #16

(1864)
Buildings #239A and B. This frame two-family residence was built in the Army Victorian style with open porches.

Funston Street

Barracks Quarters #17

(1864)
Building #241. A simple, low, wood-frame building, this was built as a barracks for fourteen men at a cost of $1,059.

Barracks Quarters #19

(1864)
Built as a barracks, this wooden

Army Victorian is now used as a dispensary. The original porch, shingled roof, brick chimneys and roof vents have been removed, making the building less distinctive.

SAN MATEO COUNTY

Atherton

Altree Court

3
(1903)
E. W. Hopkins bought this property and two other lots, which were used for his three daughters' homes. The three houses, designed by Bliss and Faville, are: this Classic Revival house; the Colonial Revival house with impressive portico at 2 Lowery Lane (1904); and the Classic Revival house at 60 Parkwood (c. 1909).

Elena Avenue

198
(1897 and 1910)
A section of this wooden house was built in 1897 and became a canteen for soldiers in the Spanish-American War. The estate's thirty acres hosted a tent camp. 1910 saw extensive additions.

Fair Oaks Avenue

198
(c. 1918)
The Period detailing is handsome on this Italian Renaissance Revival-style house.

Glenwood Avenue

183
(1903)
The slender delicately-carved pillars of the rear porch extend the full two stories of this clapboard Victorian, built as a home and winery by Amelio Gunetti.

Larch Drive

2
(c. 1880)
This two-story wood house was originally the dairy barn for Linden Towers. Now moved from its former site and converted into a residence, it still has the original floors and hay doors.

Monte Vista Avenue

73
This well-proportioned, two-

(c. 1907) story vine-covered stucco residence was built for Sigmund Stern.

Oak Grove Avenue

198
(1868)
Originally the stables and carriage house for the Burke "Oak Grove Estate", this structure has been remodeled as a residence retaining the cupola, bracketed cornice, and hay-lift door.

198 Oak Grove Avenue

Selby Lane

374
(1890's)
Here is a sound, sober interpretation of the Victorian style. The gables and porches of this two-story wood master house are echoed in a small guest house.

420
(c. 1907)
Italian Classic features, such as a tile roof, Ionic pilasters, and balustraded portico, enhance this stucco house designed by Houghton Sawyer for Lewis Stern.

420 Selby Lane

Stern Lane

47
(1907)
Houghton Sawyer designed this Tudor half-timbered house for Abraham Stern. Named "Oak Meadows" (Robleda), it was part of the 500-acre estate of Faxon Dean Atherton. New owners in

1914 commissioned Willis Polk and John McLaren to remodel the house and grounds.

Stevick Avenue

399
(1911)
This symmetrical shingle house was designed by Bliss and Faville as a summer residence. Later it was owned by the Stevick family, for whom the street was named.

Surrey Lane

4
(1870's)
In 1906 this former barn, which belonged to "Felton Gables", was moved to Surrey Lane, where it housed baby elephants and equipment for a carnival owner. It was renovated in 1958 for use as a residence.

Tallwood Court

91
(1910)
This cedar shingle home of West Coast Shingle style is generally considered a Maybeck. It has the irregularity of plan, multi-leveled roofline, and fine workmanship typical of Maybeck.

Walsh Road

383
(1917)
George Howard designed this handsome free interpretation of Le Petit Trianon. The one-story stucco home is isolated on a hill top.

Belmont

Belmont Avenue

815
(1915)
Originally this was the tea house for the Japanese Pavilion at the 1915 Panama-Pacific International Exposition in San Francisco. It was brought to Belmont for use as a home and now is operated as a restaurant.

Emmett Avenue

900
(1861)
This simple one-story cottage was Belmont's first school, located on Old County Road. Since 1890 the small building has been used as a residence.

Fifth Street

1336
(1865)
Chapel of the Good Shepherd. Belmont's first church, this

simple stucco building was then located on Old County Road south of Ralston Avenue. Its interior has the original redwood pews, paneling, and baptismal font.

Sixth Avenue

4
(1888)
This is one of the few remaining homes built by the Spring Valley Water Company for its caretakers. Its style is an outgrowth of Greek Revival.

South Street

700
(1906-07)
A Moorish influence is evident in this stucco house, which displays a loggia and a cupola topped with a towering flagpole.

Burlingame

Adeline Drive

2150
(1907–1908)
Mercy High School is now housed in this three-story brick house, designed in the English Tudor style by Howard White for C. Frederick Kohl.

2150 Adeline Drive

Broadway and California Drive

(1911)
Broadway Train Station. Originally this was called Easton Station after Ansel M. Easton, financier and developer of part of Burlingame. The tile-roofed stucco structure was expanded in 1917 and 1928.

Burlingame Avenue

1100
(1904-5)
Formerly this was the Bank of Burlingame, the town's first bank. Flatiron-shaped, the two-story stucco building has a cor-

nice, dentil course and cartouche as decorative features.

1120
(1908)
Odd Fellows Hall. Large Roman arched windows form a pattern on the top floor of this three-story stucco building.

Chapin Avenue

1421
(1906-7)
The first brick building in Burlingame, this two-story house has unique freestanding brick columns and an "eared" circle window. It was designed and built by Matt B. Farrell.

Chapin Lane

400
(1913)
Features of this two-story stucco house include a rounded corner bay and dentil cornice under the rooftop balustrade.

Edgehill Road

1200
(1911)
This rambling two-story redwood house was built in the "bungalow" style popular at that time. It has the dormer and grouped windows associated with that style.

Park Road

267
(1913)
City Hall. A small cupola sits on top of this building's tile roof. The brick structure is almost obscured by vines.

Sanchez Avenue

1120
(1910)
Gaston Rognier designed this example of Period architecture with French details. The unique baroque windows repeat a type seen in the City of Paris, San Francisco.

Washington Park

(1888)
Gunst Cottage. Perhaps this city's oldest structure, this one-story shingle house was built by Moses Gunst as a guest house. The main house was razed in 1953 to make way for Washington Park.

Half Moon Bay

Johnson and Miramontes Streets

(1872)
Community Methodist Church.

One of the oldest Protestant Churches in the county, this Victorian Gothic structure has ogee door and window moldings. A wing was once an Ocean Shore Railroad Station.

Kelly and Johnson Streets

(1850-60)
Scalloped shingling is hung from the eaves like a bargeboard on this small shingle house.

Kelly Avenue near Main Street

(Post 1900)
Benjamin Cunha built this large Queen Anne for the Alves family. It has the scalloped shingling and polygonal tower of that style.

Main Street

270
(1870's)
Pablo Vasquez, son of one of the three original Spanish land grantees in the area, built this one-story home in Late Greek Revival Style. A livery stable still stands on the property as well.

527
(1872)
This clapboard, false-front Italianate was the first mercantile store in the area. Called Levy Brothers, it was built by French immigrants Fernand and Joseph Levy.

Purisima Canyon Road

313
(c. 1865)
This farmhouse is a small, white Victorian, whose facade is dominated by a front gable and fishscale shingling. The farm still has the water wheel once used to grind feed for the livestock.

San Benito Road

505
(1880's)
Beehive shingling and colored glass borders around the windows are decorative on this one-story Victorian, which connects with another building, once used as a bakery.

South Main Street

296
(1870's)
Of Greek Revival derivation, this frame house was built by William Metzgar. Its remodeling has included the enclosing of the porch.

Hillsborough

Aster Avenue

15
(1906–9)
Notable features of this bungalow-type stucco house include gables, dormer windows, and balustrades at the second-story windows. It is almost covered with vines.

Baywood Avenue

50
(1906)
This two-story stucco house with classical detailing was built by Eugene de Sabla for Clement Tobin. It was remodeled by Lewis Hobart.

91
(1890)
Herman Schussler, the engineer for Crystal Springs Dam, designed this half-timber residence. George Howard remodeled the house and Julia Morgan is also reputed to have worked on it.

100
(c. 1916)
A vine-covered, stucco Mediterranean-style house with tile roof and balustraded porch, this was considered the "small" house for the Durham estate, once part of the Howard property.

108
(c. 1905)
This grand Shingle Style house at one time served as the main house for the Durham Estate.

130
(1906)
Designed by Albert Farr in the style of an English hunting lodge, this house has a gray shingle exterior, leaded windows, and a massive stone chimney.

130 Baywood Avenue

Brewer Drive

636
(c. 1915)
This simple Colonial Revival house was originally owned by Dr. William Brewer, first rector of Saint Paul's Episcopal Church,

Burlingame, and Mayor of Burlingame.

680
(c. 1915)
Built for Misses Edith and Helen Chesborough, this handsome shingle Colonial Revival house was later remodeled by John Drum.

Bridge Road

130
(c. 1910)
This three-story tile-roofed residence, Italian in spirit, was built for John B. Casserly.

Crystal Springs Road

91
(1906)
This redwood Bay Area Shingle house was designed by Maybeck. Details include fine carving of the entrance and diamond-paned windows. A wing was added to the rear.

891
(1914–17)
Bliss and Faville designed this Mediterranean-style residence for Count Christian de Guigne. The tile-roofed stucco house has a lovely metal spiral stairway near the back wing, which was added in 1959.

El Cerrito Avenue

252
(c. 1907)
Hillsborough Racket Club. The San Mateo and Burlingame Polo Club originally used this one-story building as a clubhouse for "El Cerrito Field." It was constructed of stucco with a colonnade and simplified classical details.

Floribunda Avenue

1615
(1890's)
(Also 141 Pepper Avenue and 50 Kammerer Court). These three houses, built by the Palace Hotel Company, were designed by A. Page Brown in an English half-timbered style with diamond-paned windows. They were used by hotel guests traveling to the Peninsula. One of the three was later used as the first Burlingame Country Club.

Forest View Avenue

2217
(1894)
Originally this was the home of Henry T. Scott, first president of the Burlingame Country Club. Although extensively remodeled, the shingle home

still retains the grace of the original mansion.

2260
(1904)
Built for George Coleman as a wedding present from his father, this shingle house is New England in feeling. The unusual solid brass hardware and leaded windows were imported from England during a subsequent remodeling.

Hillsborough Boulevard

355
(1918)
This stucco two-story English-style house was built by architect Howard White for author Stewart Edward White.

New Place Road

80
(1910 or 1911)
Originally the home of W. H. Crocker, "New Place" was designed by Lewis Hobart and landscaped by Bruce Porter. In 1954 the tile roof and shutters were removed when John Lord King remodeled the mansion for use as a clubhouse.

Redington Road

2240
(1894)
A roof of two steeply-pitched, parallel sections dominates this shingle house, built as the coachhouse for the Henry T. Scott estate. Another unique aspect of the house is the absence of side windows.

Stonehedge Road

140
(1906)
Typical of substantial residences of its era, this stucco house is a conglomerate of styles.

West Santa Inez Avenue

120
(1903)
George Howard designed this richly-detailed Shingle Style residence for Mrs. Henry Poett.

124
(c. 1905)
Lewis Hobart both designed and owned this house of ship-lapped board siding. Its most distinctive feature is the round, columned portico.

234
(c. 1910)
Green and Green, Pasadena architects, designed this wood and stucco house for Elliot McAllister. Its second-story wood balcony is reminiscent of Monterey Colonial.

310

Woodstock Road

645
(1900) A heavily-carved entrance and steeply-gabled roof line are distinguishing features of this house, built for J. H. P. Howard, Sr., whose family pioneered in the area.

La Honda

Entrata Road

(1871) La Honda School. Maurice Woodham donated the land for and financed the construction of this tiny school. The wooden building consists of a main room, foyer, and a bell tower.

San Gregorio Road

(c. 1860) Tichenor Ranch. The carpenter of one of Captain William Watkins' ships designed and built this Victorian Gothic farmhouse, which adheres to strong, basic lines.

Menlo Park

Arbor and Cambridge Streets

(1885 and 1929) Allied Arts Guild. The oldest buildings of this complex of Spanish Colonial structures are the barn and sheep sheds built in 1885 by John Jarvis Murray.

Encinal Avenue

420
(c. 1895) This small, one-story Victorian with its lacy bargeboard was originally a carriage house for Roger Reynolds' nursery. Later the house was moved to the present site, where it is now a candy store.

Fair Oaks Avenue

101
(1906–8) John McBaine designed this two-story adaptation of "Mount Vernon Colonial." The clapboard house was used as an officers' club for Camp Fremont during World War I.

Glenwood Avenue

417 Aaron W. Gale came to Menlo

(1892) Park to work as a carpenter on Linden Towers, and built this small, wood Victorian home.

Laurel Avenue

1235
(1897) This wood Queen Anne, designed by architect Curtis Tobey, was moved off its foundation by the first shock of the 1906 earthquake; the second shock replaced it.

Middlefield Road

300
(1899) Menlo Park Firehouse. Menlo's first firehouse, a simple wooden structure was built by local carpenters and volunteer firemen. It currently houses a firehouse museum.

Middlefield Road and Glenwood Avenue

(1902) Built for Joseph Frank of Frank's Tannery in Redwood City, this is a two-story wood Colonial Revival house of grand scale.

Oak Grove Avenue

250
(1880) Vallombrosa. Built for E. W. Hopkins, nephew of Mark Hopkins, this house has the flavor of early Italian Baroque. This residence, named for a Florentine Abbey, is now a Catholic Womens' Retreat.

401
(1870's) This single-story Victorian shingle cottage was built to house the architect of Linden Towers. An identical home, now gone, was built for the contractor.

401 Oak Grove Avenue

Santa Cruz Avenue

2212 Arthur Brown, Jr., designed

2212 Santa Cruz Avenue

(1919) this graceful two-story stucco house in the French tradition with some Mediterranean influence.

Millbrae

California and Irwin Place

(1907) Southern Pacific Railway Station. This wood building is typical railroad station architecture. It has a station master's house adjacent.

El Camino Real

1200
(1861) This false-front wood building served as the "sixteen-mile house" on the stage route south from San Francisco. It has been used also as a hotel, gambling hall, general store, speakeasy, and dinner house.

San Andreas Valley Road

(1868) The Spring Valley Water Company originally owned this simple, clapboard house with fragile porch and low eaves. It was the best of the Company's caretakers' homes.

Pescadero

North Street

(1870's) H. B. Adair House. Scalloped shingles on the pediments and gables and pierced columns grace this two-story clapboard Carpenter's Gothic home.

(1875) Van Allen House. This white clapboard house has a front porch supported by pierced

columns. Smooth boards outline each corner.

Pescadero Creek Road

(1858) Although now used as a storehouse for the Braddock Weeks house, this exceedingly simple one-room building was originally Pescadero's school.

San Gregorio Street

(mid-1870's) The James McCormick house could be even earlier than the 1870's. Porticoed and balustraded, the wood home is late Classic Revival with solid pillars.

(1861) The former Methodist Church, on the other hand, appears to look newer than 1861. Its profusion of lancet windows and bracketed spire convey thoughts of Victorian Gothic.

Portola Valley

Portola Road

555 An early design of Stanton
(1914) Willard, one-time head of the State Architectural Committee, this stucco house was built for timber baron E. D. Conolley in the Mediterranean manner around an inner courtyard.

765 Portola Valley School. White
(1910) paint highlights the decorative detailing of this shingle Dutch Colonial one-story schoolhouse.

930 Our Lady of the Wayside Catho-
(1912) lic Church. Funds raised by a private shooting club financed the construction of this Spanish Colonial Style church originally serving itinerant fruit workers. The church is a basilica of white stucco with tile roof, buttressed side walls, and an arcade of rounded arches.

Redwood City

Arguello Street

728 This redwood house, first
(1906) owned by Sheriff Robert Chatham, is a curious blend: Japanese sweep to the roof, leaded windows, and simple columns

supporting the front porch.

833 Here is an excellent example
(1860's) of late Greek Revival: dentil cornice, flat corner boards, slab-like window moldings, and split pillars with twig-like arches.

833 Arguello Street

1200 This house offers another ver-
(1880–85) sion of late Greek Revival. It has the quoining and roof line fins also typical of the style.

Brewster Street

1114 Built for George H. Gerwin,
(1915) this stucco, shingle and half-timbered Tudor-style house has steeply-pitched gables, overhanging upper stories, and a broad wooden porch.

1114 Brewster Street

Broadway

(1909) Redwood City Railroad Station. This one-story stucco station has a broad colonnade on three sides.

Broadway and Main

(1900) This two-story stone-faced building once housed the Bank of San Mateo established by

Ludwig P. Behrens in 1891. The architecture is Renaissance Revival with pilasters, acanthus capitals, pediments, and cupola.

Chestnut Street

312 This two-story clapboard house
(1855–60) has the distinction of being the third residence built in Redwood City.

Edgewood Road

502 The lumber for this simple,
(c. 1890's) two-story house with encompassing porch, slender columns, and fishscale-shingled gable was purchased from the San Francisco Mid-Winter Exposition of 1893–4.

610 Donald Williams sent his archi-
(1915) tect to New Hampshire to copy his ancestral home. The result is this stately wood Colonial Revival home.

Heller Street

414 This is the oldest church in
(1876) Redwood City. Made of wood, it possesses a handsome simplicity with lancet windows, bracketed roof and quoining.

Orchard Avenue

302 Originally the hunting lodge of
(1900–1910) Frederick William Henshaw, once a California Supreme Court Justice, this house was built on Selby Lane in Atherton; later it was moved to this site. The lodge was constructed of logs with the refinements of leaded windows and panels of imported wood added.

Second Avenue

325 Dr. S. S. Stambaugh, Surgeon
(1860) General to San Francisco Hospital in 1852, originally owned this two-story redwood house, built at the corner of Cedar and Stambaugh Streets, and moved to this site in 1930.

San Carlos

El Camino Real

1 Designed and built by Herman

(c. 1890) Schussler, engineer for Crystal Springs Dam, this was once the largest pump station west of Chicago.

Elm Street

408
(1913) Classic Revival in concept, this house (now a rest home) sits starkly on a large lot.

520
(c. 1890) W. B. Kraeger designed and built this two-story shingle house, later owned by the family of Charles H. Hosmer, one of the fourteen original San Carlos pioneers.

San Gregorio

Stage Road

(c. 1880) Seaside School. This stark clapboard school building with small belltower is no longer in use.

San Mateo

Claremont Street

353
(1890's) Fishscale shingles, Eastlake brace and detailed carving distinguish this Victorian cottage, built for the foreman of the Howard Estate.

Crystal Springs Road

801
(c. 1900) This Victorian cottage once belonged to the Parrott estate. It housed the man who controlled the estate's pumphouse.

Elm Street

137
(c. 1890) An unusual roof line, a fan set in the gable, and fishscale shingles are highlights of this two-story late Victorian, whose original barn is still in the rear.

Highland Avenue

343
(1880's) Designed and built by John Wisnom, this wood house is late Greek Revival—early Victorian in style.

Hurlingham Avenue

615 This two-story Colonial Re-

(c. 1906) vival house (built for George Shafer) has classical embellishments including a dentiled cornice, columned porch, and unique window treatment on the first floor.

Lawrence Road

809
(c. 1900) Of late Victorian persuasion, this wood house boasts a bracketed roof cornice, three-sided window bay, and windows (all double) with either arched or rounded moldings.

Oregon Avenue

(1885) Saint John's Cemetery. Built on the property of John Parrott, this Florentine Renaissance stone tomb was presented to Saint Matthew's Catholic Church in his memory.

Oregon Avenue

San Mateo Drive and Second Avenue

(1906) Jean Perichon built this three-story wood Victorian as a hotel-restaurant on property once owned by San Mateo House, the area's first hotel, which was built in 1851.

Second Avenue

15
(1911) Mrs. Whitelaw Reid (Elizabeth Mills) gave this two-story stucco house, originally built for Dr. Walter H. Cambridge, to Saint Matthew's Episcopal Church for use as a rectory.

South Delaware Street

2
(1892) This board and shingle Queen Anne house with tower, fishscale shingles and Eastlake carving was built by Robert Wisnom for W. H. Brown, Jr.,

blacksmith and county supervisor.

319
(1880–1890) This simple late Greek Revival wood house built by J. J. Moore, an early stage coach driver, is a good representative of its style. Its features include the wood siding with strips at the corners and horizontal fins suggestive of a pediment.

319 South Delaware Street

Third and South Ellsworth

(1899) Saint Matthew's Catholic Church. This brick basilica with pediment, dentil molding and narrow rounded windows is capped by a square tower with Tuscan arches.

Third and South Ellsworth

West Poplar Avenue

134
(1905) Coxhead and Coxhead designed this two-story house in the Bay Area Shingle style for which they were renowned.

San Mateo Coast-side Stations

Ocean Shore Railroad

(1906–7) The Ocean Shore Land Company, formed May 18, 1905, built a railroad to carry vacationers and freight to coastal resorts. The automobile and truck soon encroached on its business. The State Railroad Commission insisted the Company continue operations; a strike finally ended its service. There are seven stations remaining, all built between 1906 and 1907.

El Reino Del Mar and Route 1, Pacifica

Vallemar Station. Although the wooden facade is unchanged, the station is now a pizza parlor.

Danmann Avenue, Pacifica

San Pedro Station. At San Pedro Point (Mussel Point), stands this stone station with a pagoda-like roof, now a residence. It was sometimes known as Tobin Station.

Second Street, Montara

Montara Station. This station has field stone walls two feet thick, constructed with black mortar by Italian stonemasons. The arched doorways and original beams remain on the altered residence.

Princeton Road, Princeton

El Granada Station. The tile roof is all that is recognizable as part of the original station, now functioning as a real estate office.

Railroad Avenue, Half Moon Bay

Arleta Park Station. This, the largest of the stations, has a roof with very deep eaves that once projected over the railroad's tracks.

Johnson and Miramontes Streets, Half Moon Bay

Half Moon Bay Station. This station is now the social hall for the Methodist Church.

Tunitas, Tunitas Glen Station

Although its redwood sides are now covered with aging corrugated iron, this station looks much as it did originally. The wide plank floor and the ticket window remain.

South San Francisco

Old Mission Road

1076
(1853) This original "twelve-mile house" was one of the places to stop on the arduous ride along the old El Camino Real. The wood for it was supplied by the Tripp's Woodside Store.

Woodside

King's Mountain Road

481
(1850's) Next door to the Woodside Store (see main text) is the winery and its storehouse. These buildings have been greatly remodeled, but original sections remain in the tower and portions of both sides.

La Canada Road

985
(1870's) This one-story simple board-and-batten farmhouse still has its original front porch and shuttered windows. Its barn remains at the rear of the property.

1224
(1880) A broad porch with arbor and dormer windows at the second story distinguish this wood house. An old water tower still stands on the property.

Moore Road

137
(1906) The notable feature of this shingle bungalow is its wide veranda, whose roof extends to form a *porte cochere*. The property also includes a stable with wrought-iron stalls.

Mountain Home Road

475
(1875) Victorian Gothic flourishes appear in the peaked cupola and scrollwork ending the steep-pitched gables of this white board barn.

582
(1904) Built on a portion of Charles Brown's Mountain Home Ranch property, this redwood shingled house was designed for a daughter of John Albert Hooper. John Ralston Hamilton designed the long, low bungalow with early modern grouped windows and some Period detailing.

745
(1910–15) Julia Morgan was responsible for the design of this low, shingle-style bungalow with pergola and grouped windows.

Skyline Boulevard

(1840 to 1846) The Arguello Adobe. Built by the Arguello Rancho for use as a bunk house, this one-room structure was made of redwood slats filled in with adobe mud with a dirt floor.

Woodside Road

3763
(1900) The Precious Blood Mission Fathers presently own this two-story English stone and half-timbered home, built for William Matson of the Matson Navigation Company.

Woodside Road and Whiskey Hill Road

(1848) Pioneer Hotel. The false front is the only original part of this structure, built by lumbermen Hanson and Ackerman. The small red barn behind the hotel is of the same vintage and ownership.

MARIN COUNTY

Belvedere

Alcatraz

38
(1909) The rounded corner bay of this large shingle and wood house is cut off by an overhanging gable. It illustrates late Queen Anne moving into Shingle Style.

Bayview

140 D. A. McLean, who with his

(1894)	brother Neil designed and built most of Belvedere's early houses, constructed this gingerbread cottage for his own family. The house displays shingle patterning in the gable ends.

160
(1896) The "Pagoda House" derives its name from the sweeping Oriental lines of its roof. The upper floor of the shingle house is cantilevered from a massive base.

201
(1898) A polygonal turret and an outside staircase characterize this shingle and stucco Victorian house as do the buttresses that support the upper deck.

261
(c. 1880) Because seafaring men built this house it earned the name of the "Crow's Nest". The brown shingle house is the third oldest residence in Belvedere.

Beach Road

(1906) Belvedere City Hall Building. This structure was built by the Belvedere Land Company and was designed by Albert Farr. It and similar structures across the street were originally rented out as summer cottages.

52
(c. 1890) Old photos show this minute summer house here prior to 1890. It was originally the deck house of the *China*, one of the last paddle wheel ocean steamers.

100
(1916) This stucco and wood Period one-story house was designed by architect Clyde Payne, Jr., for his father, Dr. Clyde S. Payne. Much of the material in the formal little house came from the Panama-Pacific Exposition.

180
(1897) The Eastlake spindle work on the gable ends, bee-hive shingling and delicate verandas combine to make this Queen Anne a picturesque residence.

228
(c. 1915) Charles Crocker lived in the beach house on this property from the late 1890's until he built this three-story stucco and wood house.

251 This fine three-story split-level

(1907) house was built by John W. Mailliard who obtained John McLaren's assistance to landscape the garden. Many of the architectural details suggest the influence of Willis Polk.

251 Beach Road

266
(1894) The simple lines of this redwood shingle house foretell the later move away from Victorian elaborateness. However, a number of different window shapes are in evidence.

281
(1865) Its redwood log exterior unchanged since it was built, the "Log Cabin" became a Christian Science church in the early decades of the twentieth century before becoming a home once again.

Bella Vista

118
(1890's) John Farr was the architect and D. A. McLean the builder for this rambling summer house. The simpler third floor was added later; it stands in contrast to the arched lower verandas.

158
(1902) The square lines, heavy beams and massive effect of this two-story shingle house reflect the trend in California architecture in the early 1900's.

206
(1890's) The lines of the roof join to form a squared-off cupola on this house. The upper floor is cantilevered on eighteen-inch beams, and balconies jut out from both stories.

350
(1893) This handsome four-story shingle house is of particular interest for the manner in which it adapts to the precipitous hillside. It has a graceful encompassing porch.

Corinthian Yacht Club

(1896–
(1906) This example of Greek Revival with its two-story Corinthian columns is still used as a clubhouse. The building which has undergone several remodelings sits at the southern tip of the island.

Golden Gate Avenue

29
(1909) Albert Farr designed this as a clubhouse for the Belvedere Golf and Country Club. Its vast redwood dining room with beamed cathedral ceiling was the center of local activity from 1910 to 1930, when the club sold its golf course for development, and the clubhouse for a residence.

332
(1903) Clarence Ward was the architect for this house which is distinguished by an unusually wide roof overhang, paneled windows and superb interior design.

340
(1905) Great character is evidenced in this shingled house (built by contractor Daniel McLean). Especially attractive are the gambrel roof and latticed windows.

416
(1895) Designed by Willis Polk for Mrs. Florence Cornwall Moore, this house started out as a cottage and was enlarged over the years. The exterior is half-timbered and multi-gabled.

Laurel Avenue at San Rafael Avenue

(late
1890's) The Belvedere Presbyterian Church had Albert Farr design a church at Bayview and Laurel. In 1939 it was remodeled into a residence. Then in 1946 the building was sold to the City of Belvedere and moved to its present location. In 1967 an excellent remodeling enlarged it to house the City offices without sacrificing its character.

Madrone

160
(1890's) Seen in the earliest photographs of Belvedere, this three-story shingle house built by Mr. Morgan, Superintendent for the

Belvedere Land Company, is characterized by its polygonal tower.

260
(1890's)
A fine example of the Belvedere "box house", this brown shingle house was built by Emery Foest Mitchell. Of particular interest are the brackets and the doorway's arched and spooled openings.

San Rafael Avenue

10
(1890's)
Indian relics have been found on the property of this one-story frame cottage, one of the original San Francisco and San Rafael Railroad Company worker's homes.

West Shore Road

8
Originally constructed in San Francisco at 1818 Broadway, this house was built for Dr. H. C. Moffitt. In 1914, it was enlarged under the supervision of Willis Polk. In 1962, when it was marked for destruction, two real estate brokers bought the house. They had it sliced in two, put on a barge and floated across the Bay.

8 West Shore Road

Bolinas

Bolinas and Olema Roads

(1870's)
Wilkins Ranch: In 1869 W. W. Wilkins was the original owner of the 1,367-acre dairy ranch on which this frame house stands. A copper mine discovered on the land in the 1850's was worked through World War 1.

(1908)
Bolinas Grammar School: Louis Petar designed and built this handsome 30' by 100' wooden

building. He achieved the Classical Revival aura so essential to public buildings of that period.

Brighton Street

(c. 1888)
Bolinas Villa: This was the second house to be built on the Grande Vista Tract. The Tract had been bought from Juan Briones by Frank Waterhouse, a Sacramento banker, whose wife, Nellie, subdivided it.

(1890's)
Petar House: Louis Petar built this frame house (also in the Grande Vista Tract) for his parents. Standing unchanged, the house has only a few decorative touches, including pillars supporting the porch roof and scalloped shingling.

County Road

(c. 1900)
Druid's Hall: This tall, narrow structure was built as a meeting place for the Druids and stands, as it did then, in American Gothic severity. It is now a Christian Science church.

(1875)
Gibson House: John Charles Gibson, the area's first storekeeper, postmaster and a county supervisor, built this Classic (Greek) Revival house. After his death in 1895, the house became a stage stop and hotel; now it serves as a restaurant.

Highway One

(1878)
Audubon Canyon Ranch: Sailor Peter L. Bourne built this gabled farm house which now belongs to the Audubon Society. The original upper-story balcony has been removed, and a chimney was shaken loose in the 1906 earthquake.

Olema Road

(1875)
Sunrise Ranch: This farm house was originally part of the Randall Ranch. It was later used as a stage stop which gave the building its name, the Halfway House. The house stands unchanged with pediments and bargeboard.

Terrace Avenue

(1910)
Locke House: William L. Locke

gave this house to his daughter, Florence, when it was built by Maybeck student Harris Osborne. The two-story living room is reminiscent of Maybeck as are the diamond-paned windows.

**Mira Monte Lodge,
East of Highway 101,
Burdell Island
North of Novato**

(1894–98)
Here in this marshy location (once the site of an Indian camp) this stucco building was first used for a hunting and fishing club. Later, the Lodge became a speak-easy. Now it again serves as a resort.

Corte Madera

Corte Madera Avenue

425
(1890's)
This stucco "castle" was built by Edmund Chapman who faithfully reproduced the gabled facades and peaked turrets seen in Hanseatic towns. Two reservoirs on his land led him to found the "Chapman Water Works".

Dillon Beach

Lawson's Landing

(c. 1881)
Once a hotel, this wood building is now used as a grocery store and rental office. The dormer windows are effective; otherwise the building is almost devoid of detail.

Lawson's Landing

Inverness

Sir Francis Drake Boulevard

(1880's)
Brock's Boathouse: Its pier is gone, and the structure has fallen into disuse, yet this landmark harks back to the days when Tomales Bay was a busy waterway.

The Gables

(1890) Known as the oldest house in Inverness, this was built by Captain Alex H. Bailey as a summer home. The cottage derives its name from the gables that top every angled wall.

Kentfield

Laurel Way

3
(c. 1871) This simple frame structure was the first house on the Kent Estate. The glass and other materials were brought around the Horn, and square nails were used in its construction.

Orchard Way

7
(1871) What is now the two-story center section of this house was originally a clapboard house built for the Kent Estate foreman. This section was shingled in 1910, and over the years has been considerably expanded.

Larkspur

East Manzanita Street

(c. 1900) "Villa Madera": The sensitive handling of both the interior and exterior of this wood house would suggest that Maybeck could have been the architect.

King Street

105
(c. 1880) This is one of the few remaining residences in an increasingly commercial neighborhood. It has an exceptional veranda that surrounds the whole house.

Laurel Avenue

95
(c. 1890) The colored glass borders of the windows, the brackets under the broad eaves, the scrolled panel in the peak of the roof line and the balconied entrance porch make this house outstanding.

Magnolia Avenue

707
(c. 1880) This brick facade was once part of the John Escalle winery, situated by Corte Madera Creek.

The twenty-three acre vineyard was one of the largest in the county.

Mill Valley

Ward and Magnolia Streets

(1895) Blue Rock Hotel. First known as Hotel Larkspur, this building was later renamed when its first story was faced with blue basalt rock during a remodeling.

Corte Madera Avenue

216
(1892) Victorian vivacity is achieved here by alternating fishscale and diamond shingles that cover the entire house. The house also boasts graceful verandas.

Eldridge

315
(1911) There has been rather extensive but well-integrated remodeling on this Maybeck-designed shingle house. A bedroom, bath and deck have been added. The door onto the deck was, in fact, the original entrance.

Hillside

164
(1903) Typical of Harvey Klyce, this steeply-roofed shingle house has an enclosed porch that imparts the feeling of being an integral part of the whole house.

Lovell Avenue

21
(1897) This small wooden house has a plethora of interesting details, including fishscale shingling and angled-off corner windows on the first floor that are tucked under the squared-off second story.

64
(1891) Thomas F. Kelly had this house built as his residence, the first year-round home in Mill Valley. It remains virtually unchanged: a simple wood frame house with a long covered porch.

Miller Avenue

36
(1870's) This simple flat-front has been used over the years as a bar, laundry, grocery store and pool hall.

230
(c. 1895) The original carriage house still stands at the rear of this wooden house. Its pedimented and Doric-columned porch is matched by a twin pediment above first-floor bay.

239
(c. 1880) Gardner Villa: Designed as a hotel, this house, which shows a New England influence, became instead the family home of Casper Gardner.

Molino Avenue

125
(1890's) Treehaven: James Alden Thompson had this house built for his family which included daughter Kathleen Norris. It is a balconied shingle house, rustic in flavor.

Ralston Avenue

45
(1910) Harvey Harris designed this shingle house whose most distinctive features are the carved front door and clearstory.

Summit Avenue

100
(1907) Tamaledge: Louis Mullgardt designed this sturdy "tour de force" on a steep hillside. He gave the home heavy redwood beams, redwood horizontal siding, and a cantilevered porch.

100 Summit Avenue

Throckmorton Avenue

418
(1896) Built as a home for Dr. Reginald Kingwell and now used as an apartment, this presents an example of late Victorian architecture with Classic Revival details.

448
(1894) Falch house was built for restaurateur W. C. Falch. His son, Otto, made the residence famous be-

cause of his reptile collection housed there. The house itself offers much: a dome-topped tower, many gables, and a dentil course.

465
(1896)
Willis Polk designed this Colonial Revival house. Its interior has many handsome details: an imposing fireplace, redwood paneling, and a billiard room with special seating for spectators built into the leaded-window bay.

Novato

Delong Avenue

745
(1880's)
This simple white frame house with front veranda is typical of many homes in the Novato area.

Grant Avenue and Reichert Avenue

(c. 1850)
Known as the oldest standing and first frame building in Novato, this small, false-front shop once stood near the Baccaglio vineyard.

Railroad Avenue and Hancock Street

(late 1880's)
This rambling stucco house, now converted to apartments, will soon be demolished to make way for a freeway. It was originally the home of Judge Randolph, also known for his cheese factory.

Redwood Highway

7533
(1870's)
State Legislator and Supervisor John Atherton built this simple wood house on the 400-acre tract that he acquired in 1864. After World War II, the house was moved to its present location from a hilltop site.

Reichert Avenue

853
(1890's)
The corner, squared-off bay of this wood house is free-standing. Scalloped shingling is seen on this tower as well as on the gables of the house.

Sherman Avenue at Delong Avenue

(1889)
City Hall: Once a Presbyterian church, this crisp, trim building is an attractive version of Victorian Gothic with lancet windows and belfry.

South Novato

1416
(1850's)
Novato's first post office was apparently located here. The wood Greek Revival house is reminiscent of many seen on the San Mateo coastside.

Point Bonita

Point Bonita Lighthouse

(1855)
In 1855 a light was placed in a tower, but in 1877 the lighthouse was moved to its present location. The light shines from a hexagonal brick tower, and its white fixed rays are visible seventeen miles at sea.

Ross

Glenwood and Fernhill

(1891)
Kirk House: Richardson Romanesque in style, this was constructed of stone, an uncommon material for Marin. Its appearance, especially the corner tower, is massive in effect.

Glenwood Avenue and Lagunitas Road

(1906)
This impressive stucco house was once part of a large estate owned by Henry Bothin.

Lagunitas Road

2
(1876)
An open, lace-like bargeboard follows the roofline of this Victorian Gothic house, part of the exterior of which is covered with wisteria.

(1909)
Lagunitas Country Club: The club is housed in this fine rustic shingle building with leaded windows, designed by John White.

Lagunitas Road and Shady Lane

(1912)
Saint John's Episcopal Church: The entrance to this pristine stucco church is through the the square corner tower.

Lagunitas Road and Willow

(1893)
The changes made to the porch of this white frame house detract little from the original design.

Laurel Grove

96
(c. 1890)
This is a handsome stucco house with a covered porch that extends the width of the house. Doric columns support the porch roof, and a double stairway leads to the porch.

110
(1917)
A Period composite, this square stucco house has French windows, Doric columned portico, and tile roof.

Near Phoenix Lake

(1890's)
Porteos House: This summer house was designed with Victorian features, then the exterior was faced with redwood logs. The Marin Municipal Water District bought the property in 1916 as a residence for their caretaker.

Redwood

111
(1908)
An Eastern architect named Lamb designed this house, a version of West Coast Shingle Style.

Shady Lane

51
(1902)
Architect John White remodeled this three-story shingle house in 1919.

181
(1904)
The front porch of this frame house is supported by lovely, delicate columns.

Upper Road

(1906)
(Next house after One.) John White, who was the architect of a number of houses in this area, designed this spacious shingle residence which is set in handsome gardens. It was built for the Benjamin Dibblees.

(1903)
(Corner of Woodhaven.) Another John White design: a typical example of his rustic shingle houses.

(c. 1909)
(Opposite Upper Road West.)

John White also designed this two-story shingle house which was built for Seward McNear.

34 This Victorian house with its hexagonal corner tower was pictured in *Souvenirs of Marin County* in 1893, as one of Ross' earlier homes.

Willow Hill (end of Willow Road)

(1904) Some consider this West Coast Shingle house to be a Maybeck. Its window and roof treatment in particular are in the Maybeck tradition.

San Anselmo

Calumet

122
(1911) Architect Frank Farnkopf designed this one-story, rambling shingle house for himself. The house has remained in his family.

Parkway

50
(1869) Minthorne Tompkins, one of the area's early settlers, was the original owner of this frame home which still remains in the same family. The second story was removed before 1920.

Prospect

9
(1906) Harris Osborne designed this handsome redwood house. The thoughtful use of the redwood makes the home compatible with the Maybeck, Julia Morgan and Coxhead houses in the neighborhood.

160
(1904) A Coxhead-designed Bay Area Shingle, this had an upper-story bedroom added later by Harris Osborne.

San Rafael Avenue

43
(1905) This simple frame house was once part of considerable acreage owned by the early-day Butler family and still belongs to that family.

San Rafael

B Street

840 The first floor of this building

(1880) is commercial, but the second shows finely-detailed Stick-Eastlake workmanship.

B and Second Streets

(1868) Flatiron Hotel: Once known as Welsh's Hall, this building derived its later name and flatiron contour from the shape of its lot, caused by train tracks crossing the block diagonally.

(late 1870's) Once the Cosmopolitan Hotel, now offices and stores, this was first owned by William Barnard, Jr., who was a supervisor and operator of a stage between San Rafael and San Quentin.

Belle and Marinta Street

(late 1880's) This house (once part of the Coleman Tract) has a polygonal turret and circular balcony that juts out from the second floor.

Culloden Place

1
(early 1890's) William Barr built this Dutch Colonial house for Judge Frank M. Angelotti. It later belonged to Harry Lutgens, then owner and publisher of the *Independent Journal.*

43
(1906) Maybeck-designed, this half-timbered stucco and shingle residence has a low sloping roof cut by a cross-gable.

Deer Park Avenue

97
(1900) There is a strong Mediterranean feeling to this stucco and tile-roofed house which was built as a summer home. The redwood interior is unusually fine.

E Street

814
(1868) The fame of this simple frame and shingle house lies in the fact that writer Ambrose Bierce roomed in it while commuting to San Francisco.

Fairway Drive

46
(1910) Julia Morgan designed this house for Cary W. Cook, President of American-Hawaiian Steamship Company. Its stucco exterior and red tile roof give it a Spanish-Mediterranean air.

Fifth Street

1510
(1894) One of the few stone buildings in the area, this church falls quite naturally into the Romanesque classification.

1607
(1870's) Built for S. F. Barstow, publisher of the *Marin Tocsin*, this house has lost the entrance hood. There are unusual pent roofs over the windows.

1629
(1870's) There are Classic (Greek) Revival touches to this cottage. A veranda stretches across the front and sides.

Forbes Avenue

230
(1870's) A moon-shaped porch, gable roof, and graceful Victorian details are effective on this two-story house.

Fourth Street

709
(1880's) This structure was originally a slaughter house, then a hotel and bar, and now a candy store. The Italianate facade is heavily ornamented.

Fourth and C Streets

(1889) Peters Building: The second story of this building presents an example of busy Victorian architecture with hexagonal corner tower, many bays, heavily dentiled cornice, and carved pediments.

Fourth Street

1225-C
(1870's) A portion of a gable end appears interestingly above the flat-front facade of this Italianate structure, whose first floor is given over to commerce.

1321
(1870's) The Hotaling Bank was once located on the ground floor of this Italianate building, whose pedimented windows are sensitively handled.

G Street

333
(1880) The original owner of this Victorian Gothic house was William Bushnell Bradford, a descendant of Governor Bradford of Massachusetts. Its many interesting features include: crossbeamed and hooded gables,

elaborately-turned porch columns, and small roofs over the windows. The greenhouse and barn still remain.

Grand Avenue

1644
(1908)
A handsome, shingled cottage reminiscent of those seen often on the East Coast, this two-story residence was designed by John Ralston Hamilton for George C. Martin.

Grove Street

46–48
(1885)
Once the carriage house for the Sloss Estate, this building was made into a senior citizens' home in 1941. It has now become a private residence. The windows in the frame house have been modernized, but the house retains its cupola.

H Street

307
(1880's)
Built for San Francisco contractor Thomas Hansen, this house as pictured in 1893 was much as it looks today. The obvious difference is the addition of the upstairs porch.

Highland Avenue

301
(1911)
George A. Hind of Hind Rolph Steamship Company commissioned William Knowles to design this Dutch country-styled house. Mr. Hind, also a lumberman, selected the woods for his home. The interior is richly ornamented.

J Street

115
(1891)
This residence exemplifies controlled Queen Anne although it does have gables, fishscale shingling and yawning arches.

Linden Lane

201
(1906)
This many-gabled shingle house, which was designed by T. J. Welsh, was almost completed at the time of the 1906 earthquake. However, it was torn down and rebuilt with steel reinforcement. The spacious home was actually built as a summer home for James Follis, who had John McLaren plan the extensive gardens. It was later the home of Almer M. Newhall.

Locust

120
(c. 1878)
The restrained use of decorative touches on this unpretentious wood house show care for a well-finished job done in exceptionally good taste.

Lucas Valley Road

2201
(1886)
Originally the Loma Alta School, this small shingle building was converted to a home in 1952.

Margarita Drive

75
(1906)
Pony Express Retreat: This Spanish-style building housed the Marin Golf and Country Club until 1939; during World War II, the Seventy-Fourth Field Artillery took over the building's facilities, and later the Air Force moved in. The present owner has made the building into a residence and has converted the men's locker room into a museum to house his collection of Pony Express memorabilia.

Marin and Bayview

(1904)
Short School: The oldest school in the district still in use, this was named in honor of San Rafael's earliest developer in the 1850's, Mr. Gray Short. The building is a fine example of Classic Revival.

Marin Street

11
(1880's)
A Captain Merchason had this house built as a replica of a sea captain's house in Canada. It is a neat, trim, symmetrical building with a cupola on top.

21
(c. 1870's)
Built in the West End, this house was moved in 1903 to Marin Street. The porch that surrounded the house has been reduced to an entrance porch, and the house has been raised. The home still has its attractive bargeboard, carved pent roofs over the side windows, a spindle balustrade and double chimneys.

107
(1890's)
An elementary frame house, this nevertheless has an entrance made imposing by a pediment, arch, and brackets. It was built for the Hallowell family.

McNear Ranch

(1880's)
The only building left of the original McNear Ranch, this dairyman's cottage is a modest frame house with encompassing porch.

Mission Street

822
(1880's)
A conical corner tower highlights this Queen Anne house. Heavy ornamental bargeboard can be seen along the gables, and scrolled brackets add interest to the porch pillars.

1428
(1865)
This old wood Victorian Gothic house looks much as it did when built. It has retained the sharply peaked gables, deep eaves, and ornamented veranda.

Mountain View

102
The shuttered second-story windows of this attractive Colonial Revival house are abbreviated.

129
(1916)
Harrison Dibblee commissioned John Osborne as the architect for this graceful Classic Revival residence. Palladian windows and a columned entrance portico and dentiled cornice enhance the style of the house.

Pacheco Street

10
(1880's)
This large house with its deep veranda preserves the feeling of many of San Rafael's older homes. It once faced the road leading to the San Rafael Hotel, but the house had to be moved back to make way for a highway.

Palm Street

160
(1900)
This bungalow was built for the Lucas family, one of Marin's oldest families and owners of the Lucas ranch. John Lucas inherited the land from his uncle, Don Timoteo Murphy, San Rafael's first alcalde.

Quarry Road

27
Rich and robust features of the

(late 1880's) Queen Anne style (carved pediments, gables, porches) are displayed on this large house.

San Rafael Avenue

127
(c. 1883)
There are pediments over the arched windows on this Italianate house as well as restrained decorative features.

230
(c. 1898)
This cottage presents a fine example of Carpenter's Gothic. It has distinctive bargeboard and pedimented windows.

Sentinel Court

14
(mid-1880's)
Built in imitation of 241 West End, this residence has the same carved embellishments, brackets, and colonnettes between the bays.

Treehaven and Forbes

(1890's)
The only building remaining of "Fairhills", the estate of A. W. Foster, this gate house is a one-story cottage with fish-scale shingles and carved decorative panels on the sides of the bay.

West End Avenue

241
(1869)
Now hidden by newer structures, this house was built by Isaac Jessup. Notable are the Mansard roof, double-bracketed cornices over the bays, and rhythmic facade.

Sausalito

Alexander

26
(1890)
"Craig Hazel": Possibly designed by Willis Polk, this house was originally located on part of the Harrison tract. It has a distinctive rippled roof.

64
(1880)
This simple one-story redwood house was the honeymoon cottage for members of the Spreckels family.

Atwood

60
(1887-93)
Sea Point: The stone foundations of this contemporary house were the beginning of what was to be William Randolph Hearst's palatial Sausalito residence. However, Hearst left town before the house itself was constructed.

Bickbur Street

(1907)
Gilead: Built on an old Indian mound in the Marin City area, this gabled wooden house stands on the site of the home of Colonel O. Livermore. His stable remains in the rear.

Bridgeway

(1885)
Glad Hand Restaurant: Captain Matt Lange originally used this wooden building for his launch rental business. Lange's company also operated a 3:00 a.m. boat which brought the early papers and late revelers from the city. From 1917 until 1937 it was used by the Sausalito Land and Ferry Company.

(c. 1884)
Castle by the Sea: Jack London is said to have written some of his stories in this Queen Anne building which now faces an uncertain future.

Bridgeway (corner of Nevada)

(c. 1893)
American Distilling Company: John Mason built the first brewery in San Francisco but then came to this location where the fine water could be utilized. American Distillery then used the plant from around 1920 to 1965.

505
(1893-4)
Eastlake chalet bracing has been added to this wooden set of flats.

749-51
(1890's)
The Tides: In the mid-nineties this wooden building was bought by Frank Daroux, politician and gambling czar. In 1906 open gambling was closed down in Sausalito during a period of reform. Ironically, the wood building later became the headquarters of the local weekly newspaper—the paper that had put an end to Daroux's business.

1417
(1890's)
Central School: Moved one block at the turn of the century, this school later became a furniture store and is now a billiard parlor. The upstairs still has classrooms and blackboards.

Bridgeway & El Portal

(1915)
This Mission Revival building was erected where the Arbordale Hotel and beergarden restaurant once stood. Prohibition closed the restaurant and the old building was remodeled in 1915.

Bulkley

100
(1905)
First Presbyterian Church: The L. M. Hickmans gave this wood shingle church to the congregation in memory of their three children. A fine cypress tree, "The Founding Tree", still stands in front of the church.

109
(1888)
Laneside: H. C. Campbell designed this shingle Queen Anne house for his bride. During World War I, the Red Cross used the residence for its quarters; in 1920 it was converted into apartments.

156
(1889)
Casa Madrona: Now a residential hotel, this building was originally the home of the William Gallagher family. It has undergone many changes over the years.

Central Avenue at San Carlos

(1913)
Sausalito Woman's Club: One of Sausalito's outstanding architectural achievements, this redwood shingle clubhouse was designed by Julia Morgan. The Club began when a group of women saved the Presbyterian Church's cypress tree from threatened destruction.

Central Avenue

108
(1903)
Thomas Church recently designed the garden for this home, one of Sausalito's finest.

Harrison Avenue

168
(1877)
Tanglewood: Major H. A. Cobb, who had spent some years with the British Army in India, had this house built to resemble summer houses he had seen in the Indian hills.

Miller Avenue

33
Now converted into apartments,

(c. 1880) this sprawling residence once featured a ballroom, hotel-sized kitchen, oriental paneling, and a mahogany stairway.

Pine Street

517
(1874)
Thomas Wasser, the Chief Engineer on the Tamalpais, (the first ferry to come to Sausalito), was the original owner of this brown shingled bungalow, which has remained in the same family.

Princess Street

6
(1885)
Schnell House: Sausalito's first postmaster, Jacob Schnell, had this structure built. The shingle building was the corner saloon for years. Now it houses small shops.

San Carlos

87
(1901)
Sweetbriar: Lieutenant John C. Cantwell of the U. S. Coast Guard had this house designed and built.

172
(1870)
Bellevue Cottage: There is a patent (the Elford Patent) on the construction method used on this pre-fab. The method is similar in concept to Lincoln Logs.

Santa Rosa

48
(1879)
Cod Fish King Tashiera, one of the early Portuguese settlers, was the first owner of this Eastlake-detailed wood house.

South Street

215
(late 1860's)
For years this Victorian (brought around the Horn) was the only house in its area. The house has been enlarged by the addition of several ship cabins to the rear.

Spencer Street

54
(1880)
Red Gables: Englishman Frederick Russell had this house built behind a trim hedge (characteristic of old Sausalito and ideal for insuring privacy as well as protection from wind).

Fort Baker

(1866)
The Fort became known as Lime Point Military Reservation after its purchase in 1866. Its name was changed to Fort Baker in 1897 in honor of Colonel Edward Dickerson Baker, United States Volunteers.

Post Commander's Residence

(1903)
This typical Army house stands exactly as it did when first built and is still used as the Deputy Commander's residence. It is a basic gabled structure with covered porches.

Residence of Chief of Staff

(1903)
To the right of the Post Commander's house is this building originally used as Headquarters. It stands as an unadorned rectangle with large windows and a covered porch running along its facade.

Old Guard House

(1902)
This simple one-story frame house has a porch across its facade. It has now been put to use as a store house.

Lighthouse

(1900)
A fog horn was here as early as 1883. This building, which became automated in 1959, now stands under the Golden Gate Bridge.

Stinson Beach

Grand Hotel

(1915)
This bungalow-style building was originally known as the Sea Beach Hotel. Broad steps lead to the front veranda of the building whose broad cross-gable provides a third floor under the roof.

Marconi's Station Shoreline Highway between Marshall and Point Reyes Station

(1914)
Named for the inventor of the wireless, these stone and concrete tile-roofed buildings stand fortress-like overlooking Tomales Bay. They were built to accommodate R.C.A. wireless station employees at the first trans-Pacific communications center.

Tiburon

East Strawberry Drive

355
(1880)
Benjamin Lyford built this two-story wooden structure, encircled by a veranda, as a rest home for his patients. It is now a retreat house for the Sisters of Mercy.

Mar West

(1900's)
This row of one and two-story houses was built for the superintendents and station masters of Peter Donahue's railroad company. The homes look as they did in early twentieth century photos.

Paradise Drive

1920
(1882–1884)
The oldest building in Tiburon was moved from Petaluma by Peter Donahue as a freight and ticket office for his Railroad Company. It now serves as a decorating studio.

2900
(1909)
Annabel Powers Tilley had Berkeley architect W. H. Ratcliff, Jr., design this Spanish tile-roofed villa at the beginning of California's Spanish Revival architecture.

Woodacre

San Geronimo Valley Drive

(1870's)
This Classic Revival frame house was once part of a 500-acre dairy ranch. It has the shuttered windows and porch (with pierced columns supporting the roof) associated with that style.

(1880)
Roy Ranch: Built for the Roy family, this frame house is an outstanding structure. A bracketed cornice, scalloped edging under the eaves, and carved railings on the veranda give it distinction.

GLOSSARY

Included here are drawings and selected terms from the glossary of Time's Wondrous Changes, *written by* Dr. Joseph A. Baird, Jr., *and published by the California Historical Society. Terms appropriate to this book have been added with the generous assistance of Dr. Baird.*

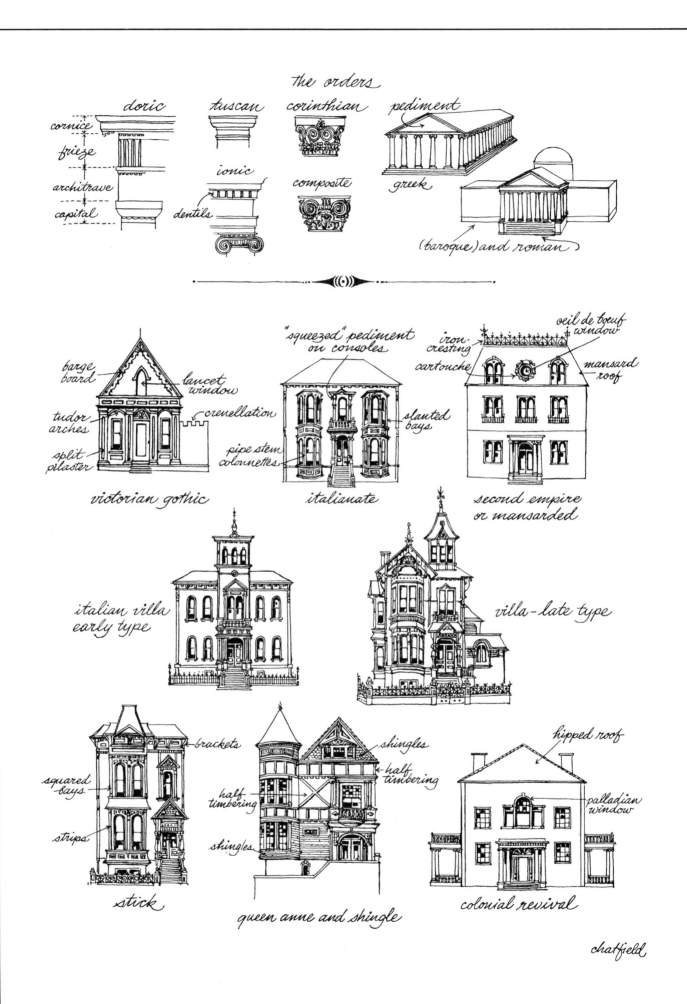

the orders

doric   tuscan   corinthian   pediment

cornice
frieze
architrave
capital

ionic

dentils

composite

greek

(baroque) and roman

barge board
lancet window
tudor arches
crenellation
split pilaster
pipe stem colonnettes

victorian gothic

"squeezed" pediment on consoles

slanted bays

italianate

oeil de bœuf window
iron cresting
cartouche
mansard roof

second empire or mansarded

italian villa early type

villa-late type

brackets
squared bays
strips

stick

shingles
half timbering
half timbering
shingles

queen anne and shingle

hipped roof
palladian window

colonial revival

chatfield

Adobe: Mud brick dried in the sun.

Architrave: See Entablature.

Balustrade: A row of balusters, or turned posts, supporting a handrail.

Barge board: A decorated wooden strip under a gable; usually a flat board, pierced with jig-saw ornament.

Baroque: Style of architecture and art common to the western world in the seventeenth and eighteenth centuries A.D.; sometimes divided into phases (especially in Italy) of Early, High and Late Baroque. Usually characterized by a controlled organization of major and minor parts, leading to a dramatic focus of design elements, and often showing strong contrasts as well as movement of parts forward and backward.

Bay Area Shingle: A particular interest in use of exterior shingles in the Bay Area comes out of the "Shingle Style", part of widespread medieval revivals in that era. It is most obvious in domestic architecture. Given a strong statement in the works of Maybeck, Coxhead and others, it became a generalized residential type in the early twentieth century, showing increasing fusion of modern, oriental and other design elements with the basic medievalisms of the Shingle Style. It has continued to be a useful and flexible wooden building manner to the present day.

Bay window: A window which projects from the envelope or mass of a building, permitting more illumination of the interior; a "slanted" bay has slanted sides and flattened top and bottom, meeting at the vertical front section, while a "squared" bay has sides at right angles to the building and vertical front section.

Beaux Arts: By exact definition, a school of architecture and art in Paris. By extension, the term refers to more conservative design of a Classicist French Baroque style.

Bracket: A support or pseudo-support (often it was used decoratively rather than structurally), based on a 90 degree angle shape; usually of extremely variable decorative character, and to be clearly distinguished from the more invariable classicist forms that are related to it in shape and function.

Buttress: A strong, projecting vertical support for a wall. In Victorian Gothic it was usually a pier (solid vertical pier attached to wall) rather than a flying buttress (arches brought from upper parts of building to piers at some remove from the wall).

Cantilever: Construction which projects from the main mass of a building, anchored firmly in that mass; from below it appears structually to be free-standing since its extension has no support; used particularly for balcony construction and wherever a "floating" effect is desired.

Capital: The carved top of a column.

Casement: A window with two upright sections opening in the center and hinged at the sides; in American architecture it was the invariable type of pre-Georgian building after which it was replaced with the double hung window; this form persisted into the twentieth century; the casement window was revived in the later nineteenth century.

Carpenter's Gothic: The craftsman's or carpenter's simplified and informal interpretation of Gothic Revival, using stock members that could be fabricated easily by a carpenter.

Cartouche: An elaborate frame with scrolled and decorated parts, resembling curled paper.

Chicago School: A general term to group architects and progressive building tendencies of the late nineteenth century in Chicago, where skyscraper construction of a metal skeleton with a sheathing of protective surface was first developed; the group included engineers like Jenney, early-modern architects like Sullivan, the young Frank Lloyd Wright, and its forms ranged from monumental commercial and civic building to houses.

Clapboard: A long narrow board, originally of cleft oak in New England but often of sawn woods of various types today; used for covering the exterior of timber-framed buildings.

Classic: The highest phase of any style or era of art. Often used as a synonym for Classical.

Classical: Ancient Greek or Roman forms, or directly imitative of them (As in Classical Revival).

Classical Revival: (Neo-Classical): The revival of interest in Classical antiquity, dating from the mid-eighteenth century, and especially notable in architecture; divided into two phases—Roman and Greek—in the United States, although they usually overlapped and both often included elements of Baroque planning continuing from the Georgian era.

Classicist: Derived from Classical forms, but variously interpreted in a new context (as Renaissance or Baroque Classicism).

Coffered: Deep, regular geometric panels (or coffers) sunk in the surface of a ceiling, vault, or dome.

Colonnade: A row of columns.

Colonnette: A small column, usually very tall and slender in proportion, approaching a "pipe-stem" in appearance in later nineteenth-century San Francisco architecture.

Colonial Revival: A phase of late-nineteenth-century American architecture which revived Georgian plans and forms, especially in domestic building; there were usually some differences from historic Georgian architecture—especially in the use of deep front or side porches, and in the inevitable touches which lingered from other late-nineteenth-century fashions.

Column: An architectural support of definite proportions, usually cylindrical in shape with shaft and capital (and sometimes, a base). May be free-standing or attached ("engaged") to a wall as a half-or three-quarter column.

Composite: One of the Roman orders— related to the Corinthian, but combining in its capital the leaves of the Corinthian and volutes of the Ionic.

Console: In architecture a support or pseudo-support (often used decoratively) with a scrolled top curving down into a reverse scroll; the scrolls are generally called volutes.

Corinthian: One of the Greek and Roman orders—originally taller than the Doric and Ionic; having a fluted shaft, capital with acanthus leaves and small corner spirals, and base.

Cornice: (1) The topmost part of the entablature in Classical architecture. (2) Any projecting horizontal molding which crowns an exterior elevation, sometimes a window or door; or a molding used internally at the junction of wall and ceiling.

Course: A continuous layer of masonry (brick, stone, etc.) of equal thickness, in a wall.

Cupola: A dome-like convex roof form used to surmount a larger mass of building or tower, especially in the Queen Anne fashion of the later nineteenth century.

Crenellation: A form of battlement, created in idea with indentations (crenels) of a low wall; in fact often made by alternating squared blocks or merlons (sometimes with pyramidal tops), with embrasures or empty spaces between. Originally intended for protecting defenders on the upper walls of a fortress; nineteenth-century crenellation was decorative.

Dentil: Tooth-like ornaments, in a row or "course"; originally associated especially with the Ionic order.

Doric: One of the Greek and Roman orders; the Greek Doric had a simple capital with block (abacus) and curved "cushion" (echinus) over a plain, fluted shaft. The Roman and Renaissance Doric was closer to the Tuscan.

Dormer: A window, framed and roofed like a miniature house, which projects from the main roof—providing additional light and air to the top floor or attic area.

Eastlake: A period term derived from the name of Charles Eastlake, English author of *Hints on Household Taste;* Eastlake was attempting to restore some measure of simplicity, dignity and good taste to domestic interiors, and his ideas were commendable. Unfortunately, his ornamental and material "hints" were misunderstood or wantonly transcribed into as excessive forms as he decried. The term Eastlake, especially meaningful for the Stick Style, implied in the United States the use of chamfered corners on pillars and furniture, incised decoration in flat wooden surfaces (usually of floreate form-often wheat patterns), variegated combinations of material and especially the interior use of "golden" oak.

Eaves: The lower edge of a sloping or gabled roof.

Entablature: The horizontal bar above columns or pilasters. In Classical architecture and its derivatives, the entablature is divided into three sections from bottom to top; the architrave, the frieze and the cornice. Each of the orders had a characteristic entablature.

Facade: The front, or frontispiece, of a building.

False or flat front: With the gradual standarization of commercial and domestic American architecture in the nineteenth century (especially with use of balloon frame construction), buildings became, increasingly, units of the same basic form. To provide facade variety was the only easy way to create "individuality"; proliferation of ornamental forms and variation of these forms on the ". . . front of buildings gave rise to rows of similar wooden boxes, with seemingly different fronts, now called "false" because of their purely applied decorative, (rather than functional) character. Often these facades gave an exaggerated verticality to the building." (Delete the remainder.)

Federal: (1) Period of American architecture from about 1790 to 1810, characterized by slender uprights and ovoid shapes. (2) Relating to U.S. Governmental design in general.

Finial: A terminal part, usually on a high vertical building element such as a church spire or decorative roof feature.

Flatiron: A wedge or triangular-shaped building which appeared in American cities at the end of the nineteenth century, accommodating early high-rise construction to irregular triangular sites created by intersection of standard gridiron city plans with main transverse streets.

Fluting: Vertical channeling of a columnar or pilaster shaft.

Fret work: Intersecting decorative patterns, particularly those made possible by fret saws working in wood.

Frieze: The middle part of the entablature in Classical architecture.

Gable: A high, peaked roof form-actually the vertical, triangular part at each end of such a peaked roof.

Gambrel: A roof of double slope, like a flexed leg (French: *jambe*).

Gazebo: A garden pavilion, usually in a fanciful, decorative style.

Georgian: A period term derived from the names of English sovereigns of the eighteenth century; divided into various phases in American architecture—Early, High and Late. Classicist Baroque in general character, it utilized features from fifteenth and sixteenth-century Italian architecture as seen through English eyes of the seventeenth century and eighteenth century. Its historic time span was 1700-1790, but its forms were revived in the late-nineteenth-century Colonial Revival.

Gothic: A style of architecture and art, essentially of the twelfth to sixteenth centuries A.D. Usually characterized by pointed arches of varied shapes-some high and narrow, others low and flat or depressed; occasionally using arches of double curvative or ogival shape.

Half-timbered: Large timbers framed and filled with brick, plaster, etc., creating a "half-timbered" wooden framework exteriorly—often painted to create greater contrast with plaster between. In early American building, half-timbering was covered with horizontal clapboarding. Half-timbering was revived by Richardson especially, and it appeared in structural or purely decorative forms in the Queen Anne period and later.

Hipped roof: A pyramidal or truncated pyramidal roof form.

Hood mold: A projecting molding over an opening, to throw off rain water; often used in a purely decorative manner in the Victorian Gothic.

Ionic: One of the Greek and Roman orders, especially characterized by its capital with large spirals or volutes at the corners.

Italianate: A period term which included forms and ornament derived especially from fifteenth and sixteenth-century Italian architecture, notably from the Mannerist and Early Baroque era in Italy (ca. 1530 to 1590); the fashion was especially common between 1850 and 1875 in northern California.

Italian Villa: A picturesque house type, of varying plan; usually it had a high, off-center tower (the first Italian Villas had a central tower), and a plan that changed from central hall with flanking rooms to a more rambling interior arrangement of rooms. The Villa was a formal type or building shape that continued through many changes of fashion in the later nineteenth century. In California there were some true Italian Villas; many were Stick Villas with enrichments of other fashions.

Jacobean: Architecture and furniture types of the reign of James I in England—late medieval in form.

Keystone: The top stone or voussoir in a true arch; the keystone makes an arch the resilient, dynamic building form it is.

Lancet: A tall, narrow pointed opening, like a lance.

Mannerism: A style of architecture and art, now especially associated with the mid and later sixteenth century A.D. Characterized by tension, ambiquity, lack of balance, crowding of parts and a proclivity for elongated shapes. Italian Mannerism was both structural and ornamental, and was particularly common to Rome, and the provinces of Tuscany, Lombardy and Venice.

Mansard: A roof form, probably named for the French architect, Francois Mansart (1598–1666); it was a type which permitted the combination of roof and extra story. Usually it had a steeply inclined face (sometimes with a secondary change of angle face above) and a flattened roof top; this permitted a top story to have walls that were virtually vertical. Tall windows or French doors, opening onto balconies, lighted the interior as on lower floors.

Medallion: A circular or oval plaque fixed to a surface.

Mission Revival: Difficult to characterize in any exact manner, the so-called Mission Revival is a combination of exterior and interior features which varied as the style developed; it bears almost no direct connection to the Mission architecture of old California but is rather a conglomeration of late Arts and Crafts "simplicity" (honest use of materials, etc.), special features such as tile roofs, stucco walls and pseudo-Mexican Colonial design elements with vestiges of Richardson Romanesque heaviness and some early modern interest in plain surfaces.

Modillion: A support or pseudo-support (it was often used decoratively) resembling a console with its flat side uppermost.

Mullion: The major bar, dividing a window into "lights".

Muntins: The minor bars, dividing a window.

Oeil de boeuf: "Eye of a bull"-a circular window.

Orders: In architecture, the basic columnar or pilaster types of the Classical world: the Doric, Ionic and Corinthian of the Greeks and the Doric, Tuscan, Ionic, Corinthian and Composite of the Roman, Renaissance, and later eras.

Palladian window: A window form with high arched central section and flanking rectangular sections – derived from the name of the Italian architect, Andrea Palladio (1518-1580); extensively used in the Late Georgian era, and again in the Colonial Revival.

Pediment: The triangular space at the end of a Classical temple's gabled roof – the latter usually rather low in pitch. Originally an important sculptured area of the temple, it was reduced in size during the Renaissance and especially used at the tops of windows, either in a triangular or lunette form. Prior to the Mannerist period, these window pediments were "supported" on columns flanking the window (imitating a small Classical temple front); in the Mannerist era, and in San Francisco architecture inspired by it, the pediments were squeezed into small triangles at the top center of the window cornice.

Period: In this book, Period architecture refers to work done after about 1895 when designers began to build in more traditionally "correct" imitations of periods of the past. During most of the mid and later nineteenth century, a fairly free and inventive ("incorrect") approach to the past was followed; partly through disinterest in architectural scholarship of a more precise kind, largely through the funneling of main styles into a vast new explosion of technology and decoration in building, the eclectic vagaries of the later Victorian era became increasingly fanciful and capricious. "Period" design was a characteristic reaction against the excesses of the 1880's. Architects were now academically schooled and travelled widely; they found a generation of clients who, although *nouveau riche*, desired the genteel and "correct" taste of an idealized Europe long past. There ensued a great new wave of construction in all the various periods known to architecture, researched and studied to the last detail. If the faults of the late Victorian were those of excess, the faults of Period architecture were those of restraint and careful imitation, verging sometimes on dullness. However, because of its superb use of fine materials and equally excellent construction (often involving steel and concrete), Period architecture is again receiving the attention it deserves on the technical level, whatever its design conservatism (as compared to the more "progressive" work of Wright and other early-twentieth-century architects).

Pilaster: A flattened columnar form, rectilinear in shape, always attached to a wall. Pilasters can be of all standard or Classical columnar types (Doric, Tuscan, Ionic, Corinthian, Composite) and of any decorative variation of other columnar forms.

Portico: A porch-like roofed projection from a building, derived from the columned porticoes of Classical temples.

Quadrant: By definition, a quarter circle; by extension, a more generalized curved shape or area.

Queen Anne: The incongruously-named architectural fashion of the late nineteenth century, which derived from the work of Norman Shaw in England; it usually emphasized rounded corner towers, shingles and a mixed ornamental language derived from other late-nineteenth-century architectural fashions.

Quoins: Derived from the French, coin or coign (corner); stones, often simulated in wooden blocks, to create an effect of strength or ornamental finish at the corner.

Renaissance: A style of architecture and art of the fifteenth and sixteenth centuries A.D. Characterized by harmony of parts (symmetrical), balance and clarity, and strongly influenced by Classical sources. Sometimes divided (notably in Italy) into Early and High Renaissance.

Richardsonian or Richardson Romanesque: An important phase of later-nineteenth-century American architecture, derived from the work of Henry Hobson Richardson (1838-1886). Richardson had been inspired by French and Spanish Romanesque building, and by Early Christian architecture of the Near East; from these, and other later medieval sources, he evolved his highly personal Romanesque manner, later popularized in most parts of the United States.

Rinceau: A foliate ornament, often in garland form (plural, rinceaux).

Romanesque: A style of architecture or art, essentially of the tenth to twelfth centuries, A.D., persisting in variant forms later. Generally characterized by use of semicircular arches, extremely solid masonry construction, heavy piers.

Rose window: A round window, usually with tracery.

Rustication: Stone construction in which the joints are emphasized or rusticated, usually in a regular pattern of bevelled edges.

Second Empire: The nineteenth-century architectural fashion which derived from the Neo-Baroque work of French architects during the Second Empire of Louis Napoleon, or Napoleon III as he was called.

Shingle Style: The late-nineteenth-century architectural fashion which derived from sources in New England of the late seventeenth century, and from certain progressive eastern architects' variations on them; it often combined features of other late-nineteenth-century architectural fashions, especially Richardson Romanesque and Queen Anne. The phrase was described especially by V. Scully, *The Shingle Style*, New Haven, 1955.

Spire: An elongated point on top of a tower.

Stick Style: The late-nineteenth-century architectural fashion derived from the ideas of Eastlake, often combining various local features; the phrase was especially described by Vincent Scully. It might as well be called Strip Style in San Francisco. A sub-phase emphasized "Moorish" details, such as horseshoe arches, etc.

Tracery: Patterns in carved stone in a window or door.

Tudor: (1) A term used for the period from about 1500 to 1600 in England. (2) A type of flattened, four-centered arch in this period, and again in the Victorian Gothic.

Tuscan: Roman and Renaissance variant of the Doric order with a very simplified capital, and use of a base rare in the Greek Doric.

Volute: A spiral.

ARCHITECT BIOGRAPHIES

Following are biographic sketches of those architects who have made especially important,
individual contributions to the history of West Bay architecture.

Applegarth, George A. (1877–). A native of Oakland, California, Applegarth, like many of his contemporaries in the architectural field, had his training at L'Ecole des Beaux Arts in Paris. Between 1911 and 1915 he was a partner in the firm of McDonald and Applegarth, while from 1938 until 1947 he was a member of the firm of McDonald and Applegarth. In 1946 he opened his own office. Applegarth's feeling for the French is manifested in his noteworthy California Palace of the Legion of Honor and the Spreckels house on Washington Street.

Bakewell, John, Jr. (1872–1963). Kansas-born Bakewell had his training at the University of California and L'Ecole des Beaux Arts. In 1905 he and Arthur Brown, Jr., formed a partnership which was to last until 1927. The following year Bakewell joined forces with Ernest Weihe, and they maintained their partnership until 1942. Two of Bakewell and Brown's most memorable efforts (showing their concern for traditional modes of architecture) were San Francisco's City Hall and Temple Emanu-El.

Bliss, Walter D. (1873–1956). Bliss left the New York firm of McKim, Mead and White in 1898 in order to return to his native San Francisco with his co-worker, William Faville. Upon their arrival in San Francisco the two men formed a partnership, which was dissolved in 1925, when they opened separate offices. Bliss practiced architecture for fifty years and left a fine legacy, which includes the St. Francis Hotel and the Bank of California.

Brown, A. Page (1859–1896). Born in the east and educated at Cornell, Brown joined the New York office of McKim, Mead and White as a draftsman. Later, he continued his architectural studies in Europe and in 1885 opened his own New York office. In 1889 Brown came to San Francisco where he practiced until his accidental death some years later. Brown was responsible for many especially important San Francisco buildings, including the Ferry Building and Trinity Church.

Brown, Arthur, Jr. (1874–1957). Like his partner, John Bakewell, Jr., Brown was educated at the University of California and L'Ecole des Beaux Arts. Brown was supervising architect of the University of California, a Chevalier of the French Legion of Honor, and, at the time of his death, one of the three chief advisors on the remodeling of the United States Capitol. When Brown died, Herbert Hoover was one of his honorary pall bearers. Among the major civic buildings he designed were the San Francisco Opera House and Coit Tower.

Burnham, Daniel H. (1847–1912). Although his firm was based in Chicago, Burnham had a strong influence on the architectural look of San Francisco through his protege, Willis Polk. Burnham was originally brought to the city in 1904, when he was asked to prepare a plan for the beautification of San Francisco similar to plans he had done for Cleveland, Detroit, and Manila. The following year he presented Mayor Eugene Schmitz with the finished "Report on the Improvement and Adornment of San Francisco." After the 1906 fire, Burham was called back to San Francisco by a citizen's committee anxious to rebuild their city. For some reason Burnham's plans were never adopted, but he did open offices in San Francisco with Willis Polk in charge. Perhaps Burnham's most notable contributions to the cityscape of San Francisco were the Mills Building, done in conjunction with his one-time partner, John Root, and the old Chronicle Building, which he redesigned after the fire. It has since been reworked.

Coxhead, Ernest (1863–1933). Before coming to the United States from his native England, Coxhead was elected a member of the Royal Institute of British Architects. In 1886 he arrived in Los Angeles, where he built many fine houses and churches. For ten years he was associated with his brother, Almeric, in San Francisco but later practiced alone. For a while Bernard Maybeck worked for Coxhead and was said to have influenced Coxhead's approach to architecture. Certainly they had similar interests in the Bay Area Shingle Style with an early understanding of the relationship of a home to its environment and a careful handling of details. His domestic architecture, especially his own home at 2421 Green Street, has added to the character of San Francisco.

Curlett, William (1846–1914). Although he spent the later years of his life in Los Angeles, Curlett was associated closely with San Francisco architecture after coming to the city from Warrenpoint, Ireland, in 1871. Curlett first worked in association with Augustus Laver, whose most important work here was the Pacific Union Club. The Citizens Federal Savings and Loan Building (originally the Mutual Building) was one of Curlett's designs.

Faville, William B. (1866–1946). This Californian both attended and taught at M.I.T. Then in 1895 he joined the New York firm of McKim, Mead and White. It was there that he worked with Walter Bliss, who came to San Francisco with him in 1898. In 1922 Faville was elected the head of the AIA. Among the San Francisco buildings which show his concern with the Renaissance theme are Sacred Heart Convent (the Flood Mansion) and the University Club.

Geilfuss, Henry (born 1850). Geilfuss came to the United States from his native Germany in 1876 and later became a practicing architect in San Francisco, building many important residences, including 1198 Fulton and 294 Page. A slight infusion of his Germanic-European background is seen in his concept of the American Victorian mode.

Hobart, Lewis P. (1873–1954). Born in St. Louis, Hobart studied at the University of California, the American Academy in Rome, and L'Ecole des Beaux Arts. Hobart came to San Francisco in 1906 after practicing two years in New York. In 1932, he became the first president of the San Francisco Art Commission. Although Grace Cathedral will probably be Hobart's most enduring work, he will also be remembered for his Peninsula mansions, especially Rosecourt and Strawberry Hill.

Kelham, George W. (1871–1936). Kelham followed his Harvard years with studies at L'Ecole des Beaux Arts. He began his architectural career in New York, and while working there for Trowbridge and Livingston, Kelham was sent by them to San Francisco to supervise their work on the Palace Hotel. He decided to stay in San Francisco and went on to design such notable structures as the Public Library, Standard Oil Building, Russ Building and Shell Oil Building.

Maybeck, Bernard (1862–1957). Maybeck, the son of a woodcarver, was born in New York and at the age of seventeen was himself apprenticed to a woodcarver. At eighteen Maybeck went to Paris to study furniture design but later transferred to L'Ecole des Beaux Arts. His actual architectural work began in St. Petersburg, Florida, where he was hired by a former roommate, who was a partner in the firm of Carrère and Hastings. In 1889 Maybeck came to San Francisco, where he was first employed by Coxhead and then in 1891, by A. Page Brown. It was in Maybeck's work for Brown on the Swedenborgian Church that he first began to show what his capabilities were. Maybeck's work soon displayed his knowledge of engineering, his feeling for materials (especially wood), and his

early experimentation with modernism, all combined with a romantic regard for gothic and classical forms. Maybeck understood the idea of incorporating garden areas with living areas and the importance of infusing an interior with natural light before most of his contemporaries did. In San Francisco, San Mateo County and Marin County it is mainly Maybeck's residences that show his special flair although his pièce de résistance was surely the original Palace of Fine Arts.

Morgan, Julia (1872–1957). Miss Morgan, a San Franciscan by birth, achieved many firsts in her career: she was the first woman to be graduated in Engineering from the University of California (in 1894), the first woman to receive a master's degree from L'Ecole des Beaux Arts, and the first woman architect licensed in California. After her return from Paris, Miss Morgan studied with Maybeck, who was to strongly influence her style, especially her Bay Area Shingle residences. Miss Morgan became the personal architect for William Randolph Hearst, for whom she designed "Wyntoon" in Shasta County and her masterpiece, San Simeon.

Percy, George W. (1847–1900). Percy went from his hometown, Bath, Maine, to Portland to serve his architectural apprenticeship. In 1876 he came to San Francisco, where he opened an office; but four years later he decided to join forces with F. F. Hamilton. He was identified with a number of commercial and public buildings, including the Children's Playhouse at Golden Gate Park and the Kohl Building.

Pissis, Albert (1852–1914). Born in Guaymas, Mexico, Pissis came to San Francisco in 1858. Later he studied at L'Ecole des Beaux Arts and traveled extensively in Europe. He was one of five architects to serve on the advisory committee of architectural procedure for the 1915 Exposition. Pissis is best known for his fine office buildings including the Hibernia Bank, the Flood Building, and the Emporium.

Polk, Willis Jefferson (1867–1924). Polk was born in Kentucky but grew up in St. Louis. At the age of thirteen Polk was apprenticed to an architect, and two years later the teenager submitted a design, in

answer to an ad, for a six-room schoolhouse in Hope, Arkansas. His design was accepted and the architect Polk was on his way. Polk came to San Francisco as an assistant to A. Page Brown, but it was his later association with D. H. Burnham that probably played a more significant part in his development. Polk first worked for Burnham in Chicago but was placed in charge of Burnham's San Francisco office after the fire in 1906. In 1910 the office was turned over completely to Polk and renamed Willis Polk & Co. Those years after the fire found Polk, who liked to be known as a master builder, playing a major role in the rebuilding of the city. Many of his residences and some of his commercial buildings reflect Polk's free use of traditional architectural forms, the knowledge of which probably developed from Polk's European trips. However, Polk's own relatively simple house on Vallejo Street expressed his comprehension of the more indigenous Shingle Style, and the Hallidie Building expressed his imaginative spirit and willingness to experiment. The faith of the ebullient, playful and dramatic Polk was expressed by his friend, Bruce Porter, in a eulogy: "His vision, to the last, was always of this city of San Francisco as the most noble architectural opportunity of the New World."

Swain, Edward H. (1852–1902). Swain had his architectural training in the office of David Farquharson. In 1877 he began his own practice in San Francisco although in the early 1890's he assisted A. Page Brown with plans for the H. S. Crocker Building and the Ferry Building. He moved later to Honolulu, where he carried on his architectural practice. Swain will be best remembered in San Francisco for his California Historical Society and McLaren Lodge in Golden Gate Park, both manifestations of Richardson Romanesque.

Whittlesey, Charles F. (1867–1941). A native of Alton, Illinois, Whittlesey was trained in Louis Sullivan's office in Chicago. In 1900 he was made chief architect of the Santa Fe Railroad Company, in charge of designing hotels and stations. Following the 1906 fire Whittlesey came to San Francisco from Los Angeles. He was one of the first architects to use reinforced concrete for construction. The Pacific Building is probably his best known in the area.

INDEX

Starred items are also mentioned in the Appendix. Entries in *italic* refer to photographs; those in parentheses to old photographs.

All photographs by Morley Baer with the exception of the following:

From the collection of Ansel Adams: B134
Courtesy of Bancroft Library: 82, 83
Richard Bare: 204
Richard S. Bodman: T159, T308, 309, TB311, T312, TR313
The W. Alan Bonners: 155, 313
Courtesy of the California Historical Society: B28, 29, T42, B69, R90, 113, L195, R275
Courtesy of the California State Library: T169
Courtesy of Citizens Federal Savings and Loan Asso.: 85
Courtesy of Mrs. Ernest Evans: 316
H. W. Frank: 252
Paul Hassel: L288
Courtesy of Mrs. William Hilbert: 142
Winton Hill: 258
Bob Hollingsworth: 15, 18, T22, T24, B24, 25, 26, TL28, 29, 36, 37, L54, 56, 57, B58, T59, BL73, BR73, TR73, 105, 108, L109, 116. T117, 118, R119, T121, 122 125, BR127, TR127, 161, 166, 177, 189, TR195, B197, 203, 205, 207, 209, 211, 212, T213, BL214, 217, 218, 221, 223, 224, B225, 226, 227, 229, 230, BL231, CR231, TR231, B236, T237, 240, 241, 242, 243, 244–245, 246, 264, 266, 271, RTB274, L275, 277, 283, B286, R288, L300, 304, RB313, 315
Merritt Hosmer: C170, B170
George Knight: 53, R54, 55, T58, 94
Maritime Museum: 13, B48, L90, 114–115
Moore and de Pue Lithograph, courtesy of Redwood City Tribune: B169
Courtesy of Mr. and Mrs. David Clayborn Mosby: 128–129
Moss Photography, courtesy of Bank of California: TR79
Moulin Studios: 68, T69, 76, L79, 285
Courtesy of the National Park Service: R103, RTB274
Courtesy of Pacific Gas and Electric Co.: T236
Norton Pearl: 162, 180, 181, 184–185, T186, TL195, 199, 206
Courtesy of Public Utilities Commission: R280
From the collection of Morton Rader: BL62, T62
Courtesy of the Redwood City Tribune: T170
Courtesy of the St. Francis Hotel: L91
Courtesy of the San Francisco Chronicle: T44
Courtesy of the San Francisco Convention and Visitors Bureau: B17, 4
Courtesy of Richard Shellers: B312
Courtesy of Security Pacific National Bank: 93
Mrs. Bonsal Seggerman: 276, L286
Courtesy of Mr. William Slater: L316
Courtesy of The Society of California Pioneers: TL214, R316
Courtesy of Southern Pacific: L298
Courtesy of Charles H. Stanyan, IV: B117
Dr. John Tobin: L280, R290
Mrs. Hans Von Briesen: 296
Mrs. Eckard Von Estorff: 267
Courtesy of Mrs. John West: 303

Code is: T=Top B=Bottom C=Center L=Left R=Right

CHANGES

A number of the buildings shown or mentioned have undergone changes of status since this book was first published. The following is a list of such changes.

Gone Today

Page 3   **946 Eddy Street:** "Inadvertently demolished" by Sacred Heart High School to make way for a new playground. Number 946 was part of a larger row of houses which is now reduced to one building (two if one counts the Maybeck Family Service Agency, which is of a different style and period). Of the row, 946 was considered the most significant architecturally.

Page 47   **1098 Lombard:** Demolished for townhouses. Trees and garden gone; environmental review process subverted.

Page 65   **150 Sansome:** The Seawall Warehouse, demolished in 1968 for a waterfront development that never happened; now a vacant lot.

Page 77   **520 Pine:** Kong Chow Temple, demolished to make way for an office building which has not been built.

Page 120   **1051 McAllister:** Firehouse, demolished by the Western Addition Redevelopment Program. The facade was removed by hand and reinstated as part of a housing project, for which it forms the entrance.

Page 121   **633 Laguna:** Mowry's Opera House, demolished by the Western Addition Redevelopment Program to make way for Ammel Park subsidized housing.

Page 199   **Montara Lighthouse and Pigeon Point Lighthouse:** still there, but no longer open to the public.

Page 202   **Lobitos Creek Cut-off, Half Moon Bay:** The Tunis District School burned down.

Page 206   **Pescadero:** The Alexander Moore House burned down.

Page 235   **Fourth Street, San Rafael:** The San Rafael Court House, formerly scheduled for demolition, was instead destroyed by fire.

Threatened

Page 13   **Fort Mason:** Administered now as part of the Golden Gate National Recreation Area, which recommends heightened recreational use of the fort. Must be watched for unnecessary demolition.

Page 85   **108 Sutter:** The French Bank Building.

Page 111   **236 Monterey Boulevard:** Owner wants to demolish structure and sell vacant land to developers for an apartment building. It is a city and county landmark.

Page 293   **1 Sansome Street:** California Office, Crocker-Citizens National Bank.

Page 181   **565 Remillard Drive, Burlingame:** Carolands, built by Harriet Pullman, is once more for sale, and in a further state of deterioration.

Converted